Brian Groom is a journalist and a leading expert on British regional and national affairs. His career was spent mainly at the *Financial Times*, where he was assistant editor and worked in various capacities. He is also a former editor of *Scotland on Sunday*, which he launched as deputy editor and which won many awards. Originally from Stretford, Lancashire, he returned to live in the North – in Saddleworth, South Pennines – in 2015. This is his first book.

NORTHERNERS
A HISTORY

FROM THE ICE AGE TO THE PRESENT DAY

BRIAN GROOM

Harper
North

HarperNorth
Windmill Green
Mount Street
Manchester M2 3NX

A division of
HarperCollins*Publishers*
1 London Bridge Street
London SE1 9GF

www.harpercollins.co.uk

HarperCollins*Publishers*
Macken House, 39/40 Mayor Street Upper
Dublin 1, D01 C9W8, Ireland

First published by HarperNorth in 2022
This paperback edition published by HarperNorth in 2023

1 3 5 7 9 10 8 6 4 2

A catalogue record for this book
is available from the British Library

ISBN: 978-0-00-847123-1

Printed and bound in the UK using 100%
renewable electricity at CPI Group (UK) Ltd

To our grandsons Oscar and Sidney and
the next generation of northerners
who make it all worthwhile.

CONTENTS

INTRODUCTION

Imagine northern England in 1911, perhaps as glimpsed in the rediscovered archive of Sagar Mitchell and James Kenyon, Blackburn-based film makers. Workers streaming out of factory gates, crossing the street, visiting a fairground or watching football. A few come and stare or wave at the camera. 'What they show is a world now lost to us: the busy world of north Britain in its manufacturing, mining heyday,' writes journalist Ian Jack. 'In Mitchell and Kenyon's films you can see it as an independent civilisation, glorying in its own easements and enjoyments such as electric trams, professional sport, street parades and pageants and seaside holidays.'[1]

That was also the year in which the north's share of England's population peaked at 36.5 per cent (in a series dating back to 1801), according to the Office for National Statistics.[2] It was still in its pomp as the founding region of the Industrial Revolution, which had begun nearly a hundred and fifty years earlier. For all the apparent serenity, this was a society facing major economic and social change. The militant suffragette movement, founded in the north, was in full swing. Strikes were common as workers demanded their share of increased prosperity. The seeds of relative industrial decline had already taken root. The north was over-dependent on industries such as textiles, coalmining, iron, steel and shipbuilding. Some had failed to innovate as fast as global competitors and the region was not developing new ones.

Roll forward more than a century and the north is at the centre of Britain's often ill-tempered debate about the future. Northern votes were crucial in the 2016 referendum decision to leave the European Union. At the 2019 general election, northerners helped Boris Johnson to achieve the biggest Conservative majority since Margaret Thatcher's time, making significant inroads into the so-called 'red wall' of former Labour seats. Johnson promised to 'level up' Britain and improve the fortunes of left-behind towns, though there were questions about how realistic this ambition was. The north's share of England's population has slipped to 27.5 per cent and its share of Britain's economic output has shrunk from 30 per cent just after the First World War to 20 per cent.[3] While northern England may not be an 'independent civilisation', however, its economy remains bigger than that of countries such as Argentina, Belgium, Denmark, Ireland, Norway and Sweden.[4]

Dramatic events have played out in the north – waves of migration, invasions and battles. It has made its mark on European culture and the global economy and played a huge part in shaping modern Britain. The Industrial Revolution, viewed by many economic historians as the key event in human history, is obviously of fundamental importance, but there is far more to the story. At least six Roman emperors ruled the empire from York. The Anglian kingdom of Northumbria became for a period Europe's leading cultural and intellectual centre. For a thousand of the past two thousand years – in Roman times and in the Middle Ages – northern England was the site of border warfare with what is now Scotland. The past has shaped the present in myriad ways. The devastation wrought by factory and pit closures in the 1980s, for example, evoked for some a folk memory of the trauma of William the Conqueror's Harrying of the North. Echoes of the Wars of the Roses, Tudor rebellions and seventeenth-century civil war divisions could be discerned in the

Brexit referendum. The north also played a leading role in creating the Labour Party and the trade union movement.

This book aims to tell the north's story through the experiences of the region's people, famous or not, including characters such as Cartimandua, queen of the Brigantes, the first northerner known by name; St Oswald, Bede and Richard III; Richard Arkwright and the Stephensons; William Wordsworth, the Brontës and Elizabeth Gaskell; Emmeline Pankhurst and Gracie Fields; Sir Robert Peel, William Gladstone, Ellen Wilkinson and Harold Wilson; Kathleen Ferrier, The Beatles and David Hockney; Marcus Rashford, Lemn Sissay and Nicola Adams. It describes the history from the earliest times to the present day and explores topics such as the significance of sheep, the north–south language divide, why the Industrial Revolution happened in the north, ethnic diversity, the legacy of slavery, northern women and the contribution of northern writers, artists and comedians. It is a story that raises many intriguing questions. Had the kingdom of Northumbria survived, northern England might today be at the heart of a northern-focused nation instead of an outlying region of one governed from the south. The Norman Conquest shifted England's strategic orientation southwards, while William's Harrying arguably laid the foundation for centuries of economic disadvantage.

But where is the north and what is a northerner? A liberal, inclusive view is taken in this work. The north is considered to be broadly where the people who live there think they are in the north. A northerner is someone who thinks of themself as a northerner. The region has rarely been a single administrative unit, so the question is more cultural than constitutional. Around the world there is a diaspora of people born or raised in the north who consider themselves northerners. Others come from families with northern roots. Equally, the region has many people born elsewhere who live or have lived in the north and consider themselves adoptive northerners.

Insofar as boundaries have been drawn for one purpose or another, these have shifted over the centuries. For modern government and statistical purposes the north comprises three regions: the north-west (historic counties of Lancashire, Cheshire, Westmorland, Cumberland), north-east (Northumberland and Durham), and Yorkshire and Humber (Yorkshire, north and north-east Lincolnshire). Two sides are bounded by the sea, and the Scottish border has changed in only a couple of ways since it was agreed at the Treaty of York in 1237. That leaves the southern boundary, on which most debate focuses.

The grey area includes Derbyshire, Nottinghamshire and Staffordshire. Cheshire now officially belongs to the north, while in Anglo-Saxon times it was in Mercia rather than Northumbria. Where significant events happened in the grey zone, this book generally includes them. Family tradition, place of work and leisure activities all affect where people perceive themselves as living. Writing in 1967, Graham Turner was surprised to find that some south Yorkshire dwellers 'think of themselves as midlanders', with two Rotherham waitresses informing him: 'We're midlands. Don't forget when they talked on t'radio about bombing raids in t'war, they put us wi' them.'[5] On the other hand, it is hard to see Derbyshire textile towns such as Glossop and New Mills as anything other than northern. And Arnold Bennett entitled his 1898 novel about an aspiring Staffordshire author in London, *A Man from the North*.

Geology created a dividing line, a 'Jurassic divide', from prehistoric times. A ridge of Jurassic limestone runs through England from Dorset to the Yorkshire coast. To the north-west lies largely a highland zone, suitable for pastoral farming, and to the south-east a lowland zone suitable for arable farming, which created a generally wealthier society. It is not a simple division – the north has arable areas such as the Vale of York and the Northumberland plain – but geography has had an influence.

When the Romans divided Britain into Britannia Inferior (north) and Superior (south, so called because it was closer to Rome) around 200 CE, the boundary stretched from the Mersey to the Wash, meaning that Lincoln fell in the northern province while Chester was in the southern.[6] The kingdom of Northumbria stretched at its fullest from the Forth to below the Humber. Its south-west boundary is less clear and has been put at the Mersey or the Ribble. It probably fluctuated. Northumbria's Æthelfrith campaigned in Chester in 616 and Edwin seized Anglesey, suggesting that Northumbria controlled territory down to the Mersey, but by the 920s a West Saxon and Mercian alliance extended its power into south Lancashire.[7]

Viking settlement created another division, with northern and eastern England forming Danelaw. This created a diagonal divide at right angles to the Jurassic divide, cutting against geography and tradition. In the thirteenth century, royal officialdom created yet a further dividing line: the River Trent. The administration of lands escheated to the crown (property that fell to the crown when an owner died without legal heirs) was divided between escheators operating north or south of the Trent, *ultra* or *citra Trentam*. The royal forest administration and Duchy of Lancaster were similarly divided. Confusingly, this divide never followed the precise course of the river; the northern administration spread south of it. At the universities of Oxford and Cambridge in medieval times, students divided themselves into northerners and southerners, which is said to have provoked riots up to the sixteenth century.[8]

Then there is the question of how far northerners see themselves as northerners. The north has for good or ill often been characterised by stereotypes, what television playwright Denis Potter called 'slate-grey rain and polished euphoniums … eh-bah-goom heritage'.[9] Allegiances to cities, towns, counties and sub-regions are often greater than those to the wider region. Tyneside, Merseyside and Yorkshire have a particularly strong sense of distinctiveness. People can hold multiple identities, however. Identification with class and ethnicity exists alongside that with locality, region or nation. Identity is often fashioned against an 'other'. In the case of the north, that other is the south.

Stuart Maconie, writer and broadcaster, argues that 'there's no conception of the south comparable to the north'. He adds:

> Good or bad, 'the north' means something to all English people wherever they hail from. To people from London ... it means desolation, arctic temperatures, mushy peas, a cultural wasteland with limited shopping opportunities and populated by aggressive trolls. To northerners it means home, truth, beauty, valour, romance, warm and characterful people, real beer and decent chip shops. And in this we are undoubtedly biased, of course.[10]

Donald Horne, an Australian writer, in 1969 described the contribution of northern and southern values to Englishness in terms of competing metaphors. In the Northern Metaphor, Britain was 'pragmatic, empirical, calculating, Puritan, bourgeois, enterprising, adventurous, scientific, serious, and believes in struggle'. In the Southern Metaphor, Britain was 'romantic, illogical, muddled, divinely lucky, Anglican, aristocratic, traditional, frivolous, and believes in order and tradition'.[11] These values describe the end of the nineteenth century better than today's England, in which the southern spirit seems more enterprising than in the past.

Consciousness of a divide goes back at least as far as Bede in the eighth century. In his *Ecclesiastical History of the English People*, Bede refers nine times to the Humber as the boundary between north and south. He tells us that the monks of Bardney, in Lincolnshire, initially objected to housing the bones of Northumbrian king Oswald because 'as he was a native of another province, and had obtained the sovereignty over them, they retained their ancient aversion to him even after his death'.[12]

Southern chroniclers in the Middle Ages tended to portray northerners as ferocious, obstinate and unyielding, though at least William of Malmesbury pointed to explanations in hard living conditions, border disturbance and distance from the king.[13] Northerners were obstinate because they would not do what southerners, who expected to rule, dictated. When northern troops were used to fight battles in the south during the Wars of the Roses, it provoked alarm. 'The people in the north rob and steal and be appointed to pillage all this country and give away men's livelihoods in all the south country and that will ask a mischief,' wrote Clement Paston, of a Norfolk gentry family, to his brother John.[14]

Historians have tended to write off the north before the nineteenth century as backward or barbaric. Medievalist G.W.S. Barrow, writing in 1969, said northern England had typically been little more than 'an agglomeration of intensely conservative and relatively poor communities'.[15] Thomas Babington Macaulay in 1848 suggested that before the discovery and exploitation of coal, 'physical and moral causes had occurred to prevent civilisation from spreading to that region'. He put it down to centuries of armed conflict with the Scots, leading inhabitants to sleep with weapons at their side. Even in the seventeenth century people on the upper Tyne were, he said, 'scarcely less savage than the Indians of California … half-naked women chaunting a wild measure while the men with brandished dirks danced a war dance'.[16]

Eric Musgrove, author of the only previous general history of northern England, published in 1990, identified four periods of 'particular northern distinction, importance and power'.[17] The first spanned the third century when Britannia Inferior was created. At the beginning and end of this period Roman emperors (Septimius Severus and Constantius Chlorus) ruled the empire from York. The second was the spectacular 'age of Bede', when Northumbria enjoyed cultural and religious influence on an international scale, culminating in Alcuin's appointment as leading scholar at the court of Charlemagne, the Frankish emperor.

The third period was the military age of the Nevilles and Percys from the mid-fourteenth to the late fifteenth centuries, when the north's importance in supplying manpower for wars in Scotland and France brought wealth and influence to its aristocratic families. This was also the age of John of Gaunt, Duke of Lancaster, and Edward of Woodstock, the Black Prince, Earl of Chester and prince of Aquitaine. The fourth period was the Industrial Revolution, from the late eighteenth to the end of the nineteenth century.

There have of course been significant developments outside these periods, notably at the start of the thirteenth century when Anglo-Norman barons from the north instigated the revolt against King John that led to Magna Carta being agreed at Runnymede. History is in any case not just about politics and wars, but about ordinary people's lives. But Musgrove's four periods do emphasise that there is more to the north's past than the Industrial Revolution or even the north–south divide. During the age of Bede, Northumbria was at the crossroads of cultural influence in north-western Europe. It is a rich and varied history that deserves to be told.

BEGINNINGS

CHAPTER 1

FIRST NORTHERNERS TO THE ROMANS

Life was hard for the first northerners, almost certainly a hunting group of an early human species, taking advantage of a warmer interlude during the last ice age to range north in search of food at least half a million years ago. Britain, on the north-west corner of north-west Europe, was at the edge of their range. It was occupied intermittently by small groups who ventured across the land bridge known as Doggerland. There were at least ten separate waves of occupation as people were repeatedly driven out by extreme changes in the environment.

All that these intrepid venturers will have known about the north was that it presented a physical challenge in a hostile landscape. Northernness, a state of mind as much as a feature of geography, was fashioned over subsequent millennia. It is as well, though, to start at the beginning. Only by seeing how each stage built upon another can we know how northerners' collective experience began to form. The physical environment was an important factor.

Britain's climate fluctuated between Mediterranean-like conditions and long stages of cold in which ice sheets up to three miles thick covered the land as far south as the Thames valley. In warmer periods, vegetation was like today, a mix of woodland and grassland, though animals were more exotic. Remains of lions, straight-tusked elephants, mammoths, rhinoceroses, hippopotamuses and hyenas have been found at sites in the north.[1]

Much earlier, there were dinosaurs. We may not know exactly who the first humans were, but there is a name for the north's – indeed Britain's – earliest identified sauropod dinosaur. It lived 176 million years ago in what is now Yorkshire. It is nicknamed Alan. A fossil vertebra of the creature was identified in 2015, having been found on a beach near Whitby after it fell from a cliff face; it is in the Yorkshire Museum in York. Alan was named after Alan Gurr, an amateur geologist who found it.[2]

The earliest evidence of people in the north is indirect. Hand-axes found in Waverley Wood, Warwickshire, are made of andesite rock likely to have come from the Lake District about 500,000 years ago.[3] The axes were wielded by *Homo heidelbergensis*, tall and heavily built people, who used stone blades to butcher large animals. These may have followed an earlier, unidentified species similar to *Homo antecessor*, so far found only in Spain.

Next came *Homo neanderthalensis*, small and stocky. Creswell Crags in Derbyshire, south of Sheffield, contains Neanderthal stone tools. It also has the northernmost cave art in Europe: twenty-five engraved figures depict deer, birds, bovids (probably aurochs, extinct wild cattle) and horses.[4] Theses were made by *Homo sapiens*, or modern humans, whose presence in Britain, initially sporadic, has been continuous since about 12,000 years ago.

As the last ice age ended, sea levels rose, cutting Britain off from continental Europe permanently. There is evidence of occupation. A large circular building at Howick in Northumberland dating from about 7600 BCE is thought to have been a permanent dwelling.[5] An even older one has been excavated at Star Carr in Yorkshire, sometimes described as 'Britain's oldest house', dating from about 9000 BCE. It may have been a hunting camp.[6] Finds at Star Carr include headdresses made from red deer skulls (possibly used by shamans in ritual practices), barbed points used in hunting and fishing, and the earliest evidence of carpentry in Europe.

The Neolithic period brought farming and a more settled way of life. The best-known monument is Stonehenge, but there are important edifices in northern England. Thornborough Henges, a Neolithic/Bronze Age complex of three circular earthworks in north Yorkshire, has been described as one of Britain's premier 'sacred landscapes' during the third and second millennia BCE.[7] Cumbria is notable for the 'Langdale axe industry', the manufacture of polished volcanic stone axes at Great Langdale in the Lake District. Axe-heads from there have been found all over Britain and in Ireland. The fact that these were widely traded, and that some appear unused, suggests they were of high value and may have had religious as well as practical purposes.[8] They may have been used in gift exchanges.

In the 1930s, archaeologist Cyril Fox identified a highland–lowland divide, described by some as a 'Jurassic divide'.[9] A ridge of Jurassic limestone runs through England from Dorset to the Yorkshire coast. To the north-west lies a highland zone, with harder rocks, suitable for pastoral farming such as raising sheep. To the south-east is a lowland zone suitable for arable farming such as grain. Pastoral communities tended to consist of isolated farmsteads or small hamlets, while arable communities created larger villages. The south-east appeared wealthier, producing more decorated pottery. This division is now seen as an over-simplification, though geography clearly has some influence.

The north is rich in Bronze Age sites such as barrows. In the Iron Age, people lived in small villages, in thatched roundhouses with wooden or wattle and daub walls and a central fire. There were also so-called 'hill forts', communal spaces possibly used for ceremonies or trading; Northumberland, with 271, has the largest number in England.[10] Iron Age Britons are thought to have spoken variants of Brythonic, the southern group of Celtic languages that now consists of Welsh, Cornish and Breton.

Did Iron Age people indulge in human sacrifice, as Julius Caesar and others suggested? A body known as Lindow Man, discovered in

1984 and preserved in Lindow Moss, a Cheshire peat bog, is cited as probable evidence of ritual killing.[11] He was about twenty-five years old, of robust frame, bearded and naked apart from a fox-fur band round his left arm. He appears to have been of high social rank because his manicured fingernails showed he had done little manual work. He suffered blows to the head, was garrotted, swallowed mistletoe and then drowned in the waters of the bog. Why he met this grim fate is unknown.

Northern England's principal Iron Age tribe was the Brigantes, centred on Yorkshire and occupying much of Lancashire, Northumberland and Durham – the first sign of a northern geographical identity emerging. Their name means high or elevated – *brig* is a top or summit in modern Welsh – which could refer to the Pennines. Their territory, the largest in Britain, was bordered by five other tribes: the Carvetii in the north-west, Votadini in the north-east, Parisii to the east and, to the south, Cornovii and Corieltauvi.

Cartimandua, queen of the Brigantes, in power around the time of the Roman conquest, ought to be as famous as Boudica or Cleopatra. She is the first British queen known to history and the first northerner we can identify (Tacitus consistently names her as a queen, but does not describe her contemporary, Boudica, as such[12]). While Boudica, leader of East Anglia's Iceni, is seen as a resistance heroine, Cartimandua tends to be relegated to a few disparaging lines in history books. She collaborated with the Romans, divorced her husband, married one of his aides and was overthrown by a revolt. She was portrayed by Roman historians, despite her loyalty, as an adulterous betrayer of British men, a picture that modern accounts often do little to challenge. Yet she succeeded in keeping her territory free from annexation for up to thirty years. A more balanced assessment is justified.

The Romans invaded Britain in 43 CE and stayed until 409, no doubt aiming to exploit Britain's land, people and resources. They faced strong resistance in Wales where a guerrilla campaign was led by a chieftain called Caratacus. For the Roman governor of Britannia, Publius Ostorius Scapula, having the Brigantes as a northern ally helped to protect his flank. Finally, Caratacus's luck ran out. In 51 CE he lost a pitched battle with the Romans in Snowdonia. His wife and daughter were captured and his brother surrendered.[13] He fled to Brigantia, possibly to seek support among anti-Roman factions, but Cartimandua captured him and handed him over to the Romans. As an ally of Rome, she could hardly do otherwise. Caratacus was taken to Rome, where his capture was hailed as a great prize. He took part in Claudius's triumphal parade and made a speech so stirring that, according to Tacitus, the emperor pardoned him and allowed him to live in exile there.[14]

Cartimandua is not generously treated in Roman sources. Although Tacitus refers to her loyalty to Rome, he also talks of her 'treacherous' role in the capture of Caratacus, her 'wanton spirit', her sexual impropriety in rejecting her husband, Venutius, in favour of a common soldier and her 'cunning stratagems' in taking Venutius's relatives hostage.[15] To understand this, we need to consider women's role in the empire. No Roman woman became emperor. Female rulers on the empire's fringes were seen as exotic, but their authority was at variance with Rome's culture and so invited disapproval. They tend to be stereotyped in Roman sources either as women of loose morals (Cartimandua, Cleopatra) or as fierce and unladylike (Boudica). Sarah Pomeroy summed up the attitude to women in classical antiquity in the title of her 1975 book *Goddesses, Whores, Wives and Slaves*.

Tacitus suggests Cartimandua had ruled the Brigantes for some time and was of 'high birth'.[16] How she came to her position is not clear. Some suggest that her predecessor may have unified the diverse tribes of Brigantia, while others speculate that her marriage to Venutius, a fellow northerner, could have cemented an alliance between tribal units.[17] It is not known which tribal group Venutius came from, though some suggest he came from the north-western people known as the Carvetii.

Not long after the handing over of Caratacus, Venutius and Cartimandua divorced. Whether the causes were personal or political is not known. Fighting broke out among the Brigantes, which led to Venutius's brother and other relations being seized and imprisoned. The conflict escalated as Venutius raised support from outside the kingdom and led an invasion. A new Roman governor, Didius Gallus, sent auxiliary troops into Brigantia. There were several skirmishes before the rebellion was finally put down by a legion. Venutius probably fled to his own people.[18] Twelve years later, in 69, Venutius rebelled again over Cartimandua's decision to marry a man called Vellocatus, formerly Venutius's armour-bearer. Tacitus says her decision was reckless because 'her house was at once shaken by this scandalous act'.[19]

Venutius again attacked with external forces and there was also an internal Brigantian revolt. Cartimandua appealed to her Roman allies for help, but the governor, Vettius Bolanus, sent auxiliary infantry and cavalry instead of legionary troops. His decision cost Cartimandua her throne. The rescue mission initially struggled to succeed, according to Tacitus,[20] probably because the Roman governor had sent inadequate forces. After some 'desperate fighting' they managed to extricate Cartimandua, who would otherwise have been killed or held hostage. What became of her is unknown: she may perhaps have died soon after, or lived under Roman protection elsewhere in Britain, or lived out her days in exile in Rome. Venutius lasted less than five years as ruler of Brigantia. Bolanus was replaced as governor by Petillius Cerealis, a seasoned soldier. Cerealis advanced into Brigantia and brought it directly under Roman rule.[21] Like Cartimandua, Venutius disappeared from the record, his fate unknown.

It is hard to know what Cartimandua was like, beyond the outlines. Almost everything we know about her is from Roman sources, coupled with archaeological evidence such as a fortified site at Stanwick, near Darlington, north Yorkshire, which may have been her capital. The Brigantes themselves are shadowy. They appear to have worshipped a goddess called Brigantia, who may have given them their name, 'the people of the high one'. There were similarly named tribes in Gaul, Austria and Ireland, though it is not known whether these were in some way related.

Cartimandua arguably served Brigantia's interest by preserving quasi-independence, albeit temporarily and at the price of internal strife over whether to work with or against the Romans. She cannot be labelled a betrayer of Britons because there was at that time no British nation to betray; each tribe pursued its own interests. Boudica, by contrast, revolted against Roman rule, though she ultimately failed and her people suffered savage retribution. In the end, however, Cartimandua was unable to halt the spread of Roman rule northwards.

Another governor, Gnaeus Julius Agricola, came close to annexing Caledonia. Scotland has never been fully conquered by forces from the south: neither the Roman Empire nor English medieval kings achieved it. Agricola arguably came closest. He became governor in 77 or 78 and remained in office for about six years, an exceptionally long term. The Roman army moved steadily north throughout his governorship, building forts on the way. He reached the Forth–Clyde isthmus and then the River Tay.[22]

In 83 or 84, Agricola defeated the Caledonian tribes at the Battle of Mons Graupius. All we know about the location is that it was near a mountain. The tribes were led by Calgacus. Tacitus portrays him as making a rousing speech (certainly fabricated) in which he excoriates the Romans as 'robbers of the world': 'To robbery, slaughter, plunder, they give the lying name of empire; they make a solitude and call it peace.'[23] The battle took place on the slope of a hill where Calgacus's warriors had assembled. Agricola's cavalry broke through the tribesmen's ranks and attacked them from behind. The warriors were trapped between the horsemen and Roman infantry units, leading to great slaughter. If Tacitus is to be believed (he was Agricola's son-in-law), 10,000 Britons but only 360 Romans were killed.[24] This was the high-water mark of Roman expansion. Agricola was soon recalled to Rome. The Romans drew back to the Forth–Clyde line. Troops were needed on the Danube, where two Roman armies had been defeated by Dacians.

Early in the second century the Romans pulled back further to the Tyne–Solway. Emperor Hadrian decided to consolidate the empire's frontiers. He arrived in Britain around 122 and started building his seventy-four-mile wall, the most visible reminder of the Roman presence in Britain and a structure without equal in any of the empire's provinces. The wall is thought to have combined defence with customs control and frontier supervision. Britons on either side were treated as potential enemies.[25]

Within a few years, however, Hadrian's Wall was abandoned. Antoninus Pius, who succeeded Hadrian, had his own wall built further north along the Forth–Clyde line. The *Historia Augusta* says: 'Lollius Urbicus, his legate, overcame the Britons and built a second wall, one of turf, after driving back the barbarians.'[26] The Antonine Wall was shorter (37 miles) and simpler.[27] It marked the largest formal extent that Roman Britain ever reached. Around 158 it, in turn, was abandoned and never reoccupied, for unknown reasons. Hadrian's Wall again became the boundary and remained so until the end of Roman rule. It was a symbol of a frontier region that was to be fought over many times during two millennia. Even today it is a powerful reminder of the limits of empires and the border struggles that have formed the experience of Scots and the northern English.

Northern Britain's importance meant that six or seven emperors visited the region while holding supreme power. Septimius Severus, known as the African emperor, who was the mixed-race son of a provincial family from present-day Libya, ruled the empire from a base at Eboracum, or York, for four years until he died there in 211. The others were Hadrian, Severus's sons Caracalla and Geta, Constantius I and his son Constantine the Great, and possibly Constans. Never has such power been wielded from northern England, yet their presence was also a sign of the region's vulnerability.

The third century was a landmark as the north gained self-governing status within the empire. Britain was split into two provinces. Britannia Inferior stretched from Hadrian's Wall to south of Lincoln, while Britannia Superior (so called because it was geographically closer to Rome) covered southern England and Wales. Rarely has northern England been governed as a single entity: the other similar cases were Brigantia, which covered most of it, and the Anglian kingdom of Northumbria, which covered northern England and southern Scotland.

Britannia Inferior benefited from imperial policy that poured money into militarised zones. The third century was turbulent in the empire: soldiers made and disposed of emperors. Hardly any emperors died peacefully. The focus was on the eastern frontier, threatened by Persians, and on the Rhine and Danube, where there were invasions by German tribes. There was a rapid succession of emperors raised to power by armies in the provinces. Britannia's northern frontier, by contrast, was peaceful for much of the century.[28]

Severus's father was North African and his mother of Roman patrician descent.[29] He emerged as emperor from a series of cataclysmic events in 193, the 'Year of Five Emperors', some of whom were assassinated or executed. Severus came to Britain in 208 with his wife Julia Domna and sons Caracalla and Geta, designated as his successors. He arrived possibly in response to a barbarian rebellion, though he may also have been seeking to remove his unruly sons from Rome's temptations.[30] Setting off from Rome with a retinue of servants and officials, Severus rode a horse for the first leg, to keep up appearances, but he was sixty-three and suffering from arthritis, so he was carried in a litter for most of the way, as also happened later on his northern military campaign.[31]

On arriving in Britain, Severus left younger son Geta in the south to attend to justice and civil government. The elder son Antoninus, nicknamed Caracalla after a Gallic hooded tunic that he habitually wore, accompanied his father north. Severus made his headquarters at York. Campaigns in Caledonia took place in 209 and 210. The tribes fought a guerrilla war, as they had against Agricola, striking and then vanishing into forests and marshes.

Unlike Agricola, Severus failed to engage them in a set-piece battle. He did eventually reach north-eastern Scotland. According to historian Cassius Dio, the tribes were forced to give up a large part of their territory. Dio also tells a story that Caracalla drew a sword as though about to kill his father while they were riding to receive the Britons' surrender. Guards restrained Caracalla. Severus ignored the kerfuffle until after the surrender, when he challenged his son to murder him then and there if he wished.[32] Severus proclaimed victory, but the tribes quickly disavowed the terms and restarted the war. Severus ordered another invasion, this time with instructions that soldiers should kill everyone they came across. He was preparing for it when he died at York in February 211. His body was cremated there and his ashes placed in a purple urn that he had thoughtfully provided for himself. Caracalla and Geta became joint emperors, which Severus probably hoped would end their bitter rivalry.[33]

Caracalla became one of the most cruel and tyrannical emperors. On his father's death, he ordered the execution of imperial household attendants; thirty decapitated male skeletons found at Driffield Terrace, York, in 2004 may be the victims.[34] On returning to Rome, Caracalla killed his brother Geta, who died clinging to his mother. Orders were issued across the empire to remove Geta's name from inscriptions and destroy his statues and portraits.

It is unclear exactly when Britannia Superior and Inferior were created. It may have been a decision by Severus, who had already divided Syria. Alternatively, his intentions may have been carried out by Caracalla, or Caracalla may have decided himself to weaken the potential threat of revolt by a large province. Britannia Superior was home to the II and XX legions, while the legate of the VI legion governed Britannia Inferior. It is not known whether Britannia Inferior was in some way subordinate to Britannia Superior.

Britannia Superior had its capital at Londinium (London), while that of Britannia Inferior was York, which saw its status raised from *municipium*, or town, to *colonia*, the highest status for a Roman city. Over about fifty years, many forts in the Pennines and on the northern frontier were repaired or partially rebuilt. Towns developed mainly in the south, with a few in the north such as Chester, York, Carlisle and Corbridge. Villas were created in east Yorkshire, though fewer than in the south. The most common urban settlement in the north was the *vicus*, a civilian area around a military base. The army's presence attracted traders. However, a militarised province where the state controlled most land had limited potential for independent economic growth. It was exploited for grain and mineral wealth, such as silver-rich lead ores in the Peak District, the profits from which went to Rome rather than local communities.[35]

The fourth century saw Roman troops in Britain frequently rebel as the empire began to fragment. The long peace on the northern frontier deteriorated in the face of barbarian incursions. The start of the century brought an odd echo of Severus's story. When Constantius Chlorus was declared augustus, or joint senior emperor, he made an expedition to Britain with his son Constantine. Sources imply that he reached the far north of Scotland, like Agricola and Severus.[36] In 306, Constantius, like Severus, died at York.

Soldiers at York declared Constantine emperor, against the wishes of Constantius's co-emperor.[37] Constantine 'the Great' emerged as victor after a succession of wars. He issued the Edict of Milan, legitimising Christianity, which was already established in Britain. Later, Emperor Constans made a surprise expedition to Britain in 342–3, possibly to repel barbarian attacks or suppress a plot, though it is not known whether he came north. Security on the frontier deteriorated amid seaborne raiding by Picts from Scotland and Attacotti and Scotti from Ireland. The raids culminated in attacks in 367, which historian Ammianus Marcellinus labelled a 'barbarian conspiracy'.[38]

At the end of the fourth century the British provinces remained prosperous and Roman rule may still have seemed secure. Within a decade, however, everything had changed. Coinage ceased to arrive after 402, leaving troops unpaid. The last Roman troops were removed in 407. Amid instability in Rome, Britons declared themselves independent in 409. Greek historian Zosimus wrote, after Germanic raids:

> The barbarians beyond the Rhine made such unbounded incursions over every province, as to reduce not only the Britons, but some of the Celtic nations also to the necessity of revolting from the empire, and living no longer under the Roman laws but as they themselves pleased. The Britons therefore took up arms, and incurred many dangerous enterprises for their own protection, until they had freed their cities from the barbarians who besieged them.[39]

What was life like in the Roman north? Roman soldiers held a disparaging opinion of native Britons, if one of the most celebrated Vindolanda tablets can be taken as a general view. These tablets – letters and documents written in ink on wafer-thin slivers of wood – are a rich source of information about life on the northern frontier. One unknown author wrote (translated from Latin): 'The Britons are unprotected by armour. There are very many cavalry. The cavalry do not use swords, nor do the wretched Britons [*Brittunculi*] mount in order to throw javelins.'[40] *Brittunculi* can alternatively be translated as 'little Britons'. It is unclear whether the writer meant Britons serving in the Roman forces or the natives he was fighting. Either way, the term appears derogatory.

The tablets, first discovered in 1973 in waterlogged deposits around the early wooden forts at Vindolanda, just south of Hadrian's Wall, provide a fascinating insight. They date mostly from 90–105, when the Ninth Cohort of Batavians (from today's Netherlands) and First Cohort of Tungrians (from northern Gaul) were based at Vindolanda. The best known was written by Claudia Severa, wife of the commander of a nearby fort, to Sulpicia Lepidina, wife of the Batavians' commander, inviting her to a birthday party: 'I shall expect you, sister. Farewell, sister, my dearest soul, as I hope to prosper, and hail.'[41] The need for clothing and other comforts to withstand northern winters is a theme. One anonymous letter reads: 'I have sent you … pairs of socks from Sattua, two pairs of sandals and two pairs of underpants.'[42]

Soldiers at the fort were auxiliaries, non-citizen recruits who served for up to twenty-five years in return for Roman citizenship. They were not British. After a revolt by these very units on the River Meuse in 69, Rome followed a policy of not allowing native troops to serve within their province of origin. Names on the Vindolanda tablets suggest origins from Gaul, Germany, Pannonia, Dacia and Greece (probably Greek slaves) as well as the upper Rhine.[43] Several artefacts and inscriptions clustered along Hadrian's Wall also record the presence of Africans. Entertaining as the tablets are, they tell us little about native Britons' lives or how they felt about the occupation. While Romans brought useful innovations to Britain, including roads and towns, they were colonisers who slaughtered and enslaved people. David Mattingly estimates that between 100,000 and 250,000 Britons perished in the conquest period of 43–83, out of a British population of about two million.[44]

Romans stimulated the economy with new markets, increased demand and new tools. Theirs was a hierarchical society, ranging from landowners, administrators and military officials to peasant farmers, slaves and the urban poor. Romans expanded various industries and developed medical treatments. It was the first time in which washing, personal hygiene, fresh water supplies and waste disposal were organised in Britain.[45] On the other hand, the population was probably exposed to tuberculosis and leprosy for the first time.

Vindolanda revealed artefacts relating to women and children, suggesting that these were living not just with officers but in barracks designed for lower ranks. Native women's position was particularly vulnerable. At Chester, Pompeius Optatus, probably a soldier, paid for a tombstone for three slave children from his household, likely to have been his own children with a female slave. At South Shields, Barates the Syrian erected a memorial to his British wife Regina, depicting her as a Roman matron. He had evidently freed and married her, only for Regina to die aged thirty.[46]

Romans sometimes paired a British god with one of their own. In the north, for example, the war god Mars was often combined with Celtic warrior god Cocidius, usually depicted in a similar manner to Mars with spear and shield. This is the Roman concept of *interpretatio*, defined by Tacitus as 'the interpretation of alien deities and of the rites associated with them'.[47]

Our understanding about life in the Roman north will forever be distorted by having only one side of the story. We can never, sadly, see native Britons' experience through their own eyes. After the Romans departed, the provincial system of government gave way to something more regionally fragmented, based on the power of local rulers. There was a lack of new coins in circulation, either imported or minted locally, which indicates that the financial and taxation system ceased to operate. Manufacture of pottery and other goods declined and trade in goods with the continent halted abruptly.

Anglo-Saxon migrants had become established by the mid-fifth century, though they were not in the ascendancy until the sixth. A British leader called Vortigern was reported by historians to have invited a force of Angles and Saxons led by Hengest and Horsa to repel barbarians. Hengest and Horsa (if they really existed) turned against the Britons and defeated them in a series of battles.[48] The Romano-British rallied under the leadership of Ambrosius Aurelianus, a possibly mythical figure like King Arthur; in later chronicles he is transformed into Arthur's uncle. Ambrosius, the last Roman-type figure in Britain's history, is said to have defeated the Saxons at the Battle of Mount Badon in or around 493. Even if he did, it was only a temporary relief.

The end of Roman Britain and birth of Anglo-Saxon England and the Celtic kingdoms seems to have been a gradual process. In northern England, the Romans left a remarkable legacy. They created a network of forts and roads that tied the region into an economic and social system that stretched beyond Egypt. Two thousand years on, their impact on the north's infrastructure and geography remains visible today. The experience of having been a strategically important, self-governing province in a mighty European empire remains central to the north's self-image.

CHAPTER 2

THE KINGDOM OF NORTHUMBRIA

The 'Dark Ages' brought more than mead halls, warlords, paganism and songs of dragons and vengeful gods to northern England. The Anglian kingdom of Northumbria arguably achieved greater political power, and certainly greater autonomy, than the north has seen since. Northumbria existed from the early seventh to the late ninth century and stretched at its fullest from the Forth to below the Humber. Four of its kings – Edwin, Oswald, Oswiu and Ecgfrith – exercised a degree of dominance over other kingdoms, north and south. Northumbria vied with Mercia for overlordship over other Anglo-Saxon territories.

More remarkable still, Northumbria transformed itself in little more than a century from a pagan, illiterate society into northern Europe's leading intellectual, Christian and artistic centre. Its golden age produced scholars such as Bede and Alcuin and exquisite illuminated manuscripts such as the *Lindisfarne Gospels*; it sent missionaries to the pagans of Germany and representatives to the court of Charlemagne and assembled some of the finest libraries. Northumbria was at the crossroads of Europe, influenced from the west by Celtic Christian missionaries and settled in the east by Germanic and Scandinavian migrants.

Yet the kingdom did not endure. Like other Anglo-Saxon kingdoms, its organisation was unstable, with warrior rulers relying on conquest and exacting tribute from other kingdoms to reward followers. Instability increased in the eighth century as rivalry for the crown among noble families grew. The monarchy was weakened by giving away too much land in perpetuity to create monasteries. Sixteen kings ruled during the eighth century and their life expectancy was as poor as that of Roman emperors: most were murdered, deposed, exiled or abdicated to become monks.[1]

Viking raids began in 793 with an attack on Lindisfarne. Alcuin believed this was divine retribution for monks who preferred feasting and hunting to God's work.[2] By 867, the Great Danish Army had seized control of York, dividing Northumbria and in effect ending its independent existence. Eventually it was absorbed into the nascent kingdom of England. Had Northumbria endured, northern England might today have been at the centre of a northern-focused Britain, instead of an outlying region of one governed from the south.

The name 'Northumbrians' first appeared in 731, in Latin, in Bede's *Ecclesiastical History of the English People*, to describe those living north of the Humber;[3] in distinguishing them from southerners, he gives us the earliest exposition of north–south consciousness. For Northumbria's origins, however, we must go back to the obscure period following the end of Roman rule. Immigrants from northern Germany, Frisia and southern Scandinavia began arriving in Britain around 430, probably in small groups, with larger migration from mid-century.[4]

Scholarly opinion has largely shifted from the notion that the Germanic incomers wiped out the Celtic British population or drove them westwards to Wales, towards the view that most of the existing population stayed and gradually adopted the new arrivals' language and culture. There are similar examples of new, prestigious, minority languages displacing existing languages elsewhere. For example, Latin replaced Gaulish in France and Gaelic replaced Pictish in Scotland.[5] Archaeological evidence such as mixed burial sites points to assimilation.[6] Palaeobotany tells us there was no large-scale reforestation, which would have been expected if the native population had fled or been destroyed, unless there was compensatory immigration on an implausible scale.[7] A 2015 genetic study by Oxford academics concluded that there was no genocide or complete disappearance of Britons.[8]

While most people appear to have assimilated, the Romano-British ruling class was displaced. Bede names Ida as 'the founder of the royal family of the Northumbrians'.[9] Ida began to rule in 547, probably only over Bernicia, the province centred on Northumberland and Durham, with its capital at Bamburgh.

Ida's grandson Æthelfrith became king of Bernicia around 593 and later also Deira, the province roughly covering today's Yorkshire – thus uniting Northumbria's main constituent parts. Æthelfrith, seen as Northumbria's founding father, subjugated neighbouring British kingdoms. To Bede, Æthelfrith was a 'brave and ambitious king' who

> ravaged the Britons more than all the chiefs of the English, insomuch that he might be compared to Saul of old, king of the Israelites, save only in this, that he was ignorant of divine religion. For he conquered more territories from the Britons than any other chieftain or king, either subduing the inhabitants and making them tributary, or driving them out and planting the English in their places.[10]

Britons called him *Flesaur*, or 'the twister'.[11]

Áedán mac Gabráin, the Irish king of Dál Riata, covering parts of western Scotland and north-eastern Ireland, led an army in 603 in a pre-emptive strike against Æthelfrith's growing threat. Although Æthelfrith commanded an inferior force, according to Bede, he won a crushing victory at a place called Degsastan, in which most of Áedán's army was killed and Áedán fled.[12] Bede says Æthelfrith's victory was so great that the Irish kings in Britain would not make war on the English again, right up to Bede's time. Æthelfrith gained control of Deira around 604 – whether by force or persuasion is unknown – and apparently married Acha, daughter of Ælla, former king of Deira.[13] Later Æthelfrith turned to deal with the Welsh, defeating the kingdom of Powys in a battle at Chester. Bede tells us that Æthelfrith ordered his warriors to attack and kill hundreds of Welsh monks who had come to pray for their side's victory.[14]

During Æthelfrith's reign, Acha's brother Edwin went into exile, where he led a wandering life, never safe from Æthelfrith's efforts to exterminate Deiran opposition to his rule.[15] Some later sources suggest that Edwin spent his childhood in the Welsh kingdom of Gwynedd. If so, he would have been foster-brother to Cadwallon, with whom he eventually had a lethal feud. By the 610s Edwin was in Mercia under the protection of King Cearl, whose daughter Coenburh he married. Edwin then went to stay with Rædwald, king of East Anglia (considered by historians to be the likely occupant of the Sutton Hoo ship-burial). According to Bede, Æthelfrith attempted to bribe, threaten and cajole Rædwald to kill Edwin. Rædwald came close to succumbing, but was dissuaded by his wife. Rædwald and Edwin then attacked Æthelfrith, taking him by surprise and killing him in a battle in 616, believed to have taken place at Bawtry.[16]

The death of Northumbria's first king underlined the fragility of early Anglo-Saxon kingdoms, which had no institutions or concept of statehood. Everything depended on the person of the king. Æthelfrith's sons Eanfrith, Oswald and Oswiu survived, however, and fled into exile. Rædwald delegated rule of the north to Edwin who became king of Northumbria. Edwin invaded Elmet, a small kingdom in what is today west Yorkshire, and drove out its king. Then he took the bold step of seizing control of Anglesey and the Isle of Man. He besieged Cadwallon, by then king of Gwynedd, but failed to kill him, which was ultimately to cost Edwin his own life.[17]

Edwin was initially under Rædwald's protection, which lasted until Rædwald died around 624–5. The untried Edwin then faced a threat in southern Britain from Cuichelm, king of the West Saxons. Edwin's response was to send envoys to Eadbald of Kent, at that stage the only Christian king in England. The alliance was cemented by Edwin agreeing to marry Eadbald's sister Æthelburh, daughter of a Frankish princess. (It is not known whether Edwin's Mercian queen, Coenburh, had died or if he repudiated her.[18])

Edwin made some half-hearted promises about converting to Christianity, which he was in no hurry to keep. In 625 Æthelburh travelled north with her entourage, including Paulinus, a Roman missionary who had been preaching in Kent for more than twenty years; he was originally part of Augustine's mission to Canterbury to Christianise the Anglo-Saxons. Paulinus was consecrated bishop in the ancient Roman *principia* at York, where he began to construct the first Christian church to be built in England for more than two hundred years: a small wooden oratory. Edwin prevaricated over conversion, weighing up political pros and cons. His interference in southern politics antagonised Cuichelm, who sent an envoy named Eomer to Edwin's court beside the River Derwent. As he addressed the court, Eomer drew a short sword, smeared with poison, and rushed at the king. In the fracas Edwin was wounded and two of his thegns slain. That night, Æthelburh gave birth to a daughter whom they named Eanflæd.[19]

Edwin had to avenge the attack, but he was an inexperienced warrior. Bede portrays Edwin as an indecisive man of weak character whom Paulinus was able to persuade to his own viewpoint. He was certainly not rash; he weighed political considerations carefully before acting. Paulinus persuaded Edwin to convert, but the king made a condition: he committed himself to Christianity provided that he was granted victory over Cuichelm, which would demonstrate that the Christian God was as effective in war as his tribal totem, Woden.[20] Edwin's campaign against the West Saxons was successful: five sub-kings were slain, though Cuichelm himself survived. Edwin's victory made him the most powerful English warlord. He subsequently embarked on consultations about converting to Christianity, culminating in a theatrical conference at which his 'noblest friends and advisers' concurred with his decision to convert.[21]

In Bede's account, the first witness was Coifi, the pagan chief priest, who was keen to renounce his former religion. Another witness made a striking rhetorical allegory:

> The present life of man upon earth, O king, seems to me, in comparison with that time which is unknown to us, like to the swift flight of a sparrow through the house wherein you sit at supper in winter, with your ealdormen and thegns, while the fire blazes in the midst, and the hall is warmed, but the wintry storms of rain or snow are raging abroad. The sparrow, flying in at one door and immediately out at another, whilst he is within, is safe from the wintry tempest; but after a short space of fair weather, he immediately vanishes out of your sight, passing from winter into winter again. So this life of man appears for a little while, but of what is to follow or what went before we know nothing at all. If, therefore, this new doctrine tells us something more certain, it seems justly to deserve to be followed.[22]

Deira was now Christian, in name at least. Bede saw Edwin as laying the foundations of a Christian Anglo-Saxon state, but Christianity's hold on Northumbria at this stage was not deep. The Northumbrian church was only six years old when Edwin's army was defeated in 632 by Cadwallon and Penda, an energetic member of the Mercian royal house, at Hæthfelth, or Hatfield. Edwin was killed along with his son Osfrith. With this defeat, Bernicia and Deira reverted briefly to home-grown kings and paganism.

Edwin was eventually succeeded by Oswald, son of Æthelfrith. Oswald ruled Northumbria for just eight years, from 634 to 642, yet he stands out as one of British history's most charismatic monarchs. A warrior known as 'Whiteblade' or 'Blessed arm', Oswald was the first English king to die a Christian martyr; he became venerated as a saint. He brought Bernicia and Deira once again under a single ruler and promoted the spread of Irish Christianity. His rule, along with that of his successors – his brother Oswiu and nephew Ecgfrith

– marked the zenith of Northumbria's power. He was the embodiment of a romantic hero, as Max Adams notes in *The King in the
North: The Life and Times of Oswald of Northumbria* – the righteous
exiled prince whose destiny is to return triumphant to reclaim his
kingdom. Adams even suggests that Oswald was the model for
another claimant returned from exile, Tolkien's Aragorn in *The Lord
of the Rings* – which, though plausible, is speculation.[23]

Oswald's short rule began and ended in violence. Yet in the view
of Bede, his saintliness was derived from meek behaviour rather than
martyrdom in battle against Mercia.[24] After his death at the Battle of
Maserfelth (possibly at Oswestry, or Oswald's Tree), tales of miracles
quickly grew up around the place where he fell. A cult developed
around him that spread across Europe and lasted for centuries. His
relics were much in demand: while Oswald's head is interred in
Durham Cathedral, at least four other medieval churches claimed to
possess it.[25]

Oswald and his brothers, following their father's death and uncle
Edwin's accession, had fled into exile in Dál Riata, probably with
their mother, Acha. Oswald was twelve. Oswald and Oswiu were
educated on Iona, in the monastery of St Columba (properly Colm
Cille), where he was converted to Christianity. After Edwin was
killed at Hatfield, Northumbria again split into constituent kingdoms. Oswald's half-brother Eanfrith briefly became king of
Bernicia, but was killed by Cadwallon after attempting to negotiate
peace. Then Oswald met Cadwallon in battle at Heavenfield, near
Hexham. Before the battle, Oswald had a wooden cross erected,
then knelt and asked his army to pray with him. According to
Adomnán's *Life of Saint Columba*, Oswald had a vision of Columba,
who told him: 'Be strong and act manfully. Behold, I will be with
thee.' He defeated and killed Cadwallon despite the Welsh king's
superior numbers.[26]

Oswald's victory made him overlord of all the lands north of the
Humber up to the Forth, yet his rule began modestly by establishing
a small community of monks on Lindisfarne, an island off Bernicia.

He asked Iona for a bishop to facilitate his people's conversion. Irish Christianity was an offshoot of British Christianity, introduced to Ireland by St Patrick and other missionaries and thence to Scotland, largely by Columba. Long isolation led to significant differences between the Irish church's customs and those of Rome. The first bishop was unsuccessful. Iona then sent Aidan, probably a senior monk.

Oswald gave Lindisfarne to Aidan as his episcopal see. Bede has nothing but praise for Aidan's humility and commitment to poverty.[27] Bede, in emphasising Oswald's saintliness, recounts the king's generosity to the poor and to strangers. In one story set at Easter – possibly imaginary – Oswald was sitting at dinner with Aidan and had a silver dish full of 'dainties' before him, when a servant came in to say that a crowd of the poor were in the streets begging alms from the king. Oswald immediately gave his food to them and even had the silver dish broken up and distributed. Aidan, impressed, seized Oswald's right hand and said: 'May this hand never decay.'[28]

Oswald was king of Bernicia, Deira and Lindsey. Bede claims that Oswald 'held under his sway all the nations and kingdoms of Britain',[29] but he struggled in the face of Penda's rise to power in Mercia. Conflict with the pagan Mercians proved Oswald's undoing and he died in battle against Penda at Maserfelth. Oswald's head and hands were put on stakes and his body dragged from the field so that he would not receive a hero's burial.[30] A year after his death, Oswald's brother Oswiu journeyed to the battlefield and took away what remained of him. His head was buried on Lindisfarne (and later moved to Durham) and his hands and arms interred at Bamburgh.

After Oswald's death, Oswiu succeeded him in Bernicia. Oswiu was a devoted Christian like his brother and founded monasteries including Gilling Abbey and Whitby Abbey. Unlike his brother, he struggled to assert authority over Deira for much of his twenty-eight-year reign, the first half of which was spent in Penda's shadow. Oswiu was, though, a canny, ruthless politician who became for a short period overlord of Britain. His ruthlessness was apparent in his treatment of Deira's new ruler, Oswine, son of Deira's last independent king, Osric. After a few years of peace, Oswiu and Oswine raised armies against each other. Oswine then shied away from conflict and disbanded his army; he was betrayed by a friend and delivered to Oswiu's soldiers, who murdered him.[31]

Oswiu had married Edwin's daughter Eanflæd in an effort to make himself more acceptable to the Deirans, but still he did not take direct control of Deira after Oswine's death. Instead, Oswald's son Œthelwald was installed, probably as sub-king. Œthelwald soon took a rebellious line, however. He fought with Penda against Oswiu, after which he disappeared from the historical record. Oswiu attempted to ease tensions with the pagan Penda in the early 650s by marrying his son Alhfrith to Penda's daughter Cyneburh, while his daughter Alhflaed married Penda's son Paeda, who was then baptised a Christian at a ceremony in Bernicia. However, things broke down in 655 when Penda invaded Bernicia with a large army. Oswiu finally met Penda in battle at the River Winwaed, near Leeds, and won an unlikely victory against heavy odds in which the Mercian king was killed.[32]

The death of Penda placed Oswiu in a dominant position. He installed Alhfrith as sub-king of Deira, while Paeda became king of southern Mercia and Oswiu himself took the north of the kingdom. Oswiu's total domination lasted only about three years, however. It ended when Paeda was assassinated, supposedly poisoned by his wife, Oswiu's daughter Alhflaed. A revolt by Mercian nobles led to Penda's son Wulfhere being installed as Mercia's first Christian king.

Meanwhile religious tensions were growing in Northumbria. Oswiu followed the Celtic Christian tradition whereas his wife Eanflæd, raised in the courts of Kent and Frankia, was a Roman Christian. Oswiu's son Alhfrith, who had been brought up as a Celtic Christian, adopted Roman practices at the urging of Wilfrid, a charismatic, noble-born priest who had studied at Lindisfarne, in Gaul and in Rome. Alhfrith, exerting independence from his father, expelled Lindisfarne-educated monks from a new monastery at Ripon and replaced them with monks of Roman persuasion.[33]

To settle the religious conflict, Oswiu convened and chaired the momentous Synod of Whitby in 664.[34] The main bone of contention was differing methods of calculating the date of Easter. Other differences included the style of monastic tonsure (round for the Romans, horseshoe-shaped for the Celts) and the system of penance. The royal decision was in favour of the Roman tradition, for reasons that appear as much political as ecclesiastical. It enabled Oswiu to outflank Alhfrith, retain his political supremacy and ingratiate himself with the pope. It shored up his influence among southern English kingdoms and gave him a voice in the appointment of the next Archbishop of Canterbury. In protest, Bishop Colman of Lindisfarne and other Celtic monks left for Iona and then the west of Ireland.

One holy man who appears to have accepted the Roman customs is Cuthbert, who was called on to introduce them at Lindisfarne when he became prior there. Noted for his piety, asceticism and generosity to the poor, Cuthbert – a simple shepherd – spent much time carrying out missionary work around Northumbria before becoming a hermit; he had a brief spell as bishop of Lindisfarne before he died. A posthumous cult grew, making him northern England's most popular saint. People from Northumbria have long believed that St Cuthbert protects them at times of peril. In the Second World War, some believed that he created an impenetrable mist to shield Newcastle and Durham from Luftwaffe bombing raids.[35]

The Romanist party advanced rapidly after the synod. The see of York was revived and eventually Wilfrid was appointed to it. Oswiu extended the Church's spiritual and civil role and built the foundations of what started to look more like a state. Oswiu died in 670, the first of his line to die of natural causes. Ecgfrith succeeded his father as ruler of Northumbria. However, the luck of the ruling Iding family was running out.[36] Married twice, Ecgfrith failed to produce an heir. An impetuous military campaign was to end with his death at the hands of the Picts at Nechtansmere, near Forfar, in 685. After Nechtansmere, Northumbria never regained its dominance of central or even northern Britain.

Ecgfrith was succeeded by his half-brother Aldfrith, son of Oswiu and an Irish princess named Fín. Aldfrith was a scholar and the first literate Anglo-Saxon king. Bede says that Aldfrith 'nobly retrieved the ruined state of the kingdom, though within narrower bounds'.[37] Aldfrith was no warrior; he did not embark on wars of conquest or seek to extend Northumbria's frontiers. However, he presided over the beginning of Northumbria's golden age of creativity.

Aldfrith died in 704 or 705 and was succeeded by his young son Osred, though only after a civil war against a claimant called Eadwulf. Osred was slain, possibly by the Picts, at age twenty after an eleven-year reign. Northumbria had been ruled by a single dynasty from 634 until Osred's death in 716, but the next 150 years were to be different. Henceforward the kingship was disputed by several families with claims to royal descent.[38] Kings were murdered, deposed, forcibly tonsured, immured in monasteries or driven into exile. The turnover of kings in the eighth century was double what it had been in the seventh.

The Northumbrian monarchy had become weakened partly because, without external conquests, it was not winning spoils with which to reward followers. It was also paying the price for giving away so much land to bishops and monasteries, which had begun in earnest under Oswiu. The policy was aimed at spreading Christianity and securing the allegiance of senior clerics, but Bede warned that the permanent alienation of royal estates would deprive young warriors of lands they might otherwise have expected as a reward. Northumbrian kings were thus forced to depend on the goodwill of other members of the aristocracy, which meant a constantly shifting system of factional alliances. When Viking raids began, it was in a kingdom already weakened from within.

CHAPTER 3

BEDE, HILDA AND THE GOLDEN AGE

The Benedictine monk Bede (c.673–735) shone brightly in Northumbria's golden age. Widely seen as the foremost scholar of early medieval Europe, he was the only Englishman named in Dante's *Paradiso*. The Venerable Bede was the polymath's polymath, England's first historian and its only native Doctor of the Church. His renown could easily survive being satirised as 'the Venomous Bead' in Sellar and Yeatman's *1066 and All That*.

Northumbria's cultural flowering was eclectic and cosmopolitan. It lit up the Dark Ages. From the mid-seventh to the late eighth centuries, it melded Anglo-Saxon, Irish, Scottish and British cultures with influences from continental Christendom. It encompassed illuminated manuscripts such as the *Lindisfarne Gospels* and *Codex Amiatinus*, the Ruthwell and Bewcastle stone crosses, and scholars such as Bede and Alcuin, along with the beginnings of English poetry.

The political context was often unstable, but conversion to Christianity crucially brought literacy. Oral, pagan culture no doubt had strengths, though much of it is lost today. Christianity offered the ruling elite not just possible eternal salvation, but also opportunity for their words and deeds to live for ever, as well as a means to write laws and create a framework of administration. Literacy and scholarship were concentrated in monasteries, notably Monkwearmouth-Jarrow, Lindisfarne and Ripon. Reading and writing is unlikely to have spread quickly within secular society. Christianity itself probably took generations to spread through the population.

Bede is best remembered for his *Ecclesiastical History of the English People* (c.731), for which he is labelled the 'father of English history'. He also wrote more than sixty works on science, cosmology, biblical commentary, hagiography, orthography, poetic metre and the reckoning of time.[1] Bede wrote lucidly about how the spherical earth influenced the changing length of daylight. He had a leading role in spreading the *Anno Domini* ('year of our Lord') system of dating from Christ's birth. He worked out how tides worked and why times varied along the same coast.

Bede, probably from a noble family, was placed at age seven in Monkwearmouth-Jarrow and educated under its founding abbot, Benedict Biscop, and his successor Ceolfrith. Bede spent his life at the monastery, where he had access to one of Europe's most extensive libraries, estimated at more than two hundred books. He was fluent in Latin, in which he wrote, and able to read Greek. He seems not to have travelled much, though he may have visited Lindisfarne and York. For his *Ecclesiastical History*, he relied on information from correspondents around Britain. He devoted his life to teaching and writing and did not rise above the rank of priest. Most of his writings were commentaries on the Bible. He also composed hagiographies, or saints' lives, including two of St Cuthbert. Bede placed his scholarly activities behind the performance of his duties as a monk, such as singing the divine office. While in some ways Bede seems modern, in others his worldview was very different to our own, notably his emphasis on miracles, visions and uncorruptible bodies.

In his first work on time, *De Temporibus*, Bede offered a radical recalculation of the age of the world, which he thought was 1,200 years younger than in an influential calculation by Eusebius of

Caesarea. It led to Bede being accused, in his absence, of heresy by members of Bishop Wilfrid's household. Bede's response was a letter in which he labelled his accusers lewd rustics.[2] Bede's *De Temporum Ratione* ('On the Reckoning of Time'), one of his most influential works, was a textbook on *computus* – methods of calculating time – written in response to debate about how to calculate the date of Easter. By the end of the eighth century, scholars and clerics across Europe were using Bede's method not only to measure the cycle of Christian feasts, but also to measure dates by which biblical epochs could be linked to the present.[3] We should be wary of seeing Bede as a historian in the modern sense. His *Ecclesiastical History* had a didactic purpose, to show how the past reveals the unfolding of divine will. He celebrated the rise of the Roman Church in Britain.

The circumstances of Bede's death were recorded in a letter by his pupil Cuthbert, who says Bede spent his final days praying and teaching, dictating a translation of the Gospel of St John and making extracts from a work by Isidore of Seville. He distributed possessions among the monks, namely pepper (an expensive commodity), incense and liturgical cloths.[4] Cuthbert's letter also relates a five-line poem in Old English that Bede is said to have composed on his deathbed, known as *Bede's Death Song*. The poem was widely copied, but its attribution to Bede is uncertain because not all manuscripts name him as the author. In translation, the poem reads: 'Before setting forth on that inevitable journey, none is wiser than the man who considers – before his soul departs hence – what good or evil he has done, and what judgment his soul will receive after its passing.'[5]

Demand for copies of his works grew across Europe after his death. Some 150 manuscripts of *Ecclesiastical History* survive. From the ninth century, Bede was deemed 'venerable', a mark of holiness in the Catholic Church. It is not known whether Bede helped to produce the *Codex Amiatinus*, one of three single-volume bibles that Monkwearmouth-Jarrow created. The *Codex* was intended as a gift for the pope, though it is unclear whether he received it; it ended up in a monastery in Monte Amiato, from which its name comes. Its script and decoration owed much to Italian exemplars, with the result that its Northumbrian origin was not recognised until the nineteenth century.[6]

The *Codex* is the earliest complete Latin Bible. It contains Old and New Testaments and three elaborate paintings, one of which shows the prophet Ezra writing. Its script, decoration, parchment and contents are Mediterranean in style. Its 2,060 pages, made from parchment processed from about 1,550 calf hides, demonstrate the industry involved in producing manuscripts.[7] These required massive animal husbandry to produce thousands of sheets of vellum, along with inks and paints for writing and illumination and leather for bindings. Scribes worked in scriptoria, or centres of manuscript production. Every manuscript is slightly different, even if it is a copy, because each scribe had different handwriting and made different errors.

Magnificently illustrated books were made in other monasteries, such as the *Durham, Echternach* and *Lindisfarne Gospels*, all thought to have been produced at Lindisfarne. These are works of Hiberno-Saxon or Insular art, combining Mediterranean, Celtic and Anglo-Saxon elements. The *Lindisfarne Gospels*, produced around 715, are the most spectacular manuscript to survive from Anglo-Saxon England. They are richly illustrated and were originally encased in a fine leather binding covered with jewels and metals. The jewelled cover was lost during Viking raids and a replacement made in 1852. The book includes five elaborate carpet pages, so called because of their resemblance to eastern Mediterranean carpets. There are also full-page images of the four Evangelists. In the late tenth century, a priest named Aldred added an Old English gloss to the manuscript, the earliest rendering of the Gospels in English. He also added a colophon, or inscription, that provides evidence of the manuscript's production. Aldred credits Eadfrith, bishop of the church of Lindisfarne, with writing the book 'for God and St Cuthbert and generally for all the holy folk who are on the island'.[8] He adds that Æthilwald, bishop of the Lindisfarne islanders, bound and covered it and that Billfrith the anchorite made the ornaments of jewels and precious metals. Illustrations and ornaments were no doubt intended to impress Northumbrians, most of whom could not read and certainly could not understand Latin.

Monasteries were themselves magnificent constructions. At Monkwearmouth-Jarrow, stonemasons and glaziers came from France to create some of the first stone buildings in Northumbria since Roman days. Equally impressive are stone crosses at Ruthwell on the Solway Firth and Bewcastle in Cumbria. These are Anglo-Saxon versions of the Celtic high cross, with sophisticated iconography. The Bewcastle cross combines runic inscriptions with figures including John the Baptist, who is holding the Lamb of God, and Christ with beasts at his feet. The Ruthwell Cross, probably created by the same sculptors, features the largest figurative reliefs found on any surviving Anglo-Saxon cross, illustrating episodes including the flight into Egypt and Christ healing the blind man. The Ruthwell Cross features runic inscriptions, possibly added later, that appear to be a section of *The Dream of the Rood*, an Old English poem in which the Passion is narrated in the form of an extended speech by the cross. The Ruthwell poem reads, in translation:

> Stripped himself God almighty / when he purposed to ascend
> the gallows,
> Brave before (all people) …

> I (raised up) the powerful King, Heaven's Lord: bow down I
> dared not.
> People derided us both together. / I …

> Christ was on the cross.
> Yet the keen ones / from afar came,
> Noble people to the solitary one. / I witnessed all that …

> All pitted with arrows.

They laid him down, tortured of limbs. /
They positioned themselves (at either end of his body.) …[9]

Only a few Old English texts can be securely identified as
Northumbrian, including *Cædmon's Hymn*, *Bede's Death Song* and
the Leiden riddle, a translation of a poem originally in Latin (the
riddle is in the voice of an unnamed garment inviting you to identify
it from a description of its history). There is also a brief couplet on
the Franks Casket, a box carved from whalebone. The couplet cele-
brates the whale:

This-fish the tide raised/stranded onto mountain-mound/shore;
was ocean-beast mournful when he on the grit/beach swam/
ended up.[10]

Cædmon's Hymn, the Ruthwell Cross poem and the Franks Casket
couplet may be the oldest attested examples of Old English poetry.
Cædmon (whose name was British in origin) was 'the father of
English Sacred Song', according to a nineteenth-century memorial
in Whitby – credited as the first to use vernacular verse for a
Christian purpose. He lived at Whitby Abbey at the time of its
founder, Hilda. According to Bede, he 'was wont to make songs of
piety and religion, so that whatever was expounded to him out of
scripture, he turned ere long into verse expressive of much sweetness
and penitence, in English, which was his native language'.[11]

Bede says Cædmon was a lay brother who cared for animals. One
evening, while monks were feasting, singing and playing a harp,
Cædmon left early to sleep with the animals because he knew no
songs. He had a dream in which someone approached him and
asked him to sing about 'the beginning of creation'. After first refusing, Cædmon subsequently produced a poem praising God. On
waking, Cædmon remembered everything he had sung and added
more lines. He was taken to the abbess, who asked him for a poem
based on 'a passage of sacred history or doctrine', as a test. When he

produced this, he was invited to take monastic vows. The abbess ordered scholars to teach Cædmon sacred history and doctrine, which he would turn into verse.

Cædmon's experience can be dated to between 657 (the abbey's foundation) and 680 (Hilda's death). Bede says Cædmon was responsible for many vernacular poetic texts on Christian topics. Sadly, *Cædmon's Hymn* is the only one to survive. It reads:

Nu scilun hergan hefen-ricaes uard,
metudæs mehti and his mod-githanc
uerc uuldur-fadur swe he uundra gihuaes
eci dryctin, or astelidæ
He aerist scop aeldu barnum
hefen to hrofæ, halig sceppend.
Tha middangard moncynnes uard,
eci dryctin æfter tiadæ
firum foldu, frea allmehtig

Now we should praise / heaven-kingdom's guardian
maker's might / and his mind-thankfulness [= mercifulness]
work of-glory-father / as he [of] wonders each
eternal lord, / the-start established.
He first formed / [for] men's sons
heaven [= the sky] as roof, / holy creator
Then middle-earth / mankind's guardian
eternal lord, afterwards ordained
for-people the-ground, / lord almighty.[12]

If this seems convoluted today, that is because writers had to adhere to a regular metrical structure and construct alliterative lines. We cannot say for sure what influence Cædmon and Northumbrian poetry had on the development of Old English verse, but it may have been much greater than appears from the few poems that have survived.

While Northumbria absorbed cultural influences from other parts of the British Isles and Europe, there was also an outward flow of people, ideas and objects. Missionaries went out from Northumbria and other Anglo-Saxon kingdoms to bring Christianity to the Old Saxons of Germany. They founded some of Europe's most prestigious religious institutions and, in doing so, helped to spread Insular artistic and scribal traditions. One missionary was the Northumbrian Willibrord.[13] He entered monastic life at Ripon under Wilfrid and spent some years in Ireland before being sent to the continent. Willibrord travelled to Frankia and Frisia and then Rome to gain papal backing. Subsequently he became archbishop and established his see at Utrecht. He also founded the monastery at Echternach, Luxembourg. He is remembered as patron saint of the Netherlands and Luxembourg.

Missionaries were just part of an outflow of churchmen and women from Anglo-Saxon England. Perhaps the most influential was Alcuin (c.735–804), scholar, monk, poet and teacher. Alcuin was educated at York under Archbishop Ecgbert, a disciple of Bede. York was a centre of learning in arts, literature and science as well as religion. Alcuin was recruited by Charlemagne, the Frankish emperor who united most of western and central Europe, to join scholars at the royal court. Alcuin became an architect of the Carolingian Renaissance, a period of cultural activity inspired by the fourth-century Christian Roman Empire. He wrote theological treatises, a few grammatical works and poems. Alcuin was head of Charlemagne's palace school in Aachen, where he promoted liberal arts and established a library. Later he became abbot of Marmoutier Abbey at Tours, where he encouraged monks to use Carolingian minuscule script, ancestor of modern Roman typefaces. When Alcuin died, Northumbria's golden age was largely over.

Little of this high culture touched ordinary people. Most men and women of Northumbria are invisible as individuals, though we know a bit about their lives in general. Some graves and craftsmen's tools have survived. Their history lives on in today's surnames and names of villages and hamlets.

Northumbria was – or grew into – a hierarchical society, with the king at the top, followed by the aristocracy, who could be warriors and their families or (after conversion to Christianity) bishops, abbots, abbesses, monks and nuns.[14] Then came artisans and farmers. Below these were peasants, for whom life was hard. There were gradations even among the peasantry. Some were able to rent land from a thegn (a noble ranked below an earl). Others had tenancy rights in return for working for the thegn for one or two days a week. At the bottom were churls, who owed their entire labour to their lord.

Most free men owed military service to the king. There were also slaves, who could be peasants or artisans. Ownership of slaves was not absolute and was more like bonded labour: a slave owed his labour to his master for as long as his master owned him, but the slave could save and buy his freedom. A poor man might sell himself into slavery when his crop failed, with the aim of redeeming his freedom later. Anglo-Saxons fetched top prices in Europe's slave markets. Pope Gregory, before his papacy, noticed a blond-haired youth in a slave market in Rome and was told he was an Angle from Deira. Gregory later sent a mission to convert the English, who he reputedly said were so beautiful that they were 'non Angli, sed angeli' (not Angles, but angels). Aside from selling themselves into slavery, people could become slaves as a punishment, for example for defaulting on a loan, or if captured in battle.

A typical day's diet in Anglo-Saxon Northumbria was coarse bread with pottage made from barley or wheat, with leeks, onions or other vegetables thrown into the pot; there was cheese or milk and small (weak) beer to drink.[15] Pigs were commonly raised, but meat was usually eaten only on high days and holy days. Dental records suggest that for poor people in Northumbria there were times – perhaps ten or twelve in a lifetime – when they were eating a poor diet or starving. Meanwhile royals at Bamburgh ate fare of variety and novelty, such as cranes, porpoises and sturgeon.

Fifth-century Britain was a 'real ethnic stew', remarks Robin Fleming in *Britain After Rome: The Fall and Rise 400 to 1070*:[16] people hailed from across north-west Europe, embracing a wide spectrum of social practices and material culture. The overarching Roman state was replaced by local, improvised societies. Larger identities were eroded and new, small-scale ones forged. But in the sixth century, she adds, another set of broader identities were created, based on social distinction and regional differences. Social and economic inequality grew.[17] Where previously two or three households in a hamlet might have had a few extra resources, now there were families who owned considerably more than others. Some of this may have been down to first-generation immigrants having an edge over latecomers. In other cases, good or bad luck made the difference: a rainless summer or disease impoverished some families. Inequality was reflected in funerary practices: the number of people buried with precious objects became smaller. Inequality was evident in life too. Women from high-status families wore jewels such as triple strings of beads including amber from the Baltic or brooches with garnet from India.

Gradually, high-status families began to assemble broader social networks, which created regional cultural identities.[18] Men and women led different lives.[19] Many women spent long hours in damp weaving sheds working at looms, as they bore and tended children. Men (as is apparent from their skeletons) had lives of hard labour and got into fights.

We know more about royal women's lives. Daughters were offered in marriage, willing or unwilling, to cement an alliance with another kingdom, put an end to a feud or seal one king's submission to another. In some cases, a daughter was married off to a husband who had deposed or murdered her father. However, as Adams observes, this does not mean royal women lived passive lives as breeders of athelings (princes) or cup-bearers to their lords and masters. A number of women played active, sometimes decisive roles in the fortunes of kingdoms.[20]

For example, Æthelfrith's wife Acha (whose father Ælla, king of Deira, may have been murdered by her husband), is thought to have taken her children into exile in Dál Riata in order to avoid the risk of them being killed by her brother Edwin, thus safeguarding their lives and enabling her sons Oswald and Oswiu, grandsons Ecgfrith and Aldfrith, and great-grandson Osred to become kings in turn.[21] When Æthelburh, daughter of King Æthelberht of Kent, became Edwin's second wife, a condition of their marriage was Edwin's conversion to Christianity and the acceptance of Paulinus's mission to convert the Northumbrians. When Edwin was killed in battle, Æthelburh fled into exile in Kent with her son, daughter and grandson. She then sent them to France, where her son and grandson died, but daughter Eanflæd lived to marry her first cousin, King Oswiu.[22] Eanflæd promoted monastic endowments.[23] Brought up in the Roman tradition in the courts of Kent and Frankia, she represented the religious conflict facing her Irish Christian husband, leading to the Synod of Whitby.[24]

The growth of monasteries created opportunities for aristocratic women not destined to be queens, notably Hilda (or Hild), great-niece of King Edwin and illustrious first abbess of Whitby. She was 'the most religious handmaid of Christ', according to Bede, and her reputation for wisdom was such that 'not only meaner men in their need, but sometimes even kings and princes, sought and received her counsel'.[25] At age 13, she was baptised a Christian by Paulinus. Hilda became more influenced, however, by the teachings of Irish monk Aidan, bishop of Lindisfarne. According to Bede, Hilda lived a secular life until the age of 33, when she became a nun. She first travelled to East Anglia, intending to join her sister in a monastery in France, but returned to Northumbria at Aidan's request. She became abbess of Hartlepool and in about 657 she founded Whitby Abbey, then known as Streanaeshalch.

Nothing of the original monastery, built of wood and thatch, can now be seen. A Benedictine abbey was founded on the same site in the late eleventh century. The ruins of that monastery stand on

Whitby's headland today. The abbey was home to monks and nuns. Bede praises Hilda for a regime that required strict observance of 'justice, piety, chastity, and other virtues, and particularly of peace and charity; so that, after the example of the primitive church, no one there was rich, and none poor, for they had all things common, and none had any private property'.[26] Oswiu chose Whitby as the venue for his synod to decide between Roman and Irish Christianity, with churchmen attending from as far as Wessex. Hilda and her supporters sided with the Irish.[27] However, she accepted the result after Oswiu ruled in favour of the Roman version.

Hilda died in 680. Local folklore says she turned a plague of snakes to stone and threw them off the cliff – a medieval explanation of the ammonite fossils found in the rocks. Victorian geologists named an ammonite species after her: *Hildroceras*. Hilda was venerated as a saint, often depicted with pastoral staff and carrying an abbey church, with ammonites at her feet. She is patron of schools and colleges across the world, including St Hilda's College, Oxford. She was succeeded as abbess jointly by Oswiu's widow Eanflæd and her daughter Ælfflæd. Thus, the development of Northumbria was shaped by influential, gifted women.

CHAPTER 4

LIFE WITH THE DANES

A new and terrifying threat came to Northumbria on 8 June 793. In the (translated) words of the late ninth-century author of the *Anglo-Saxon Chronicle*, there 'were immense sheets of light rushing through the air, and whirlwinds, and fiery dragons flying across the firmament. These tremendous tokens were soon followed by a great famine: and not long after … the harrowing inroads of heathen men made lamentable havoc in the church of God in Holy-island, by rapine and slaughter.'[1]

The seaborne raid on Lindisfarne is widely taken as beginning the Viking Age in England, which lasted until the mid-eleventh century. In fact, the first known Scandinavian attack had occurred four years earlier at Portland on the south coast, where a West Saxon royal official called Beauduherd was killed. Shortly after Lindisfarne, further raids took place in Northumbria at Monkwearmouth-Jarrow, Hartness and Tynemouth. The attacks, aimed at plundering easy loot from undefended coastal monasteries, caused consternation around Christian Europe. Alcuin, at the court of Charlemagne, wrote to King Æthelred of Northumbria: 'Never before has such a terror appeared in Britain as we have just suffered from a pagan people, nor was it thought possible that an incursion of this kind could be made.'[2]

The Viking Age was a decisive period for northern England. The raiders came first to plunder treasures and probably slaves, then to conquer and settle. Northumbria became fragmented. Battles were fought. Norse and Anglo-Saxon rulers came and went. It ended with the north absorbed into a country called England, albeit ruled by Normans. The repercussions are felt today: Britain could have been a northern-centred country, but is not.

Few peoples have stirred the imagination like the Vikings. To their Christian victims they were bloodthirsty heathens. Their swift and unpredictable attacks provoked alarm, though it is uncertain whether they were more than ordinarily brutal for the age. Later, Scandinavians became Christianised and integrated with local populations; towns and trade developed. Eventually, as the Viking threat receded, they became romanticised. Every age has written its own preoccupations onto the Vikings.

Victorians saw them as prefiguring the British Empire's achievements. Children's author R.M. Ballantyne wrote in 1869: 'Much of what is good and true of our laws and social customs, much of what is manly and vigorous in the British constitution, and much of our intense love of freedom and fair play, is due to the pith, pluck and enterprise, and sense of justice that dwelt in the breasts of the rugged old sea-kings of Norway!'[3] The Viking heritage appealed to Vidkun Quisling's Norwegian fascist movement and to Nazi Germany in the 1930s. In the second half of the twentieth century, revisionist histories pioneered by British archaeologist Peter Sawyer played down the Vikings' violence and emphasised their artistic, technological and mercantile achievements.

Viking raids were part of an expansion of Scandinavians beyond their Nordic homelands as far as America, North Africa, Russia, Constantinople and the Middle East. In part this may have been opportunism. Increased trade contacts with Europe made them aware of great treasures in vulnerable locations. Their maritime expertise enabled them to develop swift, shallow-draught ships. Raids occurred when Northumbria had already been weakened by the struggle with Mercia.

The origin of the word *Viking* is uncertain. It has been linked to *víken* ('the bay'), an area of southern Norway; to the Latin *vicus* ('trading place'); to *víkingr*, Old Norse for an individual away from home engaged in endeavours on behalf of a group, and the verb *víking*, to pursue group activities such as raiding; and to the Old English *wicing*, an individual of piratical bent.[4] Scandinavians had no written history until Norwegian and Icelandic sagas came along in the twelfth century and later. The term Viking appears not to have been commonly used during the Viking Age – it was Victorians who applied it to mean anyone from Scandinavia. Latin and Old English texts refer to Northmen, Danes, pirates, heathens, dark foreigners, fair foreigners, pagans and other terms.

The historical assumption has been that Scandinavians who settled in eastern England were mostly from Denmark, while those in north-west England were from Norway, via Ireland and Scotland. That is probably broadly true, though Viking armies are thought to have been a complex mix of nationalities and ethnicities. Alcuin, in his letter to King Æthelred, castigates monks for wishing to 'resemble the pagans' in their 'trimming of beard and hair' – implying a degree of prior contact and even admiration for the Scandinavian world.[5]

After all, Anglo-Saxons were of similar ethnic make-up and came from neighbouring parts of northern Europe. They had a paradoxical attitude to the Nordic region: they characterised it as a frozen land of devils and monsters, yet at the same time Anglo-Saxons remained enthusiastic about their northern heritage and legends. These similarities ultimately helped the two peoples to live in a process of settlement, acculturation and integration. Terrifying as the raids must have appeared, there is no evidence that Vikings sought to destroy communities in areas they conquered; there was nothing like the Harrying of the North in which William of Normandy later indulged. Rather, Vikings seemed to want to share the wealth and administrative sophistication that Anglo-Saxons had developed.

After the initial raids, there was a forty-year hiatus in Viking attacks recorded by the *Anglo-Saxon Chronicle*. By the 850s, however, there was a change in the scale and nature of attacks, involving larger fleets. In 851 Vikings overwintered for the first time in England – in Thanet – rather than returning home in the autumn. In 865 a large force appeared in East Anglia that was described in the *Anglo-Saxon Chronicle* as the *mycel hæþen here* or Great Heathen Army, a loose confederation of groups that had been operating in Britain, Ireland and Frankia. This force, reinforced by the Great Summer Army six years later, would come close to overrunning Anglo-Saxon England. First it made peace with the East Angles, receiving horses and supplies, then it turned its attention in autumn 866 to Northumbria and Eoforwic (York).

The kingdom was in a state of unrest, according to the *Chronicle*. The Northumbrians had deposed their king, Osberht, and replaced him with Ælle, who was said to have 'no hereditary right' to the throne. The Vikings swept into Northumbria and were within the walls of York before any resistance could be mustered. The Northumbrians counter-attacked unsuccessfully in 867 and both Ælle and Osberht were killed. According to Norse legend, Ragnar 'Shaggy-Breeches', so called because of the trousers he wore to protect himself during a battle with two giant serpents, had earlier been killed by Ælle of York. Ragnar's five sons, including Halfdan and Ivar 'the Boneless', were said to have invaded England and killed Ælle in a gory ritual to avenge their father's death. But while Ragnar's sons are historical figures, there is no evidence that Ragnar ever existed.[6]

East Anglia was the next kingdom to fall. In 869 the Viking army defeated and killed its king, Edmund. Mercia bought off the Vikings three times, but the Great Army forced Burgred, Mercia's king, into exile and gave his throne to a client king called Ceolwulf. Wessex, which had become the dominant Anglo-Saxon kingdom, was repeatedly attacked in the 870s. King Alfred, who succeeded to the throne in 871, was twice forced to make peace. In 877 the Vikings defeated

Alfred and came close to extinguishing permanently the West Saxon royal dynasty.

Alfred escaped and built a fort on the island of Athelney on the Somerset Levels, from which he waged guerrilla war. According to later tradition, a peasant woman scolded him for burning cakes that she had asked him to watch, a legend apparently aimed at underlining Alfred's saintly humility.[7] Alfred gathered the remains of his army and defeated the Vikings at Edington in Wiltshire in 878. Their leader, Guthrum, accepted baptism and returned to East Anglia, where he became king. Later Alfred and Guthrum agreed a treaty, drawing up a boundary between their realms up the River Thames, along the River Lea and up the River Ouse to Watling Street. This treaty is often seen as the earliest definition of the southern boundary of what became known as Danelaw, the part of Britain in which Danish laws and customs prevailed. While it is broadly true that Scandinavian settlement was concentrated in areas north-east of Watling Street (a diagonal line between Wroxeter and Canterbury), the term 'Danelaw' was not recorded until the early eleventh century. It is doubtful whether there was ever an integrated Viking realm covering the whole territory.[8]

Alfred is popularly remembered as the king who saved England, yet at the time there existed no entity called England to be saved; that was to be the creation of his grandsons and great-grandsons. To Victorians and Edwardians, Alfred the Great was the ideal Englishman and embodiment of its civilisation. E.A. Freeman, in his history of the Norman Conquest, described Alfred as 'the most perfect character in history'.[9]

In the mid-870s the Great Army had split, with one leader, Halfdan, going to Northumbria while the other half under Guthrum headed to Wessex. According to the *Chronicle*, Halfdan 'overran that land and made frequent raids against the Picts and the Strathclyde Britons'. The *Chronicle* entry for 876 contains an intriguing, much-debated entry: 'The same year Halfdan divided the land of the Northumbrians; so that they became afterwards their harrowers and ploughers.'[10] The implication is clear that these Vikings had decided to make the York area their home, but how extensive was this share-out? Did the Viking army drive existing landowners off their property or did they find land vacated during the previous decade's civil wars? Or did they buy land from native lords?

The Vikings' arrival coincided with Northumbria fragmenting into four areas:[11] the Viking kingdom of Jorvik (York); the 'liberty' of the Community of St Cuthbert between the rivers Tees and Tyne; the earldom of Bamburgh; and the kingdom of Cumbria. Halfdan and his successors established what we now call the Viking kingdom of York broadly between the River Tees and the Humber. It held some sort of power in the area, albeit intermittently, until the last Viking king, Eric, usually thought to be Eric Bloodaxe, was expelled and killed in 954. How powerful this 'kingdom' was is the subject of debate. Although Halfdan divided land, it is not clear whether he became king, or whether this was any sort of kingdom with a machinery of government. No evidence of a palace has been found. There appears to have been no settled and continuous line of succession. David Rollason suggests that archbishops of York may have wielded the real power, though other historians doubt this.[12]

Viking activity was more sporadic north of the Tees. Between the Tees and the Tyne were the principal lands of the liberty (or self-governing area) of the Community of St Cuthbert, heir to the monastic community of Lindisfarne, which maintained considerable independence. At the time of the capture of York in 866–7, the community was still based at Lindisfarne, but it moved to Chester-le-Street and then Durham. The former Bernicia, the area north of the Tyne including south-eastern Scotland, was ruled for a time by Anglo-Saxon kings about whom little is known apart from their names. By the early tenth century we find a dynasty of earls ruling from the ancient Northumbrian royal palace of Bamburgh. It is possible that they were scions of the Northumbrian royal house, or perhaps of other courtiers. On the west side of the Pennines, there were incursions by Vikings from bases in Ireland. Part of north-west

England was governed from the early tenth century by rulers described as 'king of the Cumbrians'. It is uncertain whether these were Scottish kings of Strathclyde or independent kings.

When Alfred died in 899, the eventual unification of England was not far ahead, but large parts of northern and eastern England remained under the control of Scandinavians. The Vikings' legacy can be seen in place-names and above all in the English language. While Old English had as few as forty Scandinavian loan words, there are today about nine hundred in standard English, with many more in local dialects.[13] These words are not just nouns, adjectives and verbs, but also pronouns (he, she, they), prepositions (by, at) and even the verb 'to be'. It is rare for these types of words to be transferred between languages, suggesting significant integration. Many are household words such as husband, egg, knife, seat, window, flat, ugly, scowl and want. Their everyday nature contrasts with later loans from French, after the Norman Conquest, which are almost all linked to ruling-class culture.

Despite – or perhaps because of – this apparent closeness, surprisingly little is known for certain about the settlers. They had no written culture at that time, apart from runic inscriptions found in Scandinavia, mostly on memorial stones. The result has been centuries of debate about the scale of settlement and the nature of the Vikings' impact. Towns such as York and Lincoln grew and thrived; there was increased production and trade. Over time, there was intermarriage. Ethnic identity may have been less of an everyday concern than social status. The later chronicler John of Wallingford (who died in 1214) claimed that Scandinavians were popular with English women, to the chagrin of their menfolk, because they took a bath once a week, on Saturdays. The Old Norse word for Saturday is *Laugardagr*, 'bath-day'.[14]

None of this means that the invasions were not terrifying and disruptive. Religious life was upended by the pagan invaders. Many churches and monasteries were vacated or abandoned. Libraries such as Alcuin's library at York, one of the finest in Europe, were destroyed;

books were burned or plundered as treasure. While some important churches survived, in other cases church lands were seized and redistributed. Vikings were not the only reason for the Anglo-Saxon Church's decline. By the end of the eighth century, monasteries and religious houses were increasingly seen as economic assets to be exploited by their owners, whether lay or ecclesiastical. Alcuin was not alone in seeing Viking raids as divine punishment for society's moral degeneracy. King Alfred also wrote of the invasions as punishments for 'when we neither loved wisdom ourselves nor allowed it to other men; we possessed only the name of Christians and very few possessed the virtues'.[15] He lamented that south of the Humber there was scarcely a literate priest left. At Canterbury, the single active scribe had gone blind and could barely copy out a line correctly.[16]

Scandinavians soon converted to Christianity, which had the advantage of the written word and a powerful infrastructure. Its concept of a single, all-powerful God was simple to teach and grasp. Paganism was less organised, did not have a standard set of beliefs and practices, and did not exclude other gods and religions. Much of paganism's strength derived from traditional locations, such as burial mounds and springs where rites might be carried out, together with the role of local chieftains and the family. Cut off from its roots, Norse paganism withered and died.[17] It left its mark, though. A few place-names bear witness to this period of paganism, such as Roseberry Topping, a dramatic hill in north Yorkshire. Its name originated as *Othenesberg*, or Odin's hill.

In York, there is limited evidence of paganism, which suggests conversion may have come rapidly. One of the earliest Viking kings, Guthred, was buried at York Minster. Viking Jorvik underwent an economic boom. Its population has been estimated at ten to fifteen thousand, a fivefold increase.[18] Almost all York roads that predate the Norman Conquest have the suffix '-gate', from the Old Norse *gata* ('street'). Coppergate, meaning street of the wood-turners (that is, cup-makers, from Old Norse *koppari*), was excavated between 1967 and 1981. The dig found evidence of production of leatherwork and textiles, ironwork and copperwork, cup-making and carpentry, bone- and antler-craft, minting, amber-shaping and glass recycling.

In parts of former Danelaw, a third to half of place-names are Scandinavian, but distribution is uneven. While density is highest in Lincolnshire and Yorkshire, there are few examples in County Durham, Northumberland, Cambridgeshire, Essex and Hertfordshire.[19] There are about 850 place-names ending in -by, the Scandinavian word for village or farmstead. Another Scandinavian place-name element is -thorpe, referring to a secondary settlement often on inferior land. There are compounds with Scandinavian and Anglo-Saxon elements.

One noteworthy area of Anglo-Scandinavian fusion is the proliferation of stone sculptures around churches, depicting Christian themes alongside Scandinavian mythology and pagan beliefs.[20] This tradition flourished after the Vikings settled, even though stone sculpture was scarcely known in Scandinavia. For example, on a cross at Gosforth in Cumbria there are depictions of Thor, Odin and Ragnarök (the battle that destroys the Norse gods) along with the crucifixion. One possible explanation is that these sculptures aimed to present Christian teaching and art in Scandinavian terms and were thus a vehicle of integration.

There may have been a degree of mutual intelligibility between Old English and Old Norse, both Germanic languages.[21] It is thought that Old Norse continued to be spoken as late as the eleventh century or beyond in remoter parts of the north. There was assimilation in some spheres but not others.[22] Stone sculptures are an example of the former, while other forms of material culture signal a continuing difference, such as female jewellery in Scandinavian art-styles. There is no evidence, though, that cultural distinctiveness translated into political divisions. The main fault line in the tenth and eleventh centuries seems to have lain between north and south, not English and Scandinavian.

The Vikings' cultural impact continues today. Indeed, Yorkshire's Scandinavian heritage is celebrated, not least in York's Jorvik Viking

Festival and Yorkshire County Cricket Club's naming of its one-day team as the Yorkshire Vikings. But while Yorkshire's ridings were a Scandinavian creation, the county of Yorkshire was not. It dates from the 1060s, a result of English kings' creation of the shire system for tax gathering, military organisation and judicial processes.[23]

The north in the tenth century became caught between Dublin and Winchester – a struggle for control of the region between Viking kings from across the Irish Sea and English kings from Wessex. It was a messy period involving conflict, shifting boundaries and bewildering changes of ruler. Eventually, the uniting of the English crown under Alfred's descendants ended the independent existence of Northumbria. This was not the end of Scandinavian rule, however, because four Danes became kings of England in the eleventh century. From 1066, England was ruled by another descendant of a Viking, William I.

In about 902, Norse settlers in Dublin were expelled by Irish lords. According to *The Annals of Ulster*, 'they left a great number of their ships and escaped half-dead, after having been wounded and broken'.[24] Survivors scattered to various shores of the Irish Sea including north-west England, Wales and Scotland; some went as far as Iceland and France. They left their mark on the west coast. There is an abundance of Norse-derived names on the Wirral peninsula and other parts of Merseyside, such as Irby, Meols, Thingwall, Croxteth, Aigburth and Tranmere. In 917, a Viking called Sihtric in Old English (or Sigtryggr in Old Norse, Sihtric Cáech in Irish) re-established Norse control of Dublin with the help of his cousin Rægnald (Rögnvaldr in Old Norse, Ragnall in Irish). Both were grandsons of Ivar, a Dublin ruler who may have been Ivar 'the Boneless', one of the leaders of the Great Heathen Army that invaded England in 865. His nickname is thought to refer to a physical or figurative disability.

Rægnald invaded northern England and was acknowledged in 919 as king of York. This was the start of a thirty-five-year period in which Irish Norse kings intermittently succeeded in creating a kingdom linking Dublin and York, while English kings sought to bring Northumbria under their control – a tussle between the descendants of Ivar and those of Alfred.[25] Sihtric vacated his Irish throne in order to succeed Rægnald in York, leaving Dublin to a kinsman named Guthfrith, another of Ivar's grandsons. When Sihtric died in 927, Guthfrith also briefly acceded to the York throne.

Several hoards of silver have been found across the north, likely to have been buried by Viking war-bands with connections on both sides of the Pennines. The largest, the Cuerdale Hoard, is thought to have been the war-chest of an army travelling between York and the Irish Sea. Discovered in 1840 by workmen repairing the banks of the River Ribble near Preston, Lancashire, it is easily the biggest Viking Age treasure found in Britain. The nearly nine thousand items comprised silver and other bullion and also coin, much of it minted in York.[26] The hoard suggests a degree of cooperation between Dublin and York Vikings, as does Rægnald's acceptance in York. There is uncertainty, though, about how welcome the pagans from across the Irish Sea may have appeared to Scandinavians who had already settled in southern Northumbria and become Christian.

When Alfred's grandson Athelstan became king of Wessex in 924, he threw Guthfrith out and annexed the kingdom. For the first time, a single king controlled almost all the territory of what was to become England, meaning that Athelstan is often portrayed as England's first true king. It was too soon, though, to describe the nation as unified. Northumbria retained a strong sense of distinctiveness. Olaf Guthfrithsson, son of the man Athelstan had expelled, secured power in Dublin and set about pursuing his own claim to the kingship of York. He entered an alliance with Constantin, king of Scots, and Owain of Strathclyde. They fought and were defeated by Athelstan at the famed Battle of Brunanburh. More than thirty sites have been suggested for its location, including Bromborough in the Wirral. However, when Athelstan died in 939, his hegemony over Northumbria died with him, ushering in another spell of instability.[27]

Olaf, who had survived Brunanburh, became king of York apparently unopposed. Olaf was succeeded briefly by two more Norse kings, Olaf Sihtricson and Rægnald Guthfrithsson. The south Northumbrian leaders invited a man called Eric to be their king in York. Most historians believe this was Eric Bloodaxe, son of King Harald Finehair of Norway, though some suggest he may have been another grandson of Dublin's Ivar.[28] Eric's rule in York was not a success. His forces slaughtered part of an army sent by Eadred, king of the English, to punish the Northumbrians, after which an enraged Eadred threatened huge retribution, which prompted the Northumbrians to throw out Eric. They briefly recalled Olaf Sihtricson, but later threw him out as well and invited Eric back in. Eadred then applied pressure to the Archbishop of York, after which Eric was finally expelled in 954 and killed at Stainmore in the north Pennines.[29]

That was the last throw by south Northumbrians, who henceforth accepted rule by English kings – though those kings' control over northern lands remained weak. The rise and fall of the kingdom of Northumbria left a sense of loss. As John of Wallingford put it in the thirteenth century: 'From that time to the present, Northumbria has been grieving for want of a king of its own, and for the liberty they once enjoyed.'[30]

Eric's expulsion was not the end of Scandinavian kings in England, though. Viking raids in eastern England started again in the 980s during the reign of Æthelred II 'the Unready' (more accurately, 'the poorly advised'). Æthelred tried unsuccessfully to buy the raiders off, until Svein Forkbeard seized the English throne in 1013. Svein died within weeks of becoming king. His son Cnut became king in 1017 and ruled England, Denmark, Norway and part of Sweden until his death in 1035. After Cnut died, his North Sea empire disintegrated during the short and turbulent reigns of his sons Harold Harefoot and Harthacnut. They were succeeded by Edward the Confessor, son of Æthelred II.

Edward appointed Tostig, brother of Harold Godwinson, to the earldom of Northumbria, which proved disastrous. Although he had a Danish mother and a Danish name, Tostig was a southerner. He alienated his subjects through higher taxes, harsh justice and unfair laws. In 1065, when Tostig was away in the south, rebels took over York and declared Tostig an outlaw. The next time Tostig entered Northumbria was as part of Harald Hardrada's force invading England. Tostig died at the Battle of Stamford Bridge in 1066. The failed invasion by Norwegian king Hardrada ('hard-ruler') in pursuit of a claim to the English throne is often seen as the end of the Viking Age in England. Nineteen days later, King Harold Godwinson was defeated by William of Normandy at the Battle of Hastings, shifting England's political focus from Scandinavia to western Europe.

The Vikings had a vital influence in shaping the north in ways that still resonate today. At the same time, they themselves were shaped by it. The next bunch of invaders, this time from the south, caused a different kind of trouble.

CHAPTER 5

WILLIAM, THE NORTH'S NEMESIS

William the Conqueror is widely portrayed as brutal, cruel and ruth-less, although he does, to be fair, appear to have been affectionate and devoted to his wife Matilda. His chaplain, William of Poitiers, described the Duke of Normandy as inspiring 'even great love and terror everywhere'.[1] Northern England, where the most serious revolt against his rule emerged, felt the terror more than the love. There is much debate about whether his Harrying of the North was quite as barbaric as contemporary chroniclers portrayed it to be. Whatever the truth, it was a trauma that became imprinted on northern memories for centuries. It gets regularly mentioned in connection with Margaret Thatcher and 1980s deindustrialisation.

William was another Norseman, descended from a Viking called Rollo who was Normandy's first ruler. By William's day, the Normans had become thoroughly Frenchified.[2] Their customs, language and even style of clothes and hair made them more alien to the English than the Scandinavians had been. The Normans were not farmers, but soldiers who came seeking land and power.

The roots of William's severe approach lay in his childhood. He became duke at age seven or eight when his father Robert died on a visit to the Holy Land. After a brief period of calm, the duchy descended into violence as lords struggled to gain the upper hand.

There were mafioso-style killings. One unfortunate was seized by his enemies at a wedding feast and had his nose and ears cut off and his eyes gouged out.[3] William's guardians were not able to offer much protection. One was killed in a siege and another assassinated while out riding. William's tutor was murdered and then his household steward had his throat cut while sleeping in the same chamber as the young duke. William was declared to be of age at fifteen, after which he had to see off several rebellions. His reputation for cruelty was established early. At a siege in Alençon, he ordered thirty-two townsmen's hands and feet to be cut off, after which the fortress's defenders immediately surrendered, fearing similar treatment.[4]

By 1066, William felt confident enough in his control of Normandy to bid for the English throne when Edward the Confessor, his first cousin once removed, died. William was angered by the rapid coronation of English earl Harold Godwinson, the king's brother-in-law, whom Edward had allegedly named as successor on his deathbed. William argued that Edward had previously promised the throne to him and that Harold had sworn to support his claim. William built a large fleet and invaded England, where he defeated and killed Harold at the Battle of Hastings. Harold may or may not have been felled by an arrow in the eye.

After his victory, William at first sought to reconcile the Anglo-Saxon elite to his new regime.[5] While the confiscated lands of those who had fallen at Hastings were redistributed to William's followers, earls who submitted to the conqueror had their lands and titles confirmed, though they had to pay for the privilege. Resistance soon surfaced, however. A serious rising occurred in Exeter. Early in 1068 William marched into Devon and obtained the town's surrender after an eighteen-day siege. After accepting the townsfolk's submission he set about building a castle within the town walls – an early example of his policy of building castles at places of strategic importance.[6]

Meanwhile in Northumbria, William had appointed a Yorkshire thegn called Copsig to be earl of the northern part of the region, demonstrating the king's insensitivity to feelings in far-flung parts of the realm. Copsig had been a lieutenant of the hated Tostig, whose rule in the north provoked rebellion in 1065. Copsig was ambushed and murdered by local rival Oswulf within weeks of his arrival. Oswulf hacked off his head. Oswulf himself was soon also murdered, run through by a robber's lance.[7] Oswulf's cousin Cospatric offered to buy the earldom, which William accepted in another apparent attempt at reconciliation. Soon, however, Cospatric and other northern leaders became involved in a wide-ranging rebellion probably instigated by Mercian brothers Edwin and Morcar, who were seeing their power base shrink. They were joined by Edgar Ætheling, Edward the Confessor's great-nephew.[8] William responded by marching northwards, while ordering castles to be built at Warwick and Nottingham. Edwin and Morcar soon surrendered and York submitted without a fight; Edgar, Cospatric and others fled to Scotland. William reached a peace accord with Malcolm, the Scottish king, and headed back south.

The north did not remain subdued for long. At the start of 1069 William appointed yet another new earl, Robert de Comines (or Cumin). Comines came north with hundreds of armed men who ravaged the countryside by pillaging and killing. They spent the night in Durham, but at first light a band of Northumbrians burst through the gates and massacred Comines and his men. According to local chronicler Simeon of Durham, the streets were choked with bodies and awash with blood. Comines was staying at the bishop's house, where the attackers set the building on fire: those inside either burned to death or were cut down as they tried to escape.[9]

The massacre of Comines and his men triggered a new general rising in which the governor of York Castle was slaughtered along with many men. 'The English now gained confidence in resisting the Normans, whom they saw as oppressors of their friends and allies,' said Orderic Vitalis, a chronicler.[10] The insurgents were joined by northern rebels returning from Scotland, who led an attack on York. The Norman sheriff managed to get a message to the king, saying he would be forced to surrender unless York was relieved quickly. William arrived swiftly again to defeat the rebels with overwhelming force, after which his troops sacked the city and robbed its churches. The king began to build a second castle and left the city in the hands of his close ally William Fitzosbern, but it was clear that William was not yet fully in control of his new kingdom. He was getting into a vicious circle: the more castles he built and garrisoned, the heavier taxes or more estate seizures were needed to pay for it, which led to further unrest.

Since William's coronation, Englishmen had tried to solicit aid from the Danish king, Svein Estrithson. Svein eventually sent an invasion fleet commanded by his brother Asbjorn, which arrived in the Humber in September 1069. They were joined by English allies including Edgar and Cospatric and marched on York. The defenders set fire to houses near the castle, fearing that their timbers could be used to bridge its moat, but the blaze ran out of control and engulfed the city. The garrison came out to engage the Anglo-Danish army, but were quickly overwhelmed and many were killed. After destroying the two castles and plundering what remained of the city, the Danes returned to their ships.[11]

By the time William set out to confront the Danes, they were encamped on the marshy and inaccessible Isle of Axholme. The king was distracted by rebellions in south-west England and Shrewsbury. On returning, he found that the Danes had retreated again to their fleet, where they spent the winter. Their avoidance of battle suggests that their mission may have been to create a bridgehead in anticipation of Svein arriving the following year. According to later chronicler John of Worcester, William offered Asbjorn a large sum of money and permission to forage freely along the coasts, in return for a promise that the Danes would leave without fighting at the end of winter.

The second part of William's strategy was to hunt down English rebels in a way that ensured that any future army, English or Danish, would have no place to hide and no resources to live on – resulting in the so-called Harrying of the North.[12] According to Orderic, the king divided his army into smaller contingents to comb the mountains and forests where rebels were hiding, slaying many men and destroying the lairs of others. The *Anglo-Saxon Chronicle* says the king went north 'with all the force that he could collect, despoiling and laying waste the shire withal'.[13]

William went further in Orderic's graphic account, written more than fifty years after the event:

> In his anger he commanded that all crops and herds, chattels and food of every kind should be brought together and burned to ashes with consuming fire, so that the whole region north of the Humber might be stripped of all means of sustenance. As a consequence, so serious a scarcity was felt in England, and so terrible a famine fell upon the humble and defenceless people, that more than 100,000 Christian folk of both sexes, young and old alike, perished of hunger.[14]

John of Worcester said the famine was so severe that people ate human flesh as well as horses, cats and dogs. Simeon of Durham added that others sold themselves into perpetual slavery to preserve their own existence. The harrying mainly affected Yorkshire, but also included parts of Durham, Cheshire, Shropshire and Staffordshire.[15]

Some historians argue that these accounts are exaggerated, partly because it is questionable whether William had the manpower, time and good weather necessary to reduce large areas to a depopulated, uncultivated desert.[16] There is also debate about the Domesday Book of 1086, which recorded that, even fifteen years after the harrying, 480 of Yorkshire's 1,782 vills were waste and 314 more were partly waste; in the North Riding, two-thirds of estates were either waste or partly waste. While some historians believe 'waste' denotes land that has been devastated, others suggest it may refer to manors that had been amalgamated or were in disputed ownership, or that it may simply reflect lack of information on the part of the Domesday commissioners.[17] Against that, Domesday records that Yorkshire's population had dropped to a quarter of what it was in 1066 and that the average value of manors had plummeted by more than 65 per cent.[18] Geographer Richard Muir points to archaeological evidence of violent disruption that took place in Yorkshire in 1069–71, in the form of hoards of coins that were buried by inhabitants.[19] Brian Roberts in *The Making of the English Village* suggests that villages were laid out in a regular pattern as a result of reconstruction after the harrying.[20]

While a scorched-earth strategy was common in medieval warfare, the combined evidence of the chronicles, the fall in values and the widespread entries for waste suggests significant devastation. As far away as Evesham Abbey in Worcestershire, a chronicler reported that starving refugees arrived in search of food, but died from eating too ravenously. They buried five or six bodies every day.[21] Orderic Vitalis was damning in his condemnation:

> My narrative has frequently had occasion to praise William, but for this act which condemned the innocent and guilty alike to die by slow starvation I cannot commend him … I declare that assuredly such brutal slaughter cannot remain unpunished. For the almighty Judge watches over high and low alike; he will weigh the deeds of all in an even balance, and as a just avenger will punish wrongdoing, as the eternal law makes clear to all men.[22]

The harrying was effective in putting down the most serious revolt of William's reign, but it did not end rebellions. King Svein joined the Danish fleet and made common cause with Hereward, an East Anglian rebel. By now, however, the Danish force was in a sorry state because of privations caused by storms and shortages of food. Svein accepted terms from William and sailed homewards, where his fleet was scattered by a great storm. William successfully put down a further uprising at Ely.[23] The king had one more problem: Malcolm, king of Scotland, who had provided refuge for rebels and recently raided northern England as far as Durham. He had also married Margaret, sister of Edgar Ætheling. William launched an invasion and forced Malcolm to meet him at Abernethy, near the Firth of Tay, where the Scottish king swore to become his vassal and gave him hostages. Edgar fled to Flanders.[24]

By 1075 William's hold on England was more secure. If rebellions had been coordinated and organised, they might have been effective; but as events unfolded, William was able to deal with them individually. His early attempts at reconciliation with the Anglo-Saxon elite ended. Over the remainder of his reign, English magnates were largely replaced by Norman landowners. There were huge changes in the church, including a quadrupling of monasteries by the early twelfth century. In the north, where monasticism had been wiped out after Viking invasions, monasteries were founded or restored at Selby, Jarrow, Whitby, Monkwearmouth, Durham and York.[25]

The waning English appetite for resistance was demonstrated in a failed uprising in 1075 over individual grievances by two French lords – Ralph, a Breton who was Earl of East Anglia, and Roger, Earl of Hereford. They managed to implicate Waltheof, Earl of Northumbria, the most senior remaining English lord, though how far he was involved is unclear. It appeared that they were counting on more English support, but this was lacking and the revolt was put down by a combined force of English and Normans. Waltheof was beheaded.[26]

In William's later years he spent more than half his time in Normandy, dealing with threats on the duchy's borders and a conflict with his son Robert. In his absence England was governed by his half-brother Odo, bishop of Bayeux and Earl of Kent. According to Evesham Abbey's chronicler, Odo 'ruled the country at that time under the king like some tyrant' and preyed on estates 'like a ravening wolf'.[27] In 1080, Bishop Walcher of Durham was murdered in a quarrel between two servants, which developed into a rebellion. William sent Odo with an army to deal with it. According to Simeon of Durham, Odo killed, maimed and extorted money from the guilty and innocent alike, before helping himself to some of the cathedral's treasures.[28] Two years later Odo was arrested, possibly for trying to make himself pope: he spent five years in prison and his English estates were taken back by the king.

William sent his son Robert, with whom relations were patched up, on a mission to King Malcolm of Scotland, who had raided Northumbria again in 1079. Robert succeeded in reimposing the terms of the earlier Anglo-Scottish peace. On his return journey, Robert established a new outpost near the site of Walcher's murder at Gateshead – a 'new castle' upon the Tyne.[29]

In 1085, William faced a serious threat of invasion from another Danish king, Svein's son Cnut IV, who seemed keen to repeat the victories of his illustrious namesake. Cnut assembled a large fleet but in 1086 he was murdered in church by his own rebellious nobles before the ships could set sail. At the height of the invasion scare William commissioned what became popularly known as the Domesday survey, an ambitious assessment of landholdings in much of England and parts of Wales. It covered Yorkshire, though not Northumberland and Durham or much of north-west England. The survey's purpose is widely debated: it may have been to provide accurate information on military and other resources the king could count on. It confirmed landholders' title to estates acquired in the turmoil of conquest, but in return tenants owed military service and other obligations. It established that tenure was granted by the king (with a few exceptions north of the Tees), making him the ultimate lord of most people in England.[30]

Norman rule wrought substantial changes in England, including opening the way for common law, changing the system of land tenure, and building castles and cathedrals, as well as displacing the bulk of the English political and religious elites. English as a written language was driven underground for a couple of generations, replaced by Latin. It is argued that the demise of Standard Old English caused writers to diversify into regional dialects, ultimately deepening the richness of the language as it resurfaced as Middle English and clearing a path for Langland and Chaucer.[31]

The conquest shifted England's geopolitical focus southwards towards western Europe. Norman immigrants numbered perhaps 20,000, barely 1 per cent of the population,[32] but their impact was deep and long-lasting. Suppression of rebellions in the north strengthened the central state. The English felt colonised: middle-ranking natives were forced into servitude, with many that had formerly held land freely becoming rent-paying tenants, often on onerous terms.[33] Inevitably there was intermarriage, yet it was not until the end of the twelfth century that the cultural, linguistic and social barriers separating English and Normans were broken down.[34] Anglo-Norman French was the spoken language of England's kings and nobility for more than three hundred years: Henry IV, who came to the throne in 1399, was the first monarch since the conquest to have English as his mother tongue.

William the Conqueror's end was a farcical counterpoint to his domineering rule. Obese, his military reputation declining, he died in 1087 at the age of fifty-eight or fifty-nine while leading an expedition against France. Amid confusion over who was now in charge, attendants fled from his bedside in Rouen to look after their properties. Eventually the body was transported to Caen for burial, but his bloated body was too big for its stone sarcophagus. When attendants forced it into the tomb, it caused his swollen bowels to burst, spreading a disgusting odour throughout the church.

If Orderic Vitalis is to be believed, William repented of the Harrying on his deathbed:

In a mad fury I descended on the English of the north like a raging lion, and ordered that their homes and crops and all their equipment and furnishings should be burnt at once and their great flocks and herds of sheep and cattle slaughtered everywhere. So I chastised a great multitude of men and women with the lash of starvation and, alas! was the cruel murderer of many thousands, both young and old.[35]

FRONTIER
REGION

CHAPTER 6

A VIOLENT BORDER

Life on the Anglo-Scottish border was not for the fainthearted. One six-a-side football match in 1599 between men of Bewcastle, in England, and the Armstrongs of Whithaugh, on the Scottish side, was followed by 'drynkyng hard' and a thwarted ambush. The final score was two dead, thirty taken prisoner 'and many sore hurt, especially John Whytfeild, whose bowells came out, but are sowed up againe'.[1]

The Middle Ages brought 600 years of border warfare as English and Scots wrestled over the boundary. Daniel Defoe wrote on his tour through Northumberland in 1724: 'Every place shews you ruin'd castles, Roman altars, inscriptions, monuments of battles, of heroes killed, and armies routed.'[2] Northern England's border counties have spent more than half of the past 2,000 years being fought over if you include the Roman era. It profoundly influenced both nations.

For border residents, fighting could be brutal, with homes and towns on both sides sacked and burned. Nonetheless, centuries of warfare have left little legacy of bitterness between people on either side of the border – unlike, say, the Balkans in the modern day. The border must have seemed an arbitrary creation to those living there when smaller kingdoms coalesced into Scotland and England.

Stretching from the Solway Firth in the west via the River Tweed to the North Sea, it has proved one of Europe's most enduring national land boundaries. Yet it was notable for its artificiality, as it was not a natural frontier or a cultural or historic one.[3]

Thomas Carlyle described borders inhabitants as 'Scotch in features, in character and dialect'. Carlisle-born George MacDonald Fraser wrote in *The Steel Bonnets*, his history of the border reivers: 'In general, it is conceded that the Borderers, English and Scottish, were much alike, that they made excellent soldiers if disciplined, but that the raw material was hard, wild and ill to tame.'[4] The prizing of hardness, alongside friendliness, in the male culture of north-east England is often attributed to that martial tradition.

Amid the wars, exploits of border reivers encompassed cattle thieving, feuding, murder, arson and pillaging. Romanticised in ballads and known by nicknames such as Kinmont Willie, Ill-Drowned Geordie, Fingerless Will Nixon, Davy the Lady and Buggerback Elliot, reivers (from the Old English *reafian*, to rob or plunder) on both sides of the border rode out in groups at night, typically to steal livestock, though some also indulged in kidnapping and extortion. While reiving had ancient origins, the dislocation of the Anglo-Scottish wars, combined with the remoteness and weakness of central governments, created conditions for crime to grow, particularly in the fifteenth and sixteenth centuries. Those raising crops or animals had little hope of keeping them, so robbery seemed to many a more reliable route to subsistence.

Warfare and raiding were not all that was happening in northern England in the Middle Ages. East of the Pennines, especially in east Yorkshire, the twelfth and thirteenth centuries saw economic development and population growth. There were new monasteries such as Rievaulx and Fountains abbeys and Nostell and Kirkham priories. While England's population probably doubled between the Domesday survey in 1086 and the poll tax year of 1377, that of the seven northernmost counties is estimated to have grown fivefold.[5] The wars nonetheless had an impact on the whole region.

In the first phase, Scottish kings were on the offensive (1000–1250); in the second, Scotland was fighting for its independence (1250–1600). Wars occurred intermittently until the Union of Crowns in 1603. Scottish kings' obsession with capturing, or recapturing, territory down to the Tees and beyond was to bring them only grief, just as English kings were never able to translate their claims of overlordship of Scotland into reality. Scotland remained independent until it joined voluntarily with England to create the kingdom of Great Britain in the Treaty of Union in 1707. It was not obvious during the first phase of the wars that England would hold on to the northern counties. The biggest threat came from David I of Scotland, who ruled from 1124 to 1153.

When David became king, there was every reason to suppose he would serve Anglo-Norman interests well. He had spent his adolescence at the royal court in England and Normandy. Fluent in French, schooled in Norman culture and steeped in dynastic politics, he appeared to English chroniclers to be the epitome of Norman knighthood. He had served as Henry I's virtual viceroy in northern England. When he became king, David invited knightly Norman families to join him in Scotland. Already middle-aged when he took the throne, David reigned for almost three decades. Scholars use the phrase 'Davidian revolution'.[6] He promoted commercial enterprise by creating royal burghs such as Berwick, Perth and Aberdeen as centres for trade. He introduced Scotland's first coinage. The four great abbeys of the Scottish borders – Kelso, Melrose, Jedburgh and Dryburgh – were founded under David's auspices.

When Henry I died, England was plunged into near civil war as the throne was seized by the king's nephew Stephen. To the shock of English chroniclers, David launched successive invasions in support of the claims of Matilda, Henry's daughter and his own niece. One column of soldiers attacked Clitheroe with ferocity. Unexpectedly, David's army was defeated by a smaller army in 1138 at the Battle of the Standard near Northallerton, prompting a retreat. Despite this, David kept hold of territory down to the Ribble and Tees. However,

Henry II of England forced David's successor, Malcolm IV, to cede Northumberland, Cumberland and Westmorland.[7] In 1215 Scotland's Alexander II invaded unsuccessfully in support of rebel Yorkshire barons against King John. At the Treaty of York in 1237, Alexander accepted that the border counties were English. This established the border in a form that remains almost unchanged to modern times. The only modifications have been to the 'Debatable Land' north of Carlisle and to Berwick-upon-Tweed, retaken by England in 1482.

The wars' second phase began when Edward I, who had earlier conquered Wales, invaded Scotland in 1296 to exploit a succession crisis. This arose after Alexander III's three children died in quick succession and then the king died, leaving as heir his three-year-old granddaughter, Margaret. A treaty was agreed by which Margaret was to marry Edward's six-year-old son, Edward of Caernarfon. Margaret sailed from Norway to Scotland in 1290 but fell ill on the way and died at Orkney. This left Scotland without an obvious heir and led to a dispute later known as the Great Cause.[8] It was agreed that the realm would be handed to Edward until an heir was chosen. A decision was made in 1292 in favour of John Balliol, who paid homage to the English king.

In 1295, Scots lords, seeking to take advantage of Edward's problems in France, formed an alliance with the French king, which became known as the Auld Alliance. Edward retaliated by invading Scotland and won the Battle of Dunbar. Edward deposed Balliol, placed him in the Tower of London and installed Englishmen to govern the country.[9] Edward's triumph proved temporary. Resistance emerged under the leadership of Andrew Murray in the north and William Wallace in the south. They defeated a larger English army at Stirling Bridge. Edward then defeated Wallace's forces at the Battle of Falkirk, but Wallace escaped. He was captured in 1305 and hanged in Smithfield. His body was quartered and the four pieces despatched for public display in Newcastle, Berwick, Stirling and Perth, while his head was mounted on a spike above London Bridge.[10]

The situation exploded again in 1306 when Robert Bruce seized the Scottish throne and embarked on a campaign to restore Scottish independence. An ailing Edward set off on one more campaign. He developed dysentery and died in 1307 at Burgh by Sands, just south of the border. Edward II was decisively defeated by Bruce at Bannockburn in 1314. The Scottish wars continued inconclusively under Edward III. These wars shifted England's political centre of gravity northwards. The exchequer was based in York for a total of fourteen years between 1298 and 1338 to support the war effort.[11] Clerks from east Yorkshire dominated departments of state. Parliament, which usually met at Westminster, was called to York on eight occasions. Northern landowners made up more than half the members, even when parliament was not meeting at York.

During the fourteenth and fifteenth centuries, the north was supplying soldiers for wars against both Scotland and France, which brought opportunities to prominent families for profit and political influence. The Percys and Nevilles became particularly wealthy and powerful. Spoils also extended to knights, gentry, yeomen, financiers and administrators. Profits of war flowed in ransom money and pay, offices, land, pensions, influential connections, distinctions and honours.

The Neville family began their rise in the early thirteenth century. The male line was of Anglo-Saxon origin. Their principal holdings were in North Yorkshire and Durham, centred on two main castles, Middleham and Raby.[12] The Nevilles, like the Percys of Northumberland, were regularly appointed wardens of the marches, chief officers for frontier defence. They enjoyed autonomy from royal authority because of their region's remoteness and insecurity. The house of Percy was descended from William de Percy, a Norman who arrived in 1067.[13] The family purchased Alnwick Castle in Northumberland early in the fourteenth century.

Richard II's elevation of Nevilles and Percys to earldoms did not stop them from deserting him when Henry Bolingbroke rebelled in 1399. Bolingbroke was crowned as Henry IV. In 1403, however, the

Percys revolted, in part because they felt under-rewarded for fighting border wars.[14] They signed a Tripartite Indenture to divide England with two co-conspirators, Owain Glendower and Edmund Mortimer, Earl of March. The Earl of Northumberland was to have twelve northern counties, Glendower would get Wales and much of the midlands, while Mortimer would get southern England below the Trent.[15] The Percy rebellion ended in defeat by Henry's army at the Battle of Shrewsbury.

Amid all this political chaos, border reiving became more threatening. English and Scottish governments alternated between indulging or even encouraging border families, the first line of defence against invasion, and punishing them severely when lawlessness got out of hand. Reivers could certainly be violent. In 1483, Northumbrian heidsman (family head) Robert Loraine was ambushed by a Scottish raiding party on his way home from church to his peel tower in Kirkharle, then butchered into pieces and packed into the saddlebags of his own horse. The Johnston clan reputedly decorated their houses with flayed skins of their Maxwell enemies.[16]

It had not always been so anarchic. In 1249 customary arrangements ('antient and loveable custumis') for cross-border justice were codified in the Laws of the Marches. Scots and English kings, recognising that it was near-impossible to apply their own laws there, cooperated to create a legal apparatus different from those run by London and Edinburgh. Traditional meeting places along the frontier were to stage regular courts where cases were heard and judgments made. Anyone making an accusation against the subject of another realm had to swear on oath that his statements were true. No one could be found guilty unless allegations were supported by at least one compatriot.[17]

The system seems to have worked well enough in times of relative peace. On truce days, which were judicial and social occasions, large groups of reivers attended, fully armed. A jury of twelve – six from each side of the border – heard bills of complaint from those who had been robbed. Verdicts mostly took the form of reparations.

Stolen goods and livestock were compensated for by a formula of 'double and sawfey': convicted thieves had to pay double the value of goods stolen and an amount of 'sawfey' for the insult of taking them.[18] The system relied on honour. Perjurers were punished by 'bauchling and reproaching', in which liars or oath-breakers were publicly vilified by bauchlers who carried a glove on the end of a lance to point to the perpetrator, or showed a picture of him and blew hunting horns to pick him out. This was an incendiary procedure that often ended in fighting.

Reiving had parallels in other pastoral societies such as Ireland and Gaul.[19] The economics are intriguing. Why did all the livestock not end up in the overstocked barmkins (defensive enclosures) of the Armstrongs, Elliots or Grahams? What was the point of rearing animals that were going only to end up on someone else's table? Yet populations of people and livestock grew despite the plundering. Reiving flourished at a time when the pre-medieval world, in which cattle were treated as common property, was shifting into one in which personal property had a specific, transferable value. Days of truce regulated the ebb and flow of assets.[20] This fits with the borders legend that a wife would demonstrate that her larder was empty by serving her husband his spurs on a plate instead of his dinner – a message that he should mount and go reiving, or go hungry.

The main riding season was early winter when nights were longest and cattle and horses fat after summer grazing. Raiders might range from a few dozen to organised campaigns involving up to two thousand.[21] Reivers are credited with bringing 'blackmail' and 'bereaved' (or 'bereft') into the language. 'Bereaved' simply meant 'robbed' and did not apply to the loss of a loved one until the mid-seventeenth century. 'Mail', from the Old Norse '*mal*', meant 'tribute' or 'rent', while 'black' was a common collective noun for cows, bulls and oxen, which were usually black. 'Grassmail' was money paid to a landowner for grazing rights; 'blackmail' was paid for protection and recovery of cattle – a useful insurance policy. Blackmail acquired its nefarious meaning only when it was turned into a protection racket by thugs such as Johnnie Armstrong (a Scottish reiver hanged in 1530).[22]

At the most dangerous times, people built crude turf cabins, which would be little loss if destroyed. At other times they built two-storey houses known as bastle houses, with stone walls up to three feet thick and narrow slits for ventilation. Such homes could not be set on fire. While they could be captured by smoking out defenders with fires of damp straw or using ladders, this was usually not worth the effort. Wealthier people such as heads of clans built three-storey peel (or pele) towers. Loyalty to a family was expected to be absolute. The inevitable corollary was feuds. Families on the same side of the border, sometimes branches of the same family, often fell out over some slight or other. Borderers, however, owed little or no loyalty to the kings of England or Scotland. At the Battle of Pinkie in 1547, an observer noticed Scottish and English Borderers chatting with each other, then putting on a spirited show of combat once they knew they had been spotted.[23]

One of the most destructive periods was a seven-year campaign by Henry VIII, later known as the 'Rough Wooing' – an unsuccessful effort to coerce James V to betroth his infant daughter Mary to Henry's son Edward. In the years afterwards, families such as the Armstrongs, Croziers, Forsters, Grahams and Nixons were employed to burn entire towns. It became hard to distinguish reivers' activities from the clash of nations.[24] The intensity of raiding increased in the late sixteenth century, notably in the 1590s when bad harvests and hunger drove criminal activity to new depths. When Elizabeth I died, there was a violent outbreak of raiding known as 'Ill Week', resulting from a false belief that a kingdom's laws were suspended between the death of a sovereign and proclamation of the successor.[25]

When James VI of Scotland also became James I of England in 1603, he moved quickly to suppress criminal activity on the now redundant frontier. Squadrons of troops searched out and detained known reivers. Many were hanged without trial and others deported to Ireland, forming the group known as Ulster Scots. Some families moved later to North America; eleven of the US's first fifteen presidents were of Ulster Scots ancestry.[26] Borderers exerted a strong influence on the US upland south, notably Appalachia, with practices including cattle-rustling, the honour culture and feuding.

George MacDonald Fraser vividly describes a moment in 1969 when descendants of 'three notable Anglo-Scottish border tribes' gathered for the presidential inauguration in Washington, with Lyndon Johnson handing over to Richard Nixon in the presence of evangelist Billy Graham. Johnson had a 'lined, leathery northern head and rangy, rather loose-jointed frame' and Nixon had 'blunt, heavy features, the dark complexion, the burly body, and the whole air of dour hardness [that] are as typical of the Anglo-Scottish frontier as the Roman Wall'.[27]

In the borders, James's strategy was brutally effective in restoring order. By uniting the crowns, he succeeded where predecessors had failed and brought 600 years of warfare to a close.

CHAPTER 7

JOHN AND THE NORTHERN BARONS

King John, who ruled from 1199 to 1216, had one of the most disastrous reigns in English history. Conflict with northern barons, on top of misfortunes and self-inflicted blunders, was his undoing.

When John became king after his brother Richard the Lionheart died, he inherited the Angevin empire assembled by their father, Henry II. John therefore was king of England, Duke of Normandy and of Aquitaine and Count of Anjou, from which the Angevins derived their name. He was also ruler of Ireland and overlord of Wales and Brittany. By 1204, John had lost all his French lands except parts of Aquitaine. By his death, he was in the midst of a civil war. Magna Carta, the charter of rights that John reluctantly agreed to at Runnymede, would ultimately be hailed as a symbol of freedom against arbitrary authority. For John, it was a desperate gambit to save his throne.

Throughout his reign, northern barons were at the forefront of disaffection fuelled by John's schemes to extract money to fund his failing efforts to reconquer French lands. Since William the Conqueror's Harrying, northern counties had felt the impact of Norman and Angevin royal government more lightly. John's loss of French lands freed him to interfere in the north more than his predecessors. He came north in all but four years of his reign, usually bearing threats.[1]

Northern barons of French origin and middling wealth, who had acquired lands since the conquest, instigated the revolt that led to civil war. Magna Carta, a compromise engineered by moderate southerners, was a setback for those northerners who wanted tougher constraints or to get rid of John entirely.[2] In part, this political assertiveness had its roots in east Yorkshire's growing wealth and self-confidence, coupled with a sense of separateness and distance from the heart of government.[3] It was Yorkshire that had stood firm against Scotland's David I at the Battle of the Standard in 1138 and would later lead the Pilgrimage of Grace, a popular uprising against Henry VIII's policies in 1536.

John is often portrayed as evil, not least in Hollywood films about Robin Hood (pure fiction: Robin Hood tales were not written down until the fifteenth century and the earliest versions place the events in the time of 'King Edward'[4]). Medieval chroniclers judged him harshly. Anonymous of Béthune, writing for a Flemish noble who fought for John, praised the king's hospitality but added: 'He was a very bad man, more cruel than all others … He set his barons against one another whenever possible, and was very happy when he saw hate between them.'[5]

Some historians paint a more nuanced picture, pointing to his engagement in the business of government and administration of justice. He was certainly someone who, through circumstance and ambition, was placed in a position for which he proved ill-suited.[6] John was suspicious and resentful. His need for money drove him to arbitrary rule. He needlessly provoked other lords when he was strong and desperately tried to win back their support when he was weak. John was not alone in cruelty – Richard had massacred nearly three thousand Muslim prisoners at Acre – but he broke taboos and shocked other nobles, for example by apparently ordering the murder of his nephew, Arthur of Brittany. John had a penchant for starving prisoners to death, most notoriously the wife and son of

William de Braose, a former loyalist who fell out of favour.[7] John tested the principles of kingship to destruction with myriad ways to wrest money and property from his subjects and his insistence on determining senior ecclesiastical appointments. Eventually, barons came together to force him to rule by a set of principles and then, when that failed, to dethrone him.[8]

Keeping the Angevin empire together was never going to be easy: it was a fragile grouping of disparate territories. John faced a formidable opponent in Philip II of France, who was determined to expand his kingdom. It was not inevitable that everything would go so badly wrong, though. If John's allies had not narrowly lost the Battle of Bouvines in 1214 – in which Philip was dragged from his horse and only saved from death by his armour[9] – John would have become the most powerful monarch in western Europe and the barons' revolt might never have happened.

John displayed untrustworthiness even before becoming king, first by deserting his dying father, who was in conflict with Richard, and then by trying to usurp his brother's throne when Richard was captive in Austria. John, after his coronation, saw off a challenge from rival claimant Arthur in Maine and Anjou. Under the Treaty of Le Goulet in 1200, Philip accepted John's accession to all the Angevin dominions. Yet within four years the edifice came crashing down, partly through John's mistakes.[10]

Having divorced his first wife, John married Isabella, daughter of the Count of Angoulême (she was probably aged about twelve), which strengthened his hold on his southern territories. However, he did nothing to compensate Hugh de Lusignan, a Poitevin noble to whom Isabella had been engaged. Hugh appealed to Philip, giving the French king an excuse to make war. John won a battle at Mirebeau, capturing Arthur, the Lusignans and other Poitevin enemies. But then he managed to antagonise the Angevin magnate William des Roches, who defected to Philip, resulting in John losing Maine and Anjou.

John lost further goodwill by treating the prisoners taken at Mirebeau cruelly and by apparently murdering the teenage Arthur, who disappeared while captive. Philip invaded Normandy. John returned to England. Six months later Rouen surrendered and the duchy became Philip's. Meanwhile John's mother, Eleanor of Aquitaine, died. The barons of Poitou – the northern part of Aquitaine – sided with Philip; further south, Alfonso VIII of Castile overran part of Gascony. All that remained of John's Angevin empire was a small part of Aquitaine and the Channel Islands.[11]

After 1204, John spent what J.C. Holt called 'ten furious years' taking his court round England as he tried to amass treasure to win Normandy back.[12] A 1206 expedition to Poitou achieved limited success. Among John's audacious money-raising measures was the Thirteenth, a tax of about 7.5 per cent assessed on the income and goods of every man.[13] He appointed new sheriffs to extract extra money from landowners. He exploited the royal forests by establishing forest eyres, or circuit courts, which imposed heavy fines for infringing forest law such as by hunting or foraging for wood: the heaviest were on Northumberland and Yorkshire.[14] He imposed a crushingly high special tax on Jewish money-lenders: the penalty for non-payment was seizure of their assets, with the result that Christian borrowers ended up owing money to the king.[15]

Policies that hit barons directly included an expansion of Richard's practice of charging baronial widows large sums to be allowed to stay single or marry whom they wished. There were more scutages, or payments made in lieu of military service. Under feudal powers, for a tenant-in-chief to enter into his inheritance, an heir had to pay a sum known as a relief; in the case of under-age heirs, the king retained not only their estates but also all of the profits arising from them for the duration of the wardship.[16]

Resistance to John was deep and widespread in the north.[17] Tenants commonly took up arms against the king even when their lord did not. Northern barons were not the wealthiest, but came from families that were important as administrators and officials. Rebels emerged in Yorkshire, Northumberland, Lancashire and Cumberland, including a large group with estates around the north

Yorkshire moors (Ros at Helmsley, Stuteville at Kirkby Moorside, Percy at Whitby, Bruce at Skelton, Vesci at Malton, Mowbray at Thirsk).[18] The revolt against John has been described as 'a rebellion of the king's debtors'.[19] It is true that some northern barons were heavily in debt to the crown, though that was not uniquely a northern problem. Feelings of regional independence and resentment at John's actions must have played a part. John threatened northern families' hold on profitable offices. He looked to the north to find jobs for followers displaced from positions in Normandy and sought to bring the north under tighter central control. The main impetus to revolt came from the region with strong support from eastern counties.

It was mainly northern barons who objected to serving in or paying for another Poitou campaign. One argument was that their tenure did not cover service across the Channel.[20] Eventually John sailed in February 1214 without many of his barons, but with a large treasure and numerous paid knights.[21] His strategy was to divide Philip's forces. As John's allies took on the French king in northern France, John invaded from the south. He ran into difficulties and his allies were defeated at Bouvines, leaving John to return home in failure.[22] As John's continental ambitions ended in humiliation, his barons were emboldened to act on their grievances. J.C. Holt put it thus: 'The road from Bouvines to Runnymede was direct, short and unavoidable.'[23] Resistance was led by northern lords including Eustace de Vesci, William de Mowbray and Roger de Montbegon. Their aim was to bind the king to conditions.[24]

Eighteen of the forty-five barons who mustered at Stamford in early 1215 were northerners (if Lincolnshire is included).[25] War began on 5 May and the rebels gained a significant advantage when Londoners let them into the city on 17 May; it remained the principal baronial base until the end of hostilities. John was forced to submit to their demands and, after lengthy negotiations, he put his seal at Runnymede on 15 June to a charter known later as Magna Carta. It went beyond addressing baronial grievances and made clear that the king was subject to the law and should rule according to it. It included protection of church rights, protection from illegal imprisonment, access to swift justice, and limitations on taxation and other feudal payments to the crown, with certain forms of feudal taxation requiring baronial consent.[26] Under the 'security clause', a council of twenty-five barons was to be created to ensure John's adherence to the charter. If John did not conform to the charter within forty days of being notified of a transgression by the council, the twenty-five were empowered to seize John's castles and lands until, in their judgement, amends had been made. Northerners made up one-third of the twenty-five.[27]

Neither side stood behind their commitments. John issued the charter to gain time and may never have intended to abide by its detailed provisions. He asked Pope Innocent III to annul it, contrary to a promise in the security clause. The pope was happy to oblige. John had been at odds with Innocent since 1205 over the choice of an Archbishop of Canterbury, which led to the king's excommunication. But John reached a settlement with the pope in 1213, after which Innocent became his most powerful ally.[28]

The war started again. John took Rochester Castle. He led an army north, recovering Carlisle from Alexander of Scotland, capturing Berwick and ravaging Lothian. He returned south via East Anglia, burning his enemies' lands and taking their castles. The rebels offered the throne to Prince Louis of France, who landed in Kent. Louis proceeded to take Rochester, entered a cheering London and seized Winchester. Carlisle surrendered to Alexander, who came south to do homage to Louis.[29] John marched north to relieve Lincoln. As he returned from King's Lynn, his baggage train was trapped by the tide and part of his treasure may have been lost in the Wash. He contracted dysentery and died at Newark in October 1216.

John's infant son was quickly crowned as Henry III. The regency government reissued a revised version of the charter. In May 1217, Louis' forces were defeated at Lincoln; in September, the French prince abandoned his claims and returned home. A further version of the charter was reissued in November 1217, alongside a Charter of the Forest. The larger document in time became known as Magna Carta, to differentiate it. The charter became increasingly embedded into English political life. Magna Carta was John's inadvertent legacy. His reign also demonstrated that, while power in England had shifted to the south, the north was a region that kings abused at their peril.

CHAPTER 8

THE WARS OF THE ROSES

The Wars of the Roses can mean one of two things that have little to do with each other: fifteenth-century wars between the houses of Lancaster and York or the rivalry between Lancashire and Yorkshire. The wars were in no sense a conflict between the counties, but a dynastic struggle between rival branches of the Plantagenets. There were strong, if complicated, north–south dimensions to the wars. They ended in the short and stormy rule of Richard III, sometimes portrayed as England's only 'northern' king.

As for the county rivalry, that was not much of a contest until the Industrial Revolution. Yorkshire was richer and Lancashire was one of England's poorest counties. The historic high road between London and Scotland bypassed Lancashire, seen as a backwater. It was not officially acknowledged as a county until 1181, when a royal exchequer official headed a parchment with *Lancastra quia non erat ei locus in Northumberland*: 'Lancaster, because there is no place for it in Northumberland'.[1] The rivalry was largely a product of Victorian times, when the cotton industry boosted Lancastrian self-confidence and cricket became a popular crucible.

The wars have retained a powerful hold on the imagination. In a famous scene in Shakespeare's *Henry VI Part One*, Richard, Duke of York, invites supporters to pick a white rose in London's Temple

Garden while a bitter rival, the Duke of Somerset, does likewise with a red. The name 'Wars of the Roses' was popularised in the nineteenth century by novelist Sir Walter Scott in *Ivanhoe* and *Anne of Geierstein*, though there were much earlier references.[2] Sometimes it was known as the Cousins' War. Roses were among various emblems used by the two sides, not the most prominent ones, before Henry VII employed them to create his Tudor rose with red and white petals denoting reconciliation.

The wars can be divided into two main phases: the first, 1455–71, was between Lancaster and York, and the second, 1483–7, between the houses of York and Tudor. The sporadic conflict had a limited effect on the population at large: there were at most thirteen weeks of fighting in thirty-two years. Thirty-eight peers died and seven noble families became extinct, in addition to the male lines of the royal houses.[3]

Northern England featured strongly although the wars' geography was complex. In the first phase, the north and midlands were predominantly a Lancastrian stronghold, though loyalties were always mixed and allegiances sometimes fluid. Later, Richard III, the third and last Yorkist king, seized power from a Yorkshire base. His reign was seen in the south as northern tyranny; he gave lands and offices to northerners. But he was defeated and killed at Bosworth because key northerners deserted him.

Among the wars' underlying causes was the weakening of the monarchy by the ruinous cost of the Hundred Years' War against France, which ended in 1453. In some years, military operations in France, Scotland and Ireland took up to 75 per cent of England's national budget.[4] With the centre weakened, challenges to the crown often began in outlying areas such as the Welsh marches, northern England or Calais. Northern families that had risen in wealth and importance in the fourteenth century became deeply involved in national affairs in the fifteenth through offices, alliances and advantageous marriages. The Nevilles became especially influential: Yorkist kings Edward IV and Richard III were Nevilles on their mother's side.

The Percys' power had been weakened by their failed revolt against Henry IV, but they remained a family of consequence. Whatever side the Nevilles were on, Percys would usually be on the other.[5]

Other factors behind the wars included the mental infirmity of Lancastrian Henry VI and the rise of so-called 'bastard feudalism', in which men returning from the Hundred Years' War signed contracts to serve a magnate in order to make a living.[6] This created private armies and overmighty subjects. The backdrop was an agricultural depression and deterioration in law and order.

The dynastic struggle was between descendants of Edward III. His third surviving son was John of Gaunt, who became Duke of Lancaster by marriage. The house of York was founded by Edmund of Langley, Edward's fourth son, though it would base its claim to the throne on the female line, through descendants of Edward's second son, Lionel of Antwerp. The Duchy of Lancaster owned vast estates scattered through England and France, including lands in Yorkshire and Cheshire as well as Lancashire. Richard, Duke of York's main estates were in the northern Welsh marches, with others in Ireland and thirteen English counties.[7]

Events leading to the wars began with the usurpation of Richard II in 1399 by John of Gaunt's son Henry Bolingbroke, who became Henry IV. Seven-year-old Edmund Mortimer, Earl of March, arguably had a better claim as heir general (via the female line) than Henry as male heir: that claim was to remain dormant for sixty years, though its existence provided an ever-present focus for rebels against the house of Lancaster.[8] Henry IV suffered several revolts. His son Henry V governed with firmness and justice, although he crippled the crown with debts in fighting a war with France that England lacked the resources to win, which remained unresolved when he died in 1422. His son Henry VI became king when nine months old.

Henry was sensitive, pious and mentally unstable. His reign saw the gradual loss of England's French lands, leaving only Calais. He was easily swayed by select courtiers and gave away crown lands to favourites. His household was profligate, corrupt and his reign marked by lawlessness and disorder.[9] In 1445 Henry married Charles VII of France's niece, the ambitious and strong-willed Margaret of Anjou. Assertive women played a significant role in the wars, including Edward IV's wife Elizabeth Woodville (or Wydville) and Margaret Beaufort, mother of Henry VII. Margaret of Anjou was fifteen when she married Henry; by eighteen she was, in practice, ruling England.[10]

Tensions grew with Richard, Duke of York. In 1453, Henry suffered a complete mental collapse, leaving him unable to govern. York was declared Lord Protector and chief regent during Henry's incapacity. Meanwhile Margaret bore a son, Edward of Westminster. In northern England, feuding between the Percys and Nevilles escalated. There was a skirmish when Nevilles travelling to a wedding at Sheriff Hutton Castle near York were ambushed by Lord Egremont, brother of Henry Percy, Earl of Northumberland. No one was killed but it is seen as a harbinger of the wars because it drove the Nevilles to support the Duke of York.[11]

Henry recovered in 1455 and York was forced out of court. As Margaret plotted with other nobles to reduce his influence, York resorted to armed hostilities, ostensibly to remove poor advisers from Henry's side. He defeated the Lancastrians at the relatively small first Battle of St Albans. York briefly became Lord Protector again and an uneasy peace ensued. Fighting resumed more violently in 1459. York and his supporters were forced to flee the country and Henry was again restored to direct rule, but one of York's most prominent supporters, Richard Neville, Earl of Warwick (later known as 'the Kingmaker'), invaded from Calais in 1460 and captured the king yet again at the Battle of Northampton. York returned and for the third time became Lord Protector. This time he sought to claim the throne. A compromise was reached whereby he became heir, displacing Prince Edward from the succession.

Margaret fled to Scotland, where Mary of Gueldres, queen consort to James II, agreed to give her an army on condition that she cede Berwick to the Scots and that Mary's daughter be betrothed to Prince Edward. Margaret had no funds to pay her army, so she promised them booty as long as no looting took place north of the River Trent, in the Lancastrian heartlands. She marched south with her Scottish recruits, swelled by large numbers from Northumberland, Cumberland, Westmorland and Lancashire, attracted by the prospect of plundering the prosperous south.[12] When York moved north to engage them, he was killed at the Battle of Wakefield along with his second son Edmund and brother-in-law the Earl of Salisbury, Warwick's father. A paper crown was placed on York's head and the heads of all three were placed on pikes above York's Micklegate Bar.[13]

York's death left his eldest son, eighteen-year-old Edward, Earl of March, as heir to his claim to the throne. With an army from the pro-Yorkist Welsh marches, Edward defeated a Lancastrian force at Mortimer's Cross. Margaret's army marched south, where her soldiers indulged in looting and rape.[14] She freed Henry at the Second Battle of St Albans, but failed to occupy London and retreated back north. Edward was proclaimed King Edward IV in London. He gathered the Yorkist armies and won a crushing victory at Towton near York in March 1461, one of the bloodiest battles fought on English soil. On entering York, Edward ordered the rotting heads of his father, brother and uncle to be taken down and replaced with Lancastrian heads.[15]

After Lancastrian revolts in the north were suppressed, Henry was captured for the third time at Clitheroe in Lancashire in 1465. England under Edward IV came to terms with Scotland, so Margaret and her son were forced to leave for France, where they maintained an impoverished court in exile for several years. Edward was handsome, kingly and capable, but also vain and self-indulgent.[16] He fell out with his chief supporter and adviser Warwick, England's biggest landowner. The king secretly married Elizabeth Woodville, a commoner who was the widow of a Lancastrian, to the embarrassment of Warwick, who was seeking to ally with France by negotiating a match between Edward and a French bride. Tensions mounted when Woodvilles were favoured over Nevilles at court.

An angry Warwick allied with Edward's treacherous brother, George, Duke of Clarence. They captured Edward and imprisoned him at Middleham Castle in Yorkshire (Warwick briefly had two kings in custody), but later released him. They fled to France where Warwick, at Louis XI's instigation, allied with Margaret to restore Henry VI to the throne. A marriage was arranged between Warwick's daughter Anne and Margaret's son, Prince Edward.

Warwick invaded England in autumn 1470. He occupied London and paraded Henry VI through the streets as the restored king, while Edward fled to exile in Burgundy. The following year Edward landed with a small force at Ravenspur on the Yorkshire coast, rallied supporters and re-took London. Clarence abandoned Warwick, who was killed at the Battle of Barnet. Margaret and her son had landed in the West Country: the prince was killed, possibly executed, at the Battle of Tewkesbury. With no heir, Henry VI was murdered shortly afterwards, ending the direct Lancastrian line of succession.

Edward governed relatively successfully for the next twelve years. When he died suddenly in 1483, however, political and dynastic turmoil erupted again. The north was to play a different role in the next phase. It is bittersweet for the north to claim Richard III, England's most divisive king, as its own. Though not born a northerner, it is likely that Richard spent a significant part of his teenage years in Yorkshire. As chief ally of his elder brother, Edward IV, Richard built an unprecedented power base among northern magnates, which later helped him to seize the crown. It was a fragile assertion of northern strength that collapsed with his downfall and death after a reign of twenty-six months from June 1483 to August 1485.

For centuries, Richard was bracketed with King John as one of the most wicked English monarchs, portrayed by Shakespeare and other Tudor writers as a power-crazed tyrant. Recently, Ricardians have sought to present an alternative picture of a fair-minded, pious monarch, concerned about justice. He was ambitious and at times ruthless, though perhaps no more so than many medieval kings. What sets him apart is the accusation that he ordered the killing of his two princely nephews. Many historians consider it overwhelmingly likely that he was guilty, despite the absence of conclusive proof. Child murder offended even medieval aristocratic morality.

Richard was born in 1452 at Fotheringhay Castle, Northamptonshire, eleventh of the twelve children of Richard, Duke of York, and Cecily Neville. When his father was killed at the Battle of Wakefield, Richard and older brother George were sent by their mother to the Low Countries. They returned after their eldest brother, Edward, defeated the Lancastrians at Towton.

Richard, named Duke of Gloucester after Edward IV's coronation, spent three years in the household of his cousin, the Earl of Warwick, to complete his education and knightly training, up to age sixteen. Richard probably spent time at Warwick's Yorkshire castles at Middleham and Sheriff Hutton.[17] Unlike George, now Duke of Clarence, who joined Warwick in revolt, Richard became a vital prop to Edward. Edward and Richard were forced to flee to Burgundy when Warwick allied with Margaret of Anjou. Edward was restored in 1471 after winning the battles of Barnet and Tewkesbury. Eighteen-year-old Richard played a leading role in both, while George had switched sides again and was reconciled with Edward.

Richard married Anne Neville, Warwick's younger daughter. Having already been granted Warwick's former lordships at Middleham, Penrith and Sheriff Hutton, he was able to build the Neville inheritance into a powerful northern estate. Richard built a huge personal constituency in the north, probably greater than Edward intended, though it benefited the king as long as they saw eye to eye. Richard extended his possessions, followers and power step by step. He was happy to implement the king's commands when these coincided with his own interests, but he wanted to be a great magnate and establish a dynasty.[18] Though not the principal landowner in any of the northern shires, he acquired important offices including steward of the northern parts of the Duchy of Lancaster, chief forester north of the Trent, sheriff of Cumberland, justice of the peace in all the northern counties, warden of the west march on the Scottish border and later the king's commander-in-chief against the Scots.[19]

Richard harnessed and strengthened his wife's Neville connections. He offered jobs to ambitious northern gentry as custodians, keepers, bailiffs and foresters. Not all of the north came under his sway, however. In Lancashire, the dominant power was the Stanley family, with whom Richard had an uneasy relationship. The other big northern power was the Percy family, long-standing rival of the Nevilles, strong in Northumberland and east Yorkshire. Richard exerted his influence in areas regarded as the Earl of Northumberland's territory, after which an agreement was reached whereby Richard promised not to lay claim to any grants that the earl received from the king, while the earl promised to be Richard's faithful servant. Northumberland's men in effect became Richard's men at one remove.[20]

In 1480, war with Scotland loomed and Richard was appointed lieutenant-general of the north to lead the campaign. Two years later he recaptured Berwick-upon-Tweed, the last time it changed hands. That allowed Richard to boast of a military success, albeit against a weak and divided Scotland. The war was still under way when Edward died suddenly in 1483. Eventually a three-year truce was agreed.

Edward's death changed everything.[21] The king was succeeded by his twelve-year-old son, Edward V, but within thirteen weeks Richard became Lord Protector and then king. He kept his intentions concealed, so his motive in seizing the crown will never be known. It could have been naked ambition or an attempt at self-preservation since it was unlikely he would have retained the same influence at the new king's court. Earl Rivers, brother of Queen Elizabeth, was escorting Edward V from Ludlow to London, accompanied by three associates. Richard and his cousin, the Duke of Buckingham, met them at Stony Stratford and after spending an apparently convivial evening, arrested them, claiming they were not trustworthy. The four were taken to Pontefract Castle and later executed for treason against Richard.[22]

Richard became Lord Protector while the dowager queen, fearing for the lives of herself and her younger son, retreated to sanctuary in Westminster Abbey. In a frantic two weeks, Richard had Lord Hastings, hitherto a supporter, summarily executed and made several arrests, after which he claimed the throne for himself on grounds of the illegitimacy of Edward V and his brother. There was no resistance. The grounds for this alleged illegitimacy kept shifting, suggesting rushed improvisation. First, it was alleged implausibly that Edward IV was illegitimate, the product of a liaison of his (and Richard's) mother. Second, it was suggested that Edward had been previously betrothed to a foreign bride. Finally, most seriously, a petition argued that Edward's marriage to Elizabeth Woodville was invalid because he was already pre-contracted to Lady Eleanor Butler.[23]

The element of surprise made it relatively easy for Richard to seize the throne, but to keep it he needed to win over more than just his northern supporters. Small, with spinal scoliosis and reportedly fidgety, Richard had self-belief yet lacked Edward IV's personal charm.[24] He aimed to be a better ruler than Edward. Emphasising justice, he created what later became the Court of Requests, to which poor people who could not afford legal representation could apply for grievances to be heard. He abolished benevolences, the forced gifts that Edward IV had used to raise money.[25] He founded the College of Arms, or heralds' college. Most notably, he developed the Council of the North, built on a ducal council that Richard had presided over in Edward's reign. This body was to act as final arbiter in local disputes, providing a means of redress and access to justice for communities.[26]

Richard did not have long to establish his rule. Soon a rebellion broke out across southern counties from Kent to Cornwall, with the initial aim of putting Edward V back on the throne. Surprisingly, it was joined by Richard's ally the Duke of Buckingham, for unclear reasons. He was quickly captured and executed, but it took two months to suppress the revolt. Rumours grew that Edward and his younger brother Richard, Duke of York, who lodged at the Tower of London, had been murdered on King Richard's orders. The boys were never seen after summer 1483. It seems likely that Richard was to blame, since he had a motive to remove a rallying point for opposition, but the absence of firm evidence has led to extravagant theories such as that the boys survived only to be killed by Henry VII.

Richard tried to fill a power vacuum in the south by awarding lands and offices to allies, often northerners. One chronicler wrote: 'The northerners whom he [Richard] had planted in every part of his dominions [were] to the shame of all the southern people who murmured ceaselessly and longed more each day for the return of their old lords in place of the tyranny of the present ones.'[27] Rebels fled to Brittany to join Henry Tudor, the main rival for the throne after the princes' disappearance. His somewhat tenuous claim was derived from his mother, Margaret Beaufort, who was great-granddaughter of John of Gaunt and his mistress Katherine Swynford. Richard's problems deepened when his only son Edward died, leaving him without a direct male heir. A year later his wife Anne died, after which Richard was forced publicly to deny rumours that he had poisoned her and planned to marry his niece, Edward IV's daughter Elizabeth of York.

Richard came close to succeeding with a plot to seize Henry Tudor in Brittany, but Henry escaped to France where his plans for invading England won support. He landed at Mill Bay on the Pembrokeshire coast with 3,000 French troops in August 1485, gathered support as he marched on a roundabout route through Wales, and came face to face with the king near Market Bosworth in Leicestershire. Richard had a larger army, but made the error of deploying it in a way that allowed Henry to concentrate his main force against the flank of Richard's centre. Most of the king's forces were never engaged. Intervention by Thomas Lord Stanley and his brother William on Henry's side was decisive. Richard made a rash charge towards Henry's position; he was unhorsed and died fighting. He was reported to have refused the chance to escape, saying: 'This day I will die a king or win.'[28] Richard III was the last English king to be killed in battle. His naked body was carried back to Leicester tied to a horse, where he was buried at Greyfriars Church. In 2012 his remains were discovered beneath a car park. He was reburied at Leicester Cathedral in 2015.

Henry Tudor became Henry VII and sought to cement the succession by marrying Elizabeth of York. Two years later there was a rising in support of Lambert Simnel, a boy who was claimed to be Edward, Earl of Warwick (son of George, Duke of Clarence), whom Henry held in the Tower. It was crushed on Stoke Field, near Newark in Nottinghamshire. That was to all practical purposes the end of the Wars of the Roses, though another imposter, Perkin Warbeck, claimed to be the younger of the princes in the Tower. Even after his execution, there were further intrigues. It was not until Henry VIII's unchallenged succession in 1509 that the Tudors succeeded in restoring dynastic stability.[29]

The fate of Richard III demonstrated that support from northern lords was not enough to consolidate power in England. Those who hoped to govern needed the southern heartlands onside. The Tudor era showed what that would mean in practice. It was to prove a difficult period for the north.

CHAPTER 9

TUDOR REBELS

The Tudors were centralisers. 'Tudor rule meant the rule of the south over the north,' wrote historian Stanley Bindoff.[1] This happened perhaps more by pragmatism than by coherent, self-conscious policy; it was an ad hoc response to problems of law and order and government finance. The Tudors concentrated power where wealth was increasingly focused: London and south-east England.

England saw massive changes between Bosworth in 1485 and Elizabeth I's death in 1603. Population doubled, the Church was subordinated to the crown and the Reformation took hold. National identity was sharpened by Henry VIII's battles with the pope and Elizabeth's war with Spain. Central government grew stronger. The word 'state' itself became used in its modern political sense by the second half of Elizabeth's reign.[2]

For the north, this marked the start of two centuries of greater marginalisation. The region nonetheless gave the Tudors plenty of trouble. The north was conservative, particularly in religious matters. As in the twenty-first century, many northerners resisted following where the London-based governing class wanted to lead them. After the demise of Richard III, much lamented in York, northern England was the setting for two serious revolts: the Pilgrimage of Grace in 1536 and the Northern Rebellion of 1569–70. Their failure ultimately strengthened the Tudor state. To cap it all, the Union of Crowns in 1603 meant the end of the north's border defence role after 600 years.

Under the Tudors, key royal servants were recruited disproportionately from the south-east. The Tudors built or acquired eighty-six royal palaces: forty-one were in London, Surrey, Middlesex, Kent and Hertfordshire and only two were north of the Trent – former monastic properties in York and Newcastle upon Tyne to house officials of the king's Council of the North.[3] While England's wealth had trebled between 1334 and 1515, London's wealth increased fifteenfold.[4] The power of the crown combined with London merchants' stranglehold over the cloth trade with Antwerp, the main continental entrepôt, made it a formidable capital.

In Henry VIII's reign, England north of the Trent accounted for only 8 per cent of taxable lay wealth, sharply down from its medieval peak, whereas the seven counties surrounding London paid 21 per cent.[5] Some parts of the north did not do badly. London's phenomenal expansion and demand for coal pulled Newcastle upon Tyne into unprecedented prosperity. Yorkshire's West Riding also bucked the picture of relative northern decline, though east Yorkshire towns such as Beverley, Malton, Hedon and Scarborough became poorer.[6]

Henry VII, the Bosworth victor, was the most enigmatic Tudor: 'a dark prince, and infinitely suspicious, and his times full of secret conspiracies and troubles', wrote Francis Bacon.[7] With a weak claim and no experience of government, he had much to fear. Threatened by plots for the first fifteen years, he also endured the deaths of Prince Arthur, his elder son, and his queen, Elizabeth of York. Traditionally Henry has been seen as a ruler who brought stability and put the crown on a sounder financial footing, but he had a more sinister side, particularly later in his reign. His enforcers quelled the turbulence that had marked the previous century with a mixture of surveillance, blackmail and extortion. Shakespeare omitted Henry VII from his sequence of history plays, perhaps because his reign was too uncomfortable to deal with.[8]

Lambert Simnel, a baker's son, was the figurehead of a rebellion in 1487 in which he was claimed to be the Yorkist Earl of Warwick, son of Edward IV's executed brother, George, Duke of Clarence. Henry already held the real earl in the Tower and paraded him through London's streets to counter Simnel's claim. Simnel and his Yorkist followers sailed from Ireland, with an army including European mercenaries, to Piel of Fouldray Castle in Morecambe Bay. Then they marched to defeat at the Battle of Stoke Field, near Newark in Nottinghamshire. Lancashire-based Thomas Stanley had been made Earl of Derby in 1485 in recognition of his decisive support for Henry at Bosworth. At Stoke Field, his son, George Stanley, Lord Strange, was prominent on the king's side. As a sign of gratitude, the king awarded Derby several estates of defeated rebels. Simnel was given a job turning a spit in the royal kitchens.[9]

A further rising proved not so beneficial to the Stanley family. Perkin Warbeck claimed to be Richard, Duke of York, second son of Edward IV and one of the supposedly murdered princes in the tower. Warbeck made several landings in England backed by small armies, but met strong resistance and surrendered in 1497, after which he confessed to being an imposter from Tournai in Flanders. He was executed in 1499. Sir William Stanley, a hero of Bosworth and the Earl of Derby's brother, was implicated in the conspiracy, despite having been appointed lord chamberlain of Henry's household. After all, the Stanleys had changed sides in 1485 only after much hesitation. It is possible that Sir William did not think being lord chamberlain sufficient reward. He was convicted of treason and executed. Derby, though, did not seem unduly troubled by his brother's execution.[10]

In 1489, Henry Percy, fourth Earl of Northumberland, was assassinated near Thirsk while trying to collect tax on the king's behalf. Though the king feared another Yorkist rising, this rebellion may have been a genuine expression of popular anger about war taxation. The levy had been granted by parliament to enable the king to intervene on behalf of Brittany against the French crown.[11] Rebels quickly dispersed as royal troops under the Earl of Surrey arrived at York. Surrey, a southerner who fought for Richard III at Bosworth, had been released from prison and sent north to prove his loyalty. In an effort to get a grip, Henry re-established the Council of the North, nominally led by his young son Arthur. Real authority lay with Surrey, who had some success in binding parts of the north to the king. Later, at age seventy, he led a largely northern army to victory over the Scots at Flodden in 1513.[12]

Henry VII was obsessed by security and money. Unlike most monarchs, he processed accounts himself.[13] His chief servant, Reynold Bray, transformed the royal household into an apparatus that penetrated distant parts. He created a tribunal called the Council Learned in the Law to enforce the king's will. After Bray's death, the king's bidding was done by Richard Empson and Edmund Dudley. Henry and his aides forced nobles and gentry to enter into legally enforceable contracts with stiff financial penalties, obliging them to remain loyal to the crown or to perform specified duties on pain of forfeiture. As Dudley acknowledged, the king wished 'to have many persons in his danger at his pleasure'.[14]

Henry's demands increased. Polydore Vergil, a visiting collector of papal taxes, whom Henry himself commissioned to write a history of England, wrote that the people 'considered they were suffering not on account of their own sins but on account of the greed of the monarch'.[15] Bishop John Fisher said in Henry's funeral oration that the king, in his last days, had had 'full little pleasure' from 'this wretched world'.[16] But these were also the dawning years of a dynasty.

Seventeen-year-old Henry VIII, on accession in 1509, sought to draw a line under his father's regime. The crown's financial grip was relaxed, his father's tribunals abolished, and Empson and Dudley executed. The new king was '*ricco, feroce, cupido di gloria*' ('rich, ferocious, thirsting for glory') wrote Niccolò Machiavelli.[17] Henry VIII presented himself as a kind of Renaissance prince, athletic, intellectual and artistic. Sir Thomas More wrote, in a poem celebrating the coronation, that Henry VIII's arrival represented 'the limit of our slavery, the beginning of our freedom, the end of sadness, the source of joy'.[18]

It was not long, though, before similar methods of controlling subjects and squeezing money from them were asserted.[19] Henry expanded royal power with the help of chief ministers, some of whom were banished or executed when they fell from favour. Cardinal Thomas Wolsey raised revenues, though not by enough to match Henry's extravagance.[20] Thomas Cromwell strengthened central government by shifting the focus from the royal household to departments of state under a streamlined Privy Council. He also became the driving force behind Henry's Reformation.[21]

The year 1536 was a watershed.[22] Catherine of Aragon died, Anne Boleyn was beheaded and Henry married Jane Seymour. The Ten Articles, a statement of faith aiming to reconcile conservative and reformist beliefs, was issued. Parliament passed acts with implications for the north, including one to dissolve lesser monasteries with revenues below £200 a year; there were far more of these in northern England than elsewhere. A Statute of Uses was passed to restrict landowners' use of a legal device that put land beyond inheritance tax. A further act curtailed the independent jurisdiction of territorial franchises or 'liberties' and counties palatine. Liberties with autonomy in places such as Beverley, Durham and Ripon had existed in the north for more than five hundred years.

The pace of change provoked revolt, initially in Lincolnshire, sparked by rumours that jewels and plate were to be confiscated from parish churches and that taxes were to be levied on cattle.[23] A bigger rebellion began in east Yorkshire in early October under the leadership of Thomas Aske, a well-connected lawyer with grievances against Cromwell's regime. As rebels advanced to York, Aske spoke of the rising as a pilgrimage. The full title became 'The Pilgrimage of Grace for the Commonwealth'; the grace that it sought was not primarily from God, but grace from the king for his poor subjects.[24]

Pilgrims entered York possibly ten thousand strong. They wore badges of the Five Wounds of Christ; they swore an oath and pledged to strive for suppression of 'evil councillors' and reformist 'heretics'; they circulated ballads warning that the poor would suffer from loss of monastic charity.[25] Aske emphasised peaceful intentions. A further rising started in the North Riding, where rebels held assemblies in Richmond and instigated rebellions across the north, issuing calls to Durham, Westmorland and Cumberland. Barnard Castle yielded and rebels ransacked Bishop Tunstall's palace at Bishop Auckland before sending a large number to join Aske at York.

Rebels mustered in Westmorland and Cumberland, where city authorities in Carlisle rebuffed them. In central and south Lancashire, there were rumours that the Earl of Derby would join the rebellion, but the king secured his loyalty by giving him authority over much of Lancashire, Cheshire and North Wales. By late October, virtually the whole north outside central and southern Lancashire had risen, apart from a few isolated outposts. The king was caught unawares: he had disbanded a large army that had gathered to march on Lincolnshire, thinking it was no longer needed. The rebellion's leaders were hesitant, however, which ultimately gave the government its chance. While Aske wanted a show of force to give the north a voice, remove Cromwell and reverse the thrust of Henry's Reformation, he also wanted to avoid fighting. Only one man was killed during the pilgrimage and that by accident.

Royal armies led by the Duke of Norfolk and Earl of Shrewsbury were far apart and outnumbered by the pilgrims, who by now had more than thirty thousand men, leaving the duke little option but to negotiate. Aske persuaded pilgrim leaders to meet Norfolk on Doncaster bridge. Agreement was reached on a truce while Sir Ralph Ellerker and Robert Bowes carried the pilgrims' petition to the king. Norfolk advised the king to play for time and make as many apparent concessions as possible. Further negotiations were offered and rebels were asked to clarify their demands. They met at Pontefract and drew up a twenty-four-article manifesto combining grievances of commoners and the gentry.

Norfolk offered a general pardon and a freely elected parliament in the north that would reconsider acts that pilgrims objected to, but avoided committing himself as to when and where the parliament should be held. Aske accepted the peace terms and persuaded rebels to disperse, with some difficulty. He thought he had won, but weeks passed in which the king neither ratified nor repudiated the terms. Renewed risings in February gave Henry the excuse he needed to crack down. Rebels were hanged in Carlisle and Cumberland. The trials were conducted by leaders of the autumn risings, Ellerker and Bowes, showing that a gulf had opened between some of the gentry and the populace. Other gentry were rounded up and taken to London to be tried for treason, often on weak evidence. There were many executions and Aske was hanged at York.

Sir Geoffrey Elton in the 1970s portrayed the rebellion as pre-planned by a faction of nobles.[26] More recently, historians have generally argued that it was popular and spontaneous.[27] For many people it was in response to a perceived threat to traditional rituals, practices and beliefs. Rebels saw religious, social and economic grievances as linked. The revolt followed two poor harvests. Aske emphasised the monasteries' social role: they provided some rudimentary education, safe deposit for valuable documents, tenancies for farmers and a place to dispose of unmarried daughters and aged relations. For landowners, grievances included new taxes and the Statute of Uses.

The pilgrimage was the most serious Tudor rebellion and the largest popular revolt in English history. It was poorly handled by Henry and came close to succeeding. Its defeat, however, made the English Reformation possible. In the rebellion's wake, Henry gave increased authority and land to loyal gentry as a counterweight to the old magnate dynasties. The Council of the North was reorganised and filled with less troublesome nobles, knights and lawyers; previous members had included pilgrim leaders. Its jurisdiction was extended from Yorkshire to the border counties, though not Lancashire. Over the next decade it had to cope with persistent border feuds and simmering resentment towards the government.[28]

Elizabeth I's effort to achieve a Protestant settlement that Catholics could live with encountered greatest hostility in the north, where she too faced rebellion. The Act of Supremacy 1558 re-established the Church of England's independence from Rome (after Mary's reign) and made Elizabeth its 'supreme governor'. The Act of Uniformity 1559, passed by just three votes, reintroduced a Book of Common Prayer. It also required church attendance on Sundays and holy days and imposed fines for absence. Most people gradually conformed, at least outwardly, but some Catholic recusants refused to attend services, while Puritans pressed to remove what they considered papist abuses from the church's liturgy.

Lancashire, poor and isolated, remained England's most Catholic and conservative county. The Earls of Derby acted as regional agents for the crown and their convolutions reflected the uncertainty of the times. Edward, the third earl, after serving Henry VIII in imposing the Reformation, assisted Mary in the trial and execution of Protestants; during Elizabeth's reign, Edward did a further about-turn and helped to implement her Protestant policies.[29] A priest at Croston, near Chorley, said in 1533, of Elizabeth's mother, Anne Boleyn: 'Queen Catherine was queen, and that Nan Boleyn should be no queen … Who the devil made Nan Boleyn, that whore, queen, for I will never take her for queen?'[30] A substantial part of Lancashire's gentry remained Catholic, giving them safety in numbers and affording protection to recusant tenants. Leading Catholics were frequently fined or suffered other minor punishments.[31]

South-east Lancashire became fertile ground for Puritans. Bolton was known as 'the Geneva of the north' because of its early devotion to Calvinism. But central and western Lancashire were strongly Catholic. Cardinal William Allen, exiled leader of England's Catholics, was born in Rossall, near Fleetwood. He created a college at Douai in Flanders, which trained missionary priests who returned secretly to England to keep the faith alive. Elizabeth complained of

Catholic opposition in Lancashire 'as we hear not of the like in any other parts'.[32]

However, it was in the far north, not Lancashire, that rebellion arose. The queen distrusted the Percys and Nevilles and kept them away from offices of military or political importance such as wardenships of the marches.[33] The arrival of Mary Queen of Scots in England after her Scottish defeat in 1568 led to a series of conspiracies. She crossed the border expecting support from Catholics in the north. Thomas Percy, Earl of Northumberland, was among those who paid court to her.[34] Mary fled southwards seeking the protection of Elizabeth, her first cousin once removed, after being forced to abdicate the Scottish throne following her second husband's murder. Many English Catholics viewed Mary as the legitimate sovereign of England. Perceiving Mary as a threat, Elizabeth had her confined in various castles and manor houses.

After a decade of Elizabethan government, Protestantism was not yet secure. The queen was childless, so the succession remained an open question. Tensions were rising. A faction at court advocated marriage between Mary and the Duke of Norfolk, England's premier peer, believing that this would enable the queen to settle the succession and would also destroy her chief adviser William Cecil. When Elizabeth heard about the proposal, she angrily vetoed a match between her leading nobleman and the most dangerous claimant to her throne.[35]

Revolt was brewing in the north involving Norfolk's brother-in-law Charles Neville, Earl of Westmorland, and the Earl of Northumberland, who had recently reconverted to Rome. Norfolk withdrew from court to escape the atmosphere of suspicion, which the two earls took as a signal for action. However, they were forced to abandon a planned rising when Norfolk's nerve failed him and he decided not to raise his East Anglian tenantry.[36] The queen summoned Westmorland and Northumberland to court to explain themselves, which forced them into open rebellion. They had gone too far to turn back, so they mustered forces without any clear plan.

In November 1569, the rebels marched from Westmorland's castle at Brancepeth to Durham Cathedral, where they ripped apart all Protestant books, overturned the communion table and celebrated a Catholic mass. The earls declared themselves ready to remove 'those disordered and evil disposed persons' about the queen who subverted the true Catholic faith, the ancient nobility and the rightful succession.[37] Durham was the heart of the rebellion, but large numbers also joined from Richmondshire. The rebels marched south until they reached Bramham Moor near Tadcaster, where they paused for two days. The Earl of Sussex, president of the queen's Council of the North, had only 400 ill-equipped horsemen and dared not leave York to confront them.[38]

The rebels lost their nerve, however; they turned back and did not stop until they reached Brancepeth. They may have feared a massive force that was being organised against them in the south, or they may have realised they could not reach Mary, who was hastily moved from Tutbury Castle in Staffordshire. The rebels besieged Barnard Castle while a contingent took Hartlepool, hoping in vain that Spanish troops might land there. As the royal army approached, the rebels disbanded. The two earls fled to Scotland, from where Westmorland escaped to the Netherlands; his estates were confiscated by the crown. Northumberland was sold by the Scots to Elizabeth for £2,000 and beheaded at York.[39]

The rebellion failed mainly because it was poorly organised and lacked clear aims, but also because potential backers from across the Pennines failed to stir. Retribution was severe. Elizabeth ordered 700 executions among the rank and file, though the number actually carried out was smaller, possibly about 450.[40] The rebellion's failure strengthened the hand of Cecil and his Protestant colleagues, who were never seriously challenged in government again. The affair tested and toughened the Elizabethan religious settlement. For twenty years, despite Catholic plotting, Elizabeth faced no further rebellions.

As Elizabeth's reign progressed, the age saw a flourishing of English drama. There has long been interest in the intriguing question of whether William Shakespeare spent time in Lancashire as a teenager, during his 'missing' years.[41] This arises from the 1581 will of Alexander Hoghton, a Catholic landowner whose family home was Hoghton Tower, between Preston and Blackburn. In it, he recommended two men called Fulk Gillom and William Shakeshafte to his brother Thomas at Lea Hall; and, failing that, to his neighbour and kinsman Sir Thomas Hesketh. The two are assumed to have been players or musicians since the will refers to musical instruments and 'play clothes' in connection with them. Hesketh was known as a patron of players and Hoghton hoped he would either employ Shakeshafte and Gillom or 'help them find a good master'.[42]

Some scholars argue that Shakeshafte was the seventeen-year-old Shakespeare. His last Stratford schoolmaster, John Cottam, may have been a Hoghton man and might perhaps have recommended his former pupil to the Hoghtons as a private tutor. A Fulk Gillom does later appear as a servant to Hesketh. It is supposed that, if Gillom moved to Hesketh's service, then Shakeshafte, three times mentioned next to Gillom in Hoghton's will, may also have entered it as well.[43]

There are other coincidences. Thomas Savage, Shakespeare's trustee and backer at the Globe nearly twenty years later, also came from this part of Lancashire and his wife was a Hesketh. But was Shakeshafte Shakespeare? As Michael Wood points out, Shakeshafte was, and still is, a common name in Lancashire – Preston guild records were full of them in 1580–1. On the face of it, a man in a Hoghton will bearing a Preston name ought to be a local. The jury is still out on the claimed connection.[44] Shakespeare also had links to the Stanley family, whose ancestral home is Knowsley Hall on Merseyside. Ferdinando, Lord Strange, a family member who later became fifth Earl of Derby, maintained an acting troupe called Strange's Men, which performed Shakespeare plays at London's Rose Theatre and probably also performed at Knowsley Hall. It was the precursor to the Lord Chamberlain's Men, Shakespeare's company at the Globe.[45]

A curious coda to the story of the Elizabethan north was the appointment of John Dee, alchemist, mathematician, astrologer and scientist, as warden of Christ's College, Manchester, in 1595.[46] It was not a happy appointment for Dee, who some speculate may have been the model for Prospero in Shakespeare's *The Tempest*. As astrologer to Queen Elizabeth, Dee had chosen 15 January 1559 as propitious for her coronation. As a political adviser he advocated turning England's imperial expansion into a 'British Empire', a term he is credited with coining. Much effort in his last thirty years was spent trying to converse with angels, who he thought would reveal the divine language that God had used to create the universe.

Short of money, he petitioned Elizabeth for a remunerative position, but the best she could offer was Christ's College, a former college of priests that had been re-established as a Protestant institution. It was in a poor state and gave him little but grief. The collegiate church was in disrepair, the college buildings had been sold and its lands leased to local gentry on terms that were mired in litigation. As the representative of Elizabethan authority, Dee struggled to exercise control over Puritan fellows who despised him. He was forced to borrow and had barely enough money to feed his family and household servants.

In 1597 Dee wrote to a friend that he was overcome or 'enforced' by 'the most intricate, [c]umbersome, and (in manner) lamentable affayres & estate, of this defamed & disordred Colledge of Manchester'.[47] His wife died of bubonic plague in 1604. Dee left Manchester to return to London, but remained warden until his death in 1609.

Elizabeth's later years were difficult. Conflicts with Spain and in Ireland dragged on, taxes rose to finance the cost of war and there were poor harvests. Prices rose and living standards fell. Repression of Catholics intensified. The queen increasingly relied on spies to maintain control. Many felt relief when Elizabeth died in 1603. Scotland's James VI, son of Mary Queen of Scots, also became James I of England and Ireland. When James in turn lost popularity by the

1620s, there was a nostalgic revival of affection for Elizabeth, seen as heroine of the Protestant cause and monarch of a golden age. Despite the myth of Gloriana, the notion of a united English Protestant nation disguised a more complex reality.

CHAPTER 10

WITCHCRAFT AND CIVIL WARS

In March 1612, near the east Lancashire town of Colne, a young woman called Alizon Device encountered John Law, a pedlar from Halifax, and asked him for metal pins, relatively expensive items that could be used for magical purposes. He refused to undo his pack. She claimed she meant to buy them, but he said she was begging. A few minutes later, Law stumbled and fell down lame – possibly a stroke. A few days afterwards, Law's son took Alizon to visit his father and claimed that she confessed to having bewitched him and begged for forgiveness.[1]

Thus began events leading to the notorious Pendle witch trials of 1612, in which nine women and two men were hanged. The majority of those accused came from two families competing to scrape a living from healing, begging and extortion. The affair played to Lancashire's image as a dark corner of superstition, witchcraft and popery, but it was not alone. The trials caught a widespread mood of spiritual anxiety.

For northern England, it was an ominous start to a troubled century that displayed its poverty and political weakness. Northern counties suffered during the seventeenth-century civil wars from conflict, pestilence, disruption to trade, plundering of homes and farms, and repeated taxation. The civil wars' geography bore similarities to the UK's (admittedly less deadly) 2016 EU referendum. Royalist support was strongest in socially conservative northern and western England, similar to that for Brexit. The issues were clearly different, but the pattern suggests that England's economic and cultural divide has deep roots.

Europe was swept by witchcraft panics at the start of the seventeenth century. After the Reformation had divided Europe into Protestants and Catholics, both sides hunted witches.[2] Few were more assiduous than Scotland's James VI, raised as a Protestant. He feared that he and his Danish bride, Anne, had been targeted by witches who conjured storms to try to kill them during voyages across the North Sea. James wrote *Daemonologie*, a book that explained witchcraft as a pact between humans and the devil. It inspired Shakespeare's witch scenes in *Macbeth*.

When James also became James I of England, he faced a different threat: militant Catholics. While many Catholics had conformed to Protestantism under Elizabeth, the Gunpowder Plot of 1605 – Guy Fawkes' plan to blow up parliament and kill the king – demonstrated that the threat was still potent. The Lancashire affair combined James's two greatest fears: papists and witches.[3]

England was less witch-obsessed than many other countries. It is estimated to have contributed fewer than five hundred of about forty thousand witch executions in Europe between the early fifteenth and mid-eighteenth centuries.[4] The Pendle trials were notable for the large number hanged and also because there is a detailed official account called *The Wonderfulle Discoverie of Witches in the Countie of Lancaster*, written by associate clerk to the court, Thomas Potts, on the judges' orders. It appeared aimed to further their careers by currying favour with James.[5] (James's other connection with Lancashire was a royal visit so cripplingly expensive that one of his hosts, Sir Richard Hoghton of Hoghton Tower, ended up in debtors' prison. The visit gave rise to the probably apocryphal legend that the king knighted a loin of beef 'Sir Loin'.[6])

Economic and religious factors influenced witch-hunting, both present in the rural area around Pendle hill. Its population doubled between 1560 and 1650, creating pressure on the local economy.[7] A high proportion of witchcraft cases involved disputes over money and property or misfortunes involving milk or cattle. It was commonplace for poor people to practise magic as village healers or cunning folk. Many witches were women, often disparaged as quarrelsome, who used their supposed powers to assert their place in society.

Moderate Protestants tended to regard witchcraft accusations with scepticism, while Puritans were readier to believe them. Pendle was in the vast parish of Whalley, covering 180 square miles. Dissolution of Whalley Abbey in 1537 left a spiritual and economic vacuum, into which came a group of Puritan clergy and gentry, while lay people were more varied in religious practices.[8] Those involved in witchcraft used spells and charms based on garbled versions of old Catholic prayers.

Six of the Pendle witches came from two families, each headed by a woman in her eighties: Elizabeth Southerns (also known as Demdike, derived from 'demon woman'), her daughter Elizabeth Device and grandchildren James and Alizon Device; and Anne Whittle (alias Chattox, so called because she chattered incomprehensibly to herself) and her daughter Anne Redferne. Many of the charges concerned deaths that went back years.

Investigations were conducted by Roger Nowell, a staunchly Protestant magistrate. Demdike admitted that twenty years earlier she had given her soul to a shape-shifting spirit called Tibb. Alizon and her grandmother made accusations against Chattox and her daughter. Chattox admitted that she had in the past made a compact with a devil called Fancie. Demdike, Alizon, Chattox and Anne were sent to Lancaster Castle for trial, but Demdike died before it began.

The affair might have been limited to the four women had it not been for a meeting on Good Friday organised by Elizabeth Device at Malkin Tower, home of Demdike's family, attended by friends.

Nowell suspected a witches' sabbath. The result was that eight more were accused. The strangest allegation was a claim that participants planned to blow up the castle so as to allow the prisoners to escape. It seemed couched to appeal to King James: here was another gunpowder plot.[9]

One of the accused was Jennet Preston, who lived in Yorkshire, so she was sent to York Assizes. Jennet was charged with murder by witchcraft of a landowner, Thomas Lister of Westby Hall, her friend and possible lover. It was alleged that she had touched his corpse and it 'bled fresh bloud presently, in the presence of all' – a common belief was that a corpse would bleed if its murderer touched it. She was found guilty and hanged.[10]

The remaining trials were held at Lancaster Assizes, alongside a few accused from other places. Chattox was charged with murdering a man called Robert Nutter, who had attempted to seduce her daughter. The jury found her guilty. Anne was found innocent of Nutter's murder, but guilty of murdering his father. Alizon Device was charged with having bewitched the pedlar John Law and so lamed him that 'his bodie wasted and consumed'. She pleaded guilty and wept, asking the court to forgive her. She was condemned to death.[11]

Elizabeth Device was charged with three murders. Potts records that as she came to the bar, she screamed 'in very outragious manner' against everyone, not least her nine-year-old daughter Jennet. The judge had Elizabeth removed. Jennet said her mother had a familiar called Ball, who appeared as a brown dog, and she claimed to have witnessed conversations in which Elizabeth asked Ball to help with various murders. Elizabeth was found guilty. James Device was found guilty of four murders.[12]

Alice Nutter, seventy-year-old widow of a yeoman farmer, was convicted of causing the death of a man who had refused to give Demdike a penny she had begged from him. Katherine Hewyt, wife of a Colne clothier, was found guilty of killing a child. John Bulcock and his mother Jane were convicted of bewitching a farmer's wife to madness.[13]

The Pendle group were tried alongside three women from Samlesbury, a village near Preston: Jennet and Ellen Bierley and Jane Southworth. They were accused by Jennet's fourteen-year-old grand-daughter, Grace Sowerbutts, of killing a child by sucking its blood and then eating the child. But when the judge discovered that Grace had been coached by a Jesuit priest, he ordered the jury to acquit them. His actions appeared calculated to accord with King James's views, cracking down on popery as well as witchcraft, while avoiding fraudulent accusations. James wanted judges to be lenient towards moderate Catholics, but hard on Jesuit agents.[14]

Those condemned to death were hanged at Gallows Hill, outside Lancaster city gates. Belief in witchcraft among educated people collapsed by the early eighteenth century, but continued in the wider population into the late nineteenth century. The Pendle story's fame was assured by the popularity of William Harrison Ainsworth's romantic novel *The Lancashire Witches* (1849). In modern times the witches' story has been embraced enthusiastically by the tourism and heritage industries.

The witch-hunting era's dislocation was nothing compared with that of the wars. The first attested casualty in the civil wars in England was a northerner: Richard Parcival, a linen weaver, killed in a skirmish with royalists in Manchester in July 1642.[15] Three wars over a decade (1642–6, 1648–9, 1649–51), along with parallel conflicts in Scotland and Ireland, meant that these 'wars of the three kingdoms' were among the most destructive events in the islands' history. In England alone about 4 per cent of the population is esti-mated to have died from fighting and war-related disease, a larger proportion than in the First World War. The death rate was higher in Scotland and much more so in Ireland.[16]

As with the EU referendum, there were mixed loyalties in all parts.[17] Parliament drew strongest support from London and the south-east, the most prosperous areas, as Remain did in 2016. Royalist support was strongest in rural areas of northern and western England, Wales, the Welsh marches and west midlands, similar to that for Leave. Manufacturing towns tended to be Puritan and pro-parliament. The issues were obviously different from today and the parallels inexact. Some towns, including Hull, Bradford, Bolton and Rochdale, backed parliament in the civil wars, when they were newly prosperous, but voted Leave in the EU referendum, after prosperity had deserted them. But the broad pattern suggests that England's economic and political geography has recurring features.

Power, money and religion were the main issues at stake in the civil wars. While the wars stemmed from failure of the political process at the centre, local factors were also at play. Superior access to manpower and wealth favoured parliament, a result of controlling London and the south-east. The north's royalism was largely a continuation of the traditionalism seen in the Tudor era. The region still had a large Catholic minority, who preferred Charles's High-Church Anglicanism to the Puritan ideology.

Charles I's troubles grew when he tried to introduce a High Anglican version of the English Book of Common Prayer to Scotland. Scots formulated their objections in the National Covenant. Charles's forces were humiliatingly defeated in the Bishops' Wars (1639–40), in which a Scottish army captured Newcastle.[18] Desperate for money, Charles summoned what became known as the Long Parliament in 1640. It sought to force reforms on the king and condemned Thomas Wentworth, Earl of Strafford, his former lord deputy of Ireland, to death for 'high misdemeanours' there, fearing that Strafford was encouraging the king to redeploy troops from Ireland to suppress opposition in England. Strafford, of Wentworth Woodhouse near Rotherham, had also alienated some powerful Yorkshire landowners, who sat on the committee that drew up the indictment.[19] Charles reluctantly signed his death warrant and Strafford was executed. Parliament also abolished the Council of the North, over which Strafford presided.

In January 1642 Charles unsuccessfully attempted to arrest five members of the Commons on a charge of treason. A few days later, Charles fled to York and set up court there, with the aim of rallying northern supporters. He was disappointed: he had lost the confidence of some gentry, partly the legacy of Strafford's heavy-handedness.[20] Charles tried to secure the port of Hull, which had a large arsenal, but was rebuffed by Sir John Hotham, the military governor appointed by parliament.

Lacking recruits in Yorkshire, Charles raised his standard at Nottingham. His best sources of support were to be Wales, the Welsh marches, Cheshire and Lancashire.[21] At first, people were reluctant to join the war on either side, but it is estimated that eventually at least a quarter of the adult male population at some stage bore arms.[22]

Parliament appointed Ferdinando, Lord Fairfax, as commander-in-chief in the north, though in practice he and his son Sir Thomas, general of horse, controlled only the clothing towns of the West Riding.[23] Yorkshire-born William Cavendish, Earl of Newcastle, a horse breeder and patron of playwright Ben Jonson, was given command of northern royalists, largely because he was willing to pay for his own troops. Having recruited in the four northernmost counties, he marched to York and set about adding Yorkshire regiments. The north-east was itself important because London needed its coal: royalists controlled Newcastle, so parliament aimed to take Sunderland to get coal out (achieved in April 1644), marking the origins of Tyne–Wear rivalry.[24]

In June 1643, the Earl of Newcastle marched towards Bradford, where he inflicted a calamitous defeat on the Fairfaxes at Adwalton Moor. They retreated to Hull, leaving royalists in control of almost all of Yorkshire. The Marquis of Newcastle, as the king had now made him, besieged Hull unsuccessfully for six weeks before retreating to York. Further south, Charles came as close as he would ever do to gaining the upper hand. The northern royalist army could have tipped the balance in his favour, had it not been fruitlessly employed in the Hull siege. In Lancashire, however, parliament was gaining the upper hand over royalists led by the Earl of Derby.[25]

The war turned decisively in 1644 after parliament allied with Scottish Covenanters, prompting 15,000 Scottish troops to invade northern England. A contingent besieged the city of Newcastle, which fell later in the year, while the main force joined the Fairfaxes in besieging York. Prince Rupert, the king's nephew, was sent to relieve York, but first he had to try to settle Lancashire, both to gain control of the port of Liverpool and to impose his uncle's authority. Rupert sidestepped the heavily defended town of Manchester and sacked nearby Bolton. After that battle, up to a thousand parliamentary soldiers and civilians were killed in one of the war's worst massacres. Liverpool was also taken, after which Rupert crossed the Pennines via Preston and Clitheroe to York.[26]

The parliamentarian siege was abruptly lifted and Rupert engaged the allied armies at Marston Moor, hoping to catch them retreating, but he was handicapped when the York garrison arrived ten hours late and three regiments short of its full strength. The battle, decided in parliament's favour in little more than two hours, was the bloodiest of the war and possibly the largest ever fought on British soil. The northern royalist army was destroyed. The battle enhanced the career of Oliver Cromwell, who led the parliamentary cavalry. His men routed Rupert's horsemen and destroyed Newcastle's infantry. 'God made them as stubble to our swords,' he said. York subsequently surrendered, leaving only a few isolated royalist strongholds in the north.[27]

In 1645, parliament's reorganisation of its main forces into the New Model Army, under the command of Sir Thomas Fairfax with Cromwell as his second-in-command, led to decisive victories at Naseby in Northamptonshire and Langport in Somerset. In Lancashire, Liverpool fell to parliamentary forces and Lathom House, the Earl of Derby's seat, was captured. The first civil war ended in May 1646 when Charles sought shelter with a Scottish army in Nottinghamshire and was handed over to parliament.

The war's end solved little because the winning side was divided between the army, which championed independent religious views, and parliament, which favoured Presbyterianism. This was an era of unorthodox political and religious sects. One London MP observed: 'Those that came out of the north are the greatest pests of the nation.' Gerrard Winstanley, leading theorist of the Diggers, was born in Wigan; Lawrence Clarkson, the Ranter, came from Preston; James Webster, the Grindletonian, became a schoolmaster at Clitheroe; the Seekers would also attract several Lancashire congregations. George Fox, founder of the Quakers, had a vision of a 'great multitude waiting to be gathered' on Pendle hill.[28]

Charles took advantage to negotiate a secret treaty with Scottish Covenanters known as the Engagement, under which the king agreed to impose Presbyterianism in England for a trial period of three years and suppress independents and sects. A poorly trained Engager army under James, Duke of Hamilton, marched into England. This second civil war was intended as a series of royalist risings in England and Wales, with the Scots providing support, but by the time Hamilton's army entered Lancashire in August 1648, the other revolts had been suppressed. Cromwell routed the Scots at Preston and crushed the remainder at Winwick, near Warrington. Hamilton was beheaded in London.

Parliament created a tribunal to try Charles for treason. Thomas Fairfax, who had succeeded his father as Lord Fairfax, was a constitutional monarchist and declined to have anything to do with the trial. He resigned as head of the army, clearing Cromwell's road to power. The king was beheaded on 30 January 1649. Fairfax sat out the Cromwell era at his home near York. Andrew Marvell, tutor to Fairfax's daughter, wrote a poem celebrating its 'fragrant gardens, shady woods / Deep meadows, and transparent floods'.[29]

Cromwell campaigned brutally against Catholics and royalists in Ireland. Charles II, who in exile had been proclaimed successor to his father, arrived in Scotland after reaching agreement with Covenanters. Cromwell defeated a Scottish army at Dunbar in September 1650 and occupied much of southern Scotland. After Dunbar, thousands of Covenanters were taken to Newcastle, where about 1,600 starved, and then to Durham, where 1,700 died in captivity. Their remains were rediscovered in 2015.[30]

Cromwell's victory did not prevent Charles from marching into England. He reached the west of England, but fewer supporters joined than he hoped. Cromwell defeated him at Worcester in September 1651, ending the third civil war. Charles II escaped via safe houses and a famous oak tree to France. The Earl of Derby, who helped the king to get away, was tried for treason and beheaded at Bolton for his part in the earlier massacre.

England was ruled by a republican government under the Commonwealth from 1649 to 1653. After infighting among factions in parliament, Cromwell became Lord Protector (in effect military dictator) until his death in 1658. His son Richard succeeded him, but the army had little faith in him. The army dissolved into factions, threatening anarchy. A royalist-inspired rebellion by Sir George Booth in Cheshire, Lancashire and North Wales reflected disillusionment with disintegrating central authority.[31]

Into this atmosphere General George Monck, governor of Scotland under the Cromwells, marched south with an army and organised a new Convention Parliament, which declared that Charles II had reigned as lawful monarch since his father's execution. Charles returned from exile in 1660 and was crowned in 1661. The Restoration was greeted with relief by some, while those who disagreed kept quiet. Warden Heyrick, a one-time Puritan preacher in Manchester, remembered with hindsight that, in fact, he had always supported the monarchy and liturgical worship.[32]

Northern counties had a tough time during the wars, though a few people prospered. John Lawson, a coal-carrying sea captain from Scarborough, found fame and fortune, achieving high naval rank, a knighthood and a valuable pension.[33] For most there was hardship but, in time, a degree of healing. Lancashire's population, for example, is thought to have recovered within a couple of generations, certainly by 1700. The wars' end brought only partial relief from conflict, however. The next hundred years saw further political and religious disputes, dissent, plots and counter-plots.

War-weariness was underlined by the extent to which Manchester, which had been a parliamentary stronghold, celebrated Charles II's coronation. There was a military procession, a public dinner, church services, fireworks, bonfires and the public water supply was made to run with wine. William Heawood, steward of the court leet, a local government body, wrote to a London relation:

> The Gentlemen & Officers drunck his Majesties health in Claret running forth at three streams of the said Conduit, which was answered from the Souldiery by a great volley of shot, and many great shouts, saying 'God save the King'; ... during the time of dinner, and until after Sun-set, the said Conduit did run with pure Claret, which was freely drunke by all that could, for the crowd came near the same.[34]

The short reign of James II, a Catholic, was marked by struggles over religious tolerance and his assertion of a right to dispense with acts of parliament. Events in 1688 sparked a crisis. His son James Francis Edward was born, threatening to create a Catholic dynasty. Anti-Catholic riots in England and Scotland provoked fears of civil war.

A group of seven Protestant nobles invited William of Orange, stadtholder of the Dutch Republic and grandson of Charles I, to bring an army to England. Three of the seven were northerners: Lord Lumley of County Durham, William Cavendish, Earl of Devonshire and Thomas Osborne, Earl of Danby. After William landed at Brixham, James's army deserted and he went into exile in France. William and his wife, James's eldest daughter Mary, became joint rulers in what became known to Protestants as the Glorious Revolution. James landed in Ireland to try to recover his kingdoms, but was defeated at the Battle of the Boyne. After James's fall, a crowd in Newcastle tore down his statue and tossed it into the Tyne.

A significant minority refused to accept William and Mary as sovereigns, instead believing that monarchs were appointed by divine right. Over the next fifty-seven years Jacobites pressed for restoration of James and his heirs. There were Jacobite revolts in Scotland or England in 1689, 1708, 1715, 1719 and 1745. In England, Jacobitism was strongest in northern areas with a high proportion of Catholics such as west and north Lancashire, Northumberland and County Durham. Jacobite clubs sprung up, meeting seemingly innocuously in inns. Jacobites adopted the white rose as a symbol.

In this climate of suspicion came the so-called 'Lancashire plot' of 1694, in which eight members of the gentry were tried in Manchester for allegedly planning to murder or overthrow William and Mary and reinstate James II. The chief witness was John Lunt, who claimed that he and others were given the task of eliciting commissions from James to be distributed among Lancashire Jacobites, including the accused, preparatory to an uprising. Defence witnesses described Lunt as a scoundrel, bigamist and highwayman. They said Lunt had offered them payments in return for helping to denounce the gentry. The jury quickly found the defendants not guilty. Lunt and his associates were drummed out of town.[35]

Mary died in 1694 and William in 1702. He contracted pneumonia after breaking his collarbone following a fall from his horse, Sorrel. The horse, confiscated from Northumbrian Jacobite Sir John Fenwick, had stumbled on a molehill at Hampton Court. Jacobites reputedly toasted the mole, 'the little gentleman in the black velvet waistcoat'.[36] When William's successor Queen Anne died in 1714, Jacobites saw another opportunity for Stuart restoration. They were disappointed when George I of the House of Hanover became king. After James II died in exile in France in 1701, James Edward Stuart, the Old Pretender, was recognised as James III by France's Louis XIV. On the Old Pretender's birthday, 10 June 1715, there was violence in some parts of England. A Manchester mob drank the health of King James, led by a blacksmith called Thomas Sydall, and ravaged the town for several days. Sydall was tried and jailed at Lancaster.[37]

The 1715 Jacobite rising began in Aberdeenshire, while a smaller Scottish force moved south through Cumberland and Westmorland and into Lancashire. It linked up with an English Jacobite force raised in Northumberland by the Earl of Derwentwater and his cousin. The level of support in Lancashire was low, however. The rebels released prisoners from Lancaster Castle, including Thomas Sydall, and declared James III king at the market cross. The rebels occupied Preston, where they dallied and socialised for three days. Government forces surrounded them. Some rebels escaped northwards but the rest surrendered. Sydall was among those hanged, drawn and quartered at Knott Mill, Manchester. The leaders were sent to London for trial, where the Earl of Derwentwater was beheaded.[38]

The 1745 rising was an attempt by Charles Edward Stuart, the Young Pretender, to gain the British throne – now occupied by George II – for his father, the Old Pretender. English Jacobitism had weakened, however. Charles began by landing in the Outer Hebrides. There were early successes as he captured Edinburgh and won the Battle of Prestonpans. Many in Charles's council of war argued that they should consolidate, but his strong advocacy of invading England was carried by one vote.[39]

The Duke of Cumberland, George II's son, was sent to the midlands to command defences while General George Wade was despatched to Northumberland, where the invading army was expected. Newcastle's garrison was strengthened and Jacobite suspects arrested. The Hanoverian era was a period of security and prosperity for Tyneside. The town's support for King George is one of several possible explanations for the origin of the term Geordie (another is that it was a common nickname for coalminers in ballads and songs).[40] John Wesley, founder of Methodism, was living in Newcastle and became worried about the redcoats' bad language. He wrote to the commander of his horror at the 'shameless wickedness, the ignorant profaneness, of the poor men to whom our lives are entrusted'.[41]

However, Charles avoided Newcastle by invading to the west with an army of 6,000. He marched rapidly via Carlisle to Preston, picking up little support before he reached Manchester. There, the congregation of the Collegiate Church was Tory and sympathetic to the Stuart cause (whose supporters met at the Bulls Head Inn, destroyed in the 1940 Blitz), while that of St Ann's sided with the Whigs (whose secular base was the Angel Inn). Tories held offices as justices of the peace, churchwardens or officers of the court leet, while Whig dissenters included many rising manufacturers and merchants.[42]

Many residents evacuated the town ahead of Charles's arrival. The first that Manchester saw of the army was the arrival of one Sergeant Dickson, a girl and a drummer (giving rise to a legend that Manchester had been taken without resistance by a sergeant, a drummer and a whore). Charles entered to cheers and the sound of church bells.[43]

Local people made a show of enthusiasm, but few signed up. Whereas the Jacobites hoped for more than one and a half thousand volunteers, eventually a Manchester regiment of two to three hundred was formed, led by Colonel Francis Towneley, from an old Lancashire Catholic family. Manchester also hedged its bets by subscribing nearly £2,000 for a troop of soldiers loyal to George II to be commanded by the Earl of Derby. None of the leading northern families sided with the rebels. The poet John Byrom reflected those who felt confused loyalties:[44]

God bless the King! (I mean our faith's defender!)
God bless! (No harm in blessing) the Pretender.
But who Pretender is, and who is King,
God bless us all! That's quite another thing!

Charles marched to Derby, where he was persuaded by commanders to head back to Scotland, fearing that three large Hanoverian armies were approaching. He stopped for a day in Manchester, where crowds stoned and threatened him. His soldiers responded by looting. Charles, outraged at his treatment, fined the town £5,000 and took a hostage against payment. He was persuaded to reduce the fine by half and the money was raised. Charles gave a written undertaking to repay the sum as soon as 'the Country is in quiet and Tranquility under our royall Government'.[45]

Heading north, Charles paused at Carlisle and gave the Manchester regiment the hopeless task of meeting Cumberland's pursuing army. Eventually they had no choice but to surrender. Towneley and several others were hanged, drawn and quartered, including Thomas Sydall, son of the earlier Thomas Sydall. While St Ann's congregation gave thanks for their deliverance, unruly elements in Manchester attacked the houses of widow Sydall and other Jacobite sympathisers.[46]

The rebellion ended with defeat at Culloden, north of Inverness, in April 1746. After six months in hiding in the Western Isles, Charles Edward Stuart escaped to France. Much of northern England was relieved.

INDUSTRIAL
REVOLUTION

CHAPTER 11

WHY THE NORTH?

Life in the Industrial Revolution could be tough. William Dodd, a factory reformer who started work in a Cumbrian woollen mill aged six, later described it as a period of 'uninterrupted, unmitigated suffering'. Long hours and an unnatural posture left him with seriously bowed knees.[1] Yet there was also opportunity. Benjamin Shaw, a mechanic from the village of Dent, found 'good work & wages' in Preston, Lancashire, where he made a living fixing spindles and making fly frames, mules and other parts of the machines that kept the town's cotton industry going.[2]

French social commentator Alexis de Tocqueville was shocked and awed by what he observed in fast-growing Manchester in 1835: 'From this foul drain the greatest stream of human industry flows out to fertilise the whole world. From this filthy sewer pure gold flows. Here humanity attains its most complete development and its most brutish, here civilisation works its miracles and civilised man is turned back almost into a savage.'[3]

The Industrial Revolution from about 1760 to 1840 transformed northern England and the world's image of it. A region frequently written off as backward starred in what many economic historians view as history's key event, allowing populations to grow and living standards to rise – eventually – without a Malthusian check from disease or famine. For those living through it, there was also wrenching social change.

Britain's population quadrupled between 1700 and 1870 and there was massive internal migration, with Lancashire growing faster than any other county. The outlines of the modern north–south cultural divide took shape and for about a hundred years the north became the engine of growth. By 1871 more than half of Britain's thirty largest towns were in northern England. Manchester's population grew from 10,000 in 1700 to an astounding 303,000 in 1851. Liverpool, Leeds and Sheffield also saw strong increases.[4] Middlesbrough, lauded by William Gladstone as 'an infant Hercules' and 'the youngest child of England's enterprise', had just twenty-five inhabitants in 1801; by 1891, it had more than 75,000.[5]

Migrants flooded in, notably from Ireland but also from Scotland, Wales and the midlands. It was a chance to escape rural poverty. Andrew Ure, a Scottish writer on factories, argued that cotton workers benefited from high wages, easy labour and a healthy working environment, that they were less susceptible to cholera, and they suffered from deformity or accidents only through their own careless misuse of the machines.[6] Yet Charles Dickens presented a dystopian vision of the fictional Coketown in *Hard Times*, shortly after visiting Preston:

> It was a town of red brick, or of brick that would have been red if the smoke and ashes had allowed it; but as matters stood, it was a town of unnatural red and black like the painted face of a savage. It was a town of machinery and tall chimneys, out of which interminable serpents of smoke trailed themselves for ever and ever, and never got uncoiled. It had a black canal in it, and a river that ran purple with ill-smelling dye, and vast piles of building full of windows where there was a rattling and a trembling all day long, and where the piston of the steam engine worked monotonously up and down, like the head of an elephant in a state of melancholy madness. It contained several large streets all very like one

another, and many small streets still more like one another, inhabited by people equally like one another, who all went in and out at the same hours, with the same sound upon the same pavements, to do the same work, and to whom every day was the same as yesterday and tomorrow, and every year the counterpart of the last and the next.[7]

The term Industrial Revolution was first used by French writers and popularised by Victorian economic historian Arnold Toynbee. Few periods in history provoke so much debate. How is it defined? When did it begin and end? Was it really revolutionary? Why did it start in Britain before spreading to western Europe, the US and Asia? What was its human impact? The UK economy grew slowly in the eighteenth century before picking up speed in the nineteenth. Britain's reign as top manufacturing nation was to prove fairly short-lived. Its industrial output did not overtake that of China until almost 1860, according to economic historian Paul Bairoch, and before 1900 Britain had been overtaken by the US.[8]

It is hard to overstate the shock when rural dwellers, who formerly worked in agriculture or in cottage industries such as spinning and weaving, found themselves in factories. It was not just long hours and bad conditions. There was also irksome discipline: the peremptory summons of the factory bell, long lists of rules and payment of wages in the form of overpriced goods. Workers could be fined for singing, whistling and laughing. In the cotton industry, children worked fifteen-hour days in dirty, hot factories filled with cotton dust that affected their eyes and lungs. They were often beaten to keep them awake. One mill had so many accidents that it was known as the 'Cripples Factory'. At another, 14 lb in cast-iron weights were attached to the back and shoulders of a nine-year-old throstle spinner to stop her running away.[9]

Then there was the slum housing, smoke and filth of explosively growing towns and cities into which workers crowded. Charles Mott, an assistant Poor Law commissioner, was horrified by the 'pitiable condition' of manufacturing districts in 1838, inhabited by people 'scarcely removed from savages' who lived in a 'state of moral degradation' and whose children were 'reared to habits which totally annihilate every moral and social obligation'.[10]

Conditions in factories and cities alarmed Victorian intellectuals. William Wordsworth wrote of the 'outrage done to nature'. Benjamin Disraeli's *Sybil* drew attention to the gulf between rich and poor – the 'two nations' that formed the novel's subtitle. Friedrich Engels, in *The Condition of the Working Class in England*, portrayed workers' losses as including the disappearance of stable family and community relationships, homes in a clean rural environment, health and contentment.[11]

Northern England was at the forefront, not least in cotton textiles, the revolution's foundational industry. A nation that was a marginal producer in 1760 – and lies thousands of miles from where raw cotton is grown – was by 1860 home to two-thirds of the world's cotton spindles, notably in Lancashire.[12] Inventors such as John Kay (flying shuttle), James Hargreaves (spinning jenny), Richard Arkwright (water frame) and Samuel Crompton (spinning mule) are celebrated. Arkwright holds a prominent place as creator of the factory system.

Breakthroughs in steam power and iron making were largely a midlands affair, but Benjamin Huntsman in Sheffield invented crucible, or cast, steel in the 1740s. In 1855, Henry Bessemer's process for making cheaper steel revolutionised structural engineering. Joseph Whitworth, a Manchester-based pioneer of machine tools, created a standard for screw threads, thus laying the foundation of modern mass production. Joseph Aspdin, a Leeds brickmaker, invented Portland cement. William Armstrong, an artillery and warship manufacturer, turned Tyneside into the arsenal of the British Empire. Charles Parsons, also in Newcastle, devised the steam turbine, which transformed marine transport and naval warfare.

Britain's first proper canal, the Bridgewater, opened in 1761 between Worsley and Manchester. John Metcalf, 'Blind Jack of

Knaresborough', was the first professional road builder. George Stephenson and his son Robert built the first steam locomotive to haul passengers on a public railway, the Stockton and Darlington Railway, and built the first public inter-city railway, the Liverpool and Manchester Railway. Northerners outside the north also made an impact. Leeds-born John Smeaton is credited as the father of civil engineering. Cumberland-born John Wilkinson was a pioneer of cast-iron manufacture, while Henry Cort, thought to have been born in Lancaster, transformed the puddling process for refining cast iron. Yorkshire-born Joseph Bramah invented the hydraulic press.

Victorian writers such as Samuel Smiles liked to attribute Britain's early lead to the genius of its inventors, an approach that has gone out of fashion. Underlying causes often cited today include: plentiful coal and iron ore; tolerance of religious dissenters; colonial resource extraction; profits from the slave trade; expansion of the navy to protect world trade; an agrarian revolution that enabled population and consumer demand to increase; navigable rivers; and a framework of social and political institutions favouring entrepreneurship, encouraged by economic liberalism.

Most of these theories have been disputed or downplayed as insufficient explanation, though multiple factors surely played a part. Sven Beckert, in *Empire of Cotton: A New History of Global Capitalism* (2014), said Britain was 'hardly a liberal, lean state with dependable but impartial institutions … Instead it was an imperial nation characterised by enormous military expenditures, a nearly constant state of war, a powerful and interventionist bureaucracy, high taxes, skyrocketing government debt and protectionist tariffs – and it was certainly not democratic.' He attributed Britain's success to 'war capitalism' – slavery, expropriation of indigenous peoples, imperial expansion and armed trade.[13]

An influential theory advanced by economic historian Robert Allen is that Britain had unusually high wages compared with other countries (a legacy of having more colonial trade) and easy access to coal. High wages and cheap energy made investment in labour-saving technology profitable in Britain where it would not have been elsewhere. Elements of this account have been challenged.[14] Joel Mokyr emphasises cultural factors. In western Europe during the Enlightenment, he says, conditions coincided to create a 'republic of letters', a ferment of public debate and innovation.[15] He argues that largely random factors led to Britain coming first, including good artisan skills, availability of coal and the country's island status, which enabled it to keep the Napoleonic Wars off its soil. He points to groups such as Birmingham's Lunar Society and literary and philosophical societies in Manchester and Newcastle where scientists and industrialists rubbed shoulders and exchanged ideas.[16]

And why did so much happen in the north? In 1831 more than half of England's adult male industrial jobs were in Lancashire and the West Riding of Yorkshire.[17] In 1835 Edward Baines, author of *History of the Cotton Manufacture in Great Britain*, outlined the north-west's geographical advantages: rivers to provide water power, coal for steam engines, connection to the port of Liverpool, soft water and easy access to sources of iron and chemicals.[18]

Proximity to Liverpool allowed easy importing of slave-grown cotton, initially from the Caribbean and later from the American south. Lancashire already produced linen and wool and had a tradition of small-scale cotton production dating back to 1600. In addition, newly growing towns were relatively free of medieval guilds and restrictive regulations on trade. South-east Lancashire made fustians, a coarse cloth that was often a linen–cotton mix, so it was easy to change to pure cotton. The county had skills, a network of rural cottage workers and an array of middlemen.[19] Another helpful factor was that south Lancashire had a strong tradition of watch and clockmaking. Clock and watchmakers devised cheap, accurate gears, which revolutionised the design of machinery. Arkwright hired clockmakers for his mill at Cromford, Derbyshire.[20]

Industries fed off each other. Steam power drove cotton machinery, mainly from the 1830s. Chemicals essential to textile production

1. Cartimandua. "Caractacus, King of the Silures, deliver'd up to Ostorius, the Roman General, by Cartimandua, Queen of the Brigantes" – print by Francesco Bartolozzi. Published 1788. Via Wikimedia Commons.

2. Cuddy's Crag, Hadrian's Wall, Northumberland, England. © Kevin Standage/Shutterstock.

3. Statue of Constantine the Great, outside York Minster. Via Wikimedia Commons.

4. King Oswald of Northumbria. Stained-glass window of St. Oswald in St. Oswald's Church, Grasmere. © inspirepix / Alamy Stock Photo.

5. Bede, Nuremberg Chronicle.
© Historic Images / Alamy Stock
Photo.

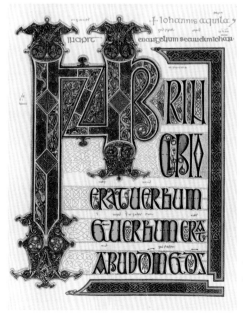

6. Illuminated manuscript page of
the Lindisfarne Gospels, England,
circa 700 AD. © North Wind
Picture Archives / Alamy Stock
Photo.

7. Clifford's Tower, scene of a massacre of York's Jews in 1190. Via Shutterstock.

8. Battle of Towton, Wars of the Roses. Painting by John Augustus Atkinson (1775–1833) © Picture Art Collection / Alamy Stock Photo.

9. Alice Nutter, one of the accused Pendle witches. Via Wikimedia Commons.

10. John Kay, inventor of the fly shuttle. Ford Madox Brown mural, Manchester Town Hall. © Sue Heaton / Alamy Stock Photo.

11. Richard Arkwright. Via Wikimedia Commons.

12. A statue of George Stephenson at the Oxford University Museum of Natural History. Via Wikimedia Commons.

13. The Peterloo Massacre, 16 August 1819. Cartoon by George Cruickshank. © Pictorial Press Ltd / Alamy Stock Photo.

14. The Brontë Sisters, c. 1834. © Matteo Omied / Alamy Stock Photo.

GRACE DARLING.

15. Grace Darling rowing out to sea, to save sailors from a shipwreck, in a furious storm. Colour wood engraving by E. Evans after C.J. Staniland. Wellcome Collection via Wikimedia Commons.

16. Manchester from Kersal Moor, William Wyld 1857. © The Picture Art Collection / Alamy Stock Photo.

were supplied by the developing cluster around Widnes, Runcorn and the Mersey valley. Steam power and coal made railways possible, while cotton-fuelled population growth created a market for the Liverpool–Manchester line. Manchester became a world centre of engineering and machine tool manufacture. Textile machinery needed iron and steel, boosting Sheffield, while high-quality steel in turn fed shipyards in Tyneside, Barrow and Liverpool. All these changes created a marked shift in economic geography. In 1693, Lancashire was thirty-fifth wealthiest of England's thirty-nine counties; by 1843, it was second. Durham, Cheshire and Yorkshire also moved up the scale.[21]

The notion that industrialists were largely self-made is a Victorian exaggeration. Smiles wrote in *Industrial Biography* that early Lancashire cotton manufacturers were 'men originally of the smallest means'. Certainly, some were from modest backgrounds. Arkwright was the seventh surviving son of a tailor; his parents could not afford to send him to school and he was taught to read and write by a cousin. Crompton had to spin yarn from the age of five after his father died. However, more than 70 per cent of industrial entrepreneurs were sons of middle-class fathers such as merchants, traders, manufacturers, craftsmen and yeoman farmers.[22]

Several entrepreneurs were nonconformists.[23] Barred from parliament, military and civil service before 1829, dissenters made their way as artisans and merchants. Unitarians such as cotton manufacturer Samuel Oldknow were prominent, along with Congregationalists and Quakers. Methodism, at its nineteenth-century peak, was to become the dominant faith of much of northern England. Most investment in new inventions came through family, social and faith networks or from other industrialists until a national banking system started to develop.[24] The failure rate was high. Oldknow, who wove muslins or fine fabrics, saw his Cheshire, Derbyshire and Manchester-based empire crumble in the 1790s and he died owing the Arkwright family and others more than £200,000.[25]

Rapid industrialisation caused concern. Thomas Carlyle, who coined the expression the 'Condition of England' in 1839, thought that the 'working body of this rich English Nation has sunk or is fast sinking into a state, to which, all sides of it considered, there was literally never any parallel'.[26] But not everyone saw things so bleakly. Edwin Chadwick, whose pioneering research into urban slums formed the basis for the earliest public health measures, believed that 'wages, or the means of obtaining the necessaries of life for the whole mass of the labouring community, have advanced, and the comforts within the reach of the labouring classes have increased with the late increase of population'.[27]

There is much debate about the revolution's impact on living standards. Many historians argue that gains for workers were slow and late and that modest improvements in real wages before about 1850 were outweighed by factors such as poor life expectancy in cities, relentless factory discipline and weakening of family bonds. Against that, when Emma Griffin studied hundreds of working-class memoirs, mostly by men, she found optimism and a new sense of personal freedom. One anonymous writer, recalling his seven-year apprenticeship in a Lancashire factory, declared that he 'was never as happy as I was at that time'. Still working at the mill during the early years of his marriage, he and his wife enjoyed plenty of money and good furniture.[28]

Many found better opportunities for steady work in cities than they had in the countryside, where wages were poor and work irregular. Labour was in demand, so workers sometimes sought to exercise bargaining power. When Benjamin Shaw's master decided that workmen should 'not go out to [their] drinkings', or tea breaks as we would now call them, Shaw and his mates continued to leave work for their breaks in defiance of his order. The master fined them all two shillings from their wages, to which the men responded by summoning the master before the mayor. They got their two shillings returned, but also got the sack. Shaw managed to find a new employer.[29]

In cities, conditions could undoubtedly be hard. Workers were crammed together in badly built housing with no amenities. Unpaved, undrained streets were augmented by manure from pigs that fed on refuse. Factories, slaughterhouses and gasworks added to the smells and waste. One Liverpool family slept on a bed over a well four foot deep in the bottom of their cellar home, into which privies in the street above drained. In lodging houses, up to eight people shared beds and disease spread quickly. Families with no access to a privy threw the contents of chamber pots into the street or on to a dung heap. In Manchester in 1839 the average age at death for mechanics, labourers and their families was a shocking seventeen years.[30]

There was resistance to change from those whose livelihoods were threatened by mechanisation. Inventors saw their equipment destroyed by mobs. The machine-breaking Luddite movement began in Nottinghamshire and spread to west Yorkshire and Lancashire. None of these protests halted the Industrial Revolution's progress.

Women faced a mixed experience.[31] Mechanisation meant the decline of cottage industries, in which married women could work and raise a family, while land enclosure reduced the number of agricultural jobs. The early factory system relied heavily on women and children, seen as cheaper and easier to manage than men. By 1841 there were slightly more women than men working in the cotton industry. But as the Victorian age progressed, opportunities for married women outside a few areas such as textiles declined and there was a move towards a sole male breadwinner. Few women found jobs in the railways, blast furnaces and engineering firms that formed a growing part of the economy.

The rise in child labour[32] provoked major controversy. It existed before, and indeed was widely accepted, but opportunities had previously been limited by children's lack of physical strength. The premium on strength declined as heavy work was taken over by machines. Moreover, children were found to be more trainable and malleable than adults. Technology created jobs best done by children, such as coalmine cart 'drawers' and 'trappers' (the latter operated large wooden doors to control air flow) and cotton mill 'piecers' who tied broken threads. Chimney sweeps used 'climbing boys' as human brushes. Children were cheap because of rising birth rates. Those as young as four were employed.[33]

A campaign grew against child labour, in part because of moral outrage about the danger of the work. Some children's health was ruined and lives were cut short by coal and cotton dust, accidents and skeletal damage caused by repeated mechanical operations. Parliament passed repeated laws that limited employment of children. Early ones were widely evaded, but the laws had a cumulative effect. Child labour fluctuated and eventually declined, in part because young men were less resistant to factory work than their fathers had been.

The north–south divide took clearer shape. There had always been differences between northerners and southerners, but as George Orwell later put it: 'It was the industrialisation of the north that gave the north–south antithesis its peculiar slant.'[34] Historian Asa Briggs observed that a '19th century conflict between north and south was as much a theme of English as American history'.[35] Northerners saw themselves as independent, straight-talking, knowledgeable and practical. Southerners perceived northerners as truculent, lacking social graces, over-competitive and unsophisticated. When travel writer Walter White visited Hull in the 1850s he saw 'evidences enough of – to use a mild adjective – an unpolished population. The northern characteristics were marked.'[36] The north's competitiveness drove small, traditional manufacturers in southern counties out of business, leaving the south more fully occupied by agriculture and the leisured classes.

Elizabeth Gaskell in *North and South* (1854) looked beyond stereotypes in a story that explored the geographical divide alongside those between town and country, Anglicanism and dissent, rich and poor, paternalism and *laissez-faire*, men and women. Her protagonist Margaret Hale, a young gentlewoman from Hampshire, moves to

Milton-Northern, a fictionalised Manchester, when her vicar father turns dissenter. She has 'almost a detestation for all she had ever heard of the north of England' and arrives to find a cityscape of 'long, straight, hopeless streets of regularly built houses, all small and of brick'.[37]

She observes strikes, feels sympathy with the poor and clashes with cotton magnate John Thornton, an example of the Manchester school of self-help. The novel traces her growing understanding of the complexity of labour relations, the role of mill owners and her conflicted relationship with Thornton. Her faith in rural innocence falters, notably when she returns to her village and hears of horrific superstition that has led to a cat being roasted alive.

Victorians' pride in the Industrial Revolution reached its high point in the 1851 Great Exhibition, housed in a crystal palace in London's Hyde Park. Astonishing things had been achieved, but British leadership was on borrowed time. The free market could not solve problems such as disease, poor sanitation and housing and inequality. Self-taught skills of the artisans who created the Industrial Revolution were no longer enough to sustain further progress. Britain needed a more thorough system of technical education – an issue that persists to the present day. It was only a matter of time before other countries caught up.

CHAPTER 12

COTTON EMPIRE

It was the 'land of long chimneys'. Cotton created almost three hundred factory towns and villages in eastern Lancashire, plus adjoining bits of Cheshire, Derbyshire and Yorkshire.[1] From small beginnings, employment in Britain's cotton industry reached 425,000 in the 1830s and accounted for 16 per cent of jobs in manufacturing and 8 per cent of national income.[2] Most of it was in north-west England.

As Friedrich Engels described Lancashire in 1844, cotton 'has thoroughly revolutionised this county, converting it from an obscure, ill-cultivated swamp into a busy, lively region, multiplying its population tenfold in eighty years'.[3] It was an extraordinary turnround for one of England's poorest counties. It was also the first time in human history that such a major industry had been built in a part of the world that lacked locally procured raw materials. Mill owners boasted that they met the home market's needs before breakfast and devoted the rest of the day to supplying the world.

Parisian journalist Léon Faucher wrote:[4]

An order sent from Liverpool in the morning, is discussed by the merchants in the Manchester Exchange at noon, and in the evening is distributed among the manufacturers in the environs.

In less than eight days, the cotton spun at Manchester, Bolton, Oldham or Ashton, is woven in the sheds of Bolton, Stalybridge or Stockport; dyed and printed at Blackburn, Chorley or Preston and finished, measured and packed at Manchester.

The north-west's cotton industry was built on slavery, without which it might never have got under way. The slave trade supplied cheap raw cotton from the West Indies and the US via Liverpool. Lancashire textiles were sold to slave traders in West Africa in return for slaves. Some slave trade profits were reinvested in cotton manufacturing. Even after slavery's abolition in the British Empire in the 1830s, raw cotton came from southern American slave states until the civil war in the 1860s.

The system also relied on exploiting children, especially pauper or parish apprentices. A mill owner could pay £5 to a workhouse overseer, provide clothes and essentially take ownership of a child. Children were brought in some cases hundreds of miles from cities and towns including London to mills, where they were given bed and food in return for work. Robert Blincoe, a former pauper apprentice, described life at Litton Mill in Derbyshire:

Palfry, the smith, had the task of riveting irons upon any of the apprentices, whom the masters ordered, and those were much like the irons put upon felons. Even young women, if suspected of intending to run away, had irons riveted on their ancles, and reaching by long links and rings up to the hips, and in these they were compelled to walk to and from the mill to work and to sleep.[5]

Lancashire had a cottage-based handicraft industry making woollen textiles at least as far back as the thirteenth century and also made linens.[6] Flemish refugees brought 'new draperies' to England in the later sixteenth century, including fustians, comprised of a linen warp and cotton weft, giving a fairly coarse and cheap cloth. In 1601 the name of George Arnould, fustian weaver of Bolton, appeared in the records of quarter sessions.[7]

Things were not easy for inventors who transformed cotton technology. Few apart from Sir Richard Arkwright became wealthy. Innovations often brought down the wrath of their neighbours, who dreaded job losses. Inventions were widely adopted without royalty payments and efforts to enforce patents were fraught with difficulty.

John Kay, a serial inventor from Bury – the fifth son of a yeoman farmer who died before John was born – struggled to profit from his flying shuttle, patented in 1733. This small wooden tool shaped like the hull of a ship revolutionised weaving by automatically throwing the weft thread back and forth across the loom where previously it had been passed by hand, thus doubling the productivity of weavers. It was adopted slowly at first, initially in the woollen industry, but by the 1760s it was widely used in cotton. Weavers who used it often reneged on royalty payments of 15 shillings per shuttle. Kay took some to court but his awards were less than the cost of the lawsuits. Users formed a 'shuttle club' to defend themselves against Kay. Eventually he moved to France and sold his technology to the French government for less than he expected. He died there in poverty and obscurity.[8]

Kay's invention created extra demand for cotton yarn. Breakthroughs in spinning solved the problem. James Hargreaves, an illiterate handloom weaver from near Blackburn, is credited with inventing the spinning jenny in 1764.[9] The jenny – a Lancashire term for an engine – consisted of a hand-operated wheel that would rotate a number of spindles (initially eight or sixteen) within a frame, enabling the operator to spin the yarn onto several spindles at the same time. When word got out that Hargreaves had made a spinning machine, neighbours broke into his house and destroyed the jenny and much of his furniture. He moved to other premises, where jennies were again destroyed, before relocating to Nottingham. He belatedly patented his invention, but failed to reach agreement with users on payment and was unable to enforce his rights because he had sold some jennies before patenting it. Use of jennies spread rapidly, despite rioting and arson as spinners protested against them. By the late 1780s about twenty thousand were in operation.[10]

Arkwright, a barber and wig-maker from Preston, patented the spinning frame in 1769, also known as the water frame after it was adapted to use water power. The frame consisted of four rollers that drew out the cotton strands before a spindle twisted them into thread, which allowed for continuous spinning. In 1779, Samuel Crompton combined elements of the jenny and the water frame to make a complex machine called the mule. This could produce yarns that rivalled the finest in India and laid the basis for Britain's superiority in cotton goods in the nineteenth century. Mules became the dominant spinning machines for the next 150 years.

Crompton, from Bolton, had been spinning thread from age five when his father died. He was a skilled musician, mathematician and craftsman who gained an education at night school. During the seven years it took him to perfect the machine, he supported himself by spinning, weaving and playing the violin at the Bolton theatre. He kept his invention secret, but rumours spread. He could not afford a patent and so made the machine public in 1780 in exchange for funds raised by a public subscription. This raised only about £50, though it did ensure the mule was made widely available. A sullen and solitary character, Crompton had little talent for business and never managed to reap big rewards. Parliament awarded him £5,000 when he petitioned it for recompense for his efforts, whereas he had been hoping for ten times as much. The bleach works he set up with the money failed and he died with just £25 to his name.[11]

The industry's towering figure was Arkwright, not only for the water frame but above all for his driving role in creating the factory system. Thomas Carlyle described him as an 'historical phenomenon' who had given England the 'power of cotton', enabling her to finance wars against Napoleon and without which 'imperial kaisers were impotent'.[12] Samuel Smiles said: 'Arkwright was a man of great force of character, indomitable courage, much worldly shrewdness, with a business faculty amounting to genius.'[13] He could also be arrogant and exasperating. James Watt, the steam engine pioneer, wrote:

> Some years ago, he [Arkwright] applied to us at two different times for our advice which we took the trouble to give him, in one or more long letters, which he never had the manners to answer but followed his own Whims till he threw away several 1000£s and exposed his ignorance to all the world, & then in disgust gave up the scheme.[14]

By 1772, Arkwright had installed his frames, together with picking, washing, carding and packing facilities, in a five-storey, water-powered mill in Cromford in Derbyshire. It was not the first mechanised factory – arguably that was John Lombe's 1721 silk mill at Derby – but Arkwright's genius lay in organising a system of factory production. He worked out how water power would operate, how work would flow without hold-ups or overstocking, where each part of the operation needed to be located, how workers were best placed to run and repair machines, what its costs would be and what profit he would make – all this for a man trained as a wig-maker.[15] His timing was perfect, as demand for cotton goods was rising rapidly. The template became widely copied and is seen as the beginning of the factory age.

He also displayed political skills. The 1721 Calico Act had imposed duties on the sale of printed calicoes in order to protect British woollen textiles from Indian imports, but it was also hurting the domestic cotton industry. In 1774 Arkwright persuaded parliament to pass an act that distinguished home-made from Indian cotton. British cloth would have three blue threads in the selvage (the edge that prevents the fabric unravelling) and would be stamped 'British Manufactory'. The result was a massive increase in investment.[16]

Arkwright built further mills in Derbyshire, Nottingham, Manchester, Staffordshire and Scotland and licensed his spinning frame to other mill owners, though his mill at Birkacre in Lancashire was destroyed in anti-machinery riots. He also fought landmark legal cases against spinners who infringed his patent. As part of these, it was alleged that he had stolen the original idea for the spinning frame from a man called Thomas Highs. Lancashire industrialists, who objected to Arkwright's high charges, rejoiced when a judge refused to extend his patent. Nonetheless, as *Gentleman's Magazine* put it, he 'died immensely rich, and has left manufactories the income of which is greater than that of most German principalities ... His real and personal property is estimated at little short of half a million.'[17]

Weaving was slower to mechanise than spinning. Edmund Cartwright, a Wakefield-educated Anglican vicar, created the first power loom in the 1780s, though the factory he built at Doncaster to make his machines failed. Further refinements included William Radcliffe's Dandy loom, patented in 1802, and the semi-automatic Lancashire Loom, invented by James Bullough and William Kenworthy in 1842. Power looms were unsuitable for all but coarser cloths until the 1840s, and handlooms were still a sizeable minority by mid-century.[18] Use of steam power finally spread in part because of a shortage of sites for water wheels. At one time there were sixty water-powered mills on one three-mile stretch of the Mersey near Manchester.[19] Steam-powered mills were sited near sources of coal.

Cotton's explosive growth meant that by 1811 more than one-third of Lancashire's population was employed in the industry; overall numbers continued to rise, though that proportion later shrank as the industrial base widened.[20] The influx of new workers remodelled towns and cities and brought big changes to family life. Females over the age of thirteen comprised the majority of employees, though these were subordinated to male overlookers, while men held on to supposedly skilled jobs such as mule spinning. Women earned much less than men.[21]

Among jobs done by women or girls were those of 'tenters' or 'stretchers', who worked carding machines that straightened cotton fibres ready for spinning. One said she had to 'fight for her breath every night when she came home' because of 'fly', the cotton dust fibres in the atmosphere where she worked. 'Drawers' and 'rovers' were in charge of drawing and roving machines, which stretched out cotton and twisted it. Women spinners worked on small mules and 'throstles' making strong warp thread. They worked barefoot in the hot, damp spinning room, which for the sake of the cotton had to be kept warm and moist for processing; they took off clothes 'as far as decency will allow'. One hazard for those working nights was unwelcome personal attention from the overseer. Female weavers operated steam looms, helped by child tenters, whom they paid out of their own wages.[22]

Most women gave up work on marriage to look after their children, but a sizeable minority stayed at work out of necessity. Pregnant women worked right until their baby was due and occasionally a child was born while a mill girl was tending machinery. New mothers returned to work a few days after giving birth. Some gave opium mixtures to their children in order to get a night's sleep, with disastrous results. If the mill was close by, mothers rushed home to feed their babies at dinnertime; sometimes an older daughter or neighbour brought the baby to the mill to be fed in a meal break. The advent of penny banks enabled some married women to save a few pence for when their next baby was due, so they would not have to rush back immediately.

Factory work carried dangers for men and women.[23] Workers lost fingers in machines or could be 'scalped' if their hair became caught up. Women's and girls' long clothing was especially prone to getting caught in machinery, which could result in them being crushed. The machines' clattering meant that weavers were deafened (comedian Les Dawson used to do sketches in which women mouthed words silently, the only way mill girls could communicate). Male mule-spinners contracted cancer of the groin from oil used on the spindles. Weavers who 'kissed the shuttle', threading it by sucking through the thread, could catch TB or suffer mouth cancer. Cotton dust caused byssinosis, a lung disease.

While migrants flooded from far and wide into cities such as Manchester and Liverpool, most workers in smaller textile towns came from the surrounding countryside. A study of Preston found that 83 per cent of residents in 1851 had been born in the town or within thirty miles.[24] Workers integrated factory routines into their lives by building family and community networks, meaning that mill towns escaped some of the worst social dislocation caused by rapid industrialisation.[25] Temperance, building and friendly societies, savings clubs and educational groups made an early appearance, supported in some cases with middle-class patronage. The most spectacular example of formal collective activity was the cooperative movement. Boosted by the Rochdale Pioneers in 1844, it spread rapidly through the cotton districts of east Lancashire over the next two decades.

By the later nineteenth century there was more time for leisure, resulting in societies and clubs catering for interests from fishing and football to photography and pigeon racing. Some working-class people could afford a piano for their parlour. The coming of the railways meant that workers could escape briefly to the entertainment mecca of Blackpool during the wakes – local festivals, originally religious, during which mills closed.

Towns developed specialisms. South-east Lancashire specialised in spinning: Oldham in coarse thread and Bolton in fine thread. Weaving was more common in north Lancashire: coarse cloths in Blackburn and Burnley and finer ones in Nelson and the Colne valley. Manchester became a centre for warehouses where merchants displayed their products. Oldham showed particularly strong growth. By 1870 it had more spindles than Manchester. By 1914 the town housed 29 per cent of UK spindles.[26] A big factor behind Oldham's growth was the presence of Platt Brothers, the world's largest textile machinery manufacturer. There was a boom in 'Oldham

Limiteds', joint stock companies whereby local people could invest in mills and receive dividends.[27]

There were spells of boom and bust. The cotton famine of the 1860s is thought to have been caused by massive overproduction of cotton goods, though it also coincided with disruption of raw cotton supplies during the American civil war. Some towns coped better than others. Blackburn, for example, began successfully producing bordered dhotis (loincloths) for the Indian market. Distress was intense in many places. Some expressed their pain in poetry. In *A Song of the Cotton Famine*, the anonymous author asks: 'Shall I again permitted be / To send my kids to schoo', / Where they con larn to read and write, / Do sums by figures too?'[28]

The period 1870–1914 was an Indian summer, when the cotton industry benefited from a large increase in global trade.[29] Lancashire, especially Manchester, tended to see this as vindicating liberal economic policies promoted earlier by Richard Cobden and the Anti-Corn Law League, but there were danger signs. India, Brazil and Japan started to build their own cotton textile industries. Britain was slow to adopt developments such as 'ring spinning' and the automatic Northrop loom, both American. It missed out on an international trend towards vertical integration, whereby large firms sought market power by bringing together various stages of production and distribution. Britain's industry remained dominated by small and medium-sized firms.

In 1913 Lancashire supplied two-thirds of world trade in cotton cloth, but by 1938 that had shrunk to 25 per cent and output and employment had halved.[30] Indian production and Japanese exports grew. UK capacity fell, but not by enough. There were strikes: the town of Nelson, for example, became known as 'little Moscow'. After a modest recovery following the Second World War, decline was relentless from the early 1950s. Lancashire's cotton producers had lost their comparative advantage to the Indian subcontinent, Hong Kong and China. By the late 1950s, Britain was importing more cotton cloth than it exported for the first time in two centuries. Import quotas between 1958 and 1992 failed to stem the decline.[31]

Lancashire's once-mighty cotton industry shrank as rapidly as it had originally grown. It is doubtful whether more could have been done to counteract its decline, since similar descents were occurring in older industries across the developed world. As economies become wealthier, labour-intensive work naturally shifts to cheaper producers. It was nonetheless painful for those whose jobs were lost. North-west England could only mourn the demise of its cotton empire.

CHAPTER 13

ENGINE POWER

Joseph Whitworth was an irascible, obsessive man. The letter-writer Jane Carlyle said he had

> a face not unlike that of a baboon; speaks the broadest Lancashire; could not invent an epigram to save his life; but has nevertheless 'a talent that might drive the Genii to despair' and when one talks with him, one feels to be talking with a real live man, to my mind worth any number of the Wits that go about.[1]

Less celebrated than figures such as Isambard Kingdom Brunel or George Stephenson, he has arguably had an even greater impact on the modern world.

Stockport-born Whitworth, together with other precision engineers such as Henry Maudslay, helped to pioneer a manufacturing revolution that transformed Britain from a craft economy to a fully mechanised one within two generations. Without their innovations the railways and industries such as textiles and shipbuilding would have struggled to grow.[2]

Whitworth's breakthroughs, achieved in Manchester in the 1840s and 1850s, included perfectly flat surface plates against which other items could be measured, and a measuring machine that could detect differences of less than one millionth of an inch. He even invented the Besom Cart, a horse-drawn street-sweeping machine. He is best known, however, for creating a standard system of screw threads. Before him, there were no standard measures for nuts and bolts. Standardisation allowed components to become interchangeable, enabling mass production. Parts could be made in different factories and they would all fit together. The Whitworth Standard remained in place in much of the world until after the Second World War.

Aside from cotton, the Industrial Revolution in the north encompassed steel, machine tools, chemicals, construction, armaments, shipbuilding, roads, canals and railways. It changed irrevocably the nature of places such as Sheffield, Tyneside, Teesside and Barrow. While Lancashire saw a stunning 133 per cent population growth between 1761 and 1801, there were also big increases in Yorkshire's West Riding (65 per cent), Derbyshire (48 per cent), the East Riding (44 per cent), Cheshire (42 per cent), Cumberland (37 per cent) and Durham (34 per cent).[3] Developments in engineering spread the revolution across the north as the nineteenth century progressed. It was a male affair with many 'fathers': George Stephenson is characterised as the father of the railways, Whitworth as the founding father of modern production engineering, the Duke of Bridgewater as the father of British inland navigation, and road builder John Metcalf as one of the fathers of the modern road.

Enabling what Thomas Carlyle described as the 'Age of Machinery' were the north's large deposits of coal and iron ore. If the first phase of the revolution was 'organic', involving water power, cotton and canals, the second phase from about 1820 was about converting coal into mechanical energy via steam engines.[4] It enabled higher output and faster growth at the expense of an environmental impact that polluted Britain and in its modern form has become critical to climate change.

Benjamin Disraeli in *Sybil* (1845) described the scene around a coalmine:

> Far as the eye could reach … a wilderness of cottages or tenements that were hardly entitled to a higher name, were scattered for many miles over the land … interspersed with blazing furnaces, heaps of burning coal, and piles of smouldering iron-stone; while forges and engine chimneys roared and puffed in all directions and indicated the frequent presence of the mouth of the mine and the bank of the coal-pit.[5]

Coal production increased from three million tons in 1700 to more than thirty million in 1830 and 128 million in the 1870s.[6] Much coal was mined in Northumberland and Durham and shipped to fast-growing London, where house design changed to accommodate tall, narrow chimneys. Climbing boys were used to clean them, some of whom died of cancer, suffocation or heat exhaustion. The practice continued until 1875 despite effective brushes and even a mechanical sweeper being available from 1803.[7]

An important shift was the replacement of charcoal with coke, or coal with impurities removed, to produce cast iron in blast furnaces from 1709. Steam power was relatively slow to spread, despite James Watt's steam engine patented in 1769, but during the nineteenth century steam became widely adopted in factories, locomotives and steamships, consuming vast quantities of coal. Newcomen's steam pump made it possible to sink deeper coalmine shafts without flooding.

Coalmining enriched aristocratic landowners, thus helping to ensure that they did not obstruct industrial development. It also created many dangerous jobs.[8] Boys and girls as young as five or six were used as trappers, to operate wooden doors that helped control the air flow. To save on candles, they sat through a whole shift in the dark. The Mines and Collieries Act 1842 forbade women and girls of any age to work underground and introduced a minimum age of ten for boys employed in underground work.

Steel was to become vital to the industrial economy, valued for workability, strength and durability, but it was complex and difficult to make. Sheffield was known for knife-making from the fourteenth century – the miller in Chaucer's *The Reeve's Tale* has a 'Sheffeld thwitel' (small knife or dagger) in his hose. By the eighteenth century it had also become a centre of steel-making. In the 1740s, Benjamin Huntsman, a Quaker clockmaker working in the Handsworth district, devised a process that revolutionised steel production. Huntsman managed to make satisfactory cast steel in clay pot cruci-bles, each holding about thirty-four pounds of blistered steel. A flux was added and they were covered and heated by means of coke for about three hours. The molten steel was then poured into moulds and the crucibles reused. Huntsman did not patent his method, preferring to keep it secret. There is an old legend that a competitor, Doncaster iron-maker Samuel Walker, disguised himself as a beggar and was allowed into the Huntsman works to warm himself, where he memorised the process; whatever the truth of this, Walker appears to have acquired a clay crucible by November 1749.[9]

At first Sheffield cutlers were reluctant to use Huntsman steel, considering it too hard to work with, but they were forced to adopt it after it was taken up by rivals in Paris, Berlin, Geneva and St Petersburg. Its uses spread well beyond the cutlery trade. A further Sheffield metal invention came from Thomas Boulsover, who acci-dentally created Sheffield Plate, a fusion of silver and copper. With this, he was able to make buttons at a fraction of the cost of solid silver ones.

In the 1850s, inventor Henry Bessemer devised a process that made steel quicker and cheaper to manufacture.[10] His converter, an egg-shaped furnace, was open at one end so that air could be blasted into molten pig iron; the oxygen rapidly burned the carbon and other elements and thus converted the iron into steel. No fuel was required. Steel could now be made in much greater quantities at about a fifth of its previous price. Bessemer's steel was quickly in demand for railways, ships, bridges and other heavy engineering work. He announced his invention in London in 1856 and two years later moved to Sheffield to open his own steelworks. Other steelmakers took out licences to install converters and the age of bulk steel-making was born. Thousands were employed at Sheffield steelworks, such as John Brown, Charles Cammell and Vickers. High wages attracted migrants. Workers lived in rows of brick terraced houses, blackened by smoke. John Murray's *Handbook for Travellers in Yorkshire* (1874) said that Sheffield was 'beyond all question the blackest, dirtiest and least agreeable' town in the county: 'It is indeed impossible to walk through the streets without suffering from the dense clouds of smoke constantly pouring from great open furnaces.'[11]

A further innovation came in 1912 when Harry Brearley, a metallurgist at Sheffield's Brown-Firth Research Laboratory, discovered a low-carbon steel containing about 12 per cent chromium, which resisted corrosion. At first he called it 'rustless steel', but the name that caught on was 'stainless steel'.[12]

Iron and steel was also the making of Middlesbrough, which had astonishing population growth.[13] Henry Bolckow, a businessman from Mecklenburg, and John Vaughan, a works manager on Tyneside, opened an iron foundry in 1841 using ore from the Cleveland Hills. It became the chief supplier of iron rails to railway companies in England, Russia, Austria and India. Middlesbrough became known as 'Ironopolis' or the 'iron smelting centre of the world'. There was a severe setback when steel replaced iron in rail manufacture in the 1870s, but the company responded by opening a steelworks. Teesside also acquired a chemical industry from 1863, when Bolckow Vaughan accidentally discovered salt while drilling for water.

The north's other big chemical cluster grew on Merseyside, attracted by coalfields, salt supplies from Cheshire and proximity to the glassmaking industry. James Muspratt was the first in the UK to make alkali on a large scale by the Leblanc method for glassmaking, at first in Liverpool and then St Helens and Newton-le-Willows. Two brothers named Pilkington took over a glassmaking firm in St Helens in 1826 and made it a success. Also in chemicals, in the

1820s a Leeds brickmaker called Joseph Aspdin achieved the high strengths needed in construction by burning finely pulverised lime with clay at high temperatures. His product became known as Portland cement.[14]

In 1886, Bolton-born William Lever and his brother James, in their company Lever Brothers, became one of the first to manufacture soap from vegetable oils. Their product, Sunlight Soap, was initially made at Warrington, after which they created a works and 'model' village at Port Sunlight in the Wirral. It was run on paternalistic lines.

In addition to inventors and industrialists, the north also produced scientists such as Cumberland-born John Dalton, best known for introducing atomic theory into chemistry and for research into colour blindness, sometimes referred to as Daltonism. Salford-born James Prescott Joule, who managed a family brewery, was in his spare time a physicist who established that the various forms of energy – mechanical, electrical and heat – are basically the same and can be changed for one another. Thus, he formed the basis of the law of conservation of energy, the first law of thermodynamics.

In the north-east, iron and steel helped William Armstrong, arms manufacturer and warship builder, to turn Tyneside into a region bristling with military production. It has a long tradition of shipbuilding: the first recorded vessel built on the Tyne was the *Tyneside Galley*, commissioned by Edward I in 1294 for his wars against the Scots. In the seventeenth century Sir Ambrose Crowley supplied the Royal Navy with 108 varieties of nail from his ironworks near Gateshead.

Armstrong, a Newcastle-born solicitor turned inventor, came from a clan of border reivers and served as a bridge between older Northumbrian martial traditions and mechanised industrial warfare. Apart from supplying Britain, Armstrong sold ships and guns all over the world, notably to Japan. The *Newcastle Chronicle* noted with pride that 'Tyneside has become one of the world's greatest centres for the production of the weapons of death'. Pubs in Armstrong's fiefdom of Scotswood carried names such as the Rifle, the Gun, the Vulcan, the Blast Furnace and the Ordnance Arms.[15]

Unlike his near-contemporary Alfred Nobel, Armstrong had no qualms about selling weapons. He believed that applying science to armaments would increase deterrence and reduce bloodshed.[16] In the nineteenth century he was seen as a national benefactor, improving security and the defence of empire. He said in a speech: 'We as a nation have few men to spare for war, and we have need of all the aid that science can give us to secure us against aggression – and to hold in subjection the vast and semi-barbarous population which we have to rule in the east.'[17] His reputation in the modern day has been affected by imperial guilt and revulsion against arms manufacture.

Another north-east contribution was Charles Parsons' 1884 invention of the steam turbine, which raised the efficiency of electricity generation tenfold and transformed marine transport and naval warfare. Parsons was an Anglo-Irish aristocrat. His breakthrough came while working for Clarke, Chapman and Co., ship engine manufacturers, near Newcastle. Later he founded C.A. Parsons in the city to produce turbo generators. His Wallsend-built steamship *Turbinia* astonished onlookers at Spithead for Queen Victoria's Diamond Jubilee in 1897 by travelling at an unprecedented 32 knots (38 miles per hour). Other north-east innovations included George Stephenson's 'Geordie lamp' for mining safety in 1815, John Walker's friction match in 1827, Joseph Swan's incandescent electric light bulb in the 1870s, and John Henry Holmes's quick-break light switch in 1884, the basis for modern wall-mounted light switches.

Transport was vital to the Industrial Revolution. Turnpike trusts emerged in the seventeenth century, allowing trustees to charge tolls in return for maintaining roads. By the mid-1830s about 17 per cent of Britain's road network had been 'turnpiked'.[18] One pioneer of road construction was Jack Metcalf from Knaresborough in Yorkshire. Blind from age six, Metcalf had already had a colourful career as a fiddle player, gambler and horse-trader before setting up as a carrier of goods from Leeds to Manchester and Knaresborough to York.[19] When a turnpike trust was set up in his area in 1765, the trust commissioned Metcalf to build roads that could carry heavy wagons and withstand wet weather. He innovated by building strong foundations under the road surface and used a convex surface to enhance drainage, with gutters running down either side. Metcalf used rafts to build roads across bogs. He went on to build further roads across northern England. When he died in 1810 aged ninety-three he was a hero in his hometown, if little known outside Yorkshire.

Waterways were an alternative for transporting bulky goods. Francis Edgerton, third Duke of Bridgewater, built the first purpose-built canal in the 1760s between Manchester and his coalmines at Worsley (later extended to Runcorn and Leigh). The canal halved the price of coal in Manchester, though it took the duke decades to make a return on his huge investment. The Bridgewater sparked a spate of canal building, with fifty-two canal acts passed in the next fifteen years.[20] Construction was slow, however. It took sixty years to complete about 2,200 miles of canals. They were expensive to build and maintain, with ingenuity needed to construct aqueducts, embankments, bridges, locks and tunnels.

The railway revolution was also slow to get going, though spectacular when it did so. The first coal-powered steam locomotive was constructed by Richard Trevithick in 1804, yet the Stockton and Darlington Railway did not open until 1825 and even then used both a locomotive engine and horses to move the wagons along.[21] But once a really effective steam locomotive – George and Robert Stephenson's *Rocket* – was developed in the 1820s, its superiority over horses was quickly recognised and the railway age took off.

Trevithick ran his locomotive along nine miles of track at the Pen-y-darren ironworks at Merthyr Tydfil. Colliery owners also tried out steam. At Wylam colliery in Northumberland, Christopher Blackett commissioned local engineers including Timothy Hackett to build a locomotive; the necessary steam power was generated, but there were problems with adherence to wooden tracks. John Blenkinsop, agent at the Middleton estate near Leeds, which contained several coalmines, commissioned Leeds engine-builder Matthew Murray to build a locomotive. The result was the *Salamanca*, a twin-cylinder locomotive that was so successful that Blenkinsop ordered three more, all of which ran successfully for twenty years.[22]

George Stephenson, born at Wylam in 1781, found fame as an engine-builder, surveyor and rail-maker. His father was a miner and the family could not afford schooling. George was illiterate until, at the age of eighteen, after starting work at Newburn colliery as a hand on the winding gear, he paid for night school and learned to read and write. Life remained a struggle. His daughter died in infancy and his wife died of tuberculosis. He left his son Robert with relatives and went to Scotland in search of better-paid work, but was forced to return when his father was blinded in a mining accident.[23]

Stephenson's skills won him a position as engineer at Killingworth High Pit and he began to be recognised as an expert in steam engines. He built twelve locomotives there. George was hired to build the Stockton and Darlington Railway. He and Robert built the engine *Locomotion*, which ran on the opening day. Though originally planned as a colliery line, it was also the world's first public steam railway, with passenger cars as well as coal wagons. It made him a national figure.[24]

Canals could not keep up with the cotton industry's needs, so Liverpool and Manchester merchants appointed Stephenson as chief engineer to build a railway between their cities. The thirty-five-mile line included the Wapping Tunnel beneath Liverpool and crossed Chat Moss peat bog using brush floats, a technique learned from Metcalf's road-building. Trials were held at Rainhill in 1829 to decide whether locomotives were suitable – as opposed to having stationary engines pulling wagons via cables – and if so which were the best. The *Rocket*, designed by George and Robert, was the only entry to survive the trial. It pulled 13 tons at an average of 12 mph and a top speed of 30 mph. The Stephensons were given the contract to produce locomotives for the first inter-city railway.[25]

The Liverpool and Manchester Railway was opened with fanfare on 15 September 1830 when almost eight hundred people, including the Duke of Wellington, prime minister, boarded the first trains from Liverpool. Actress Fanny Kemble had been given a demonstration ride three weeks earlier: 'When I closed my eyes the sensation of flying was quite delightful, and strange beyond description; yet strange as it was, I had a perfect sense of security and not the slightest fear.'[26] The first journey was marred by tragedy when, after the train stopped to take on water, politician William Huskisson stepped down on to the parallel track and was hit by a locomotive. He was taken to the nearest place on the line, Eccles, but died later that day.

Sir Joshua Walmsley, a businessman and politician, wrote:

Tragic as the occasion was, Stephenson could not resist a quiet thrill of satisfaction as he remarked to me, on returning to Liverpool, that the *Northumbrian* 'had driven Mr Huskisson to Eccles at the rate of 40 miles an hour. Five years ago,' he added, 'my own counsel thought me fit for Bedlam for asserting that steam could propel locomotives at the rate of 10 miles an hour.'[27]

After Rainhill, the railway era dawned. In 1829, just fifty-one miles of track had been laid; fifteen years later, the length had already reached that of the canals – 2,200 miles. By 1852, 7,500 miles were in existence and by 1872 this had doubled again to 15,736 miles.[28] The rail network encouraged trade and personal mobility and was pivotal to the creation of a national postal service and telegraph service. Since lines were built by individual enterprises, the network was fairly haphazard, with many routes duplicated and multiple stations in the same town serving different lines. Rotherham, for example, a town of about forty thousand, had three stations.[29]

The Stephensons built more engines and railways, including the first engines to be used in the US. Other engineers such as Joseph Locke and Isambard Brunel entered the fray, sometimes in competition and occasionally in partnership with George Stephenson. Southerners sometimes struggled with his accent. Asked once whether it would be serious if a cow got on the railway in front of the engine, he replied: 'Yes, vary aakward – for the coo.'[30]

Stephenson's gauge was mandated for all Britain's railway tracks in preference to Brunel's wider gauge. Railways, while popular, were expensive to build. In the late 1840s almost half of all British capital investment was going into transport, treble the figure of the 1820s.[31] Some engineers were profligate with investors' money. Robert Stephenson estimated that the London–Liverpool line would cost slightly above £21,000 per mile, whereas the actual cost was more than £50,000. Brunel underestimated the cost of his London–Bristol line by 150 per cent. Railway companies built extravagant, architect-designed stations. Estimates of the railways' net economic benefit tend to be fairly modest.[32]

George Stephenson was confident, tenacious and sometimes bloody-minded and insensitive to other people's feelings. Robert, by contrast, struggled with self-doubt.[33] He nonetheless managed to become one of the Victorian age's pre-eminent engineers, building railways in Britain and around the world. He also built tunnels and long-span railway bridges, including the Britannia Bridge over the Menai Strait in North Wales.

The genius of all these inventors and industrialists may not alone have created the Industrial Revolution, but they helped northern England to take advantage of its lead. The north's share of UK gross domestic product increased from 22 to 27 per cent between 1861 and 1911.[34] Together, these entrepreneurial spirits conjured up an enduring image of the north as a land of engineers.

CHAPTER 14

TROUBLE AT TH'MILL

'Uncle Enoch sent me to tell you,' pants a young man in Phyllis Bentley's novel *Inheritance*. 'There are three thousand men coming over Marthwaite Moor now – they're Chartists or Lancashire Turn-outs or something, and they're stopping at all the mills.'[1]

Inheritance (1932) opens a trilogy about the textile-mill-owning Oldroyd family in a West Riding valley covering 150 years from the late eighteenth century. It encompasses a mill owner's murder by Luddites, a riot in which plugs are removed from factory boilers to stop them working, and a weavers' pay strike. Granada Television serialised it in 1967, starring John Thaw and James Bolam, which turned the expression 'there's trouble at th'mill' into a catchphrase. The genre had already been satirised in Keith Waterhouse's novel *Billy Liar* (1959), when Billy and his friend mimic clichéd Yorkshire scenes: 'Father! The men! They're coming up the drive!'[2]

There is no doubt that 1790–1850 in Britain was turbulent. Suffering and dislocation were at times severe. Problems included explosive population growth, food shortages caused by climatic disruption, stresses of urbanisation and industrialisation, economic fluctuations, and diseases such as typhus and cholera. It was not just the north that faced hardships. The agricultural south experienced riots in 1830 in which supporters of a mythical 'Captain Swing' destroyed threshing machines, burned ricks and maimed cows in protest against wage cuts, church tithes and mechanisation.

The north arguably suffered less. Whig historian Thomas Babington Macaulay asserted in 1830 that poor rates to relieve distress were lower in northern counties because demand for labour in the towns had pushed up wages and reduced the need for relief in neighbouring agricultural areas.[3] When journalist and reformer William Cobbett reached Tyneside in 1832 after years of rural rides in the south, he found relative prosperity in both mining and agriculture: 'The working people seem to be very well off; their dwellings solid and clean, and their furniture good.'[4]

Nonetheless, significant unrest and radical movements took root in the north, fed by factors such as displacement of workers by mechanisation, harsh turns of the trade cycle and lack of democratic representation. This period included Luddite machine-breaking, the Peterloo Massacre, the working-class Chartist reform movement and a successful, employer-led campaign to abolish the Corn Laws. It was not always coherent, which is understandable given the uncertainty: no one knew whether all these social and economic changes would lead to wider prosperity or mass starvation.

It is not easy to interpret the early nineteenth century in modern political terms. Paternalist 'High Tories', for example, favoured state intervention to defend the vulnerable and high spending on welfare, whereas liberal Whigs favoured *laissez-faire* economics, tax cuts and harsh welfare restrictions.[5] While other European countries had revolutions in 1830 and 1848, Britain muddled through without one, despite Friedrich Engels' prediction in 1845 that it would sooner or later see 'a revolution in comparison with which the French Revolution, and the year 1794, will prove to have been child's play'.[6]

Much agitation came from self-employed workers such as handloom weavers, stockingers and framework knitters whose livelihoods were threatened by factories. Weavers' piecework rates dropped by more than half between 1805 and 1819 and many had little or no work.[7] The Luddite insurgency began in 1811 among Nottinghamshire hosiery workers, led by a probably mythical Ned Ludd, and spread to Yorkshire and Lancashire. A Luddite attack on a mill near Huddersfield led to the assassination of a mill owner, William Horsfall. Across the Pennines, a crowd of several thousand tried to break into the Middleton mill of Daniel Burton, an early power loom adopter. Burton's men shot four or five dead and more were killed by a troop of Scots Greys when hostilities resumed the next day. The coroners returned a verdict of 'justifiable homicide'.[8] Lord Liverpool's government deployed 12,000 troops in affected areas and magistrates were given extra powers. Ten rioters were hanged at Chester and Lancaster and a further seventeen at York. Harsh penalties eventually quelled the riots, despite a resurgence in 1816. The Luddites did not succeed in halting the spread of power looms.

The Napoleonic Wars' end in 1815 brought no relief. Twenty-three years of war with France had left Britain with unprecedented tax levels (23 per cent of gross domestic product) and a huge national debt of £800m, more than 250 per cent of GDP – a larger burden than in 1918 or 1945.[9] Radicals complained that wartime taxes had gone to line the pockets of the Tory government's cronies. Cobbett called it 'Old Corruption'. Hasty demobilisation of the armed forces and spending cuts led to unemployment and a deeper slump. A Whig–Radical alliance forced the government to abandon income tax, leaving it more dependent on regressive indirect taxes. To make matters worse, the eruption of Mount Tambora in Indonesia in 1815, the largest volcanic explosion known to history, darkened skies and created the worst European food shortages for more than a century in 1816–17. England's spending on poor relief rose to compensate partially, but all these factors led to riots and demonstrations culminating with Peterloo.

Hampden Clubs – radical campaigning and debating societies – became popular in the north, but were suppressed. In 1817, a march by Blanketeers set out from Manchester to London (with rolled blankets on their backs), aiming to petition the Prince Regent for urgent help for the cotton industry and to protest against parliament's repressive measures and resistance to reform. The march was broken up violently and leaders imprisoned. An armed uprising at Pentrich in Derbyshire was quashed.

The reform movement, which had been in retreat because of reaction against the French Revolution and the effect of William Pitt's anti-sedition laws, was revived. Parliamentary reform was a key demand. Those entitled to vote were mostly wealthy landowners, about 15–16 per cent of adult males in England and Wales, down from 24 per cent a century before.[10] Population growth had been concentrated in northern industrial areas that contained few parliamentary boroughs. Half of all English constituencies lay south of a line between London and Bristol; Manchester and Salford had no dedicated MP. A petition to parliament for manhood suffrage gathered three-quarters of a million signatures in 1817 but was flatly rejected by the House of Commons. Reformers also wanted to restore civil rights and repeal the Corn Laws, which excluded imports of grain until the price reached near-famine levels. The government had introduced these laws in 1815 to protect landowners from loss of government contracts to feed the armed forces, but this raised the price of bread at a time of hardship.

A crowd of about forty thousand gathered at St Peter's Field, Manchester, on 16 August 1819 to hear a speech by Henry 'Orator' Hunt, a Wiltshire farmer and reformer. As Hunt arrived, magistrates called in the Manchester and Salford Yeomanry to help constables to arrest him and other leaders. The yeomanry, who were mill-owner and shopkeeper volunteers, became stuck in the crowd and started to hack about them with sabres. After Hunt was arrested, the yeomanry tried to seize flags in the crowd, 'cutting most indiscriminately to the right and to the left to get at them', according to John Tyas of *The Times*. Only then were objects thrown at the military: 'From this point the Manchester and Salford Yeomanry lost all command of temper.'[11] William Hulton, the magistrates' chairman, summoned the 15th Hussars and Cheshire Yeomanry to disperse the crowd, but the main exit route was blocked. One Hussars officer was heard trying to restrain his own men and the Manchester and Salford Yeomanry, who were 'cutting away' at everyone they could reach: 'Gentlemen! gentlemen! for shame! Forbear! The people cannot get away.'[12]

An estimated eighteen died of injuries received on the day and almost seven hundred were seriously injured, including two hundred by sabre wounds.[13] Many were women and some were children. More than one in three of those injured were handloom weavers, along with shoemakers, hatters and tailors; only about one in twenty were factory workers. It all happened in a few minutes of confusion. There were Waterloo veterans on both sides. The name 'Peterloo' was coined five days after the massacre by James Wroe, editor of the radical *Manchester Observer*, ironically comparing the cowardly attacks on unarmed civilians to the brutality suffered in the battle against Napoleon.[14]

After the event, Hunt was jailed for thirty months. The government feared armed rebellion: a planned uprising was suppressed in west Yorkshire and the Cato Street conspiracy to blow up the cabinet was foiled. Legislation known as the Six Acts was passed to suppress radical meetings and publications. By the end of 1820, every significant working-class radical reformer was in jail. The government congratulated itself on having seen off a threat, but the legacy of Peterloo contributed to the reform bill crisis of 1830–2.

A somewhat blue-blooded Whig cabinet under Earl Grey (from a Northumberland family) took office in 1830. It eventually passed the Reform Act 1832, which increased the electorate to about 20 per cent of adult males and achieved some geographical redistribution. It enfranchised towns including Manchester, Salford, Bury, Bolton, Rochdale, Oldham, Ashton and Warrington, increasing the number of Lancashire MPs from fourteen to twenty-seven. But it did not widen the social mix; if anything, the opposite. The act created uniform voting qualifications based solely on ownership or occupation of property, strengthening the influence of landowners and wealthy urban elites. The number of working people with the vote may actually have fallen as the standardised borough franchise of '£10 householders' ended some relatively democratic local franchises, notably Preston.[15]

Whigs won the 1832 election by a landslide and passed a mixed bag of reforms including abolition of slavery in 1833 and the Municipal Corporations Act 1835, which enabled towns such as Manchester to acquire an elected corporation. Pressure to improve factory conditions, limit working hours and protect child and women workers came, however, from paternalist Tories such as Richard Oastler (a Leeds cloth trader turned land steward), his friend Michael Sadler (a Leeds linen draper) and philanthropic aristocrat Lord Ashley, later seventh Earl of Shaftesbury. These were evangelical Anglicans who had opposed both slavery and Catholic emancipation and were horrified by the moral and social effects of unregulated factory labour. 'I heard their groans,' wrote Oastler, 'I watched their tears; I knew they relied on me.'[16] Utilitarians and liberals fought what they saw as attempts to shackle the labour market and pile costs on employers. A watered-down Factory Act was passed in 1833, establishing an inspectorate. After many rejections, an act limiting daily working hours for women and children in textile mills to ten was passed in 1847. It was piloted through the Commons by John Fielden, mill owner and radical MP for Oldham.

The Whigs' Poor Law Amendment Act 1834, resulting from a royal commission, was intended to curb the cost of poor relief and address abuses of the old system. While rising in cash terms, the cost was stable as a share of national income at about 2 per cent, but fell heavily on some local ratepayers. In one Yorkshire parish, Newburgh, the annual bill to the thirteen ratepayers rose from £34 in 1817–18 to £130 in 1836–7.[17] Under the new system, relief would be given only in workhouses; conditions in them would be such as to deter any but the truly destitute from applying for relief. The act was passed by large majorities, with only a few Tories and Radicals objecting. Benjamin Disraeli said the act 'disgraced the country'. Annual spending on poor relief fell from £6.3 million to £4 million and the percentage of the population aided from 10.2 to 5.4 per cent.[18] The changes were resisted by local authorities in northern England, where it was argued that cyclical unemployment meant any new workhouse would be empty for most of the year and thus a waste of money. The new Poor Law was never fully implemented. Bradford, for example, had a workhouse that could accommodate 260 people, but more than 13,000 were claiming benefits in 1848.[19]

Anger about the Poor Law helped to spur the Chartist campaign, described by Robert Tombs as 'arguably the greatest – if not the only – class war England has ever seen'.[20] Chartism was created in 1838 during an economic slump. It began in London, where a People's Charter was drawn up demanding the vote for every male inhabitant of Britain and Ireland, a secret ballot, equal electoral districts, payment for MPs, abolition of the property qualification for MPs, and annual parliaments. The movement gained traction in the north, particularly in Manchester, where the National Charter Association, viewed as the world's first prototype working-class political party, was launched. The *Northern Star*, a Chartist newspaper, was based in Leeds.

Joseph Rayner Stephens, a Methodist preacher, told a rally at Kersal Moor outside Manchester that the vote was a 'knife-and-fork question', meaning that political power was needed to relieve hunger.[21] The senior military commander in the north, Charles Napier, wrote: 'There may be and there may not be a general insurrection; but the people menace the use of the pike and fire in all directions, which is perfectly practicable.'[22] A petition for the charter, bearing 1.2 million signatures, was rejected by parliament. In 1842 there were waves of strikes and riots across the north and midlands, including the 'plug plot' riots in which tens of thousands of strikers forcibly closed down factories by removing the plugs from their steam engines. The protests were suppressed, with hundreds sentenced to transportation.

Chartists found it hard to win over London, with its vast size and occupational diversity. They lost momentum in 1848 when leaders organised a rally on Kennington Common, on the wrong side of the Thames, and decided not to defy a police ban on a procession to parliament. Several hundred Chartists and Irish Confederates were arrested in London and the north, leading the movement to collapse. In the short term it was a failure, though by 1918 all the charter's points had been achieved except annual general elections.

Why did these events not spark a revolution similar to upheavals in 1848 in countries such as France, the Netherlands, Italy, the Austrian Empire and the German Confederation? Macaulay believed that England had had its revolution in 1688, that liberties had already been won and that the ruling class made a timely concession in 1832. Left-wing historians emphasise the authorities' willingness to use force, though that did not stop popular movements elsewhere from bringing down repressive states.[23] Some have pointed to the moderating influence of Methodism. It was probably a combination of factors.

The Manchester-based Anti-Corn Law League, also founded in 1838, was more successful. Its objective was quickly achieved when Sir Robert Peel, the Bury-born Conservative prime minister, repealed the Corn Laws in 1846 with Whig and Radical support, splitting his own party. Peel, son of a wealthy textile manufacturer and MP, was Britain's first prime minister from an industrial background and is seen as creator of the modern Conservative Party. The league's leaders were Richard Cobden and John Bright, promoters of what Disraeli called the 'Manchester school' of liberal economics. Cobden was a self-made calico printer and Bright a Quaker mill owner from Rochdale.

The movement was dominated by cotton merchants and manufacturers, sometimes called the 'cottonocracy'. They saw cheaper bread and potentially cheaper labour as expanding world trade, to the benefit of British manufacturing. Their cause aligned in one major respect with that of working-class radicals – abolition of the

Corn Laws had been a demand at the time of Peterloo – but not in others. The cottonocracy opposed factory reforms. The same parliamentary session that achieved Corn Law repeal also saw Bright resist the ten hours bill. The Corn Law campaign, modelled on the anti-slavery movement, involved pamphleteering, petitioning and public meetings. It was one of the most successful single-issue pressure groups in history. Free trade became Britain's settled orthodoxy until the 1930s and still has a strong influence today.

Repeal of the Corn Laws marked a symbolic shift in Britain's image of itself as primarily agricultural. This was now an urban, industrial nation. By 1851 more than half the population lived in towns; from the 1820s, more people worked in manufacturing than in farming.[24] But while the cottonocracy's economic victory endured, it was never so politically assertive again. Having gained the vote and free trade, many northern capitalists were content to leave governing to the liberal-imperial elite.

The century's second half was calmer, helped by growing prosperity in which many working people shared. Class conflict was deferred until the twentieth century, when industrial wealth began to contract and working-class living standards levelled off or fell. The Victorian age was one of self-congratulation in which school textbooks assured children that they belonged to 'the greatest and most highly civilised people that the world ever saw'.[25] An average of 43,000 people flocked every day for six months to the 1851 Great Exhibition in London, seen as the embodiment of commercial, technological and political progress. Macaulay concluded that 'there is as much chance of a revolution in England as of the falling of the moon'.[26]

It was an age of mutual self-help and respectability – of friendly societies, trade unions and the cooperative movement, boosted by the Rochdale Pioneers in 1844, a group of twenty-eight weavers and other tradesmen who banded together to open a shop selling food items they could not otherwise afford. Samuel Smiles, who delivered evening classes for working people in Leeds, had an international bestseller with *Self-Help* (1859), which promoted thrift and claimed that poverty was caused largely by irresponsible habits.

Trade unions and friendly societies were hard on shirkers: benefit claimants were medically checked, banned from drinking and required to accept any suitable work. Temperance was promoted by campaigners such as Joseph Livesey, founder of the Preston Temperance Society in 1833 and author of The Pledge: 'We agree to abstain from all liquors of an intoxicating quality whether ale, porter, wine or ardent spirits, except as medicine.'[27] One story attributes the word teetotal to Richard Turner, a society member, who said: 'I'll be reet down tee-tee-total for ever and ever.'[28] (The prefix tee- was sometimes used in Lancashire to emphasise resolve.) Alcohol consumption declined continuously from the 1870s.

Real wages rose from mid-century, particularly from the 1870s, when cheap imports led food prices to fall. Wages were highest in coalmining, factory industries and engineering. People were able to consume more; they ate more meat and acquired goods such as household furnishings and clothes. Children were better fed and stayed longer in their parents' home. The home became the focus of urban family life for all classes. As men's wages rose, working-class mothers increasingly stayed at home. The Trades Union Congress, founded in Manchester in 1868, defined one of its aims in 1877 as 'bring[ing] about a condition … where wives should be in their proper sphere at home, instead of being dragged into competition for livelihood against the great and strong men of the world'.[29]

Working hours declined after 1850, creating what envious foreigners called the 'English week' of five-and-a-half days. There was more time for leisure. Workers in Lancashire cotton mills sang in choral societies and went on holiday together. Brass bands were formed in mining and other industries. Works outings took place well into the twentieth century.

The Second Reform Act 1867 extended the vote to a wider number of urban working men, prompting politicians to court skilled working-class voters. Six pieces of legislation enhanced the status of trade unions, including the Trade Union Act 1871, which recognised them as corporations and entitled them to protection under the law. Robert Applegarth, a Sheffield trade unionist who became leader of the Amalgamated Society of Carpenters and Joiners, was a leading figure in the spread of moderate trade unionism. The unions' growth was not always trouble-free. In the 'Sheffield Outrages', William Broadhead of the Grinders' Union admitted, after being given indemnity from prosecution, that he had ordered a murder and other crimes to intimidate non-unionists.[30]

Not everyone was impressed by all this apparent social harmony. Intellectuals such as John Ruskin and Matthew Arnold were scathing about the materialism and ugliness of industrial society. Even Engels, though, grudgingly accepted in 1885 that a revolution had not happened because the working class shared in the benefits of 'England's industrial monopoly'. He continued to predict that when the monopoly broke down, 'there will be socialism again in England'.[31]

CHAPTER 15

HAIL TO THE SHEEP

Northern England, especially Yorkshire, owes a huge debt to sheep. This versatile animal lay at the heart of the region's fortunes from medieval times, when Cistercian monks helped to fuel a wool export boom, to the Victorian era when the West Riding became the world's capital of woollen cloth manufacture.

Sheep, raised for fleeces, meat and milk, were first domesticated in England about 4000–3500 BCE. Their wool – warm, water-resistant, soft – is arguably the most useful fibre ever made into clothing. By the time of the Domesday survey in 1086, sheep may have outnumbered people by more than two to one.[1] People kept far more sheep than other animals put together, including cattle, pigs, fowl and goats.[2] The wool trade was the backbone of England's medieval economy, particularly 1250–1350, when exports supplied cloth industries in Flanders and Italy. As exports of raw wool declined in the later Middle Ages, those of cloths rose.[3] While wool made some people wealthy, however, it was a volatile trade affected by war, taxes and disease.

Wool production lay partly behind an economic upsurge in the north during the twelfth and thirteenth centuries, especially in east Yorkshire,[4] though it was far from the only area of England raising sheep. Cistercians were particularly associated with northern

England. Between 1128 and 1153 they established fifty-six houses for monks throughout England, of which 18, almost a third, were in the northern counties. They were mostly in rich, if remote, valleys.[5] The 'white monks' were one of a number of reformed orders created in response to what were seen as luxurious ways of the Benedictines ('black monks'). Led by St Bernard of Clairvaux, Cistercians spotted an opportunity to develop sheep-rearing in England, which was mostly local and piecemeal, and export wool on a massive scale to abbeys in Flanders that specialised in spinning, weaving and dyeing.

Monks enclosed large areas of land, a departure from traditional strip farming; eventually this changed the face of the British Isles and radically altered social structures. Wool was brought to each abbey from granges, or monastic farms, then cleaned, sorted, taken to a regional collection point and despatched to a port.[6] Cistercians created a second tier of monks, drawn from society's lower echelons, known as lay brothers, who did the agricultural work. These were fed and clothed but did not receive wages, so costs were low. While Yorkshire wool was not considered the best, Cistercians achieved above-average quality by taking care in sorting and packing.[7]

Rievaulx, the north's first Cistercian monastery, founded in 1132, quickly grew to be a community of 140 monks and 500 lay brothers under its best-known abbot, Aelred. According to some estimates, the four most important northern Cistercian houses, Rievaulx, Fountains, Byland and Jervaulx, each had more than thirteen thousand sheep, with Fountains, the largest, having almost nineteen thousand.[8] In the fourteenth century, abbeys met setbacks, including Scottish invasions, an epidemic of sheep scab and the Black Death. The system of lay brothers fell apart as a result of labour shortages. Cistercians, along with other estate owners, were forced to rent out land to tenant farmers. Some recovery was achieved by the time monasteries were dissolved by Henry VIII in 1536–41, but monks never matched their earlier success.[9]

Apart from rearing sheep, Rievaulx is known for having operated a prototype blast furnace, in use at the time of dissolution – a technology for making iron not previously thought to have been used in England until the early eighteenth century. This led some historians to speculate that industrialisation might have begun earlier if monasteries had remained, though that is conjecture.[10] The wool trade also made some merchants wealthy, notably William de le Pole of Hull, who died in 1366. He rose from obscurity to become a royal moneylender and created one of the prime families of the realm. His descendants became earls of Lincoln and earls and dukes of Suffolk.

From the fourteenth to the sixteenth centuries, northern England suffered relative economic decline. Cloth replaced wool as England's principal export and its manufacture flourished in East Anglia and the south-west.[11] High-quality Cotswold wool was in demand, but northern wool was not. Old industrial towns of east Yorkshire such as Beverley, Malton, Hedon and Scarborough became poor, probably not helped by guild restrictions and urban taxation.[12] The West Riding bucked the declining trend and by the late Middle Ages was a centre for wool textile manufacture, though not yet as important as southern locations. Merchant-employers created the 'putting-out' system: merchants supplied wool for spinning and weaving by farming families and then had the products finished and took them to market.[13]

During the eighteenth century, the West Riding became the dominant manufacturing area, helped by supplies of coal for domestic heating, the soft water necessary for textile production and relatively low living costs. Southern counties appear to have stopped manufacturing because they could get a better return from improvements in agriculture.[14] The West Riding also eclipsed York as the north's main wool textile producer since rural production was cheaper.[15] Daniel Defoe, in his travels through Britain in 1724, marvelled as he approached Halifax to find the steep hillsides littered with small houses, each standing in its own patch of land. Perplexed to find so many people living in such desolate places, he attributed it to the bounty of nature in providing coals and running water: 'This seems to have been directed by the wise hand of Providence for the very purpose which is now served by it, namely, the manufactures, which otherwise could not be carried on.'[16]

Defoe went on to Leeds, whose cloth market 'indeed is a prodigy of its kind, and is not to be equalled in the world'. He explained how on two days each week, cloth merchants and small producers brought finished pieces that were laid out on trestle tables. Deals would be struck in silence: 'Thus you see ten or twenty thousand pounds value in cloth, and sometimes much more, bought and sold in little more than an hour.'[17] His sums may be exaggerated, but Leeds was clearly a commercial centre. The open market in Briggate (moved from the river bridge when it became too large) was for coloured cloth only; a hall was built in 1711 for trading white cloth. Leeds later acquired a coloured cloth hall and two more white cloth halls.[18]

Mechanisation came to Yorkshire wool later than to Lancashire cotton, partly for technical reasons: improvements to early machines had to be made before wool could be spun effectively. It was even longer before efficient power looms were evolved for the woollen trade. Yeoman clothiers described by Defoe remained important figures for at least a century.[19] John Kay's flying shuttle, however, was patented in 1733 for woollen weaving. Kay, from Bury in Lancashire, went to Leeds, where cloth producers adopted his shuttle but refused to pay royalties. He used up his money fighting abortive legal battles.[20]

Woollen cloth production was overtaken by cotton around 1800. It was well into the nineteenth century before Yorkshire could boast of many large woollen mills. Britain's first worsted spinning mill was erected at Dolphinholme, near Lancaster, in 1784. Yorkshire's first equivalent, Low Mill at Addingham, was built in 1787. The machinery was designed by factory pioneer Richard Arkwright; the mill supplied yarn to Bradford.[21] One of

Yorkshire's main factory pioneers was Benjamin Gott, a Leeds merchant turned manufacturer. In 1792 he opened his first mill at Bean Ing on the banks of the Aire; only a few processes were mechanised. Gott benefited from demand for army clothing and blankets as a result of war with France. His Armley Mills, leased in 1804, became the world's largest wool factory. John Marshall built the magnificent, Egyptian-style Temple Mill in Leeds for flax-spinning in the 1830s.[22]

Industrialisation was boosted by better transport. Turnpike roads came to Yorkshire from the 1730s. Canal building began in earnest in the 1760s and lasted for about seventy years. During this time, the Pennines were crossed by three canals and the main centres were connected to each other and to the Humber ports. Then came the railways. West Riding towns developed specialisms. Bradford, Huddersfield, Halifax and Keighley focused on worsted, a high-quality yarn made from longer wool fibres, whose name was derived from Worstead, a village in Norfolk. Bradford grew into the world centre for worsted, nicknamed Worstedopolis. Halifax began to specialise in carpets. Batley, Dewsbury and Ossett were centres of the shoddy and mungo trade, which recycled rags into blankets and uniforms.[23]

There was violent resistance to mechanisation. Machine-breaking began among hosiery workers in Nottinghamshire, who declared themselves followers of 'General' Ned Ludd. On the night of 11 April 1812, William Cartwright, owner of Rawfolds Mill in the West Riding town of Liversedge, with the help of soldiers beat off a raid by 100 Luddites from Huddersfield, killing two raiders. Anger turned against two local masters: Enoch Taylor of Marsden, who made both the hated weaving machines and the hammers often used to smash them, and William Horsfall, a wealthy cloth finisher and merchant who said he would 'ride up to his saddle-girths' in Luddite blood. Horsfall was shot dead and three men were hanged for the murder. At the same time, sixty-three others were tried for the raid on Cartwright's mill; seventeen were executed and six transported to

Australia. Resistance was fruitless. By 1835, more than four thousand power looms were in use in Yorkshire.[24]

Wool merchants and manufacturers were prominent in the campaign to repeal the Corn Laws. Working-class causes included the anti-Poor Law movement, Chartism and efforts to create trade unions. A Bradford wool-combers' strike in 1825 involved 20,000 men and ended in bitter defeat after five months.[25]

Rapid population growth created dire conditions including cholera and poor life expectancy. Friedrich Engels wrote of Bradford in 1844: 'Heaps of dirt disfigure the lanes, alleys and courts. The houses are dirty and dilapidated and not fit for human habitation.' Charles Dickens described Leeds as 'the filthiest and most awful place I have ever seen'. There was an influx of Irish workers after the potato famine. While some Bradford leaders tried to persuade them to leave, many Irish joined the Chartists and trade unions.[26] Child labour was endemic. Rosetta Baker, a ten-year-old spinner in Bradford, told an inquiry: 'I come at six in the morning. I go at seven ... The overlooker is my grandfather. The overlooker brays [hits] us if we do not mind our work, with his hands over the head. He does it very often. He brays the others with a strap; he does not take the strap to me.'[27]

A few mill owners such as Titus Salt in Bradford realised that it was not in their interest to have workers dead or maimed. To help them escape the city's pollution, he created the factory and town of Saltaire near Shipley. Although a confirmed authoritarian, he cut down hours of work and built homes with gas and fresh water. He began in worsted but diversified into cloth that mixed cotton with the fine wool of the Alpaca.[28]

Bradford's exports were boosted from the 1830s by German Jewish merchants such as Charles Semon, Jacob Behrens and Jacob Moser, who created the area known as Little Germany. At the end of the century, Leeds's burgeoning clothing industry benefited from immigrants such as Montague Burton, a Lithuanian Jew who arrived to escape persecution in tsarist Russia. After starting his chain of tailoring shops in Sheffield, he moved operations to Leeds. By the mid-twentieth century his Burmantofts factory was believed to be the world's largest clothing factory. Joseph Hepworth, a Methodist tailor, created a chain of clothing shops in Leeds in 1864; it grew to 100 outlets by 1884 and today survives as the fashion chain Next. By 1914 Leeds was home to 100 wholesale clothiers, with perhaps eighty factories and a host of small tailoring sweatshops.[29]

By the late nineteenth century, industrialisation had transformed west Yorkshire. Many industrialists were inspired by Scots-born but Leeds-based Samuel Smiles, author of *Self-Help*, who outlined his philosophy of hard work, thrift and competition in the 1840s. Although life was materially and culturally richer for the middle classes and skilled workers, many others lived in poverty. Foreign competition was growing. The *Bradford Observer* commented after Paris's 1867 Industrial Exhibition: 'The German spinners compete with us in our own markets, Roubaix attracts our buyers of fancy goods and Belgium undersells us in worsteds abroad.'[30]

Employment in the UK wool textile industry peaked at almost 280,000 in 1912.[31] Exports slumped after the First World War and things got worse after the Wall Street crash: unemployment in Bradford reached 20 per cent as 400 textile firms closed in 1928–32.[32] There was a recovery in the later 1930s, but companies were slow to invest in new technologies such as manmade fibres. During the Second World War, manufacturers supplied cloth for military uniforms as well as the civilian market and exported to the US and the Empire, despite losing workers to the forces. In Bradford there was full employment and high wages.

After the war, Bradford coped with labour shortages by employing east European immigrants and, after 1955, large numbers of Asians from Pakistan and India. As post-war recovery petered out, there was rationalisation and many smaller family businesses disappeared. The world economic crisis of 1979–81 coincided with a wool crisis and caused even more firms to go under. Yorkshire's woollen industry is much reduced, though niche producers survive such as Hainsworth in Pudsey, Abraham Moon in Guiseley and Camira Fabrics in Mirfield. They would make Rievaulx's monks proud.

IMMIGRATION
AND SLAVERY

CHAPTER 16

MIGRANT LAND

At about 10 p.m. on 5 June 1919, Charles Wootton, a twenty-four-year-old Black sailor from Bermuda, who had served in the Royal Navy during the First World War, was pursued for more than half a mile through the streets of Liverpool by a white mob two to three hundred strong. Eventually he was cornered on the water's edge at Queen's Dock, by which time the hostile crowd had grown to two thousand. Wootton was torn out of a police officer's grasp. Stones were thrown, driving him into the water, and some shouted 'let him drown'.

The *Liverpool Echo* reported that as Wootton floundered in the water, 'a detective climbed down a ship's rope and was about to pull the man out of the water when a stone thrown from the middle of the crowd struck Wootton on the head and he sank. His body was later recovered by means of grappling irons.' No arrests were made. An inquest found insufficient evidence to determine how he got into the dock. It returned the near-meaningless verdict of 'found drowned'.[1]

The lynching of Wootton was just one shocking episode in the riots of 1919 in seaports including Liverpool, South Shields and Hull. Five people were killed and hundreds injured when white soldiers returning from the war blamed Black people, Asians and

Arabs for taking their jobs and homes. The 'fit country for heroes' promised by the prime minister, David Lloyd George, had failed to materialise and lack of jobs was aggravated by an acute housing shortage. Black men became scapegoats, even though many were themselves out of work and destitute, having been dismissed from ships to make way for demobilised white men.

The north has had an equivocal and often less-than-welcoming attitude towards ethnic minorities, though not always as dire as this. On occasions, the welcome was warm. Less than ten years after the events of 1919, people in Nelson, north-east Lancashire, took the West Indies' Learie Constantine to their hearts as a professional at their cricket club, creating a joyful, decades-long tradition in which the game's biggest Black stars charmed Lancashire's small White towns.[2] Many people had never seen a Black man. 'Schoolchildren were peeping through the window to see him,' said one resident. Constantine said: 'I had a job to do to satisfy people that I was as human as they were.' He lived in the town for nineteen years and became a barrister, a knight and then Britain's first Black peer.

Northern England has been entirely shaped by migrants including *Homo heidelbergensis*, *Homo neanderthalensis*, Britons, Anglo-Saxons, Vikings, Normans and the Irish as well as African-Caribbean people, Africans, South Asians and Chinese people, along with Jews from central and eastern Europe. Slavery inevitably overshadows the topic (see next chapter). Liverpool came to dominate the slave trade, profits from which made fortunes and helped to build cities and towns across the region, leaving a shameful legacy. All the north's minorities, however, have played a role in the region's history.

The Romans brought greater ethnic diversity than was once supposed. An altar stone found in 1934 in the Cumbrian village of Beaumont records that, in the mid-third century, a unit of North Africans was stationed at the fort of Aballava, at the western end of Hadrian's Wall.[3] It is one of several artefacts and inscriptions clustered along the wall that record the presence of Africans. In York, forensic science has enabled archaeologists to unlock the stories of

200 human skeletons from the Roman era. While most were of European ancestry, 11–12 per cent were of African descent.[4] They were in two burial grounds, one for poorer and one for wealthier people, suggesting that they moved in all levels of society.

The most famous individual to emerge from work on York's third-century citizens is the Ivory Bangle Lady, discovered in 1901 in a stone sarcophagus with luxury goods, suggesting high social status. One of her bracelets was made of African ivory. Analysis of her remains indicates that she is likely to have been of mixed race and that she, her parents or grandparents had come from North Africa.[5] She was between eighteen and twenty-three when she died.

Ethnic minority migrants to Britain were rare between the end of the western Roman Empire in the fifth century and Europe's age of exploration 1,000 years later. Romani travellers, who originated in northern India, have been in Britain since at least the early sixteenth century. Black people have been continuously present since around then. Sir Francis Drake, an intermittent slave trader, circumnavigated the globe in 1577–80 with four Africans in his crew.[6] England became closely involved in the slave trade under Charles II and his brother James from the 1660s and was a major participant until abolition in 1807.

From the seventeenth century, Indian servants and ayahs (nannies) arrived with English families returning from India, while Indian sailors, known as lascars (via Portuguese from the Urdu and Persian *laskari*, meaning soldier), crewed East India Company ships.[7] Some ended up destitute and eventually many settled in ports such as Liverpool, Hull and South Shields.

There were a few thousand Black people in Georgian England including domestic servants (or slaves), sailors, tavern workers, musicians and prostitutes.[8] Most lived in London, but by the late eighteenth century Liverpool had one of the largest Black communities. Slaves were bought and sold at coffee houses.[9] Some escaped their owners and were joined by runaways from other parts of Britain. They settled in the Toxteth Park area, one of the poorest parts. Liverpool's Black population in the nineteenth century, as in other seaports, was largely male. These men often married local women. Sometimes there was opposition to interracial relationships and prejudice against their children. Liverpool produced the first British-born Black councillor, alderman and mayor – John Archer, born in the city in 1863 to a Barbadian father and an Irish mother, who became mayor of Battersea in 1913.[10]

Chinese seamen began to lodge in ports outside London, primarily Liverpool and Cardiff, after the East India Company's monopoly on trade in Asia ended in 1834.[11] Numbers increased in Liverpool from 1866 when the Blue Funnel Shipping Line, part of Holt Ocean Steamship Company, ran steamers directly between Liverpool and China. Boarding houses for Chinese seamen opened near the docks. There was a sprinkling of other occupations. Chinese jugglers and magicians, for example, were popular in music halls across Britain. Liverpool's Chinatown, then clustered around Cleveland Square and Pitt Street, grew rapidly from the 1890s. A 1906 report identified thirteen boarding houses and seven shops run by members of the Chinese community, along with forty-nine laundries (spread across the city). There were accusations that gambling and opium-smoking were rife and that Chinese men were corrupting young British girls.[12]

Groups of Muslim seamen in Britain included Somalis along with Yemenis from Aden, a British colony. Muslims settled in ports and established distinct communities. The north's booming textile industries also attracted white migration. Manchester drew in Germans (both Jewish and gentile), French, Russians, Italians, Greeks, Dutch, Spanish, Armenians, Danes, Swiss, Turkish, Portuguese, Swedes and Moroccans.[13] The Great Famine in Ireland in the 1840s drove many Irish to settle in northern cities, especially Liverpool and Manchester (see chapter 18).

Northern England's relationship with Judaism began shockingly with the massacre of York's Jewish population in 1190. Jews had come to England after the Norman Conquest because early Norman kings needed to borrow money to build castles and secure their kingdom, while moneylending was forbidden to Christians, but hostility grew during the crusades. Stories were spread of Jews murdering Christian children, now known as the 'Blood Libel'. Jews were expelled from England by Edward I in 1290 and did not return until the 1650s, when Oliver Cromwell invited them to resettle.

The York massacre happened amid widespread attacks against Jews in several cities. The houses of York's Jews were set on fire and they were besieged for a week inside the castle, where they had fled for safety. Most took their own and their families' lives, while a few were tricked into leaving the castle and massacred. The attack had a partly financial motive, as local magnates were unwilling or unable to repay debts to the Jews. York's Jewish community recovered to some extent until the expulsion.[14]

The north's first synagogue appeared in Liverpool in 1753. Manchester's Jewish community was founded by fourteen families in 1786; their first synagogue was a rented room in Long Millgate.[15] By 1851 there were about one and a half thousand Jews in Liverpool and one thousand one hundred in Manchester, with smaller communities in Sheffield, Leeds and Hull.[16] Manchester, which saw an influx of German Jews, was to become the largest community outside London. German Jewish merchants also helped to make Bradford a major exporter of woollen goods. Samuel Montagu, who founded merchant bank Samuel Montagu & Co., was the son of a Liverpool silversmith and watchmaker. Nathan Mayer Rothschild, of the Rothschild banking dynasty, established a textile trading and finance business in Manchester at age twenty-one before moving to London and founding N.M. Rothschild.[17]

Between 1881 and 1914 came Jewish immigration from tsarist Russia and Poland, giving the community a poorer cast until the mid-twentieth century. Pogroms were the catalyst but the underlying driver was economic: the growing Jewish population was denied access to the tsarist empire's industrialising cities and regions.[18] Many came to Manchester. Leeds's small community also expanded rapidly as migrants worked in its burgeoning men's clothing industry; by the First World War it was the third largest Jewish community after London and Manchester. Polish-born Michael Marks, co-founder of Marks and Spencer, began as a pedlar visiting villages around Leeds.[19]

Midway through the nineteenth century, Britain's reforming spirit, which led to abolition of the slave trade in 1807 and the act to abolish slavery in most of the empire in 1833, gave way to a climate that was more threatening towards ethnic minorities. 'Scientific' theories emerged in which whites stood conveniently at the head of a hierarchy of races, just as European countries were scrambling to colonise Africa and Asia. Exhibitions put Africans on show in human zoos. At the 1904 Bradford Exhibition, organisers booked a group of 100 men, women and children from Somalia. The Somalis constructed and lived in an 'African' village where Yorkshire crowds could watch them washing clothes, wrestling, throwing spears and making handicraft items. They departed wearing English suits and it transpired that they were a professional outfit touring the European circuit, thus undermining the notion that Africans were unworldly.[20]

During the First World War, ethnic minorities found their labour in demand. More than one million Indian soldiers fought, including on the western front, and there was increased employment of Indian sailors, some of whom jumped ship in search of better pay in factories.[21] Soldiers from Britain's African and Caribbean colonies were deployed to fight in Africa and the Middle East rather than in France: the War Office did not want Black volunteers to fight alongside white soldiers and kill white men, seen as a precedent that could endanger colonial rule.[22] This was in contrast to France's mass deployment of African battalions. A few Black men did outmanoeuvre the colour bar and fight in Europe. One combatant was Ernest Marke from Sierra Leone, who was accepted into the army at a Liverpool recruiting office.

Britain's Black and Asian populations had swelled as men from across the empire served on merchant ships or worked in factories.

At the war's end, Ernest Marke noted that in Liverpool 'things became different with the demobilisation of thousands of men from the armed forces and the closing down of munitions factories. It now became scarcity of jobs, not men, with the demobbed men wanting their old jobs back and negroes being sacked to make room for them.'[23]

The 1919 riots started in Glasgow and spread to South Shields, London, Hull, Newport, Barry and Cardiff. In Liverpool, the homes of Black people were ransacked and contents set on fire. Hundreds had to take shelter. Marke recalled encountering a mob of men on Brownlow Hill: 'They started chasing us the moment we were spotted, shouting, "Niggers, niggers, stop them niggers."' A woman helped them to escape through a back lane, but they were spotted by another mob. 'A tram car was going southward where we lived; we ran for it, the mob on our heels. I caught it but my friend was unlucky. That was the last time I saw him. I learned later that he was beaten unconscious and left for dead.'[24]

Police went on strike. Three battalions of soldiers, supported by tanks, were deployed and a battleship accompanied by destroyers sailed up the Mersey – an overreaction by a government made twitchy by the 1917 Russian Revolution.[25] During the 1920s and 1930s, a colour bar operated in certain trades and workplaces. Repatriation schemes were tried and failed. The 1920 Aliens Order and the 1925 Special Restriction (Coloured Asian Seamen) Order required all Black and Asian seamen domiciled in Britain to register with the police and prove their nationality – thought to be Britain's only state-sanctioned enactment of racial discrimination.[26]

Passport controls were tightened to restrict the flow of Indians of 'low standard of education and limited means', particularly from the Punjab, coming to earn a living as pedlars.[27] M.K. Gandhi, leader of India's anti-colonial movement, while visiting London for a conference in 1931, took time out to visit the cotton town of Darwen in Lancashire, invited by the mill-owning Davies family. They wanted him to see the hardship suffered by east Lancashire's textile industry, badly hit by the independence movement's boycott of British goods. Gandhi was polite, but said the boycott would stay until there was progress towards independence.[28]

The Jewish community suffered from xenophobia in the First World War. German-born Jews were accused of supporting enemy interests. Numerous families legally changed names to escape harassment. Immigrants from eastern Europe were reluctant to fight on the same side as the hated tsarist regime, leading to a popular belief that Jews were shirkers, stealing British soldiers' jobs and growing rich. In 1917, a mob wrecked houses and looted shops in Leeds's Jewish quarter.[29]

The war, however, boosted the cause of Zionists, who wanted a Jewish homeland in Israel. A key figure was Chaim Weizmann, later Israel's first president, who lectured in chemistry at Manchester University between 1905 and 1918. He also invented a process to produce acetone in large quantities, which helped the war effort by removing a bottleneck in producing explosives.[30] Weizmann and allies argued that a British-sponsored Jewish homeland would protect the Suez Canal, the lifeline to India. Their reward was the 1917 Balfour Declaration.

After 1918, Jewish immigrants and their children started to move up the economic ladder. This had begun in a modest way before the war. Michael Marks, for example, had made the transition from pedlar to market trader and then, in Manchester, to shopkeeper and eventually co-founder of Marks and Spencer. Prosperity was accompanied by new levels of ill-will. Golf, tennis and motor clubs banned Jews; admission to public schools and some universities became more difficult. Anti-semitism was less severe than in central Europe, but in the 1930s members of Oswald Mosley's British Union of Fascists invaded Cheetham, Manchester's Jewish district, four or five times a week, making insulting remarks and attacking Jewish youth.[31]

The Second World War brought a clamour to intern enemy aliens. By mid-1940, 30,000 people, most of them Jewish refugees who had fled the Nazis, were held in makeshift detention camps, the largest of which was in the Isle of Man. The government started deporting them to Australia and Canada, fearing implausibly that they might aid German troops in an invasion. After news that British and Canadian soldiers had robbed and mistreated deportees, and after a German submarine sank the Canada-bound *Arandora Star*, public opinion turned against deportation and mass internment. The government began releasing internees.[32]

Many from Britain's Black communities joined the services or did war work. In Liverpool, many worked in munitions factories. Indians worked in construction and factories in Newcastle, Bradford, Huddersfield, Leeds, Manchester and Sheffield.[33] The war's outcome prompted widespread repudiation of social Darwinist racial theories, which had led to Nazism and the Holocaust. Prejudice was hard to undo, however. The post-war Labour government of Clement Attlee tried to tackle labour shortages by using Polish and Irish immigrants, while discouraging Black people. Attlee enquired as to whether the *Empire Windrush*, which arrived at London's Tilbury docks in 1948 with 492 men from the West Indies, could be diverted to east Africa.[34] However, the Nationality Act 1948 continued the British tradition of open borders by giving the empire's people who formerly held the status of 'British subject' the new status of 'Commonwealth citizen'. MPs of all parties imagined the act would simply enable the continued flow of two-way traffic between Britain and Canada, South Africa, Australia and New Zealand. They did not foresee the mass migration from the West Indies and south Asia that would occur over the next two decades.[35]

In a disturbing echo of 1919, there were attacks on Black people's homes and clubs in Liverpool in 1948. The National Union of Seamen worked to replace Black and Asian sailors with White people. When a 2,000-strong mob attacked a Liverpool hostel where Black sailors lived, the police, instead of arresting aggressors, raided the hostel and arrested the Black men trapped inside.[36]

The Home Office decided in 1945 to expel Chinese seamen who were not British citizens. Those who did not leave by a specified date were rounded up by the police, placed on ships waiting in the harbour and taken away. Those who had married British women were supposed to be spared repatriation, but there was confusion and many Chinese seamen simply vanished, largely from Liverpool, never to be seen again by their families.[37]

The number of Chinese people working on ships or in laundries declined and Chinese restaurants became popular. Chinese communities grew in cities and some moved into small towns and suburbs. When Lily Kwok opened a restaurant in Middleton, Manchester, in 1959 she attracted locals by adding chips with curry sauce to her repertoire. Chinese restaurants' popularity was partly achieved by offering a meal for less than competing establishments, while late opening hours appealed to those wanting a meal after the pub.[38]

As Black immigration grew, so did hostility. Black migrants across Britain were consigned to menial jobs and poor parts of cities. Interracial relationships were a sensitive issue. White mobs attacked Black people and homes in Nottingham and London's Notting Hill in 1958. The 1962 Commonwealth Immigrants Act applied controls to those whose passports were not issued directly by the UK government. The 1965 Race Relations Act outlawed discrimination on grounds of race, but further immigration acts from 1968 to 1971 removed the remnants of Commonwealth citizens' rights of entry and residence.

Riots in 1981 by young Black people who felt marginalised and persecuted by police spread from London's Brixton to Moss Side in Manchester and Toxteth in Liverpool. Kenneth Oxford, Liverpool's chief constable, suggested that the riots' underlying cause was 'the problem of half-castes' who were 'the product of liaisons between Black seamen and White prostitutes'.[39]

Migrants arrived from various parts of south Asia, notably Pakistan, in the 1950s and 1960s. Significant concentrations of Muslims formed in Bradford, Blackburn, Dewsbury, Leeds, Manchester, Oldham and Rochdale. Many were in areas that became blighted by manufacturing decline in the 1970s and 1980s, making it hard to break from deprivation. Tensions grew. Copies of Salman Rushdie's novel *The Satanic Verses* were burned at a protest organised by the Bradford Council of Mosques in 1989. There was a riot in Bradford's Manningham district in 1995. Disorder in 2001 in Oldham, Burnley, Bradford and Leeds prompted concern that Pakistanis and Bangladeshis were insufficiently integrated into British life. Fear about radical Islam was heightened by the 2005 London bombings, which killed fifty-two commuters and the four suicide bombers; two of them came from Leeds and one from Dewsbury. In the 2017 Manchester Arena bombing, twenty-three died including the attacker.

On a brighter note, national surveys in the 1990s and 2000s showed a decline in racist sentiment as a younger generation emerged who had not experienced the post-war battles and who saw the world in less racist terms.[40] This picture is not without hope. All the north's waves of migrants, from Anglo-Saxons and Vikings to African-Caribbeans and South Asians, have added new layers of richness to the north's identity.

South Asian communities, in particular, have supplied MPs, councillors, mayors and professionals. Business people include Mohsin and Zuber Issa, low-profile brothers from Blackburn who created the petrol filling station chain Euro Garages, with 6,000 forecourts in ten countries. In 2020 they acquired the Asda supermarket chain. Others include Mahmud Kamani, co-founder of online fashion retailer Boohoo, and Simon and Bobby Arora, who built up the B&M discount store chain.

Business people from other ethnic groups include Lord (David) Alliance, born in Iran to a Jewish family, who co-founded textile giant Coats Viyella (now Coats); and Assem Allam, Egyptian-born manufacturer of industrial generators, who also owns Hull City football club. Black and Asian figures have made their name in sport, including Marcus Rashford, Manchester United and England footballer and anti-poverty campaigner, and Leeds-born boxer Nicola

Adams. Cultural figures include Wigan-born poet Lemn Sissay, of Ethiopian heritage.

In politics, Calcutta-born Marxist academic Dipak Nandy studied English literature at the University of Leeds in the 1950s and later became a leading figure in race relations. He was deputy director of the Equal Opportunities Commission, based in Manchester. His daughter, Lisa Nandy, MP for Wigan and shadow secretary of state for levelling up, housing and communities, is a campaigner for the interests of former industrial towns.

One of the most difficult issues has been the child sexual abuse scandals in Rochdale and Rotherham, in which British Pakistani men were convicted of offences against young white girls. The Rochdale case brought to prominence prosecutor Nazir Afzal, who became a campaigner for women's rights and against forced marriage, female genital mutilation and honour killings.

It remains fair to say, though, that almost two thousand years after the Romans, northern England's efforts to integrate ethnic minorities remain a work in progress.

CHAPTER 17

TAINTED WEALTH

On 3 October 1699, Liverpool's first known slave ship, the *Liverpool Merchant*, set sail for Africa, from where it carried 220 enslaved Africans to Barbados.[1] It was a trade to which Britain and Liverpool came late, but from which they were to profit handsomely. Between the mid-fifteenth century and 1870, Europeans are estimated to have carried more than 12 million Africans to slavery in the Americas. Liverpool merchants transported about 1.4 million, or more than 10 per cent.[2]

Wealth generated by this inhuman trade and the sale of goods that slave labour produced helped to turn Liverpool and Bristol into boom towns. Liverpool was dominant for more than half a century until the British slave trade was abolished in 1807. Between 1780 and 1807, Liverpool ships were responsible for 80 per cent of all slaving voyages from British ports and 50 per cent of voyages originating in Europe. A contemporary described Liverpool as 'the metropolis of slavery'.[3] The trade benefited Lancashire's burgeoning cotton textiles industry and profits permeated across the north. Lancaster and Whitehaven took part in the slave trade on a smaller scale. Chester, Preston and Poulton-le-Fylde also sought to get into it by undercutting bigger rivals, though with limited success.[4]

Slavery was common in Britain for centuries before the Norman Conquest and slaves were sometimes exported. Slaves comprised about 10 per cent of England's population in the 1086 Domesday survey,[5] though slavery appears to have died out by 1200. The British were slower than the Portuguese and Spanish to establish colonies in the Americas and were also latecomers to the slave trade. British participation began properly in the 1640s when Caribbean colonies were established in Barbados, St Kitts, Nevis, Antigua, Barbuda, Montserrat and Anguilla. The seizure of Jamaica, which already had a nascent sugar industry, from Spain in 1655 placed Britain in a leading position.[6]

The slave trade north of the equator operated on a triangular basis. Ships carried goods to West Africa including textiles, weapons and alcohol. Captains bartered with slave traders and exchanged these goods for Africans, whom they transported across the Atlantic, a journey known as the 'middle passage', which normally took six to ten weeks. Conditions were dreadful and many died. Africans resisted enslavement and revolts on ships were a common occurrence. Captives were sold to work in plantations, after which ships returned home carrying goods such as sugar, coffee, tobacco and eventually cotton. The whole voyage lasted between nine and twelve months, sometimes longer. The northern trade over time transported nearly seven million Africans. A southern trade, operated bilaterally mainly between Brazil and West Africa, transported almost 5.5 million.[7]

London merchants initially dominated the British trade. They came together as the Company of Royal Adventurers Trading to Africa, which was granted a monopoly in 1660. In 1672 it became the Royal African Company, whose aristocratic investors included Charles II's brother James. The 'Glorious Revolution' of 1688 introduced a more liberal economic policy, which led to the monopoly being rescinded in 1698. Bristol was first to benefit. Liverpool was limited because the Mersey's tidal range meant large ships had to anchor mid-river to avoid beaching at low tide. The answer was to build an enclosed wet dock, which opened in 1715; a further five followed. By 1750, Liverpool was sending more ships to Africa than all other British ports combined.[8]

Reasons for Liverpool's dominance are still debated. Success required a larger outlay of capital than other types of trade, a good network of contacts on the African coast, detailed knowledge of African merchants' requirements and easy access to appropriate trade goods. Liverpool could get textiles from Lancashire, pottery, copper and brass from Staffordshire and Cheshire and guns from Birmingham. It built up expertise and appeared willing to take greater risks by opening up new areas of the African coast for trade. It also developed a more efficient system of payments. A Bristol rival commented that 'the people of Liverpool, in their indiscriminate rage for commerce and for getting money at all events, have nearly engrossed this trade'.[9]

In Liverpool, the trade's financing and organisation was in the hands of a core group of about two hundred merchants, many of whom held public office. Slaving families included the Earles, Tarletons, Hodgsons, Heywoods, Gregsons and Aspinalls. Usually one merchant took charge of organising a voyage and was known as the 'ship's husband'. Ownership of each ship was made up of sixty-four shares, typically distributed among half a dozen investors. There were sometimes small investors, such as the ship's captain. Other merchants supported the trade in various ways – by building ships or supplying goods, provisions and equipment.[10]

The slave trade was lucrative for some. A drunken actor, George Cooke, cried out when booed off stage in Liverpool in 1772: 'I have not come here to be insulted by a set of wretches, there is not a brick in your dirty town but what is cemented by the blood of a negro.'[11] Analysis of 110 voyages organised by merchant William Davenport suggests an average return of almost 11 per cent on his investments, which was better than other businesses. However, some made serious losses as a result of shipwreck, capture by foreign privateers, high mortality or poor management.[12]

Slaving merchants supported local institutions and charities such as schools, hospitals, churches, theatres and libraries. Some built large houses, mainly on the northern outskirts such as Everton, Kirkdale and Walton, or country houses as far afield as the Lake District and Shropshire. Financial benefits spread through every level of society and helped stimulate other sectors of Liverpool's economy, particularly shipbuilding, port facilities and banking. Founders of Liverpool banks, including Arthur and Benjamin Heywood (Arthur Heywood Sons & Co., now part of Barclays) and Thomas Leyland and Richard Bullin (Leyland and Bullin, part of HSBC), were heavily involved in the slave trade as participants and provided credit for other slave traders.[13]

The British movement to abolish the slave trade began as a rumbling of discontent among religious groups in the 1770s and 1780s and then gathered pace. The *Zong* case, which emerged in 1783, shed a shocking light on the slave trade's secrets.[14] In September 1781, the *Zong*, a Liverpool-registered slave ship, sailed from Accra in Ghana with 442 slaves, about twice the number a ship of that size could transport without risking heavy loss of life. After navigational errors, it was running out of water and disease broke out. To ensure some slaves reached Jamaica alive, the crew gradually threw 133 of the sickliest slaves overboard. The case came to national attention only when the *Zong*'s owners filed an insurance claim against loss of 'cargo', demanding £30 for each slave cast overboard. Their insurance underwriters refused to pay. Newspaper reports of this were spotted by Olauda Equiano, an abolitionist and former slave. It was explained in court that the captain had reasoned that, if the slaves died a natural death, it would be the owners' loss, whereas if the slaves were thrown alive into the sea, the loss would be the underwriters'. Lord Mansfield, chief justice, privately admitted that the case 'shocks one very much'; he found against the ship owners.

The abolitionist movement was formally born at a meeting in 1787 when twelve men – nine Quakers and three evangelical Anglicans – formed the Society for Effecting the Abolition of the

Slave Trade.[15] They included Quaker banker and philanthropist Samuel Hoare and Durham-born Granville Sharp, a lawyer. Also present was Thomas Clarkson, author of an influential essay against the slave trade, who became the cause's driving force. He formed an effective partnership with William Wilberforce, MP for Hull (crucially, not a slaving port), who led the parliamentary campaign for twenty years.

These men's hostility to slavery stemmed from their moral and religious views. A number of Enlightenment philosophers and even economists had also condemned the practice. Adam Smith, in *The Wealth of Nations* (1776), suggested that slave labour was less productive than free labour because it artificially constrained individuals from acting in their own interest.[16] Abolitionists mounted an unprecedented campaign of public education, persuasion and political lobbying. It has been calculated that 1.5 million people signed petitions against the slave trade at a time when Britain's population was twelve million.[17] There were boycotts of slave-produced rum and cane sugar. The testimony of former slaves such as Equiano also had an impact.

Unsurprisingly, there was strong opposition in Liverpool, where there were just a few abolitionists including William Roscoe, who became an MP in 1806. When Clarkson visited Liverpool in 1788 as part of his mission to collect evidence, a group of sailors attempted to push him off a pier and he narrowly escaped with his life. Clarkson went on to Manchester, which he found more welcoming – even though it sold £200,000 of goods each year to slave ships, mostly cloth that was traded for slaves, and used slave-grown cotton in its mills. It may have been receptive because its tens of thousands of workers uprooted from the countryside knew what it was like to be strangers. Manchester's campaigners collected a petition with more than ten thousand names, one out of every five people in the city.[18]

The climate became tougher for abolitionists in the 1790s as fear of the French Revolution and repression of radicalism during the war against France, coupled with a bloody slaves' revolt on San

Domingo, the French colony that became Haiti, made it harder to win support. Wilberforce plugged away, putting forward parliamentary motions. Among his adversaries was Colonel Banastre Tarleton, elected an MP for Liverpool in 1790, a dashing hero of the American Revolutionary War. Known as 'Bloody Tarleton' after his troops bayoneted a group of Americans who had surrendered, he was missing two fingers that had been shot off. 'These gave I for king and country!' he would cry, waving his hand at campaign rallies.[19]

Wilberforce was conservative on almost every issue except slavery, which arguably helped to make him listened to by the ruling class. Eventually the Slave Trade Act 1807 was passed, prohibiting the slave trade in the British empire. The last slave ship to leave Britain, the *Eliza*, left Liverpool on 16 August. For the next half-century, Britain's West Africa Squadron attempted to stop slave trading by other nations, with limited success. The navy rescued 150,000 Africans from foreign slaving ships and returned them to Africa, though some were re-enslaved. Over the same period a further three million Africans were transported, mainly to Cuba and Brazil. The last slaving voyages took place to Cuba in the mid-1860s and by 1870 the transatlantic trade had finally ceased.[20]

Abolitionists hoped that ending the British slave trade would lead slavery itself to wither, but that proved optimistic. A renewed campaign was necessary to achieve the Slavery Abolition Act 1833, which abolished slavery in most of the empire. There were strings. Although the enslaved became technically free in 1834, anyone over the age of six was indentured as an apprentice for a further four years. Slave owners were compensated for every slave freed, costing £20 million, equivalent to 40 per cent of annual government expenditure. The largest sum, £106,000, went to Liverpool slave owner Sir John Gladstone, father of the future prime minister.[21] William Gladstone, born in Liverpool to Scottish parents, served four times as premier. As a young politician he joined his father in opposing abolition of slavery, but later he came to see it as a great achievement.

Abolition had little impact on Liverpool's economic fortunes, despite dire warnings from opponents. Most merchants already had diverse interests and were able to adjust. Many continued to trade goods on two sides of the triangle with West Africa and the Caribbean. There was also another opportunity to exploit: importation of slave-produced raw cotton from America's southern states, which increased dramatically. By 1850 raw cotton imports and manufactured cotton goods exports comprised half of Liverpool's trade. It helped to sustain slavery; by then more than 1.8 million enslaved Black people were working on southern America's cotton plantations.[22]

Lancashire had about two and a half thousand cotton mills and factories. Britain's cotton industry directly employed 430,000 people and up to a fifth of the country's population in some way depended on it. The 1860s cotton famine was caused by overproduction at a time of contracting world markets, but it coincided with disruption caused by the American civil war. At least three-quarters of raw cotton came from the US, so Britain was vulnerable when the war broke out in April 1861 and the Union blockaded southern ports. By October 1862 more than half of Lancashire's looms were idle.[23]

People trudged from town to town looking for work. Public works schemes included sewers, canals, parks and roads. Soup kitchens ran out of food. In Stalybridge, in which all but five of the sixty-three factories had been forced to close, a riot broke out and soldiers with fixed bayonets patrolled the streets. There was suffering on a smaller scale in Cheshire, Derbyshire and parts of Scotland and Northern Ireland.[24]

Britain was officially neutral on the war and opinion in Lancashire was divided. Liverpool, unsurprisingly, sided with the southern states and became in effect the Confederacy's European headquarters. The Confederacy established an unofficial embassy there and organised its business affairs through a Liverpool company, Fraser, Trenholm & Co. Liverpool's traders defied neutrality rules and its shipyards built at least thirty-six blockade-running vessels for the south, many crewed by Liverpool seamen.[25]

In the first two years of the war, there was a tendency among all classes in Britain, including Lancashire's mill workers, to support the south. Mill workers formed pro-Confederate clubs, seeing the south as a land where white working-class men were given opportunities denied them in Britain. In April 1862 in Ashton-under-Lyne, 6,000 unemployed mill workers gathered to condemn the northern blockade. The following year 8,000 met in Oldham to support the south. Areas worst affected by the cotton famine tended to be those where support for the Confederacy was strongest.[26] Yet many workers did support the north, even if that meant acting against their immediate economic interests. Towns from which unions and cooperative societies emerged were most strongly anti-slavery, notably Rochdale, where abolitionist societies had been active long before the war. John Bright, Quaker and Liberal MP for Birmingham, whose family owned mills in Rochdale, continued to pay his workers two-thirds of their salaries through the cotton famine.[27]

British opinion shifted against the Confederacy in late 1862 when Abraham Lincoln issued the Emancipation Proclamation, which promised to free southern slaves on 1 January 1863. Up to that point Lincoln had said the war was waged to preserve the Union; after the proclamation, the war was understood in Britain as an armed struggle against slavery. Previously many had accepted the south's presentation of itself as a new nation seeking freedom. Some had even believed that the south was likely to abolish slavery of its own accord. Now the north's campaign seemed a logical extension of Britain's ending of slavery.[28]

In the last weeks of 1862, pro-north meetings were held across the country. The most dramatic was at Manchester's Free Trade Hall on 31 December, which drafted an address to Lincoln saying: 'Heartily do we congratulate you and your country on this your humane and righteous cause.' Lincoln replied in his letter 'To the Working-Men of Manchester': 'Under the circumstances I cannot but regard your decisive utterances on the question as an instance of sublime Christian heroism which has not been surpassed in any age or in any country.' There was even a meeting of three to four thousand people in Liverpool in February 1863 that affirmed support for Lincoln and emancipation.[29]

In January 1865 as the war approached its end, the US Congress passed the thirteenth amendment to the Constitution, abolishing slavery. Later that year, the captain of the Confederate vessel *Shenandoah*, after sinking thirty-eight Union ships, mainly whalers off America's west coast, refused to surrender in an American port but travelled halfway round the world to Liverpool, where on 6 November it surrendered to the Royal Navy in the Mersey between Toxteth and Tranmere. So, bizarrely, the Confederate flag was lowered for the last time 4,000 miles from where the conflict started.[30]

One American slave, James Johnson from North Carolina, escaped amid the confusion of war and made his way to Liverpool, where he was robbed of his few possessions. He walked 'friendless and hopeless' from town to town 'where I took to singing, dancing and rattlebones, which … was easier than begging'. He joined a boxing troupe and performed at fairs around the country, before deciding to stay in Oldham, where he found work and married a cotton worker.[31]

Of course Manchester, like other cities and towns, profited from slave-grown cotton, as it previously had from the slave trade.[32] A big historical argument has been whether profits from Britain's sugar colonies and slave trade made a significant contribution to financing the Industrial Revolution, as Eric Williams argued in *Capitalism and Slavery* (1944). Efforts to calculate slavery's impact have produced varying results, some suggesting that slave trade profits amounted to just 1 per cent of Britain's domestic investment.[33] But Klas Rönnbäck, Professor of Economic History at Gothenburg University, has estimated that by 1800 the triangular trade alone generated 5.7 per cent of UK gross domestic product and the value of all slave-related industries amounted to 11.1 per cent of output.[34]

There were significant connections. The need for trade goods to barter for slaves boosted Lancashire textiles, metal industries and Staffordshire potteries. Development of canals was driven partly by desire to get these goods to Liverpool more quickly. Some slavers invested in other industries, such as Thomas Hodgson, who built a cotton mill in his native Caton in north Lancashire in 1784. Liverpool bankers such as the Heywoods participated in the slave trade and lent money to cotton manufacturers. The trade helped Liverpool and Manchester to develop into important banking centres. A reasonable judgement seems to be that slavery had an important, though not decisive, impact on Britain's long-term economic development.[35] Britain made a lot of money out of slavery and much of it still forms part of the country's wealth in property, loan capital and equity.

CHAPTER 18

IRISH INFLUENCE

For Irish families fleeing the Great Famine of 1845–9, their first sight in Liverpool was an Irish pub run by former champion boxer Jack Langan with an effigy of St Patrick, shamrock in hand, high on its walls.[1] If they managed to evade the 'sharpers' – fraudsters, often themselves Irish, who tried to trick them and leave them penniless – most went on to America. A significant number settled in Liverpool and other northern cities, where soon they found themselves scapegoats for the ills of rapid industrialisation.

The Irish were the largest group of immigrants to Britain until the post-1945 wave from the Caribbean, India and Pakistan. Up to one in four Britons claim Irish ancestry.[2] Their experiences reflect contorted relations between people of Britain and Ireland, who have criss-crossed the Irish Sea throughout history. It was an Irish priest, Aidan, who restored Christianity to Anglo-Saxon Northumbria. Irby on the Wirral peninsula is thought to be a Viking name for 'settlement of the Irish'. Numbers of Irish migrants to Britain accelerated from the late eighteenth century, with many seeking either temporary harvest work or opportunities in industrialising parts of northern England and Scotland. Steamships were introduced in the 1820s, cutting the passage's cost and duration. Before the famine, migrants tended to be from Ireland's prosperous regions; afterwards, most were poor.[3]

The famine, caused by potato blight, doubled Ireland's emigration rate. More than two million departed in little more than a decade, including up to three hundred thousand to Britain.[4] Conditions on ships were often appalling. In 1848, more than seventy passengers suffocated on board the steamer *Londonderry* from Sligo to Liverpool when the crew packed them into a tiny space below deck in a storm.[5] For migrants who survived the crossing, Liverpool offered little except damp cellars and soup kitchens. Many died, some from starvation, but usually of disease.

The term 'Irish fever' became a common epithet to describe the clutch of diseases, especially typhus, that the Irish suffered and spread. During the 'Black '47', William Henry Duncan, medical officer of health, described Liverpool as the 'city of plague'.[6] The scale of arrivals swamped Liverpool's authorities and fed a groundswell of anti-Irish feeling. By 1851 the Irish-born accounted for 22 per cent of Liverpool's population compared with 18 per cent for Glasgow, 13 per cent for Manchester and almost 5 per cent for London.[7] Many arrivals went on to other destinations in Lancashire, Cheshire, Yorkshire and the midlands. Some failed to make it, such as Bridget Callaghan, whose corpse was found beside her crying children, lying under a hedgerow in the village of Knotty Ash, which had been their bed for one rainy night.[8]

The Irish suffered a backlash, prefiguring the experience of later migrant groups in the twentieth century. The influx came in a country already unnerved by urbanisation and social unrest. It had seen the French Revolution of 1789, Napoleonic Wars and failed Irish risings in 1798 and 1803. Of those injured in Manchester's 1819 Peterloo Massacre, an estimated 22 per cent of casualties had Irish names, well above the likely percentage of Irish in the population.[9] Catholic emancipation in 1829, via an act that permitted Catholics to sit in parliament, was resented by many Protestants.

The idea took hold that the Irish were to blame for their own misfortune. They were routinely portrayed as stupid, drunk, violent and content to live in squalor. James Phillips Kay, a Manchester public health doctor and reformer, wrote in a now-infamous 1832 essay: 'The Irish have taught the labouring classes of this country a pernicious lesson … Debased alike by ignorance and pauperism, they have discovered, with the savage, what is the minimum of the means of life, upon which existence may be prolonged … and this secret has been taught the labourers of this country by the Irish.'[10] Not everyone saw things the same way. A registrar in Manchester's Angel Meadow slum district blamed poverty and overcrowding for deaths from disease: 'The houses are very badly ventilated and the unhealthy odour arising from so many persons huddled together in a confined apartment must have a very injurious effect. It cannot be surprising, that while such a state of things exists, the mortality should be so great.'[11]

Concern about the Irish fed into the 'Condition of England' debate that exercised writers such as Benjamin Disraeli and Elizabeth Gaskell. Essayist Thomas Carlyle in 1839 described the Irishman as 'the sorest evil this country has to contend with. In his rags and laughing savagery, he is there to undertake all work that can be done by mere strength of hand and back – for wages that will purchase him potatoes.'[12]

Friedrich Engels, who spent two periods in Manchester, accepted in *The Condition of the Working Class in England* (1845) Carlyle's arguments that the Irish had lowered working-class morals, living standards and wages. He said the Irish were at home with filth and drunkenness, lacked furniture and shared their domestic space with pigs. His views are all the more remarkable for the fact that he set up home with his lover Mary Burns, a second-generation Irish mill worker, and her sister Lizzie. Engels' analysis later became more sophisticated after visiting Ireland with Mary and Lizzie.[13]

By the 1850s, violent reprisals against the Irish were widespread for religious, cultural and economic reasons. Pope Pius IX's recreation in 1850 of the Roman Catholic hierarchy in England, which had been extinguished in Elizabeth I's reign, aroused anti-Catholic feeling among Protestants; it was dubbed the 'Papal Aggression' by

The Times. There were disturbances in towns such as Birkenhead. Rioting in Stockport, near Manchester, in 1852 led to one dead, fifty-one injured and ransacking of a Catholic church.[14] 'No popery' lecturers such as William Murphy made dangerous livings by denouncing popery in towns and villages, some with large Catholic communities. His career ended when in 1871 he was severely beaten in Whitehaven and died a year later.[15]

There were also intra-Irish tensions. Manchester was the scene of the first riot between Irish Catholics and Irish Protestants in Britain in July 1807. A local newspaper reported:

> Monday last a body of Orange-men, as they are termed, paraded in their sashes and favours to hear divine service, being the anniversary of the Battle of the Boyne; when, on their return, a very serious and alarming affray took place between them and a body of the Greens, as they are called ... The conflict was desperate; several were wounded on each side.[16]

Protestants were a significant part of Irish migration to Britain, especially pre-famine, including recession-hit textile workers moving to Scotland, Cumbria and Lancashire; others worked in iron ore and coalmining, metal manufacture and shipbuilding. The Orange Order, through its lodges, provided a drinking club combined with friendly society-type benefits and a vehicle for public expressions of group unity, which helped to align working-class Protestants with Tory Unionism. Orangeism grew strongly in northern England from the 1840s, with a particularly large concentration in Liverpool, which had fifty lodges by the early twentieth century.[17]

Irish male workers were at the frontier of industrial expansion, hewing canals, laying railways and blasting docks. They dominated building trades in towns and cities. Many fell into the worst jobs in textiles, tanning or chemicals, or heavy work such as dock labour. Some became street traders hawking old bones, tools or clothes. The claim that they drove down wages lacks evidence: often the Irish went to areas where labour was in demand, helping the economy to shift its balance quickly. Immigration slowed in the later nineteenth century and there was a wider spread of settlement, including in the mining, shipbuilding and heavy-engineering regions of Durham and Northumberland. Journalist Hugh Heinrick found in 1872 that in Newcastle some of the Irish 'have worked their way to competence, a few to independence, while the great bulk of them find constant employment at good wages, and are in a condition of comparative prosperity'.[18]

There was workplace tension as the Irish reached into many industrial areas. During a cotton strike at Preston in 1854, employers imported Irish hands as blackleg labour; after the strike, some children that had been imported from a Belfast factory were shipped to poverty in Dublin.[19] Some of the worst fighting was among railway builders in northern England and Scotland during the 1840s, when navvies were laying north–south lines. At Penrith, a riot began when an Irish navvy allegedly ignored his English ganger's order to use a shovel and not his pick. The Irish retaliated, leading 2,000 Englishmen to attack them before the yeomanry restored order.[20] The Irish faced many forms of workplace prejudice, including job advertisements specifying 'no Irish need apply'.

One unusual feature of Irish emigration was the high number of females. Numbers of men and women departing were roughly equal during the nineteenth century; by the century's end, and between the world wars, women accounted for the larger share. During the famine era families migrated; later, migrants were more often single. Some women found work in mill towns such as Preston and Oldham. In Barrow-in-Furness in the 1870s, where iron, steel and ships attracted thousands of Irish males, local industrialists also developed flax and jute mills to provide work for women so as to hold on to their male workers. Around the country, poor women and widows took in washing. Many women did home-based work such as making pegs or brushes or dressmaking. Some ran lodging houses; these had a bad reputation for disease, though things improved after legislation set standards and inspection regimes. Even the better classes of women's work were only a short step from domestic-type chores: nurses, governesses, cooks and teaching assistants. Irish women were unfairly disparaged as bad household managers, as likely to drink excessively as the men and in some cases wilder.[21]

Sharon Lambert, who interviewed women who migrated to Lancashire in the twentieth century, found that most moved for a mix of social and economic reasons. Farm incomes were not enough to support them and they did not want to be a burden. Their remittances often paid for younger siblings' education. They tended to go to places where relatives were already living. They were trying to help their families, not to escape family control.[22]

Irish migrants in the nineteenth century embraced a bewildering variety of social and political movements, initially including the Society of United Irishmen, which sought republican government in an independent Ireland, and Ribbonism, a Catholic secret society. There was rivalry between Daniel O'Connell, a moderate nationalist who wanted to restore an Irish parliament through repeal of the 1800 Acts of Union, and Chartist leader Feargus O'Connor. The repeal and Chartist movements came together briefly in a meeting at Manchester Free Trade Hall in 1848, once O'Connell was dead. Another failed Irish nationalist uprising took place that year, led by the Young Ireland group.

Then came the Fenians, precursor of the modern-day Irish Republican Army. The Irish Republican Brotherhood, as the Fenians (from *Fianna*, mythological warriors) were originally known, was founded in Dublin in 1858; it had an American arm called the Fenian Brotherhood. It quickly spread among migrant communities. In February 1867, Fenians made a botched effort to seize the arsenal at Chester Castle. Young Irishmen travelled from Liverpool, Manchester, Preston and Halifax, but the plan was scuppered by an informant.[23]

In November 1867, Fenians in Manchester launched a daring raid on a police van to rescue two prominent prisoners, IRB chief executive Thomas J. Kelly and his aide Timothy Deasy, as they were moved across the city. Shots were fired and a police officer, Sergeant Charles Brett, was killed. The prisoners escaped: Kelly hid in a water cistern and swapped clothes with a priest. He and Deasy were sheltered by sympathisers and eventually they made it to New York. After a trial in Manchester, three men involved – William Allen, Michael Larkin and Michael O'Brien – were hanged. These were commemorated for decades as the 'Manchester Martyrs'. A widespread bombing campaign feared by the authorities never happened, however, and many Irish communities disavowed Fenianism.[24]

In the 1870s the constitutional home rule movement emerged, led by Irish MPs at Westminster. The Home Rule Confederation of Great Britain spread quickly in northern England; Bradford alone had six branches. The confederation was replaced by the Land League after unrest over a bad harvest in Ireland in 1879. In a feverish atmosphere, American Fenians bombed Liverpool town hall in 1881.[25] The Land League was succeeded in 1882 by the Irish National League, founded by Charles Stewart Parnell. Journalist T.P. O'Connor became MP for the Liverpool Scotland constituency in 1885 and held it until his death in 1929, the only constituency outside Ireland ever to return an Irish nationalist party MP. Hopes for home rule rose when William Gladstone's Liberal government introduced the first home rule bill in 1886, but it was defeated in the Commons. A second bill was defeated in the Lords in 1893. A third bill was passed in 1914 shortly after the outbreak of war, but implementation was suspended until the war's conclusion.

Hard-line nationalism revived in the early twentieth century and the 1916 Easter Rising galvanised radicals. By 1918 there was an extensive network for trafficking arms via the Clyde and Mersey to Ireland. Éamon de Valera, president of Sinn Féin, which won three-quarters of Irish seats in the 1918 election, was sprung from Lincoln jail and hid in Manchester before returning to Ireland. The Irish Republican Army, the army of the newly declared Irish Republic, waged a guerrilla war against Britain from 1919 to 1921.

IRA units attacked targets on Tyneside and in County Durham and set off fires in Liverpool. Factories, hotels and warehouses were attacked in Manchester.[26] A treaty was reached and the Irish Free State was created in 1922, with Northern Ireland opting out.

Militants opposed to partition won control of the IRA in the 1930s, after which a bombing campaign was mounted in Britain in 1939–40, including attacks in Manchester, Liverpool and Blackpool. Unlike the earlier campaign, this was carried out by outsiders from Ireland rather than by people from local communities. It was the last concerted attack against Britain until Northern Ireland's Troubles started in the 1970s.[27]

Emigration to Britain rose in the interwar period, partly as a result of US immigration controls. Many also sought to escape hardship caused by protectionist policies of de Valera's Fianna Fáil ('Soldiers of Destiny') government, which took office in 1932 and imposed tariffs on imported goods, mainly from Britain, in an effort to make Ireland agriculturally and industrially self-sufficient. Insofar as these had anti-British motives, it was ironic that they provoked more people to seek sanctuary in Britain. As a woman called Maura, who came to Morecambe in 1945 to work as a chambermaid, put it: 'You were sort o' taught to hate England and then sent here.'[28] Once again, in the 1920s and 1930s, the Irish found themselves blamed for scarcity of work in Britain, reawakening old prejudices. J.B. Priestley wrote in *English Journey* (1934) that the Irish in Liverpool 'have settled in the nearest poor quarter and turned it into a slum, or, finding a slum, have promptly settled down to out-slum it. And this, in spite of the fact that nowadays being an Irish Roman Catholic is more likely to find a man a job than to keep him out of one.'[29] The demand of post-war reconstruction in the 1940s and 1950s attracted still more Irish into Britain.

The Irish have given much to northern England, culturally, economically and personally. Despite all these strains, Irish migrants have managed to integrate, yet at the same time retain a strong sense of Irishness.[30] They have felt the pressure at times of conflict, particularly during the thirty-year Troubles. This included the Provisional IRA's 1993 bomb attack in Warrington, which killed two children and injured fifty-six people, and the 1996 Manchester attack, the biggest bomb detonated in Britain since the Second World War, in which 200 were injured but amazingly there were no fatalities. Many people of Irish extraction have had generations to adapt to British life. For some, though, there lingers a sense of not wholly belonging to English or Irish society.

THE VICTORIAN
AGE

CHAPTER 19

THE GREAT CITIES

Newcastle's neoclassical Grey Street, built in the 1830s just as Victoria became queen, has many admirers. William Gladstone described it on a visit in 1862 as 'our best modern street'. Known nowadays for bars and restaurants as well as architecture, it was voted 'best street in the UK' by BBC Radio 4 listeners in 2010. Grey Street forms part of the magnificent town centre created by developer Richard Grainger, which prompted Nikolaus Pevsner to describe Newcastle as 'the best designed Victorian town in England'.[1]

Classicism gradually gave way to an exuberant cacophony of styles as the merchants and manufacturers who built Britain's nineteenth-century cities set out to demonstrate that they were not simply money-making philistines. Temple Works, John Marshall's Egyptian-style flax-spinning factory in Leeds, modelled on the temple of Horus at Edfu, looks as startling and incongruous today as it did when built in 1840. The city's castle-like Armley Gaol (1847) is a brooding example of the revival of medieval Gothic, the dominant early Victorian idiom. Liverpool's St George's Hall (1854) is one of the world's finest neo-Grecian buildings. Manchester's cotton merchants built warehouses resembling *palazzi* of Renaissance Florence. Its town hall (1877), designed by Alfred Waterhouse, a

Liverpool-born Quaker, mixes elements of English medieval and Venetian Gothic styles.

'Our age is pre-eminently the age of great cities,' wrote Robert Vaughan, president of Lancashire Independent College, Manchester, in 1843.[2] In 1800, there were no cities or towns in England and Wales outside London with a population of 100,000 or more; when Victoria came to the throne in 1837 there were five; by 1891 there were twenty-three.[3] As Asa Briggs put it: 'The building of the cities was a characteristic Victorian achievement, impressive in scale, creating new opportunities but also providing massive new problems.'[4] Would-be merchant princes aimed to marry commerce with culture and civilisation, but were slow to tackle squalor that accompanied urbanisation.

Humankind had never experienced the modern city and many were bewildered and horrified. An 1843 Select Committee on Smoke Prevention described how Manchester's 'nearly 500 chimneys discharging masses of the densest smoke' rendered the air 'visibly impure, and no doubt unhealthy, abounding in soot, soiling the clothing and furniture of the inhabitants'.[5] French social commentator Alexis de Tocqueville called it 'this new Hades'.[6] Rural migrants kept pigs, cows and horses in city centres. Rivers and canals in places such as Bradford and Leeds were clogged with industrial waste and human excrement. Charles Thackrah, a Leeds surgeon, said that a terrible diet, poor housing, long working hours and industrial poisoning were producing a 'small, sicky, pallid, thin … degenerate race – human beings stunted, enfeebled, and depraved'.[7] Cities were blamed for crime, irreligion, promiscuity, loneliness and despair.

The backlash prompted a yearning for the supposed simplicity of medieval times, an infeasibly idyllic 'merrie England'. Sir Walter Scott's *Ivanhoe* (1819), a tale of love, chivalry, the crusades and a damsel in distress, was a runaway success. Augustus Pugin, a Catholic architect, led the revival of Gothic style, which began to change the face of the Victorian city. Art critic John Ruskin championed a secular Gothic in the style of medieval Venice, which became widely applied to courthouses, town halls and athenaeums, though he was later horrified by pseudo-Venetian designs – 'the accursed Frankenstein monsters of, *in*directly, my own making'.[8]

The industrial city's defenders fought back, notably Whig historian Thomas Babington Macaulay, who mocked the notion of merrie England and argued that urban mortality rates were falling (questionable as regards inner-city life expectancy), wealth spreading and employment booming.[9] The *Manchester Guardian*, founded after the Peterloo Massacre, highlighted the 'grinding merciless oppression' of the Middle Ages and urged enthusiasts for the barbaric past to feel profoundly thankful their lot 'had been cast in the nineteenth century, rather than in the twelfth'.[10]

The cities' rise was fostered by the growth of middle-class professionals, merchants, industrialists and retailers. They tended to be Whig-Liberal and believed in low taxes, a small state and *laissez-faire* economics. Liberals often favoured Italianate architecture while Tories preferred Gothic. Many middle-class city dwellers were nonconformist, the largest number being the various types of Methodist. Unitarians, who believe that God is one entity rather than a trinity, were especially influential in northern cities. Nonconformists, with their chapels, shaped not only cities' appearance but also how people saw themselves and their society.

Dissenters' emphasis on personal liberty and free association encouraged the growth of a public sphere outside the state's control, including clubs, institutes, mutual societies, life assurance societies and other self-help groups. Literary and philosophical societies (Manchester 1781, Newcastle 1793, Liverpool 1812, Leeds 1819, Sheffield 1822) catered to the elite and had a focus on science. Mechanics' Institutes, pioneered in Glasgow, became the most popular institution of the Victorian city and were transported round the English-speaking world. Initially their middle-class founders aimed to spread knowledge to artisans while instilling in them the virtues of capitalism, personal industry and private property. But as the working classes began to take control, they shaped their own agenda. By 1850, there were 700 Mechanics' Institutes and related societies in Lancashire and Yorkshire alone.[11]

Towns and cities, controlled largely by unelected Tory oligarchies, fumbled their way towards democracy. The Municipal Corporations Act 1835 enabled the creation of a system of municipal boroughs to be governed by councils elected by ratepayers. Decentralisation and municipal self-government were hailed as embodying the spirit of Anglo-Saxon independence. The drawback was that city authorities were reluctant to tackle social problems, leading to continued decline in public health during the first half of the century.

Manchester was subject to a fierce battle over incorporation.[12] The town was governed by five separate bodies: the court leet (a medieval survival responsible to the lord of the manor); churchwardens and overseers; police and improvement commissioners; surveyors of highways; and justices of the peace. It had different police forces for day and night. Opposition to an elected corporation came from Tories, who feared losing to Whigs, and radicals angry with the Whigs over Poor Law changes.

There were petitions for and against the measure. The one against it apparently had three times as many signatories as the one in favour, but Captain Jebb, the civil servant responsible for advising the Privy Council on incorporation, weeded out dubious signatures and a charter was granted to create the new borough. Tories, claiming the outcome had been manipulated, boycotted the first elections in 1838. The two sides backed different appointees as borough coroner, who even started carrying out rival autopsies of the same bodies. There were years of legal wangles before the charter was finally established in law in 1842.

Briggs described Manchester as the 'shock city of the 1840s', attracting visitors from all countries, who saw in it a foretaste of the world's future.[13] Its population had increased sixfold in sixty years. Poet Robert Southey, a critic of industrialisation, said its smoke-blackened buildings were 'as large as convents without their antiquity, without their beauty, without their holiness'.[14] A character in Benjamin Disraeli's novel *Coningsby* (1844) says: 'It is the philosopher alone who can conceive the grandeur of Manchester and the immensity of its future.'[15]

Manchester's political influence reached a peak in the 1840s as Richard Cobden and John Bright led their successful campaign against the Corn Laws. Manchester was, however, half-hearted about the Manchester school of free-market economics. In 1841, the city chose a Suffolk squire as parliamentary candidate rather than Cobden, who became MP for Stockport. Bright's effigy was burned in Manchester (where he was MP from 1847) for his unpopular stance against the Crimean War and he was defeated at the 1857 general election. A few months later he became MP for Birmingham, a position he held for more than thirty years.

It took Manchester sixty years to sort out sanitation problems.[16] The council defended the system of privy midden toilets, from which filth soaked into surrounding soil, and resisted water closets. A sewage treatment works was not built until 1904. It took until 1874 to appoint factory chimney inspectors. The city in effect outlawed back-to-back housing in 1844, more than eighty years ahead of national legislation, and commercial development destroyed many notorious slums. But private-sector housebuilding did not keep pace, so people moved to new slums in even more overcrowded conditions.

Sensitive to charges of philistinism, Manchester in 1857 staged the Art Treasures Exhibition, one of the most impressive collections of art works ever assembled in one place. Under one glass roof at Old Trafford were 1,800 paintings including ones by Michelangelo, Raphael, Van Dyck, Turner, Constable, Holbein, Titian and Giotto along with 16,000 objects such as glass, porcelain and fine furniture. More than 1.3 million visitors attended. The *Illustrated London News* said Manchester now 'hurls back on her detractors the charge that she is too deeply absorbed in the pursuit of material wealth to devote her energies to the finer arts'. Ruskin, invited to give a lecture, was less impressed, saying the purpose was simply to encourage the production of works of art for sale.[17]

Music for the exhibition was provided by Charles Hallé (born Karl Halle), a German who had fled the 1848 revolution. He created a new orchestra and gave daily concerts. After the exhibition, a series of weekly concerts was inaugurated in 1858 and the orchestra that took Hallé's name became one of the finest in Europe. Manchester achieved city status in 1853. Other developments included Owens College, now the University of Manchester, the John Rylands Library and Waterhouse's town hall, whose great hall houses Ford Madox Brown's cycle of frescoes extolling the city's history. However, in terms of developing effective public administration, the city was less ground-breaking. As Briggs put it: 'Manchester's story lacked the excitement and public appeal of the story of [Joseph] Chamberlain's Birmingham.'[18]

Bradford grew at a startling rate as steam power turned it into 'Worstedopolis', the world centre of worsted production. There had been one mill in Bradford in 1801 and by 1841 there were sixty-seven.[19] As in Manchester, there was opposition to creating an elected borough council. This was not achieved until 1847, after a battle of petitions. A report to the Health of Towns Commission in 1844 condemned the squalor of the streets, with open sewers and rubbish heaps that were removed infrequently by local pig feeders.[20] Housing was poor and overcrowded. Things improved after 1850, but slowly and expensively. The corporation bought out the water-works company in 1854 and over the next half-century spent almost £3 million on providing water. Thirty miles of sewers were built by 1870. Slum clearance from 1877 helped to make Bradford healthier; the death rate dropped in later years of Victoria's reign.[21]

Samuel Smith, one of Bradford's first aldermen, headed the private subscription for a 'huge public concert hall'. St George's Hall opened in 1853 complete with Corinthian pillars, arched windows, a public hall and gallery to accommodate more than three thousand people. Smith said it would meet the needs not only of 'mercantile men' but also of operatives who would, after attending concerts, return to their homes 'elevated and refreshed, rising in the morning to their daily toil without headache and without regret'.[22] The Wool Exchange opened in 1867 in Venetian Gothic style, to the dismay of Ruskin, who thought it imitated the aesthetic but not the spiritual conditions of medieval society. Today it is a branch of Waterstones. The town hall opened in 1873 with Gothic façades enclosing stone statues of thirty-four English monarchs, overshadowed by a 200-foot clock tower copied from the campanile of the Palazzo Vecchio in Florence.[23]

Leeds evoked similarly mixed feelings. Charles Dickens described it on separate occasions as a 'great town' and 'a beastly place, one of the nastiest places I know'.[24] It was a town with many trades, more varied in its economy than Bradford. Its engineering industry grew strongly. Later in the century it acquired a ready-made clothing industry in 300 small workshops. A Tory oligarchy ran the city before the 1835 municipal reforms, but thereafter a Liberal hegemony was established for sixty years. Economic growth drew in outsiders who were often dissenters in religion and Liberal in politics, such as Preston-born Edward Baines, editor and proprietor of the *Leeds Mercury*.

Overcrowding was a problem. In notorious Boot and Shoe Yard, 341 people were reported to be living in fifty-seven rooms in 1839; on one occasion, seventy cartloads of manure had to be removed.[25] A sewerage network was built in 1850–62, but was far from comprehensive. The city resisted the introduction of water closets and fought to be able to build back-to-back houses until 1909. Leeds was spasmodic in acting to deal with its social problems, but its death rate began to decline in the 1870s, in line with the national pattern.

Not to be outdone by Bradford, which had just built St George's Hall, Leeds planned one of the largest town halls in Britain, combining law courts, council chamber, offices, a public hall and ceremonial rooms. It was designed in classical style by Cuthbert Brodrick, a little-known young architect from Hull. The building, completed in 1858, cost much more than original estimates because of rising prices and constant additions. John Heaton, a doctor who championed the project, believed that

> if a noble municipal palace that might fairly vie with some of the best Town Halls of the Continent were to be erected in the middle of their hitherto squalid and unbeautiful town, it would become a practical admonition to the populace of the value of beauty and art, and in course of time men would learn to live up to it.[26]

Leeds town hall became a model for civic buildings across Britain and the empire. The structure is notable for its façade, massive proportions, flight of twenty steps and stone lions. It inspired town halls in Bolton, Morley and Portsmouth along with public buildings in Melbourne, Adelaide, Cape Town and Durban.

Social conditions in Sheffield were parlous by mid-century. A reporter for *The Builder*, an architecture journal, wrote in 1861: 'These rivers ... are polluted with dirt, dust, dung, and carrion, the embankments are ragged and ruined; here and there overhung with privies; and often the site of ash and offal heaps – most desolate and sickening objects.' Sheffield was 'a town where authority is so divided ... that virtually there is no authority at all'.[27] Problems caused by explosive population growth had mounted in the 1850s. In the second half of the century, Sheffield's death rates from contagious diseases were among the country's highest.

The corporation was powerless to tackle its smoke problem and slow to meet the challenge of public health. In the worst parts of town, some privies were shared by sixty people. One reporter counted twenty-eight decomposing dogs in the river at Ball Street Bridge. The corporation began to install an effective sewage disposal system only in 1884. There was progress, however: an 1883 survey found that, although some quarters remained filthy and neglected, they were no longer characteristic of all working-class districts. Sheffield suffered a disaster in 1864 when the embankment of Dale Dyke reservoir collapsed. Flood waters poured down the Don valley, killing 240 people and 693 animals.[28]

Until about 1860, Sheffield's politics were strongly Liberal and radical. Later, it became more closely contested. The Conservatives gained their first MP in 1880 and held a narrow lead on the borough council during the 1880s and early 1890s. Sheffield finally got round to building a Renaissance-style town hall to compare with other northern cities, opened by Queen Victoria in 1897.[29]

Newcastle, despite Grainger Town's grandeur, was not spared social problems. A report in 1845 by physician D.R. Reid said living conditions in poor areas were damp and squalid inside and no better outside, where 'filth and refuse accumulate in the lanes and vacant corners'. Building regulations were virtually non-existent and any that were in place were widely ignored. Newcastle faced cholera outbreaks in the 1830s, 1848 and 1853; in the latter, at least one and a half thousand died.[30]

The city's most notable politician in the latter half of the nineteenth century was Joseph Cowen.[31] He was Liberal MP for Newcastle, as had been his father, a self-made colliery owner of the same name. Cowen Junior promoted radical, internationalist views via his proprietorship of the *Newcastle Daily Chronicle*. He was a supporter of Irish home rule and friend of European nationalists and revolutionaries. Italy's Giuseppe Garibaldi visited him on Tyneside to raise funds and volunteers to fight for Italian unification. Cowen set up the Northern Reform Union to campaign for universal male suffrage.

Newcastle's High Level Bridge, designed by Robert Stephenson, was built in 1849. Central Station, designed by John Dobson, opened a year later. Dobson argued that railway stations, as 'structures constantly seen by thousands and tens thousands of persons', might do much 'towards improving the taste of the public'.[32] In 1876 a Swing Bridge was built and paid for by arms manufacturer

William Armstrong, allowing sizeable ships to pass up-river. Novelist William Clark Russell wrote, after visiting the Tyne in the 1880s: 'Who says there is no beauty nor poetry in coal and grime and smoke, in huddled tenements, high chimneys, and such things?'[33]

Liverpool, already a major trading port whose activities included slavery, began the nineteenth century with advantages that other cities lacked, but it had to cope with an influx of poor Irish migrants fleeing the Great Famine in the 1840s. Even in 1835, de Tocqueville had written: 'Liverpool is a beautiful town. Poverty is almost as great as it is at Manchester. Fifty thousand poor people live in cellars. Sixty thousand Irish Catholics.'[34]

Municipal reforms of 1835 brought in an elected council, dominated at first by liberal capitalists who initiated programmes of educational, sanitary and health reform.[35] Their inspiration was William Roscoe, a self-taught Unitarian lawyer and banker who in a brief spell as Whig MP had been among those who ended the slave trade in 1807. An enthusiast for the Italian Renaissance, Roscoe's *Life of Lorenzo de' Medici, Called the Magnificent* won international acclaim. Sadly for him, Roscoe's collection of High Renaissance art had to be sold when a bank with which he was connected went bust. Many of the paintings remained in Liverpool and later reached the Walker Art Gallery.

The merchant elite, however, never got to fulfil Roscoe's vision of uniting commerce and culture in a Florence of the north. The Tories were back in power by 1841 and established their hegemony based on a popular platform of Protestantism and protectionism. From then until the 1970s, more than a century later, Conservatives dominated the city council and often held more than half of Liverpool's parliamentary constituencies. In part this was built on the Protestant majority's fear of Irish Catholic migrants, but the Tories were concerned to put working-class interests first and developed a Tory version of municipal socialism.[36]

A key Tory figure was Samuel Holme, local builder and first president of the Liverpool Tradesmen's Conservative Association. Like

Roscoe and the merchants, Holme admired the spirit of the 'commercial princes of Italy', but also wanted to see the latest British engineering and architectural skills applied. In fact it was neoclassical Greek rather than Italian Renaissance architecture that came to dominate Liverpool, with buildings such as the 1815 Wellington Rooms and John Foster's 1828 Custom House. St George's Hall came about when separate competitions to design a concert hall and assize court were both won by a young man called Harvey Lonsdale Elmes; the schemes were brought under one roof. Elmes died in 1847, before it was completed. When the hall opened in 1854, Queen Victoria declared it 'worthy of ancient Athens'.[37]

Classicism continued to thrive in Liverpool long after it had fallen from fashion in other cities. St George's Hall became the centrepiece of neoclassical buildings including the William Brown Library, Picton Reading Room and Walker Art Gallery. At the start of the twentieth century, when the dockside offices of Royal Liver, Cunard and the port of Liverpool were created, they became popularly known as the 'Three Graces', Liverpool's architectural answer to the original Three Graces, Aglaia, Euphrosyne and Thalia, of fifth-century Athens.

As the century wore on, conditions in the north's cities improved along with living standards, though there was waste and confusion before there was effective control. The world's attention moved southwards, first to Chamberlain's Birmingham in the 1870s with its philosophy of municipal activism and improvement (Joseph Chamberlain, as mayor, created a municipal gas company and water department and spearheaded slum clearance). London's population expanded dramatically from 2.5 million in 1851 to 6.5 million in 1901, almost one-fifth of the population of England and Wales.[38] It became the pre-eminent global city, swollen by internal and international migration. Its problems of overcrowding, criminality and child sexual exploitation created the same concern that northern cities had generated. Northern cities never achieved political influence commensurate with their industrial strength. By the 1890s, the capital was driving the country's politics and economics. Cities started to look more alike – same working-class housing, same suburbs. Local newspapers gave ground to national ones. National advertising increased and people began buying the same branded goods.

The early twentieth century brought a reaction against all things Victorian, including cities. George Bernard Shaw suggested that all British cities would have to be pulled down and built again if people were to live in a worthy environment.[39] Later in the century, the cities became valued once more, helped by Sir John Betjeman's passionate defence of Victorian architecture. At their worst, the north's cities were a 'new Hades' of sickness and death. At their best they were a bold expression of human ingenuity, enterprise and new ways of living together.

CHAPTER 20

FRIENDS OR RIVALS

In the early nineteenth century, 'Liverpool gentlemen' in insurance, finance and shipping are said to have looked down on 'Manchester men' who earned their living from smoky, dirty cotton manufacturing. Victorian Bradford and Leeds competed for civic and commercial glory. Sheffield used to see itself as morally superior to Leeds, contrasting its steel industry with the latter's easy-profit tailoring trade: '*We* have to work hard to make our money.'[1] North-easterners have at various times labelled their neighbours with derogatory terms such as 'Monkey-Hangers', (Hartlepool residents), 'Pit-Yackers' (Northumberland and Durham miners), 'Sand-Dancers' (South Shields) and 'Smog Monsters' (Middlesbrough and Teesside). Usually, victims appropriate the offending term themselves.

Cities have squabbled ever since Athens squared up to Sparta. Enmity between Melbourne and Sydney was so intense that neither became Australia's capital. The Madrid–Barcelona rivalry is rooted in football, regionalism and civil war divisions. Others include Rome v. Milan, Dallas v. Houston, Toronto v. Montreal and Beijing v. Shanghai. The UK has plenty of notable ones, including Glasgow v. Edinburgh. And of course, everyone resents London.

Football and other team sports have given these rivalries a particular intensity. Usually it is amicable banter, though that between supporters of Liverpool and Manchester United, for long vying to be the top club, has been spicy. In the high-unemployment 1980s, Old Trafford's Stretford End taunted Liverpudlians with 'Sign on, sign on, and you'll never get a job.' Later, Anfield terraces responded with 'There's only one Harold Shipman', referring to the Greater Manchester mass murderer; or 'Always look on the runway for ice', a reference to the Munich air disaster, to the tune of *Monty Python's* 'Always look on the bright side of life'.

Rivalry between Lancashire and Yorkshire, in theory the broadest and longest-established, is at times so jovial that it can seem like a mutual admiration society. It is known as the Wars of the Roses, even though that conflict had been between royal houses rather than between the counties. For centuries there was not much contest: until the Industrial Revolution, Yorkshire was richer and Lancashire one of England's poorest counties. By the Victorian era, the cotton industry had boosted the Lancastrian population and self-confidence. County cricket became popular and encapsulated the contest. Up until then, Yorkshire was not only bigger and richer than other northern counties but better connected to the centre of power and tied into the North Sea mercantile community. The historic high road between London and Scotland skirted Lancashire: it went from Stamford to Doncaster, though the Vale of York to Scotch Corner; then one branch turned north-west through the Stainmore pass to Appleby, Penrith and Carlisle. Lancashire was bypassed and isolated.

When the Romans advanced northwards, they did so on both sides of the Pennines, but they were more interested in places further east and north than Lancashire. They treated it like a transit area, though they did build towns, forts and camps at places such as Ribchester, Lancaster and Manchester, along with roads.[2] The Domesday Book, the result of a 1086 survey, records no administrative unit called 'Lancashire'. What is now south Lancashire is described *as inter Ripam et Mersham* ('between the Ribble and the Mersey') and is written up at the end of the Cheshire section, while the area north of the Ribble, together with south Westmorland and the Millom peninsula, is described as 'the king's lands in Yorkshire'.[3] Lancashire was sparsely populated and much of the land was uncultivated moss, heath and woodland.

Lancashire was accepted as a county only when a royal exchequer official, in the audit for 1181–2, wrote out a separate parchment under the heading *Lancastra quia non erat ei locus in Northumberland*: 'Lancaster, because there is no place for it in Northumberland.'[4] Official documents called it the 'county of Lancaster', then it became Lancastershire or Lancashire. The title Duke of Lancaster has been held by the reigning monarch since Henry IV's time – hence the loyal toast to 'Her Majesty, Duke of Lancaster'.

If medieval tax statistics are believed, Lancashire was thirty-eighth out of thirty-eight counties measured by personal property assessed for tax in 1334. Some argue that distance from London meant that tax gathering was less efficient, with higher levels of avoidance or evasion, but the broad picture was probably accurate. It remained thirty-eighth in 1515.[5]

It is uncertain how far the Lancastrian rose – possibly *Rosa gallica*, more pink than red – was used during the Wars of the Roses, but it later came to be adopted as the county's cricket cap badge. The Yorkist white rose also became a cap badge. In 1867 the first Roses match was staged at Whalley, which Yorkshire won by five wickets.[6] Lord Hawke, Yorkshire captain from 1883 to 1910, described Roses matches as a 'jolly rivalry'. The fixture was at its peak between the world wars. Neville Cardus wrote: 'At Old Trafford, in 1926, 78,617 Lancashire and Yorkshire folk paid to watch this annual holiday argument, and consumed almost as many pork pies … In those years, dwellers in Lancashire and Yorkshire regarded the Roses match second in importance and family pride to none; England v Australia came second.'[7]

People often seek to define local identities against an 'other'. Lancashire fashioned a self-image as softer, friendlier and more generous than its eastern neighbour. Yorkshire defined itself defiantly against all-comers. James Burnley, a nineteenth-century writer born in Shipley, said the county was 'the most birthproud member of the human race'. Yorkshire people have become adept at paying themselves backhanded compliments, as in the Yorkshire prayer:

Hear all, see all, say nowt.
Eat all, drink all, pay nowt,
and if thy ever dus owt for nowt,
All-us do it for thee-sen.

In perhaps the most famous piece of Yorkshire mockery, the *Monty Python* 'Four Yorkshiremen' sketch (first seen in *At Last It's the 1948 Show*), in which four Yorkshiremen outdo each other in ludicrous one-upmanship about their childhood privations, one part is played by Sheffield-born Michael Palin.[8]

Sometimes Lancashire and Yorkshire saw themselves as sister counties. Single-county societies were the norm among emigrants, but a Lancashire and Yorkshire Society was formed in Otago, New Zealand, in 1903, and 1891 had seen the formation of the Natal Yorkshire and Lancashire Association in South Africa. At the latter's 1894 dinner, the chairman, Lancastrian J.B. Cottam, said the 'warfare of their fathers had given place to that rivalry in commerce, arts, science, mechanics which had made the two counties so enormously great'. Guest speaker William Hartley, from Yorkshire, summed up

those characteristics of a Yorkshireman which had made him a man of the world, go where he would, as a straightforward, outspoken, determined man ... Wherever they had found him they had found the same stubbornness of character, the same determination to do the right, to pity the distress, and help on the needy in whatever country they found it. He was ... unique in that particular.[9]

The most notable 'Yorkshireman of the world' was perhaps explorer Captain James Cook, from the North Riding, who sailed thousands of miles across largely uncharted areas in three voyages in the Pacific Ocean between 1768 and 1779, making the first recorded European contact with Australia's eastern coast and the Hawaiian Islands and the first recorded circumnavigation of New Zealand. He was killed while trying to detain the ruling chief of Hawaii in order to reclaim a cutter taken from one of his ships after his crew took wood from a burial ground.

This friendly contest remains uneven, insofar as there appear to be far more Lancashire jokes about Yorkshire than vice versa. Examples include: 'A Yorkshireman is a Scotsman with the generosity squeezed out'; and 'There's no point in asking a man whether he's from Yorkshire, because if he is, he will already have told you.' The rivalry has occasionally become sharper, notably after local government reorganisation in 1974 when Yorkshire lost territory to other counties and boroughs, including Saddleworth to Oldham, in Greater Manchester. Many in Saddleworth still celebrate Yorkshire Day on 1 August and defiantly give 'West Riding of Yorkshire' as their address.

There was a bust-up in 1918 when Yorkshire fish friers formed a rival association, the Northern Counties Federation of Fish Friers, breaking away from the National Federation of Fish Friers. Yorkshire friers used beef dripping, while many Lancashire friers favoured vegetable oil. Faced with shortages of oils and fats, Yorkshire friers felt the NFFF's secretary, an abrasive Lancastrian called William Loftas, was not doing enough to support their cause.[10]

There have been other approaches. Rugby League's War of the Roses was held from 1895 until 2003. The term also applies to contests between Manchester United and Leeds United and to games between other east Lancashire and west Yorkshire football clubs. The Roses Tournament is an annual sports contest between students of the universities of York and Lancaster. In the annual World Black Pudding Throwing Championships in Ramsbottom,

Greater Manchester, contestants lob black puddings to knock off as many Yorkshire puddings as possible from a 20-foot (6-metre) platform.

Rivalry between Liverpool and Manchester, meanwhile, ebbs and flows. At the turn of the nineteenth century, Liverpool was vaunting its status as a commercial centre second only to London, 'the first town in the kingdom in point of size and importance, the Metropolis excepted'.[11] In contrasting 'Liverpool gentlemen' with 'Manchester men' it was seeking to define itself against industrial Manchester. That was partly accurate, in that by 1802 Manchester had more than fifty cotton-spinning mills,[12] but Manchester also developed rapidly as a commercial city. Manchester and Newcastle also both established literary and philosophical societies before Liverpool.

Liverpool prided itself on being a global city. As Thomas Baines' *History of the Commerce and Town of Liverpool* put it in 1852: 'The commerce of Liverpool extends to every port of any importance in every quarter of the globe. In this respect it far surpasses the commerce of any city of which we have record from past times, as Tyre, Venice, Genoa, Amsterdam, or Antwerp, and fully equals, if it does not surpass, that of London and New York.'[13]

Liverpool saw itself as in the north of England, but not of it, a view that still persists ('Scouse not English', people say). As entrepreneur Michael Swerdlow put it: 'I don't think of myself as a northerner – what have I got in common with Newcastle or Yorkshire or the Lake District? What I am is a Liverpudlian.'[14] The Scouse accent, once described as 'a mixture of Welsh, Irish and catarrh',[15] bears little relation to those of its hinterland. Liverpudlians have long disparaged inhabitants of Lancashire towns around them as 'woolybacks'. The origin is obscure: theories include the notion that they were scab workers on the docks who carried woollen bales on their backs, or men who delivered coal, while wearing sheep fleece to protect their backs.[16]

Liverpudlians were not generally called 'Scousers' – derived from lobscouse, a stew commonly eaten by sailors – until the mid-twentieth century. In the early nineteenth century, they were often known as Dick Liver (after the town's emblem, the mythical liver bird). That was superseded by 'Dicky Sam', thought to have been a corruption of Dick o'Sam's, a patronymic. Then came 'Whacker', probably derived from army slang.[17]

The opening of the Liverpool–Manchester railway in 1830 brought the two towns within less than two hours' journey of each other. As the century progressed, Manchester's cotton merchants became concerned about excessive charges levied by Liverpool's docks. Their bold answer was to build the Manchester Ship Canal, a thirty-six-mile waterway linking their city to the Mersey estuary. Opened in 1894 and wide enough to take ocean-going vessels, it enabled the Port of Manchester to become Britain's third-busiest port.[18]

The cost had soared from a projected £8.4m to £14.4m and some ordinary investors did not see a return until 1915.[19] Arguably, the biggest beneficiaries were the corporations of Salford and Stretford, which made no investment but were the main recipients of the rate-able income it created. Gradually, traffic grew and it put a dent in Liverpool docks' income. Industry grew along its banks, notably Trafford Park industrial estate, which employed 40,000 by the 1930s. Tonnage on the canal peaked in 1958 and declined after containerisation made it more difficult to use.

In the 1960s The Beatles made Liverpool appear cool even to Manchester. The two cities have long competed in music and entertainment. Manchester's music scene dominated the 1980s and 1990s with bands such as The Stone Roses, Happy Mondays and Oasis. Manchester has produced comedians including Victoria Wood, Steve Coogan and Caroline Aherne, while Liverpool yielded the likes of Jimmy Tarbuck, Ken Dodd and John Bishop.

Both cities suffered post-industrial decline in the 1970s and 1980s, but Liverpool had it worse. Mancunians were not slow to join in ridiculing Scousers. Bernard Manning, a comedian often accused of racism, said: 'I like Liverpool. I go there to visit my hubcaps.' A common Mancunian joke of the time went: 'What do you call a Scouser in a suit and tie? The accused.'[20] Yorkshire's Alan Bennett joined in, saying of the Scouse accent: 'There is a rising inflection in it, particularly at the end of a sentence that gives even the most formal exchange a built-in air of grievance.'[21] If Scousers sometimes seem like a race apart, Mancunians are widely perceived as arrogant. 'The Swagger' is a cultural trait they admire in themselves. 'What Manchester does today, the world does tomorrow' was a Victorian boast that is sometimes still heard.

Today's relationship between the cities is cordial at official level. Manchester supported Liverpool in its effort to become European Capital of Culture, achieved in 2008. Andy Burnham, elected as metro mayor of Greater Manchester in 2017, was born on Merseyside. But still there is the Manchester United v. Liverpool rivalry, described by Stuart Maconie as 'a vendetta, a blood feud that's Sicilian in intensity'.[22]

Rivalry between fans of Newcastle United and Sunderland is often popularly traced to the seventeenth-century civil wars, when Newcastle – which had monopoly coal-trading rights granted by the crown – was controlled by royalists, so parliament turned to Sunderland to get coal out. Sunderland backed an army of Scottish Covenanters that fought royalists at the Battle of Boldon Hill.[23] Connections between these distant events and today's football contests seem tenuous. Historian Bill Lancaster wrote:

> The origin of recent Tyne–Wear hostility undoubtedly lies in post-1960s football rivalry. A survey of more than a century of Newcastle United versus Sunderland derby matches reveals that the games were for most of the century manifestations of what the *Evening Chronicle* described as a 'neighbourly rivalry', conducted by fans who 'erected a holiday atmosphere with bugles, bells and rattles'.[24]

Geordies labelled Sunderland folk 'Mackems', the first recorded use of which goes back only to the 1980s, according to Oxford Dictionaries. It may originate from the shipbuilding phrase 'mack 'em and tack 'em', suggesting that Sunderland workers made ships that needed to be taken to Tyneside for the skilled tasks of fitting out and finishing.

In March 2000, more than seventy Sunderland and Newcastle hooligans took part in some of the worst football-related violence seen in Britain. The sides were not even playing each other. Sunderland's 'Seaburn Casuals' boarded a ferry towards Tyneside and fought the awaiting 'Newcastle Gremlins'. One man was left permanently brain-damaged and dozens were arrested. At the subsequent trial, the battle was likened to a 'scene from the film *Braveheart*'.[25]

Things have not always been that bad, though the north-east is no stranger to disunity. Sunderland people complained about paying local taxes to finance Newcastle's Metro and airport. In 2016, Sunderland council, with Gateshead, South Tyneside and Durham, voted to reject a proposed metro mayor for the north-east, saying the government package was not good enough. Eventually a North of Tyne Mayoralty was created, covering Newcastle, North Tyneside and Northumberland. Labour's Jamie Driscoll was elected in 2019.

If there is one thing that annoys north-easterners more than conflicts with neighbours, it is criticism by outsiders from the inner northern cities (considered by some Geordies to be in the midlands). The most famous case was when Bradford's J.B. Priestley visited Tyneside in autumn 1933 for his book *English Journey*.[26] Dosed with medicine for a heavy cold and tired of travelling, he arrived in Newcastle, where years before he had been sent to recover from the First World War and that held few happy memories.

Priestley described the Geordie accent as a 'most barbarous, monotonous and irritating twang'. While Newcastle had a 'sombre dignity' and 'more impressive buildings that one would expect', Gateshead was a town 'carefully planned by an enemy of the human race'. Walking east along the Tyne, Priestley saw 'slatternly women

… standing at the doors of wretched little houses gossiping with other slatterns or screeching for their small children playing among the filth'. Jarrow suffered from a 'thick air heavy with enforced idleness, poverty and misery' and seemed as if it had 'deeply offended some celestial emperor and was now being punished'.

To be fair, Priestley was lamenting the way London, the financial capital, had made money out of Tyneside but then left it to rot through destruction of its trades and industries. But his words were received badly in the north-east. Folk in Jarrow labelled him a 'prophet of evil'. In Middlesbrough, which Priestley described as a 'dismal town even with the beer and football', the mayor and local paper called his observations 'the height of impudence'.

Tensions between neighbours are common in most regions of the world. Despite these rivalries, it is notable for example that the whole north rallied round in sympathy with Liverpool following the Hillsborough football disaster in 1989. Except, that is, for a hard core of Manchester United fans.

CHAPTER 21

YORK, LOST CAPITAL

Medieval York and nineteenth-century Manchester are the only English cities since Anglo-Saxon Winchester to have challenged London's centrality. 'The history of York is the history of England,' the future George VI is reputed to have said in the 1920s.[1]

York has more experience than most cities of being a capital. It was capital of the Roman province of Britannia Inferior and an important royal centre of the kingdoms of Deira and Northumbria. It lay at the heart of a Viking kingdom. In the Middle Ages it became England's virtual capital for significant periods as Edward I, II and III fought against the Scots. Yet it never became England's or Britain's official capital for any sustained period, despite local rumours that that might happen when James VI of Scotland and I of England passed through on his way to London to unite the crowns in 1603.[2]

York owes its existence to the Romans. Petillius Cerialis, commander of the Ninth Legion, in 71 CE built a wooden fortress by the River Ouse. The Romans named it Eboracum, possibly derived from a Brythonic name meaning 'place of the yew trees'.[3] York became a *colonia*, the highest grade of civilian town. It flourished in the third century, when London and other southern towns were economically stagnant or in decline.[4]

In 208, Emperor Septimius Severus and his son Caracalla used York as the base for campaigns north of Hadrian's Wall. Severus died at York in 211 and Caracalla returned to Rome to secure the succession. The province of Britain was split in two, with York as the capital of Britannia Inferior, so called because it was furthest from Rome.[5] Londinium, or London, was the capital of Britannia Superior. Early in the fourth century, Constantius I also came to York with his son to campaign in the north. He died at York in 306 and troops there hailed his son Constantine as successor, though he first had to defeat other contenders. Constantine the Great proclaimed toleration of Christianity throughout the empire in 313; by 314 Eboracum was a bishopric.[6]

By the time the Romans abandoned Britain in 409, York's fortunes had declined. Two obscure centuries followed. Revival began when Edwin of Deira, Anglian king of Northumbria, was baptised a Christian in 627 in a wooden church that he had built in York.[7] Edwin ordered the church to be rebuilt in stone, a task incomplete when he was killed in battle. His successor Oswald ruled from Bamburgh; Lindisfarne became his bishop's seat and York may have been virtually deserted again. The bishopric was re-established at York when Oswald's successor Oswiu decided at the Synod of Whitby in 664 to follow Roman rather than Irish observances. York became an archbishopric in 735.

Anglian York was known as Eoforwic. By the eighth century it was a commercial centre with links to northern France, the Low Countries and the Rhineland.[8] It became an internationally recognised centre of learning, with a cathedral school and library. Its most famous pupil, Alcuin, was recruited to head Charlemagne's palace school in Aachen.[9]

In 866 part of the Vikings' Great Army captured York. Their leader, Halfdan, overran Northumbria and Viking kings ruled an area between the Tees and Humber, known to historians as the kingdom of Jorvik. How settled and continuous their rule was is uncertain. Archbishops were also influential.[10] While there was disruption to religious life, the Vikings' conversion to Christianity may have followed fairly rapidly. One of York's earliest Viking kings, Guthred, was apparently Christian and buried at York Minster.[11] The economy and trade boomed in Viking Jorvik and population is estimated to have grown fivefold to at least ten thousand, second only to London.[12] Excavations of the Coppergate area have demonstrated that textile production, metalwork, carving, glasswork and jewellery-making were all practised. Materials from as far as the Baltics, Byzantium and Samarkand have been discovered.[13]

Between 919 and 945, York was ruled intermittently by Irish Norse kings from Dublin, while English kings of Wessex sought to bring Northumbria under their control. In 927 Athelstan, grandson of Alfred the Great, conquered York, making him the first Anglo-Saxon ruler of the whole of England until his death in 939.[14] Norse kings then regained control. The last, Eric, is believed to have been Eric Bloodaxe, son of King Harald Finehair of Norway. When he was expelled, his kingdom was incorporated into newly consolidated Anglo-Saxon England.[15]

York featured in 1066 when Norwegian king Harald Hardrada ('hard-ruler') defeated northern earls at the Battle of Fulford, on the city's outskirts. Shortly afterwards, Hardrada was killed at nearby Stamford Bridge by Harold Godwinson, England's king, who in turn lost the Battle of Hastings. In 1068 William the Conqueror captured York and built two castles. Chronicler Orderic Vitalis described the city as 'seething with discontent'.[16] York had been accustomed to being largely left alone by English kings; William was determined to bring it under control. In 1069 an invasion fleet sent by King Svein of Denmark arrived in the Humber. English rebels joined the invaders in seizing York and destroying the castles. The Danes withdrew before William could confront them. After that, he devastated the countryside from York to Durham and elsewhere in the Harrying of the North. In the 1070s Thomas of Bayeux, Archbishop of York, began rebuilding the cathedral that became the current minster.[17]

In 1190 came the most infamous event in York's history, the massacre of its Jewish population. After their houses were set on fire, York's Jews fled inside the castle for safety and were besieged for a week. Most took their own and their families' lives, though some were tricked into leaving the castle and massacred.[18]

York grew in prosperity during the Middle Ages, though it also had squalor alongside wealth. From being a conquered and devastated city after the Norman Conquest, it gained a degree of independence. In 1212 King John granted a charter allowing the citizens, rather than his sheriff, to organise the city's annual payment to the crown and to appoint a mayor.[19] The city became a trading and cloth-manufacturing centre through its location as a port on the Ouse and its proximity to the Great North Road. By 1334 its taxable wealth was greater than that of any English city except London and Bristol.[20] Growth was strong between the mid-thirteenth and mid-fifteenth centuries when the minster's rebuilding was completed and buildings such as the Merchant Taylors' Hall and Merchant Adventurers' Hall were constructed. The York Mystery Plays, a regular cycle of religious pageants performed by craft guilds, grew up in this period.

York became the northern base for Scottish wars. Edward I, II and III resided frequently in the city, bringing government offices and royal courts. In 1392 Richard II made York his capital for six months, escaping Londoners' hostility. Richard III, whose power-base was in Yorkshire, favoured York with visits and privileges. His death at Bosworth in 1485 was a political setback for the city.[21] York's wealth declined between 1450 and 1550 when towns such as Wakefield, Hull and Leeds grew in significance. Its cloth industry shifted to the West Riding, where production was cheaper. The Reformation and Henry VIII's dissolution of the monasteries (1536–9) meant that monastic buildings were pulled down and some hospitals, chapels and parish churches shut.[22] Robert Aske, leader of the Pilgrimage of Grace, a rebellion sparked off by the dissolution, was executed at York in 1537. A Catholic community remained in York including Margaret Clitherow, executed in 1586 for refusing to enter a plea to the charge of harbouring priests. She was pressed to death, the standard inducement to force a plea – crushed beneath her own door on top of which was piled a huge weight of rocks.[23] Guy Fawkes, one of the Gunpowder Plotters in 1605, was born and educated in York.

York was revitalised from 1539, when it became the seat of the King's Council of the North, earlier based at Sheriff Hutton and Sandal castles.[24] This council, housed in King's Manor, was mainly a judicial body that governed parts of the north, mostly Yorkshire, on behalf of the king until 1641. Charles I fled to York in 1642 and in effect made it his capital for six months, which was not universally welcomed. As the civil wars began, he stationed a royalist army in the city, which was then besieged by parliamentarians. Prince Rupert lifted the siege but was defeated at Marston Moor, after which the city surrendered to Lord Fairfax, parliament's northern commander.[25]

After the restoration of the monarchy, York lost some national prominence. Competition from Leeds and Hull, together with silting of the Ouse, meant it lost pre-eminence as a trading centre. However, it became a social and cultural hub for wealthy northern families. Daniel Defoe, who visited in the 1720s, observed that York was full of 'gentry and persons of distinction … [who] have houses proportioned to their quality'.[26] Georgian townhouses such as the Lord Mayor's Mansion House and Fairfax House date from this period, as do the Assembly Rooms, Theatre Royal and racecourse.[27] By the end of the eighteenth century, however, York's economy was stagnating.

The growth of other industrial cities diminished York's relative importance. At the beginning of the nineteenth century it was England's sixteenth largest city; by 1901 it ranked forty-first.[28] However, George Hudson, an entrepreneur and politician who became known as the 'Railway King', ensured that it had a leading role in the railway age. Hudson helped to link London and Edinburgh by rail, presided over railway company mergers and ensured that his home town of York became a major junction. Hudson's success was built on dubious practices such as paying dividends out of capital rather than earnings. He went bankrupt and fled abroad to escape imprisonment for debt. But the railways established engineering in York: by 1900, the North Eastern Railway employed more than five and a half thousand people.[29]

The railway enabled expansion of York's other main industry, chocolate and confectionery. Unlike railways, it was a major source of employment for women. Terry's of York began making chocolate in 1886 and exported all over the world. Its famous Chocolate Orange was born in 1932[30] (its Chocolate Apple, launched in 1926, was discontinued in 1954 to allow more Oranges to be produced). Terry's factory closed in 2005 and production shifted abroad.

Quaker-owned Rowntree's was founded in 1862 by Henry Isaac Rowntree. He was joined by his brother Joseph, a philanthropist whose causes included creating the model village of New Earswick. The company grew into a global manufacturer. By the Second World War, confectionery represented 30 per cent of York's working population, while the railways employed 13 per cent.[31] Rowntree's famous Kit Kat acquired a blue wrapper, rather than the familiar red one, during the Second World War to mark the fact that it was produced with plain chocolate because of milk shortages. Rowntree's was acquired by Nestlé in 1988.

In the early twenty-first century, York has become a renowned tourist city, but has struggled with productivity, having replaced manufacturing employment with lower-wage service jobs. It may be a while before it is a capital again.

CHAPTER 22

NORTHERN WOMEN

In the early hours of 7 September 1838, twenty-two-year-old Grace Darling spotted the shipwrecked paddle-steamer *Forfarshire*, which had run aground on the Farne Islands off the Northumberland coast. Grace and her father, keeper of the Longstone lighthouse, rowed out through the stormy sea and rescued nine survivors stranded on the rocks. Her bravery in risking her life to save strangers made her the subject of a media frenzy.

Gifts and donations flooded in, including £50 from young Queen Victoria. Admirers sent silk, silverware, books and bibles. People wrote requesting her signature, locks of her hair or a piece of the garment she wore during the rescue; some letters contained instructions for her to kiss the paper and return it. Visitors arrived in hired boats daily, hoping to see her or touch her clothes. Artists arrived to paint her portrait. It was an ordeal for the modest Grace.[1]

Sadly, Grace died of tuberculosis four years after the rescue, but the Victorian age had a heroine. William Wordsworth wrote a poem, *Grace Darling*, about the 'pious and pure' maiden. Eva Hope wrote in 1875: 'She gave her thoughts and powers, with conscientious diligence and perseverance, to the common-place duties of her lot, but she was none the less ready, when the occasion came, to go forth over the stormy waters to do a most uncommon deed of daring.'[2]

The Victorian era, despite its penchant for confining women to the home, was one in which more women achieved prominence. They did not all fit the mould of Victorian sensibility as easily as Grace Darling. Many were northerners, including writers such as the Brontë sisters and Elizabeth Gaskell, social reformers such as Josephine Butler, women's suffrage campaigners such as Lydia Becker and Emily Davies, and militant suffragettes led by Emmeline Pankhurst.

Of course there were prominent women in earlier ages. The first northerner we know by name was Queen Cartimandua. Queens played an important political role in the kingdom of Northumbria, as did Hilda, founder of Whitby Abbey. In Elizabethan times, Elizabeth Cavendish, known as Bess of Hardwick (of Hardwick Hall in Derbyshire), made herself one of England's wealthiest women through four advantageous marriages and increased her assets by investing in coalmines and glass works.

The overwhelming majority of women were, nonetheless, unsung and confined to domesticity, which was the norm in the Victorian age despite stirrings of feminism. The north gained a reputation for strong-willed, independent women, notably in textile areas such as Lancashire where female employment was high. How far these genuinely differed from women elsewhere is unclear, but it became a feature of the north's self-image. Northern fiction is full of women who hold together families and social networks in the face of poverty and personal tragedy. The twentieth century produced determined, resolute young characters such as Harold Brighouse's Maggie Hobson in *Hobson's Choice*, Walter Greenwood's Sally Hardcastle in *Love on the Dole* and Willy Russell's Rita White in *Educating Rita*.[3]

The Brontës – or at least the image of them – have contributed perhaps more than anyone to the world's view of northern England. Their unsettling talents and supposedly constricted lives on the windswept moors are a constant source of fascination. They have suffered from stereotyping, as biographer Juliet Barker acknowledges:

Charlotte is portrayed as the long-suffering victim of duty, subor-
dinating her career as a writer to the demands of her selfish and
autocratic father; Emily is the wild child of genius, deeply misan-
thropic yet full of compassion for her errant brother; Anne is the
quiet, conventional one who, lacking her sisters' rebellious spirit,
conforms to the demands of society and religion.[4]

Reality was more complicated. The Brontë men have if anything
suffered even more from two-dimensional portrayals.

Charlotte herself started the process of myth-making in the way
she sought to protect the posthumous reputations of her sisters,
whose novels had shocked and titillated literary critics. Gaskell's *Life
of Charlotte Brontë*, which did much to establish the genre of literary
biography, also reinforced the stereotype of the north as uncivilised
and half-tamed. She portrayed the sisters' talents as sharpened by
living among 'this wild, rough population'. Of the Yorkshire folk
living in the moorland communities, Gaskell wrote:

Their accost is curt, their accent and tone of speech blunt and
harsh. Something of this may, probably, be attributed to the freedom of mountain air and of isolated hill-life; something be
derived from their rough Norse ancestry. They have a quick
perception of character, and a keen sense of humour; the dweller
among them must be prepared for certain uncomplimentary,
though most likely true, observations, pithily expressed.

In reality, Haworth was an industrial community with many and
varied links to the outside world. Politics and religion were hotly
disputed there and culture thrived.[5]

Cut through the myths, however, and what remains is that all
three sisters produced novels that were ground-breaking at the time
and have resonance today. Charlotte's *Jane Eyre* (1847), which traces
the heroine's growth to adulthood and love for the brooding Mr
Rochester, is an intimate first-person narrative of great intensity that

has been seen as prefiguring writers such as Marcel Proust, James Joyce and Virginia Woolf.[6] Emily's *Wuthering Heights* (1847) portrays the passionate, doomed relationship between Heathcliff and Catherine Earnshaw and its effect on those around them. Reviewers were impressed by the 'rugged power' of the novel's imagination, but taken aback by its savagery. It still has power to divide readers – for example, over how far it is a love story and how far a portrait of a toxic relationship.

For decades, Anne's literary reputation languished. That was partly down to the attitude of Charlotte, who prevented republication of *The Tenant of Wildfell Hall* (1848) after Anne's death. The novel tells the story of Helen Huntingdon, who left her husband to protect her son from his father's alcoholism and debauchery and made a living as an artist. Charlotte wrote: 'The choice of subject in that work is a mistake, it was too little consonant with the character, tastes and ideas of the gentle, retiring inexperienced writer.'[7] Anne's reputation has been rising sharply since the late twentieth century. Sally McDonald of the Brontë Society said in 2013 that in some ways Anne 'is now viewed as the most radical of the sisters, writing about tough subjects such as women's need to maintain independence and how alcoholism can tear a family apart'.[8]

Gaskell's wide-ranging work is valued for its social history, including first-hand accounts of Manchester's poor, as well as its literary qualities. Much of what she wrote was innovatory or controversial. Her first novel, *Mary Barton* (1848), tells the story of a young woman subject to the affections of Jem Wilson, a hard-working engineer, and Harry Carson, son of a wealthy mill owner. The mill owner is murdered by Mary's father, but Jem is wrongly accused. It was not the first novel of industrial strife: others included *William Langshawe, the Cotton Lord* (1842) by Elizabeth Stone (whose father owned the *Manchester Chronicle*). Both works were based partly on the assassination of mill owner Thomas Ashton in 1831.[9]

Mary Barton's strength lay in its portrayal of how the poor suffered not only in the mill but in their homes and in its moral examination of the conflict between classes. The novel was initially published anonymously, though that did not last long. The book caused furious arguments, especially in Manchester. Gaskell was married to a Unitarian minister and several rich manufacturers in her husband's Cross Street congregation were outraged. They felt the novel vilified masters and glorified workers, wilfully ignoring market forces and the capitalists' share of risks. They thought it ignored their charitable efforts and cast a slur on the city.[10]

Ruth (1853) caused a national moral storm. It was a compassionate portrait of a 'fallen woman', an unmarried orphan girl made pregnant by her aristocratic lover, and her efforts to gain a respectable position in society. Men forbade their womenfolk to read it. Old friends expressed 'deep regret' that she should have written such a book. All over the country *Ruth* was debated in drawing-rooms, clubs, churches, chapels. Gaskell was buoyed, however, by support from the likes of Charles Kingsley and Elizabeth Barrett Browning.[11]

North and South, the subtlest of the industrial novels of the 1840s and 1850s, had a troubled genesis. Charles Dickens published it in his magazine *Household Words*, but Gaskell struggled with the serial form. They tussled over style and length and the ending had to be compressed. Sales of the magazine dropped, probably because it followed too quickly after Dickens' *Hard Times*, though he blamed it squarely on Gaskell's 'wearisome' novel.[12] It tells the story of Margaret Hale, forced to leave the rural south and settle with her parents in the northern industrial town of Milton. Sympathetic to the poor, she clashes with mill owner John Thornton, but is also attracted to him. After a bitter strike, they come to a better understanding of each other and of the complexity of labour relations. She finally accepts his offer of marriage. This is a romantic novel, but more than an industrial *Pride and Prejudice*. Its theme is the need to pull down barriers between self and others – not only barriers between the sexes and classes but between cultures and faiths, town and country, north and south. It has been adapted three times for television.

Northern writing often attracts national attention at times of economic stress.[13] The 1930s produced writers such as Winifred Holtby, Lettice Cooper and Phyllis Bentley. Holtby's *South Riding* (1936) and Cooper's *National Provincial* (1938) both feature professional women returning to their native Yorkshire. *National Provincial* focuses on conflict between moderate and militant socialists in 'Aire', a city based on Leeds; like *North and South*, it involves a strike. The later twentieth century produced prominent northern-born writers including Beryl Bainbridge, Pat Barker, A.S. Byatt, Margaret Drabble and Susan Hill. There was also a clutch of popular sagas, most notably those by Catherine Cookson. Many are set in the nineteenth century or 1930s, maintaining the 'mill town' picture of the north, perhaps reflecting readers' desire to connect with a world they felt they had lost.

Scientists and mathematicians appear to be fewer in number, though one notable figure is Annabella Milbanke (1792–1860), a highly educated, serious woman from County Durham who gave birth to Ada Lovelace, the computing pioneer. Annabella is better known as Lady Byron, having married the 'mad, bad and dangerous' romantic poet in an unlikely match that ended acrimoniously in legal separation. Byron called her his 'princess of parallelograms'. She insisted that Ada receive a disciplined education, including mathematics, which she felt would calm any inherited tendency towards volatility.[14]

Beatrix Potter (1866–1943), born in London to parents from east of Manchester, was a gifted amateur natural scientist, whose study and watercolours of fungi led to her becoming an expert in mycology.[15] She developed a theory of how fungus spores germinated, on which she submitted a paper to the Linnean Society. It had to be introduced by a male expert because, as a woman, she could not attend proceedings or read her paper. In 1997, the Linnean Society issued a posthumous apology to Potter for sexism displayed in its handling of her research. She is, of course, better known for children's books such as *The Tale of Peter Rabbit*. Proceeds from the books helped her to buy Hill Top Farm in the Lake District, which, with other farms that she had acquired, she left to the National Trust.

The north's best-known social reformer was Josephine Butler (1828–1906), born in Northumberland, where her high-minded liberal father was a cousin of Earl Grey, prime minister. She was arguably the most effective campaigner for women's rights of her time, from ending coverture in English law (whereby a woman's legal rights were subsumed by her husband's) to criminalisation of child prostitution and human trafficking. She was a staunch feminist but a passionate Christian, whose favourite phrase was: 'God and one woman make a majority.'[16] Suffragist Millicent Fawcett considered Butler 'the most distinguished Englishwoman of the nineteenth century'.[17]

She and her husband George began taking fallen women into their home while living in Oxford, accelerating this when he became headmaster of Liverpool College. Josephine was mourning for Eva, their fourth child, who had died falling from a banister. She later wrote that she 'became possessed with an irresistible urge to go forth and find some pain keener than my own, to meet with people more unhappy than myself … It was not difficult to find misery in Liverpool.'[18] The couple founded two homes for women in need. She also co-founded the North of England Council for Promoting the Higher Education of Women, which aimed to raise the status of governesses and female teachers to that of a profession.

In 1869 she became involved in the campaign to repeal the Contagious Diseases Acts, legislation that attempted to control venereal diseases, particularly in the army and navy, through the forced medical examination of prostitutes, which opponents described as surgical or steel rape.[19] Butler toured Britain, often facing danger and hostile audiences. The acts were repealed in 1886.

Butler was appalled that some prostitutes were as young as twelve. She fought against trafficking of young women and children to the continent for prostitution, which led to the sacking of the head of the Belgian Police des Mœurs and the trial and imprisonment of his deputy and twelve brothel owners, all involved in the trade.[20] She fought child prostitution alongside the campaigning editor of the *Pall Mall Gazette*, Tynesider W.T. Stead, who purchased a thirteen-year-old girl from her mother for £5. The subsequent outcry led to the Criminal Law Amendment Act 1885, which raised the age of consent from thirteen to sixteen and brought in measures to stop children becoming prostitutes. Amid all this, Butler managed to write more than ninety books and pamphlets during her career, including biographies of Catherine of Siena and Protestant pastor Jean Frederic Oberlin.

The north has produced many women's rights activists, notably Newcastle-born Mary Astell (1666–1731), whose advocacy of equal educational opportunities for women led to her being described as the first English feminist. After her mother and aunt died, she moved to Chelsea where she belonged to a circle of literary women. Her books were published anonymously, starting with *A Serious Proposal to the Ladies for the Advancement of their True and Greatest Interest*, which proposed an all-female college. In *Some Reflections upon Marriage*, she said women ought to be educated thoroughly so that they would choose husbands wisely – or else not marry at all.[21]

Lydia Becker (1827–90), from Manchester, was an early leader of the women's suffrage movement who founded and published the *Women's Suffrage Journal*. She and fellow campaigners succeeded in winning the vote for women in municipal elections and inclusion of women on school boards.[22] Emily Davies (1830–1921), daughter of the rector of Gateshead, was a suffragist who edited the *English Woman's Journal* and co-founded Girton College Cambridge, the first university college in England to educate women.

In 1903, Manchester's Emmeline Pankhurst (1858–1928), frustrated by the failure of suffrage bills in parliament, formed the Women's Social and Political Union, an all-female organisation dedicated to 'deeds, not words'.[23] It was a *Daily Mail* journalist who first used the diminutive term 'suffragette', which the movement seized as its own. At first it indulged in peaceful activities such as rallies, but before long members started smashing windows and assaulting police officers. Pankhurst, her daughters and other activists received repeated prison sentences and staged hunger strikes to secure better conditions, which led to them being force-fed. Her eldest daughter Christabel became national coordinator. Another leader was Annie Kenney, a cotton-mill worker from Oldham, who was jailed thirteen times.[24] Finally the WSPU adopted arson as a tactic, while moderate suffragists increasingly spoke out against the militants. Fawcett said hunger strikes were publicity stunts and that militant activists were 'the chief obstacles in the way of the success of the suffrage movement in the House of Commons'.[25] In 1913 several prominent members left the WSPU, including Pankhurst's younger daughters, Adela and Sylvia. Adela disapproved of property destruction; Emmeline paid her to move to Australia and they never saw one another again.[26] Sylvia became a socialist.

When the First World War broke out, Emmeline and Christabel halted militant action and supported the government's stand against the 'German peril'. They urged women to take part in industrial production and encouraged young men to fight. At rallies, their supporters handed white feathers to any young man not in uniform. Emmeline was never tolerant of dissent. Sylvia and Adela, as committed pacifists, did not share their mother's enthusiasm for the war. In 1918, the Representation of the People Act removed property restrictions on men's suffrage and granted the vote to women over thirty who met minimum property qualifications. Historians differ about whether Emmeline's militancy helped or hurt the movement, though there is general agreement that the WSPU raised public awareness.[27] Some believe extension of the franchise became possible because public hostility to pre-war militant tactics had faded, while others think politicians made the concession to avoid any resurgence of militancy.

Emmeline and Christabel reinvented the WSPU in 1918 as the Women's Party, campaigning for equal marriage laws, equal pay for equal work and equal job opportunities for women. After the war, Emmeline continued to rally support for the British Empire and warned about the dangers of Bolshevism.[28] Christabel narrowly failed to get elected to parliament, after which the Women's Party withered.[29] In 1926 Emmeline joined the Conservative Party and two years later stood for parliament. She put her transformation from window-smashing radical to Tory member down in part to 'my war experience', though she may also have seen the Conservatives as the best route to secure votes for more women.[30] In 1928, the year she died, the Conservative government passed an act extending the franchise to all persons over twenty-one on equal terms.

While Victorian and Edwardian women from the north made a huge contribution to national life, some also had an international impact. Lucy Osburn (1836–91) from Leeds, having trained at a London nursing school created by Florence Nightingale, led a team of nurses to set up the Nightingale system in Australia, where she is regarded as the founder of modern nursing.[31]

None had a greater geopolitical impact than Gertrude Bell (1868–1926), born in Co. Durham, granddaughter of Tyneside ironmaster Sir Lowthian Bell. After becoming the first woman to graduate in Modern History at Oxford with first-class honours, she travelled and mountaineered independently across the Middle East, publishing her observations in *Syria: The Desert and the Sown*. In the First World War she became the first female officer ever employed by British military intelligence, known as 'Major Miss Bell'. She played an important role in defeating the Ottoman Empire, creating the state of Iraq and preserving Mesopotamian antiquities. Yet she is a problematic feminist icon, in that she campaigned against votes for women.[32]

As the twentieth century progressed, influential women emerged such as 'Red' Ellen Wilkinson, MP for Jarrow, who played a big part in the 1936 Jarrow March of the unemployed to London to petition for the right to work, and became minister of education in the 1945 Labour government; Gracie Fields, actress and singing star of the industrial world; and Barbara Castle, Blackburn MP, who became transport minister, employment secretary and health and social services secretary – and introduced the Equal Pay Act 1970. There remains further to travel, however, on the road to equality.

CHAPTER 23

AT LEISURE

Few things symbolise the north's transformation more vividly than the rise of Blackpool and other seaside resorts. By the 1880s this former coastal hamlet – a sea-bathing spot for the wealthy in the mid-eighteenth century – had become a raucous working-class pleasure ground with piers, fortune-tellers, pubs, trams, donkey rides, fish and chip shops and theatres. J.B. Priestley later described it as 'the great roaring spangled beast'.[1]

The advent of the railway in 1846, coupled with more disposable income and leisure time, turned Blackpool into the most popular destination not just for northern families, but for many from the midlands and Scotland too. By 1901 it had a population of 47,000.[2] Other resorts included Southport, Morecambe, Whitley Bay, Saltburn, Bridlington, Filey, Scarborough and New Brighton. The nineteenth century's second half ushered in a new age of popular entertainment and leisure, including music halls, variety theatres, shopping and excursions. There were new parks, libraries and museums: Birkenhead opened the world's first publicly funded park in 1847, designed by Joseph Paxton.[3] But people also wanted excitement. Northern England led the world in creating professional spectator sports, notably football and rugby league. Clubs were formed for activities including rambling and cycling.

The growth of leisure was not without stresses. The teetotalism movement, founded in Preston in 1833 in response to excessive drinking, won strong support in the north. Religious and moral campaigners objected to lewd performances in music halls and accused the halls of encouraging prostitution. The north-east was particularly noted for its culture of sociability, sentimentality, heavy drinking and weekend hedonism, no doubt a reaction to hard working lives in the pits and elsewhere.[4]

Life remained tough for many. One Bolton doctor wrote in 1875 that, over the previous decade, 'the children of the mill population were steadily, year by year, for their age, getting smaller, and physically less capable of doing their work'.[5] Reformer Seebohm Rowntree found in his 1899 investigation into poverty in York that a family of five living on 21s. 8d. a week

> must never spend a penny on railway fare or omnibus. They must never go into the country unless they walk. They must never purchase a halfpenny newspaper or spend a penny to buy a ticket for a popular concert. They must write no letters to absent children, for they cannot afford to pay the postage. They must never contribute anything to their church or chapel, or give any help to a neighbour which costs them money. They cannot save, nor can they join sick club or trade union, because they cannot pay the necessary subscriptions. The children must have no money for dolls, marbles, or sweets.[6]

Nonetheless, successive factory acts helped to reduce working hours, so that workers had more leisure time and their options widened. In textile areas, the wakes, traditionally religious festivals, evolved into 'wakes weeks' in which mills closed and families from entire towns escaped to the seaside. Morecambe became nicknamed 'Bradford by the Sea' because of its links to the West Riding. Places such as the Lake District became more accessible, to the horror of William Wordsworth, who campaigned against the railway's advance.

Outraged by a plan to extend the railway from Kendal to Windermere, he wrote in a sonnet published in most national and provincial newspapers: 'Is there no nook of English ground secure from rash assault?'[7] Railway outings to the 1851 Great Exhibition were laid on after entrance was reduced from five shillings to one shilling between Mondays and Thursdays.

Working-class living standards slowly but surely began to rise. Surplus money plus urbanisation created a dense new market, which entertainment entrepreneurs were keen to exploit. Music halls began as pub music rooms, offering an opportunity to sell more drink. Bolton had one of Britain's earliest music halls, created in 1832 as a 'singing-room' at the Millstones Inn. Landlord Tom Sharples moved in 1840 to the Star Inn, where he built on to his hostelry the Star Theatre and Museum. The museum contained wax figures, a menagerie and an axe said to have been used to execute the Earl of Derby during the civil wars. At one point, Barney the leopard killed his keeper.[8] The theatre was reportedly capable of holding up to one and a half thousand people. Programmes from the 1840s reveal an eclectic mix of entertainments: a 'Characteristic Yorkshire Dialect Singer'; a 'True Representative of Negro Character'; assorted acrobats and jugglers; ventriloquists and magicians; even readings from popular novels.[9]

According to the *Bolton Guardian*:

Mr Geoghegan, the manager, acted as chairman, and he had a mallet and called out the names of the performers. Performances began at 7.30 each night, and the curtain was wound up by hand. A well-known character called 'Museum Jack' lit the lamps and footlights with a taper, and also played the piano. If a 'turn' failed to please, Mr Geoghegan said 'You're no good' and ejected the hapless performer.[10]

Other early music halls included the Adelphi at Sheffield, which started as a circus in 1837; the Britannia at Huddersfield, 1842; and Thornton's New Music Hall and Fashionable Lounge in Leeds, 1865 (now City Varieties), though there was probably a concert room at the White Swan Inn long before that.[11] It was common for halls to contain waxworks, museums or picture galleries. Music hall was flourishing in most towns and cities by 1850. The most famous hall on Tyneside was the old Wheatsheaf in the Cloth Market, Newcastle, a pub with a built-on singing room where, in 1862, George Ridley, a crippled ex-collier, wrote and sang the 'Blaydon Races'.[12]

Among performers, George Leybourne, who co-wrote and performed songs including 'Champagne Charlie' and 'The Daring Young Man on the Flying Trapeze', was born in Gateshead and toured northern halls early in his career. He played a 'lion comique', a parody of an upper-class toff. Leybourne drank too much champagne and was over-generous to friends, with the result that he died penniless.[13] Mark Sheridan, born in Sunderland, became famous for singing 'I Do Like to Be Beside the Seaside'. Thinking that his career was in decline, he shot himself in the head in Glasgow's Kelvingrove Park in 1918.[14]

Dan Leno, a comedian who vied with Marie Lloyd as the late Victorian era's most popular entertainer, was brought up in Liverpool. At first he was in a clog-dancing double act with his brother. They and their parents appeared on the opening night of the Cambridge Music Hall, Toxteth, under the billing 'Mr and Mrs Leno, the Great, Sensational, Dramatic and Comic Duettists and The Brothers Leno, Lancashire Clog, Boot and Pump Dancers'.[15] Leno played many stage characters: one of his favourites was Pongo, an escaped monkey, at Pullan's Theatre of Varieties in Bradford.[16] He was so good at clog dancing that he won the title Champion Clog Dancer of the World at the Princess's Music Hall in Leeds, but clog dancing never caught on in southern England and he dropped it from his act.[17] In later life Leno suffered from alcoholism, like his father, and poor mental health.

Vesta Victoria was born in Leeds, but adopted a cockney persona. She was famous for singing 'Waiting at the Church' and 'Daddy Wouldn't Buy Me a Bow-Wow'.[18] Bradford-born Jack Pleasants, popular in northern music halls, is remembered for 'I'm Twenty-One Today' and 'I'm Shy, Mary Ellen, I'm Shy'.[19] Hetty King, born in New Brighton, was a male impersonator whose signature song was 'Ship Ahoy! (All the Nice Girls Love a Sailor)'.[20] Charles William Murphy, a composer from Manchester, co-wrote two hugely popular songs, 'Oh, Oh, Antonio' and 'Has Anybody Here Seen Kelly?' for Florrie Forde, an Australian who became music hall's greatest chorus singer. She performed every summer on the Isle of Man in the Edwardian era. Murphy also co-wrote 'She's a Lassie from Lancashire' and 'Hold Your Hand Out Naughty Boy' for Forde.[21]

There were some macabre acts, such as Sacco, the fasting man, who went for fifty days (so said the day-bills) without food at Hull in 1897. Admission was two pence, but when Sacco was reported to be 'sinking fast' the management raised the admission price to sixpence. He lived to fast again.[22]

Moral opposition to music halls began early. A Baptist minister, campaigning for withdrawal of the Bolton Star hall's licence in 1852, told a public meeting:

> A tall, well-dressed female came on to the platform and attracted their attention by a song. I do not say that the song was immoral, but I do affirm that the gestures of the lady who sang it, together with the stimulating influence of the drink and the whole scene, were calculated to excite the basest passions of the human mind … My heart sickened at what I heard … I felt that I was in the very suburbs of hell.

Magistrates withdrew the licence, but restored it again a month later when it emerged that no formal complaint had been made.[23]

Later in the century, campaigners led by writer and feminist Laura Ormiston Chant, a member of the Social Purity Alliance, stepped up pressure. In 1894, London's Empire, Leicester Square, was required by London County Council to place a screen to separate the auditorium from the bar – a notorious pick-up place. But the screen was torn down by a group of young bloods, among them Winston Churchill.[24] The temperance lobby exerted considerable influence in the north. Manchester's Palace Theatre of Varieties, promoted by a London syndicate, was kept dry by the lobbying of local Methodists and fellow teetotallers. Sheffield's Empire Palace also could not obtain an alcohol licence.[25]

Proprietors were themselves becoming less keen on alcohol. Increasingly, they were seeking to attract a new, lower-middle-class audience – the sober, industrious clerk or shop assistant and their families. 'Variety theatre' or 'theatre of varieties' was becoming the fashionable term. Content was similar, but new theatres were large, stand-alone venues, cutting the symbolic link with pubs. Tables and chairs were replaced by rows of theatre seats.[26]

The 1890s' variety theatre also represented a structural change in the music hall industry. A new breed of entrepreneurs had begun to build national chains. Edward Moss, from Droylsden, Manchester, joined forces with Richard Thornton, from South Shields, and later Edward Stoll to create Moss Empires, Britain's largest group. Architect Frank Matcham designed numerous theatres for Moss Empires and other proprietors including Blackpool's Grand Theatre, the Isle of Man's Gaiety Theatre, Bury's Theatre Royal, Buxton Opera House, Hull's Palace Theatre, Manchester's Ardwick Empire and Hippodrome, Wakefield Opera House and Liverpool Olympia.

Music halls and variety theatres were not the only forms of commercial entertainment. Manchester's Pomona Gardens (1845–88) and Belle Vue Zoological Gardens (1836–1980) offered entertainments such as music and dancing. Belle Vue contained an Italian garden, lakes, mazes and hothouses; it soon added elephants, lions and other exotic animals. In the 1850s both Belle Vue and Pomona had their own rival diorama of the siege of Sebastopol in the Crimean War, with nightly pyrotechnics restaging the onslaught.

Belle Vue adapted to changing fashion and became a twentieth-century amusement park.[27]

Blackpool had three piers, a Winter Gardens and Opera House, an aquarium and an electric tramway. Blackpool Tower opened in 1894, initially known as the 'Blackpool Eiffel Tower'. When the Winter Gardens Company opened its Empress Ballroom, the Tower Company responded with Matcham's equally lavish Tower Ballroom, opened in 1898. The Pleasure Beach amusement park was founded in 1896. Other 'Eiffel towers' were planned elsewhere. One in Douglas, Isle of Man, never progressed beyond its foundations. A Morecambe tower ended up incomplete. A tower was built at New Brighton, across the Mersey from Liverpool – fifty feet higher than Blackpool Tower – but the business struggled. The tower was demolished after the First World War, afflicted by rust and too costly to maintain. The ballroom below survived until a fire in 1969.[28]

Retailing expanded in city centres as shopping became popular for those with means. Bainbridge's in Newcastle, founded in 1838, claimed to be the world's first true department store, in that it began recording weekly turnover separately for each of its twenty-three departments in 1849. Now it is John Lewis Newcastle.[29] Early in the nineteenth century, clothing was still commonly home-made, but later on more was bought in shops.[30]

Men wore heavy jackets and trousers for work, an overcoat if they were lucky and a best suit with a scarf on Sundays. The flat cap became symbolic of northern men, though not universal. Robert Roberts, recalling his childhood in Edwardian Salford, says the bowler hat or 'billy pot' was compulsory wear: 'Only the lower types wore caps.'[31] When possible, children were treated with new outfits for the Whit Monday walk, an excuse for a fashion show. If money ran short, the wife often did without new clothes and made do with a blouse, patched skirt and an apron, with a shawl to wear outdoors.[32]

Working-class food was geared to hard labour, with dishes such as pie and mushy peas, black pudding, tripe, liver and onions, Cumberland sausage and lots of cheap carbohydrates. The north has a range of subtly different breads: stotties, oven bottoms, barm cakes. Local specialities include pease pudding in Newcastle, pasty and black peas in Bolton, and dripping-cooked fish and chips in Yorkshire. In the twentieth century, Chinese and Indian restaurants brought welcome diversity. Meanwhile northern dishes such as Yorkshire pudding and Lancashire hotpot have spread across the UK and in modern times there has been an effort by chefs to revive the traditional repertoire.[33]

Music hall and variety began to decline in the 1920s with the arrival of cinema, though many twentieth-century stars began their careers on the boards. Gracie Fields made her professional debut at Rochdale Hippodrome in 1910. Stan Laurel, born in Ulverston, Lancashire, began in Glasgow. London-born Charlie Chaplin appeared at Leeds City Varieties in 1897, aged eight, as the youngest member of the Eight Lancashire Lads, a clog-dancing troupe.[34] Victoria Hall, a concert hall in Settle, North Yorkshire, is reckoned to be England's oldest surviving music hall, having opened as Settle Music Hall in 1853.[35] Leeds City Varieties was the venue for the BBC's *The Good Old Days* (1953–83), which aimed to recreate an authentic Victorian-Edwardian atmosphere with songs and sketches of the era performed in the style of original artistes.

Music hall had a strand of Lancashire comedians, including Morny Cash, who billed himself 'The Lancashire Lad', and Robb Wilton. Among the best known was George Formby senior, born into poverty in Ashton-under-Lyne in 1875.[36] He played characters including 'John Willie', an archetypical gormless Lancashire lad, accident-prone but muddling through, whose cane twirl and duck-like walk allegedly inspired Chaplin.[37] For years Formby battled against consumption, making light of it by muttering asides such as 'coughing better tonight, coughing summat champion'. He was billed as the Wigan Nightingale, a reference to his croaky voice.

Formby had a miserable childhood. His mother Sarah was a prostitute and a drunk. A music-hall owner in Birkenhead, who booked him early in his career, thought that his real name, James Booth, was unsuitable for the stage and suggested 'George Formby' – George after comedian George Robey and Formby after the Merseyside town. After Formby died in 1921, his son used parts of his father's act when starting his stage career and, when established, also changed his name to George Formby. Formby junior went on to be the ukulele-playing star of successful British comedy films in the 1930s and 1940s.

The late Eric Sykes said the north-west was 'where all the good comics come from'. Aside from Oldham-born Sykes himself, Lancashire has produced comedians including Frank Randle, Tommy Handley, Ken Dodd, Les Dawson, Eric Morecambe, Ted Ray, Arthur Askey, Al Read, Hylda Baker and Jimmy Clitheroe. More recently, there have been Victoria Wood, Steve Coogan, Johnny Vegas, Caroline Aherne (London-born but raised in Wythenshawe), Peter Kay, John Bishop and Jason Manford. Industrial Lancashire's humour is considered to have been slow-building and character-based compared with quickfire patter heard in London and Liverpool.[38]

Whence comes this strain? Sykes said: 'My theory is that we are all idiots. The people who don't think they're idiots – they're the ones that are dangerous.'[39] Some attribute it to the Celtic influence from the west. A.J.P. Taylor, the Southport-born historian, attributed Lancastrian whimsicality to the 'south-west wind, bringing an atmosphere that is always blurred and usually gentle'.[40] Walter Greenwood, author of *Love on the Dole*, wrote even more fancifully of the 'wild, warm, amorous wind wenching with fat clouds and leaving them big with rain of which they deliver themselves on the Pennines' westerly slopes'.[41]

It may be simply the result of people thrown together by rapid industrialisation responding to their conditions. Anthony Burgess called it 'the bark of the underdog'.[42] Lancashire folk like to contrast their abundance of comics with an alleged dearth in Yorkshire, but Yorkshire people can point to several names, such as Whit Cunliffe and Charlie Whittle before the First World War. Others include

Jimmy Jewel, Frankie Howerd, Ernie Wise, Charlie Williams, the Chuckle Brothers, Marti Caine, Michael Palin, Vic Reeves, Ade Edmondson, Graham Fellows, Richard Herring, Reece Shearsmith, Leigh Francis and Lucy Beaumont. The north-east can point to figures such as Austin Rudd, Wee Georgie Wood, Bobby Thompson, Rowan Atkinson, Sarah Millican, Ross Noble, Mark Gatiss, Eric Idle and Alexander Armstrong.

The north did not invent major sports such as cricket, association football and rugby, but it can fairly claim to have turned them into professional spectator sports. It was the urban north that nourished sport as a mass phenomenon in the late nineteenth century. Northern teams subsequently dominated many competitions.[43]

Football took hold in the Sheffield area and in east and central Lancashire. Sheffield FC, founded in 1857, is recognised by FIFA as the world's oldest football club.[44] Professional football developed rapidly from the 1870s, when it became clear that spectators were willing to pay, especially in Lancashire textile towns where family incomes were above average and a Saturday half-holiday was available. The Football Association initially tried to outlaw professionalism, but accepted it in 1885. The Football League was created in 1888. All twelve founder members came from the north and midlands, including six from Lancashire. Preston North End won the first season, going through the twenty-two games unbeaten. They also won the FA Cup and became known as the Invincibles.[45]

Northern and midlands clubs dominated the Football League until the 1920s, by when it was eighty-eight strong. The seven northernmost counties provided at least 50 per cent of Football League clubs at all times before 1920, and usually 40–45 per cent until the later 1970s when the figure fell to about 35 per cent.[46] The proportion remains about the same today in England's top four divisions. Only in the 1980s did the north come close to losing its position as the English game's heartland. Although Liverpool and Everton dominated, overall northern representation in the First Division fell below 20 per cent.

Cricket's growth was more uniform across the country, but northern and north midlands counties were again central to its emergence as a spectator sport.[47] In 1838, William Clarke, landlord of the Trent Bridge Inn in Nottingham, laid out a cricket ground that was to become a Test Match venue; in 1846, he organised an All-England XI whose tours helped to establish professional cricket. One of his players, batsman George Parr, was nicknamed 'the lion of the north'. Lancashire and Yorkshire were among the County Championship's nine founder members in 1873. Yorkshire won twenty-one of the forty-six championships between 1890 and 1939 and a further nine titles between 1946 and 1968. The poet Francis Thompson wrote of Lancashire's early days:

And a ghostly batsman plays to the bowling of a ghost,
And I look through my tears at a soundless clapping host
As the run-stealers flicker to and fro,
O my Hornby and my Barlow long ago.

A.N. Hornby was the captain, an amateur, while Dick Barlow was a professional all-rounder.

Rugby League is one of the north's most potent symbols. It arose from the desire by industrialists who ran northern clubs to give working-class players 'broken time' payments to compensate them for lost earnings while playing, which was opposed by the London-based Rugby Football Union and by professional middle classes in the north, wedded to the amateur ethos.[48] Representatives of twenty Yorkshire and Lancashire sides established the Northern Rugby Football Union at the George Hotel, Huddersfield, in 1895. Northern Union became a separate code, particularly after 1906 when the sides were reduced from fifteen to thirteen players. The dramatic growth of association football prevented it from expanding beyond the north, though it periodically tried to do so. In the north, Rugby League established itself only in south Lancashire, west Cumbria and west and east Yorkshire, though it attracts passionate support in its heartlands.

Most sports were male-dominated except cycling clubs, which attracted a lot of female participants. In the twentieth century Beryl Burton, from Leeds, dominated women's cycle racing in the UK, winning more than ninety domestic championships and seven world titles and setting many national records.

Lesser-known northern sports include crown green bowling, whose core territory is between the River Trent and north Yorkshire (though not the north-east, where flat green prevails). Its Talbot and Waterloo tournaments were named after Blackpool hotels. Competitive rowing was hugely popular in nineteenth-century Tyneside, arising from commercial rivalry between the Tyne and Thames. In Newcastle, spectators would regularly number between 50,000 and 100,000 on the Tyne's banks to watch heroes such as Harry Clasper, Robert Chambers and James Renforth.[49] Other sports include quoits; potshare bowling, played by Northumberland miners at least until the early twentieth century; knur and spell, in which two people compete in striking a ball with a stick, popular in west Yorkshire and east Lancashire until the 1930s; Cumberland wrestling; hunting with beagle packs on foot, popular in west Yorkshire; whippet racing; and fell-running.[50]

As Dave Russell comments, sport 'has provided a powerful means of expressing a body of supposed northern values; acted as a site for the definition and symbolic resolution of differences between north and south; and facilitated the expression and construction of a range of personal and collective northern identities'.[51] Wilfred Rhodes, Yorkshire's great all-rounder from 1898 to 1930, reputedly summed up one of those self-proclaimed values succinctly: 'We doan't play cricket in Yorkshire for foon.'[52]

CHAPTER 24

ENGINEERS OR POETS?

To Arthur Conan Doyle it was clear: excellence in music, poetry and art largely existed south of Lincoln, while those who excelled in engineering, science and theology mostly came from the north. In a rudimentary 1888 study of Victorian men eminent in literature, poetry, art, music, medicine, sculpture, engineering, law and other intellectual pursuits, culled from biographical dictionaries, Conan Doyle found that Derbyshire and Lancashire came bottom for overall intellectual production. Northumberland fared better, but 'produces men of a practical turn. There are no poets and few authors in her records, but *en revanche* there is in the past the great Robert Stephenson, and in the present Lord Armstrong and Sir Daniel Gooch, engineers, with Burdon Sanderson, Sir G. B. Airy, and Birket Foster'.[1]

It is no great surprise that writers, musicians and artists should be thinner on the ground when distant from the capital's networks of patrons, agents and impresarios. From William Wordsworth to contralto singer Kathleen Ferrier, The Beatles and David Hockney, northerners have made an impact on cultural life, nonetheless. The best-known activity for many has involved hills and mills – landscapes and Lowryscapes – yet the range of subjects is far wider.

It was a radical step for Wordsworth to return to the Lake District in 1799 with his sister Dorothy and friend Samuel Taylor Coleridge to lead a poet's life in the 'grand / And lovely region' where he grew up.[2] For Wordsworth, poetry should be written in the 'real language of men', yet nevertheless be 'the spontaneous overflow of feelings: it takes its origin from emotion recollected in tranquillity'. He portrayed common people's lives and helped to launch the Romantic Age with its concern for the human relationship to nature. Before the 1790s, mountains were a source of fear. In 1724 Daniel Defoe described Lakeland as 'the wildest, most barren and frightful of any that I have passed over in England'.[3]

Wordsworth has rightly been seen as paving the way for the National Trust, national parks, rambling and environmental movements. An irony is that he helped to draw visitors, threatening to disrupt the landscape and rural society that he hoped to preserve, though he came to terms with tourism by writing one of the best guides to the region.[4] Coleridge was the first person to use the term 'mountaineering' after a nine-day 'circumcursion' of the Lake District mountains, including a terrifying descent of Scafell as a storm approached. Faced with steep drops, he found a way out via a narrow chimney, since christened Fat Man's Agony.[5]

The years of collaboration with Coleridge, 1797–1807, produced Wordsworth's most revolutionary work in the *Lyrical Ballads* and the first versions of *The Prelude*, his poetic autobiography ('look with feelings of fraternal love / Upon those unassuming things that hold / A silent station in this beauteous world'[6]). The remaining four decades until his death in 1850 produced largely forgettable verse. His sympathy for ordinary people remained, yet he came to believe that the only way to preserve their virtues was to maintain the traditional social order. Wordsworth and Coleridge's friendship became strained because of Coleridge's increasing use of opium. In December 1806 Coleridge apparently found Wordsworth naked in bed with Sara Hutchison, younger sister of Wordsworth's wife Mary. Coleridge, unhappily married yet with divorce impossible, was infatuated with Sara; he ran from the house and spent all day drinking in a tavern, yet continued staying with the Wordsworths.[7] The poets quarrelled in 1810, but were reconciled by 1828.

Art critic John Ruskin was profoundly influenced by Wordsworth. Family tours of the Lake District inspired him as a child. In later life Ruskin bought Brantwood, a dilapidated house on the shores of Coniston Water, which he transformed with a turret and lancet windows to view the fells from all angles. Ruskin corresponded with Thomas Dixon, a highly literate cork-cutter who worked in Sunderland's shipyards and whom Ruskin saw as 'the highest type of working man'. His twenty-five letters to Dixon were published in *Time and Tide by Weare and Tyne* (the superfluous 'e' on Wear appears to be either a flourish or a mistake). Dixon, who corresponded with many artistic and literary figures, was far from the north-east's only working-class autodidact. South Shields miner Tommy Turnbull was known as 'Two Williams' because he would recite William Blake or William Wordsworth at the coalface.[8]

The third 'Lakes poet' was fellow Romantic Robert Southey, who lived at Greta Hall, Keswick. Also living there was Coleridge's abandoned wife Sara, who was Southey's sister-in-law, and her three children. Like Wordsworth, Southey was a youthful radical who turned conservative. He was Poet Laureate from 1813 until he died in 1843. Wordsworth succeeded him, but only after the prime minister, Robert Peel, assured him that 'you shall have nothing required of you'; thus Wordsworth became the only Poet Laureate to write no official verses.[9] Southey's poetry is little read today. His most enduring legacy may be the original version of *Goldilocks and the Three Bears*. In 1837 Southey received a letter from a then unknown Charlotte Brontë seeking his advice on her poems. He wrote back praising her talents, but discouraging her from writing professionally: 'Literature cannot be the business of a woman's life.' Years later, Brontë remarked to a friend that the letter was 'kind and admirable; a little stringent, but it did me good'.[10]

The Brontës brought their own perspective to the link between people and landscape. Syima Aslam, director of the Bradford Literature Festival, contrasted the freedom of their Pennine moorland setting with Victorian society's constraints. 'It's in those spaces that the characters are really free to express what they want to express and yet when they are in their domestic spaces they have to behave in the way that they are expected to behave.' She made parallels with twenty-first-century Bradford:

> The social convention and the age that the Brontës were living in is very much akin in terms of social norms to where Asian or Pakistani society is now. The fact that they had to publish under aliases is very telling because of the kind of work that they were writing. This is certainly not true for everyone, but there are a lot of girls in Pakistani society who are probably living under those kinds of restrictions in terms of what they can or cannot do because of their gender.[11]

For W.H. Auden, born in York and raised in Birmingham, holidays with his parents sparked a lifelong fascination with the north Pennines and their abandoned lead mines, which feature in many poems. Until he was fifteen, he was more interested in the machinery than in the people – he expected to become a mining engineer – but above the decaying village of Rookhope he began to see himself as a creative being:

> In Rookhope I was first aware
> Of Self and Not-Self, Death and Dread:
> There I dropped pebbles, listened, heard
> The reservoir of darkness stirred.[12]

The Pennine landscape was central to Ted Hughes, born in Mytholmroyd in the West Riding and raised in the Calder Valley and Mexborough. His poetry is dominated by nature, especially by animals, though his approach is more mythical than naturalistic. One of his best-known subjects, 'Crow', is an amalgam of god, bird and man. Using rhythms and diction influenced by Old English, Hughes saw his role as challenging myths such as technological progress and offering true myths that help humans to discover 'a proper knowledge of the sacred wholeness of nature, and a proper alignment of our behaviour within her laws'.[13] Hughes's poetry remains overshadowed by controversy about the suicides of his first wife, the poet Sylvia Plath, and his partner Assia Wevill, who also killed her and Hughes's four-year-old daughter.

Simon Armitage, the current Poet Laureate, was born in Huddersfield, raised in Marsden and continues to live in the south Pennines. He is far more than a nature poet. Writing in street language accessible to young, urban audiences, he treats subjects such as death, violence and lost love with wry humour. His poetry is influenced by Hughes, Auden and Philip Larkin and echoes Wordsworth's 'real language of men'. Six of his poems are carved into stones on the Stanza Stones Trail, which runs through forty-seven miles of the Pennine region.

That other familiar pole of northernness, the industrial city or mill town, was firmly established in industrial novels of the 1830s to 1850s. Several were by outsiders, including Harriet Martineau's *Manchester Strike*, Charles Dickens' *Hard Times* and Benjamin Disraeli's *Coningsby* and *Sybil*. There is a sense of the north being prodded and probed as an anthropological exhibit, even perhaps in Elizabeth Gaskell's *Mary Barton* and *North and South*, which are generally sensitive treatments by a Manchester resident. A later classic is Walter Greenwood's *Love on the Dole* about poverty in 1930s Salford.

Northern writers' repertoire is wider than industry, however. In the late nineteenth and early twentieth centuries there was a fashion for rural novels, including those of Winifred Holtby, who portrayed small-town east Yorkshire in novels such as *The Crowded Street* and *South Riding*. Whitby appears as 'Monkshaven' in Gaskell's *Sylvia's*

Lovers and as 'Port St Hilda' and 'Danesacre' in the work of locally born writers Mary Linskill and Storm Jameson. The Lake District was popular not only with poets: it was the setting for *Swallows and Amazons*, Arthur Ransome's children's books about school-holiday adventures.

One question facing northern writers is how far they are trying to explain their region to locals and the wider world. The regional novel emerged as a Europe-wide phenomenon in the late nineteenth century.[14] Halifax-born Phyllis Bentley, from an upper-middle-class family of woollen manufacturers, embraced the form in novels such as *Inheritance* (1932). She and others sought to attribute regional character to features such as the harsh climate and hills. In 1938 a Yorkshire Authors Dinner was organised by a committee including Bentley. Chaired by J.B. Priestley, 113 Yorkshire writers met at the Great Northern Hotel in Leeds. White roses, heather and bracken adorned the top table, a map of the county was placed behind Priestley, and a vast Yorkshire pudding was brought in to the singing of 'Ilkla Moor Baht 'At'. Despite various expressions of distinctiveness, speeches stressed Yorkshire's contribution to wider society.[15]

Many northern writers have left to seek fortune elsewhere. Manchester-born Anthony Burgess left at age twenty-three and returned only occasionally, yet the city's accents and landmarks pervade his work.[16] Visiting Leningrad in 1961, he recognised pungent tannery smells that he recalled from his youth. Burgess drew on both Leningrad and Manchester to create the unspecified future urban dystopia in *A Clockwork Orange*. His novel *One Hand Clapping* is set in the fictional northern city of Bradcaster, whose inhabitants are trapped in a dreary, shallow provincial England. In his memoir *Little Wilson and Big God*, Manchester is 'an ugly world with ramshackle houses and foul back alleys': the account of his childhood is marked by grief at the deaths of his mother and sister in the 1918 flu pandemic and the loneliness he associated with his distant father and a stepmother he disliked. Yet in his novel *The Pianoplayers*, Manchester and Blackpool in the 1920s and 1930s are portrayed as places of excitement and adventure. In 1989, Burgess – also a composer – wrote *The Manchester Overture*, celebrating his home city, which was performed there for the first time in 2013.

Keith Waterhouse's 1959 novel *Billy Liar* tells the story of Billy Fisher, a teenager from the fictional Yorkshire town of Stradhoughton, who is unable to stop lying, especially to his three girlfriends. Bored by his job as an undertaker's clerk, Billy indulges in fantasies and dreams of life in London as a comedy writer. But when his opportunity to leave comes, he cannot go through with it – unlike Waterhouse, who left Leeds for a successful career as playwright, novelist and newspaper columnist. *Billy Liar* became a play starring Albert Finney, a film starring Tom Courtenay, and later a television series and a musical. It was part of the 'kitchen sink' movement of working-class novels and dramas, many set in the north, in the late 1950s and early 1960s. Shelagh Delaney's 1958 play *A Taste of Honey*, set in her native Salford (though first produced by Joan Littlewood's Theatre Workshop in east London) was about a teenage schoolgirl who has an affair with a Black sailor, gets pregnant and then moves in with a gay male acquaintance. It also became a film.

Others include Stan Barstow's *A Kind of Loving*, which became a film, television series, radio play and stage play. It is about Vic Brown, a young working-class man forced by his girlfriend's pregnancy into marrying her and moving in with his mother-in-law. John Braine's *Room at the Top*, about the rise of Joe Lampton, an ambitious young man of humble origin, became a successful film with Laurence Harvey and Simone Signoret. David Storey wrote the novel *This Sporting Life*, about a Rugby League player whose romantic life is less successful than his sporting life, and also the screenplay for Lindsay Anderson's film of it. These works represent an unusual period of northern cultural self-confidence amid economic buoyancy and growing consumer power, though the critical acclaim and fashionable status were short-lived. In recent times the north has continued to produce notable writers such as Pat Barker and Kate Atkinson.

The strength of northern theatre also ebbs and flows. A high point was Annie Horniman's creation of Britain's first repertory theatre in Manchester in 1907. It spawned the Manchester school of play-wrights, including Harold Brighouse, Stanley Houghton and Allan Monkhouse. Brighouse's *Hobson's Choice* is a comedy about the battle of wills between a hard-headed cobbler and his daughter Maggie, who defies him by marrying his downtrodden worker, Will. In Houghton's *Hindle Wakes*, mill-girl Fanny Hawthorn has a fling with the boss's son but refuses to marry him, confident in her ability to support herself. *Hobson's Choice* was first performed in New York, however, and Brighouse moved permanently to London. Houghton died in 1913, aged thirty-two. Horniman's venture was successful artistically but less so commercially and was essentially dead by 1917.[17]

The arrival of the Arts Council in 1946 with a brief to stimulate art in the regions helped to create a resurgence of regional theatre and drama from the early 1960s.[18] That spawned a generation of writers including not just Delaney, Waterhouse and Storey, but also Liverpool's Alun Owen, best known for writing the screenplay of The Beatles' film *A Hard Day's Night*, TV playwright Alan Bleasdale, author of *Boys from the Blackstuff*, and Willie Russell, author of *Educating Rita*, *Shirley Valentine* and *Blood Brothers*. John Godber, based for years in Hull, is known for observational comedies. Other popular favourites include Bill Naughton's *Spring and Port Wine* and Jim Cartwright's *The Rise and Fall of Little Voice*. North-east successes include Alan Plater and Alex Glasgow's *Close the Coalhouse Door*, a musical about mining communities, and Lee Hall's screenplay for *Billy Elliot* and play *The Pitmen Painters*, about a group of Ashington miners who took up art. Andrea Dunbar, author of *Rita, Sue and Bob Too*, an autobiographical drama about the sexual adventures of teenage girls living in a run-down part of Bradford, died at twenty-nine.

The north has had a strong tradition of music-making dating back as far as Anglo-Scottish border ballads, folksongs telling vivid tales of raids, feuds, betrayals, romances and revenge from the fourteenth century onwards. In spring 1903, Edward Elgar adjudicated at the Morecambe Music Festival and was deeply impressed by choirs from the north and midlands. 'Some day the press will awake to the fact, already known abroad and to some few of us, that the living centre of music in Great Britain is not London, but somewhere further north,' he wrote to the organiser.[19]

London dominated professional playing and teaching of classical music. Manchester was also a leading centre after the Hallé orchestra was founded in 1857, but never had as many concerts as the capital. Sir Charles Hallé insisted on being allowed to spend each summer in London and kept a house there. Northern-born composers in the nineteenth century included Sheffield's William Sterndale Bennett and Bradford's Frederick Delius, whose relationship with his German wool merchant father was so strained that he left Britain for good in the 1880s. The twentieth century produced Oldham's William Walton, Accrington's Harrison Birtwistle and Manchester's Peter Maxwell Davies.[20] Kathleen Ferrier, daughter of a Lancashire village school teacher, won many amateur piano competitions while working as a telephonist for the General Post Office, before taking up singing seriously. She became an international star with a repertoire that included folksong and popular ballads as well as classical work, but died from cancer aged forty-one at the height of her fame.

The north's strength lay in amateur music-making, notably brass bands and choirs that emerged from the 1830s and 1840s; it also produced amateur orchestras, operatic societies, concertina bands and handbell teams. These traditions grew as industrial society offered new leisure opportunities. Brass bands and choirs were particularly strong in small industrial towns and villages. The culture reached its zenith in the 1890s and declined during the twentieth century as consumer choices widened, although a significant amount remains.

Brass bands were overwhelmingly male and working-class. Wind bands, using clarinets and bassoons, emerged first after the

Napoleonic Wars: some may have been inspired by military bands, though bands formed by workers had a different purpose. They soon gave way to purely brass instruments: the first brass band may have been founded in York in 1833.[21] By later in the century there were tens of thousands, with national championships and national and international tours. They existed all over Britain, but were particularly focused on the Nottinghamshire and Derbyshire coalfields, Lancashire's coal and textile districts, west Yorkshire's coal and textile districts, and the Durham and Northumberland coalfields. Prize-winning bands almost all came from Yorkshire and Lancashire.

Choral societies were mostly mixed-voice, offering opportunities to women. Members were drawn largely from the lower-middle or skilled working classes. Initially the repertoire was dominated by Handel, Haydn and Mendelssohn.[22] This widened later in the century and included new music by composers such as Elgar. Handel's *Messiah* was never superseded as the premier choral work, though not everyone loved it. The *Slaithwaite Guardian and Colne Valley News* wrote in 1898: 'Why not form a philharmonic orchestra – musicians are tired of *Messiah* – it is like the poor, always with us.'[23]

The north's big moment in popular music came in the early 1960s with Merseybeat, notably The Beatles but also including Gerry & The Pacemakers, The Searchers and Cilla Black. Manchester had The Hollies, Freddie and the Dreamers, Herman's Hermits and Wayne Fontana and the Mindbenders, while Newcastle had The Animals. In the 1970s Wigan gained an improbable role as focus of the 'northern soul' dance scene. Manchester's music scene took off in the late 1970s, feeding on the urban bleakness of the era with bands such as Joy Division, New Order and the Smiths leading to the 'Madchester' period, Happy Mondays and the Stone Roses. With typical swagger, there were T-shirts proclaiming 'On the Seventh Day God Created Manchester' and also, with a wider regional flavour, 'Born in the North. Live in the North. Die in the North.'[24] Oasis was popular in the 1990s. Sheffield produced Pulp and later Arctic Monkeys, while Kaiser Chiefs came from Leeds and Maxïmo Park from Newcastle.

Poetry's Romantic moment in the early nineteenth century was paralleled in art. J.M.W. Turner toured the north as a young artist in 1797, making more than two hundred sketches at sites in Derbyshire, Yorkshire, Durham, Northumberland, the Scottish borders, the Lake District, northern Lancashire and Lincolnshire. They formed the basis of more than fifty major paintings and watercolours and shaped his future direction as a landscape painter. John Constable also toured the Lake District in 1806. He told his friend and biographer, Charles Leslie, that the solitude of the mountains oppressed his spirits. Leslie wrote: 'His nature was peculiarly social and could not feel satisfied with scenery, however grand in itself, that did not abound in human associations. He required villages, churches, farmhouses and cottages.'[25]

As in other spheres, many northern-born artists moved south to further their careers. George Stubbs worked in his native Liverpool and in York before spending eighteen months in Lincolnshire dissecting horses, after which he moved to London. George Romney, born in Dalton-in-Furness, Lancashire, left his wife and children in Kendal while he went to the capital, becoming a society portrait painter. Romney made more than sixty portraits of his artistic muse Emma Hamilton, mistress of Lord Nelson. After nearly forty years' absence, he returned in poor health to Kendal, where his wife Mary nursed him for two years until he died.

Newcastle-born John Martin moved to London and became a popular painter of apocalyptic Old Testament scenes that were detested by Ruskin. One artist who stayed local was Thomas Bewick, wood-engraver and natural history author, who was born in Northumberland and worked in Newcastle. He is best known for *A History of British Birds* and also illustrated editions of *Aesop's Fables*. His 'Chillingham bull' has been described by Simon Schama as 'an image of massive power, perhaps the greatest icon of British natural history'.[26] He made technical innovations that cut the cost

17. Knitting party, Liverpool. © De Luan / Alamy Stock Photo.

18. Leeds Town Hall, 1858. © Chronicle / Alamy Stock Photo.

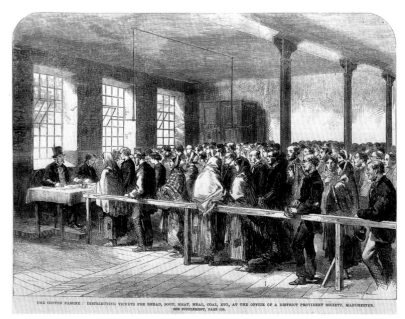

19. The Cotton Famine: Distributing tickets for bread, soup, meat, meal, coal etc. at the office of a District Provident Society, Manchester. Wellcome Collection via Wikimedia Commons.

20. The Dinner hour, Painting by Eyre Crowe. Wigan, 1874. © The Picture Art Collection / Alamy Stock Photo.

21. Josephine Butler, social reformer. LSE Library via Wikimedia Commons.

22. Emmeline Pankhurst, 1913. National Woman's Party records, US Library of Congress collection, via Wikimedia Commons.

23. Two street boys steal coal from a wagon in Manchester during a coal shortage, 1912.
© Sueddeutsche Zeitung Photo / Alamy Stock Photo.

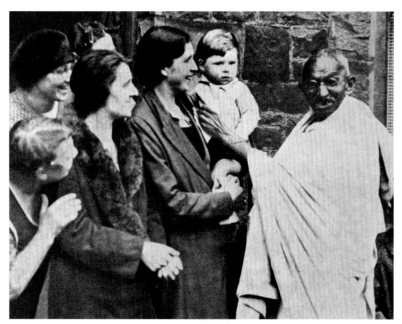

24. Mahatma Gandhi visits Lancashire's cotton mills in 1931, during his tour of England. Darwen, Lancashire. © World History Archive / Alamy Stock Photo.

25. Gracie Fields. Sheet music for 'Sing As We Go'. © Tim Mander / Alamy.

26. Beatles statue, Pier Head. © Nina Alizada/Shutterstock

27. Harold Wilson statue, Huddersfield. Via Shutterstock

28. Temple Works, Leeds: a former flax mill, designed by Joseph Bonomi the Younger and built by John Marshall between 1836 -1840, based on the Temple of Horus at Edfu in Egypt. Via Wikimedia Commons.

29. Grey Street, Newcastle. Via Wikimedia Commons.

30. Stone Roses concert, Manchester, 2016. Via Wikimedia Commons.

31. Nicola Adams with her Olympic gold medal, ExCeL Arena, London, August 2012. © Allstar Picture Library / Alamy Stock Photo.

32. The Three Graces, Liverpool waterfront. © Shaun Jeffers/Shutterstock.

of illustrations. Bewick's swan and Bewick's wren were named after him.

John Atkinson Grimshaw, painter of almost photographic nocturnal urban scenes, was based largely in his native Leeds, though he also maintained a studio in Chelsea in the 1880s. Art was a male-dominated world, yet Manchester-born Annie Swynnerton, best known for portraits and symbolist works, became the first woman to be elected to the Royal Academy of Arts in 1922.[27] She trained in Manchester and later lived in Rome. Derbyshire-born Laura Knight later became the academy's first female full member. She was one of the Staithes Group, a collection of almost forty British impressionists who worked on the Yorkshire coast near Whitby between 1894 and 1909.[28]

Sculptor Henry Moore was born in Castleford and trained at Leeds School of Art before moving south. The Yorkshire hills were a lifelong influence on the undulating form of his reclining figures. His friend Barbara Hepworth, born in Wakefield, was similarly inspired. 'Moving through and over the West Riding landscape with my father in his car, the hills were sculptures; the roads defined the forms,' she said.[29] Surrealist painter Leonora Carrington, born near Chorley, was expelled from two convent schools (including once for exposing herself to a priest) and could not wait to get away from her wealthy mill-owning family. She settled in Mexico, but Lancashire's atmosphere of legends and witchcraft fed the imagery in her paintings.[30]

L.S. Lowry, who lived for years in Salford, remains the artist most closely associated with the north. 'My ambition was to put the industrial scene on the map because nobody had seriously done it,' he said.[31] Incredibly, nobody had. He represented it so successfully that the world came to see the north through the prism of his paintings, which did not please everyone. Lowry's industrial pictures evoke both anomie and community; people move in crowds yet appear lonely. He also painted haunting portraits, Welsh valleys and empty landscapes and seascapes. 'You don't need brains to be a painter, just feelings,' he said.[32]

Lowry studied under Adolphe Valette, a French impressionist whose own work captured Manchester's damp fogginess. Although Lowry was exhibiting from the 1920s and achieved his first one-man London exhibition in 1939, he worked as a rent collector until he retired on his sixty-fifth birthday in 1952. His recurring motifs – chimney, mill, warehouse, terraced row – reflected the repetitive narrowness of factory and slum life. He used only five colours: flake white, ivory black, vermilion, Prussian blue and yellow ochre. His use of a white background to lighten the pictures was suggested early on by D.B. Taylor of the *Manchester Guardian*. After the Second World War, Lowry's painting became more upbeat, including pictures of people at play rather than at work.

David Hockney, born in Bradford and trained at Bradford College of Art, moved to Los Angeles in 1964, where he made paintings of naked young men in swimming pools. These portrayed a world of leisure, bright light and sexual openness, contrasting with Britain's greyness and repression, though a darkness lay behind them: the young men may have been waiting to hear if they had been drafted for service in Vietnam.[33] When Hockney's mother Laura first visited him in Beverly Hills, after two or three days out on the patio, she delivered her verdict on his lifestyle: 'It's strange – all this lovely weather and yet you never see any washing out.'[34] In the 2000s Hockney returned to his birth county and painted a series of vivid pictures of the Yorkshire Wolds.

Among contemporary artists, Damien Hirst, born in Bristol but raised in Leeds, is famous for preserving dead animals in formaldehyde and for reportedly being the UK's wealthiest living artist.[35] Manchester-born Chris Offili is a Turner Prize-winner renowned for paintings incorporating elephant dung. No artist has had a bigger visual impact on the north than Dewsbury-born Antony Gormley, whose public sculptures the *Angel of the North* in Gateshead and *Another Place* on Crosby beach near Liverpool, like almost all his work, use his own body as the basis for metal casts.

Gormley said: 'The angel has three functions – firstly a historic one to remind us that below this site coal miners worked in the dark for 200 years; secondly to grasp hold of the future, expressing our transition from the industrial to the information age; and lastly to be a focus for our hopes and fears – a sculpture is an evolving thing.'[36] It seems an appropriate symbol for how art has helped northerners to think about themselves, their communities and their future.

CHAPTER 25

DIVIDED TONGUES

In the Wakefield *Second Shepherd's Play*, a mystery play written about 1430, Mak the sheep-stealer affects the guise of a 'yoman … of the kyng'. The other shepherds are not fooled. One says: 'Now take outt that Sothren tothe, / And sett in a torde!' They think a southern accent is more worthless than a turd.[1] Awareness of a divide between northern and southern versions of English grew in the Middle Ages. In this example, northerners show they can give as good as they get. Over time, however, northern ways of speaking and writing became marginalised and denigrated as inferior to 'standard' English, reflecting the dominance of London and the south-east.

Dialect, according to Oxford Dictionaries, is 'the form of a language that is spoken in one area with grammar, words and pronunciation that may be different from other forms of the same language'. Northern England has many overlapping variants combining Old English, Norse and Norman roots. These are not debased or incorrect versions of standard English, which is itself a dialect, albeit one that reflects the nation's geographical and social power bases.[2]

The process of standardising written English began in the late fifteenth century, followed later and less successfully by moves towards uniform spoken English. The death-knell of northern and other regional dialects has been sounded regularly since the nineteenth century, yet still they survive. Over the past sixty years, regional identities have again become more valued. Attempts to make all educated people speak the same way have relented. The English language, originally spoken by a few thousand Anglo-Saxons, is now used by more than 1.5 billion people worldwide. A degree of standardisation, particularly of written English, helps mutual comprehension, yet standard English is a tiny part of the whole. 'For every person who speaks standard English, there must be a hundred who do not, and another hundred who speak other varieties as well as the standard,' writes linguistics professor David Crystal.[3] Efforts to impose uniformity on such a fast-changing, unruly tongue seem doomed to fail.

Scholars have traditionally identified four Old English dialects, loosely matching Anglo-Saxon kingdoms: West Saxon, Kentish, Mercian and Northumbrian, with the last two sometimes grouped together as one northern variety, Anglian. There were probably many more. The reason more variants are not identified is lack of data: only three thousand texts amounting to three million words survive from 600 to 1150. By comparison, Charles Dickens alone used more than four million words.[4] Some of the earliest texts are Northumbrian, including the Franks Casket inscription, the Ruthwell Cross inscription, Caedmon's *Hymn* and Bede's *Death Song*. This reflects the fact that, by 700, centres of learning had been established at places such as Jarrow, Durham and Lindisfarne. Northumbrian and West Saxon versions of Caedmon's *Hymn* survive, furnishing evidence of phonological differences between the dialects.[5] Later, West Saxon became the dominant dialect, but it did not become the basis for standard English because England's capital moved from Winchester to London.

The Vikings had a profound influence on English, though one that took a while to become apparent. They have left us with pronouns such as 'he, she, they' and the verb 'to be'. Everyday words of Scandinavian origin include anger, awkward, cake, crooked, egg, get, leg, neck, skill, smile and window.[6] In the north there were numerous borrowings including fell (hillside), lug (ear), laithe (barn), aye (yes) and nay (no).[7] Melvyn Bragg sees the Nordic element as 'clawing deeply' into the language in the north, 'which lies at the core of the fundamental separation – so often noted – between north and south'.[8]

The Middle English period, roughly the twelfth to fifteenth centuries, is seen by Crystal as a 'dialect age', with much regional variation reflected in written language before standardisation began: 'For a glorious 300 years, people could write as they wanted to, and nobody could say they were wrong.'[9] Some linguists point to a divide along the Ribble–Humber line, with a north–south differentiation of words such as lang/long, hoose/house and stane/stone that placed the far north in the same linguistic zone as Scotland. Even within that zone there were several dialect areas.[10]

In Geoffrey Chaucer's *The Reeve's Tale* (late fourteenth century), Cambridge undergraduates called John and Aleyn take revenge on a miller who has been stealing corn belonging to their college, and in the process cause havoc in his family's bedroom. They are from a town 'fer in the north' called Strother and talk in a north-eastern manner. Although some fun is had with the clash of dialects, it is the southern-tongued miller who is the butt of the joke.

There was tolerance of language diversity in the Middle English period, although we start to see some uncomplimentary remarks about regional speech. Ranulf Higden, author of the early fourteenth-century *Polychronicon* (translated from Latin in 1387 by John of Trevisa), wrote that the whole language of the Northumbrians, especially at York, 'ys so scharp, slytting, and frotyng, and unsshape' that 'we southeron men can hardly understand it'. The passage is borrowed from William of Malmesbury, writing in 1125. Higden attributes northern English's outlandishness to being near to 'strange men and aliens', presumably the Scots, and adds that kings of England live in the south because it has better cornland, more people, more noble cities and more profitable harbours.[11]

As London's power and prestige grew, so did belief that regional dialects were inferior. George Puttenham in *The Arte of Poetrie* (1589) advised poets not to 'take the termes of Northern-men' and to 'write as good Southerne as we of Middlesex or Surrey do'. In what could be the first 'north of Watford' joke, Richard Kereforde in 1580 thought it 'but a sport to deffraude a northeron man, ffor so he termeth all northeron men that be born xxti [twenty] mylles north from London'.[12]

The English language showed resilience in avoiding being overwhelmed by French after the Norman Conquest, in part because the French-speaking ruling class was small. English renewed itself by absorbing thousands of French words. Gradual standardisation of written English began during the fifteenth century as the language was used in a wider range of settings, rather than Latin or French. Education expanded, prompting shared usage by a broader cross-section of society. Driving forces included London scriveners such as those at the Chancery, a cross between today's law courts, tax office and civil service.[13] The basis for the emerging standard, perhaps surprisingly, was the east midlands dialect. London was rapidly expanding and drew in large numbers of migrants, particularly from the east midlands, the most populous part of the country. It was also the easiest dialect for both northerners and southerners to understand.[14]

Printing, introduced to England by William Caxton in 1476, also had an impact, though it took a while. Caxton had to cope with regional variations and there were errors and inconsistencies in typesetting. In one well-known story, Caxton described how a mercer named Sheffelde came ashore from a ship in the Thames and asked at a house for 'mete' and especially 'eggys'. The good wife answered that she did not speak French. She did not understand what he meant by 'eggs', one of few words where the northern form came to predominate, the southern plural being 'eyren'.[15] Once significant levels of standardisation took hold in printed books, however, it helped to spread the standard rapidly and widely.[16]

The drive to standardise English reached its peak in the eighteenth century, when there was a fear that the language had become too chaotic, a reaction perhaps to 150 years of social and political upheaval. Some feared English was changing so fast that readers were losing the ability to read authors such as Chaucer and that contemporary authors would themselves rapidly become unintelligible. Satirist Jonathan Swift was among those who pressed, ultimately unsuccessfully, for an academy to fix the language, such as French and Italians already had.[17] Samuel Johnson hoped initially that his 1755 *Dictionary* would be a means 'by which the pronunciation of our language may be fixed and its attainment facilitated; by which its purity may be preserved, its use ascertained and its duration lengthened'. By the time he came to write the preface, however, he had to acknowledge that complete uniformity was impossible to achieve.[18]

Efforts to standardise spoken English gathered force from the eighteenth century, but ultimately achieved less success than with written English. They reached their height in Received Pronunciation, also known as BBC English or King's English, in the twentieth century. Almost as soon as RP arrived, it started to fragment, with personal and age-related variations developing. Since the 1960s, RP's upper and upper-middle-class character has come to seem a liability. Crystal estimates that less than 2 per cent of the British population now uses it. Scholars talk instead of 'modified RP' or 'regional standards'.[19]

The Romantic movement created interest in regional dialects. William Wordsworth, in his preface to the *Lyrical Ballads* (1798), said they aimed to describe incidents and situations from common life 'as far as possible, in a selection of language really used by men'. However, Wordsworth did not write in dialect. He achieved a simpler and 'purified' form of poetic language, but it was standard English.[20]

Northern dialect literature re-emerged in the eighteenth and nineteenth centuries in forms such as broadside ballads, bucolic dialogues, almanacs (popular in Yorkshire) and journals (particularly in Lancashire). Popular writers included John Collier of Milnrow, Lancashire, who wrote as 'Tim Bobbin', and Rochdale-born poet Edwin Waugh, whose most famous poem was 'Come whoam to thi childer an' me'. John Hartley's *Halifax Original Illustrated Clock Almanac*, edited almost continuously by the Halifax-born writer from 1867 until his death in 1915, enjoyed an annual sale of about eighty thousand copies.[21]

Much dialect writing was comic, nostalgic or sentimental, with an emphasis on hearth and family and domestic pleasure. It was not overly political, though it did not shy away from hardship. While it is not much read today, it prefigured later cultural forms such as stand-up and situation comedy and soap opera. It was full of stock characters including sharp-tongued women, henpecked husbands, wise uncles and daft lads. Its largest audience was reached via public performance. Most northern writers both performed their own work and published it for performance by others. Joseph Wright, an apprentice wool sorter, was a dialect reciter in Bradford's chapel-based recreational culture in the 1870s; later he became Professor of Comparative Philology at Oxford and editor of the *English Dialect Dictionary* (1905).[22]

Music hall also flourished in the north from the mid-nineteenth century until well into the twentieth. George Formby senior, who introduced the phrase 'Wigan Pier' into the language, is said to have based his bittersweet naïve character 'John Willie' on the bronchitic condition of a typical mill worker.[23]

Pressure to conform to standard English or RP in order to succeed nationally has discomfited many a northerner. As Manchester-born Anthony Burgess put it: 'Cradle-speakers of that south-eastern dialect which has become the national language of the educated have never sufficiently realised the pain the provincials have suffered in forcing themselves to conform.' Composer William Walton, born in Oldham, is said to have been bullied at Oxford by his peers because of his accent. Linguist H.C. Wyld reduced female students to tears at Oxford by his fierce comments on their northern pronunciation.[24]

Halifax-born actor and radio presenter Wilfred Pickles was invited to read the national news early in the Second World War, apparently because Brendan Bracken, minister of information, believed that a northern voice would be an inclusive gesture and would be difficult for German propagandists to impersonate. Although BBC research found Pickles' reading popular, a torrent of abuse came through the post from people who claimed that his delivery undermined the credibility of the bulletin. Pickles claimed he enjoyed the fuss, but he eventually decided to give it up, preferring to carry on with other broadcasting work in Manchester.[25]

Attitudes have thankfully improved in the past half-century. Regional accents have become more accepted, though the south-east still dominates. While some northern dialect features have eroded, enough variety still exists to express regional and local identities. Standard English and regional dialects can coexist; many educated people deploy elements of both, depending on the context. English is nothing if not adaptable.

TWENTIETH CENTURY AND BEYOND

CHAPTER 26

ABRUPT REVERSAL

Edwardian England is often portrayed as a long, sunlit afternoon that ended in the horror of the First World War. In fact, although there was peace and relative prosperity, it was also a period of rapid – sometimes disconcerting – changes in science, technology, society and politics. Northern England was in the forefront of union militancy, the campaign for female emancipation and the creation of the Labour Party. However, its industrial self-belief was soon to be shattered by a devastating economic collapse.

On the scientific front, New Zealander Ernest Rutherford was already a celebrated figure by the time he arrived as Professor of Physics at the Victoria University of Manchester in 1907. His work there redefined the nature of matter. The atom had previously been thought the smallest particle in the universe. His experiments established that an atom's mass was concentrated in its nucleus – a particle a thousand times smaller than the atom itself – with the rest being made of a cloud of orbiting electrons.

In 1917, Rutherford achieved the first ever artificially induced nuclear reaction by firing particles from a radioactive source that disintegrated the nuclei of nitrogen atoms, resulting in the release of subatomic particles that he afterwards named protons. That is sometimes described as 'splitting the atom', a term that some prefer to apply to later experiments. His work in Manchester did, though, lead ultimately to nuclear energy and the atomic bombs that devastated Hiroshima and Nagasaki in 1945.[1]

Technological developments of the age included the motor car and aeroplane. Many breakthroughs were French, German or American. Henry Ford established his first European assembly plant at Trafford Park near Manchester in 1911, making the Model T car initially from parts imported from the US. In the 1910 London to Manchester air race, the £10,000 prize was won by Frenchman Louis Paulhan. There were some British achievements. Engineer Henry Royce was introduced to dealer Charles Rolls at a Manchester hotel, on 4 May 1904, creating the renowned luxury car marque and later aero-engine manufacturing business. After the war, Stretford-born John Alcock, with navigator Arthur Whitten Brown, piloted the first non-stop transatlantic flight from St John's, Newfoundland, to Clifden, Connemara, Ireland, in June 1919.

Overall, however, Britain, which had been so creative a century earlier, particularly in northern England, found itself with a dearth of innovative mechanical engineers. One of the few globally significant breakthroughs was development of the steam turbine, which Charles Parsons had devised on Tyneside in 1884. It transformed merchant shipping and naval warfare just in time for the start of the world war.

Britain still led the world in trade, finance and shipping, and had strong bases in manufacturing and mining, but its industrial growth fell behind those of rivals. In 1910, Britain's share of world industrial capacity stood at 15 per cent, just behind Germany's 16 per cent and less than half the US's 35 per cent.[2] It was over-reliant on northern industries: textiles, coalmining, iron, steel, shipbuilding. The north's share of UK gross domestic product grew from 22 to 27 per cent between 1861 and 1911,[3] but its industries lacked sufficient innovation, whether through complacency among manufacturers or lack of investment from the City of London, which often preferred to put its money overseas. The north also failed to develop significant new industries.

Lancashire's cotton industry was aware of growing competition, though few considered it a serious threat. In 1911, almost one in five of the county's workforce was employed in cotton production.[4] As one manufacturer put it:

> My lad, never again let anybody in Lancashire hear you talk this childish stuff about foreign competition. It's right enough for Londoners and such like, but it puts a born Lancashire man to shame as an ignoramus. It's just twaddle. In the first place, we've got the only climate in the world where cotton piece goods in any quantity can ever be produced. In the second place, no foreign Johnnies can ever be bred that can spin and weave like Lancashire lads and lasses. In the third place, there are more spindles in Oldham than in all the rest of the world put together. And last of all, if they had the climate and the men and the spindles – which they can never have – foreigners could never find the brains Lancashire cotton men have for the job.[5]

There were pockets of economic modernisation, notably Trafford Park, regarded as the world's first planned industrial estate, which opened in 1896 beside the Manchester Ship Canal, itself completed three years earlier. 'People have talked about the decline of Lancashire. But Manchester declines to decline,' opined the *St James's Gazette* about the canal.[6] Trafford Park was created by Ernest Hooley, an opportunistic Nottingham company promoter (and later fraudster) on parkland sold by a local baronet, Sir Humphrey Francis de Trafford. Hooley planned to build grand villas and a racecourse, but instead was persuaded to build an industrial estate. It attracted engineering, chemicals and food-processing firms, including leading American businesses, starting with Westinghouse, which built Europe's largest factory complex there. By 1903, Trafford Park employed 12,000. At its peak in 1945, an estimated 75,000 worked there.[7]

Alliott Verdon Roe, born in Patricroft, was a pioneer pilot who founded the Avro aircraft company in Manchester in 1910. After experimenting with model aeroplanes, in 1908 he had flown a full-size aeroplane at Brooklands in Surrey and became the first Englishman to fly an all-British machine, a triplane, on Walthamstow marshes. Avro's most popular model, the 504, became the backbone of allied flying training during the First World War and eventually more than eight thousand were built. Thus he proved wrong the *Manchester Guardian*, which said in a leader dated 11 September 1908: 'We cannot understand to what practical use a flying machine that is heavier than air can be put.'[8] Avro became a subsidiary of Hawker Siddeley in 1935. The Avro Lancaster became one of the Second World War's leading bombers and the delta-wing Avro Vulcan a stalwart of the Cold War.

Britain's steel output rose from 1.3 million tons in 1880 to eight million in 1914, but Germany overtook it in 1893 and by 1914 was producing 14 million tons, almost double Britain's total.[9] Many of Teesside's furnaces were small and their equipment elderly. Sheffield remained the leading international centre for special steels and a huge producer of guns, projectiles and armour-plate. The arms race up to the First World War swelled order books at Sheffield's main steel producers, Vickers, Brown, Cammell Laird, Hadfield and Firth.[10]

The race to build battleships also benefited the shipyards of Tyne and Wear, Barrow-in-Furness and Merseyside. Vickers acquired Barrow shipyard in 1897. On Tyneside, Armstrong Whitworth, created through a merger, was regarded as the world's most successful exporter of warships.[11] It also made ice-breakers and oil tankers. One spectacular feat was the *Baikal*, an ice-breaking train ferry sent overland in thousands of pieces and reassembled on the bank of Russia's Lake Baikal as part of the Trans-Siberian Railway. Armstrong Whitworth was, however, less successful at building cars.[12]

In 1905 Armstrong-built warships helped the Imperial Japanese Navy to defeat the Russian fleet. All this warmongering had caused a bizarre tragedy, however. In October 1904, the Russian navy, steaming to the far east, attacked a trawler fleet from Hull in the North Sea's Dogger Bank, mistaking them for Japanese torpedo boats steaming in the opposite direction. Russian warships also fired on each other in the chaos. Two fishermen and two Russians died and a further six British fishermen were injured.[13]

Industrial Tyneside enjoyed cheap electricity thanks to Charles Merz, a Newcastle-born electrical engineer who, with his consulting partner William McLellan, built power-supply systems that became the model for the National Grid. They also worked in Australia, Argentina, South Africa, India and the US. Their efforts cut Tyneside's electricity price from more than fourpence a unit in 1899 to just more than a penny in 1905. Electricity use there increased thirtyfold in the decade before the First World War, far outstripping growth elsewhere in the UK.[14]

Adoption of Charles Parsons' turbine engines, enabling faster speeds, spread from warships to passenger liners, creating an opportunity to restore some of Britain's maritime prestige. The Germans had built liners that for three successive years won the Blue Riband for crossing the Atlantic at record speed. In response, the British government gave Cunard loans and a subsidy to commission two faster, turbine-driven liners. The result was the *Mauretania* and *Lusitania*.[15] The *Lusitania*, built on the Clyde, made its maiden voyage from Liverpool to New York in 1907 and soon won the Blue Riband. Two months later, the *Mauretania*, built by Swan Hunter and Wigham Richardson on the Tyne, made her first Atlantic crossing and broke the *Lusitania*'s record. It held the Blue Riband for twenty-two years.

The Liverpool-based Oceanic Steam Navigation Company, commonly known as White Star Line, commissioned two non-turbine liners, the *Olympic* and *Titanic*, from Harland & Wolff in Belfast. More than one and a half thousand died when the *Titanic* sank in 1912 after striking an iceberg during her maiden voyage from Southampton to New York. Wallace Hartley, leader of the band that was said to have carried on playing to calm passengers, came from Colne in Lancashire. There is a plaque to the musicians in the Philharmonic Hall, Liverpool, and a monument on Liverpool waterfront to 244 engineers who lost their lives. Second officer Charles Lightoller, from Chorley, was in charge of loading lifeboats on the port side and distinguished himself by applying the 'women and children first' policy. Another Lancastrian was Fred Fleet, the lookout who first saw the iceberg. One man whose reputation never recovered was Joseph Bruce Ismay, from Crosby, White Star Line's chairman and managing director. He was blamed for cutting the number of lifeboats from forty-eight to the minimum required by regulations, sixteen, and pilloried in the press for deserting the ship while women and children were still on board.[16] The official inquiry said he had jumped aboard the last lifeboat on the starboard side after assisting other passengers.

For many northerners, the Edwardian era was a mix of optimism and hardship. Despite rising average living standards in the later Victorian era, poverty remained significant. Seebohm Rowntree calculated that, in 1901, almost 30 per cent of York's population lived in poverty and he believed that was similar in other towns and cities.[17] Most families led a frugal existence, fearing disability or unemployment. There was scope for leisure, however. J.B. Priestley listed what Bradford had to offer:

> three daily papers and a weekly; the Subscription concerts on Fridays, the Bradford Permanent series on Saturdays, and superb choral singing on almost any night; two theatres, two music halls, two or three professional concert parties; an Arts Club; a Playgoers Society; one football club that won the FA Cup not long before; several fine old pubs from the *George* in Market Street to the *Spotted House*, easily reached from the band concerts in Lister Park.[18]

A glimpse into Edwardian northerners' lives was afforded by the discovery in 1994 of a hoard of negatives of films made by Mitchell and Kenyon, a Blackburn firm that traded under slogans such as 'Local Films For Local People'. Its shots include workers leaving factories, street scenes, parades, marches, fairgrounds and football matches, including one between Sheffield United and Bury in September 1902 featuring William 'Fatty' Foulke, a Sheffield goal-keeper of legendary proportions.[19]

Society was changing. Women were no longer so willing to accept the subordinate role that Victorian England had ascribed to them. The militant suffragette movement began in the north, led by Emmeline Pankhurst and her daughters. Workers were also discon-tented, particularly as prosperity enjoyed by the middle and upper classes was becoming ever more visible. Trade unionism had grown steadily in the north's industrial districts. There was a dramatic increase in industrial conflict from 1908, with strikes in sectors including cotton, shipbuilding and coalmining.

In summer 1911 the first national railway workers' strike began with an unofficial stoppage in Liverpool, coinciding with a wider strike by dock and transport workers in the city. Herbert Henry Asquith, Liberal prime minister, and Winston Churchill, home secretary, sent 2,000 soldiers and a cruiser to Merseyside. The *Manchester Guardian* likened Liverpool to 'a city of which a besieg-ing army has just taken possession'. Police reinforced from Birmingham and Leeds baton-charged a mass meeting. A policeman was killed in the ensuing street violence and two days later hussars shot dead a docker and a carter.[20]

Working-class political consciousness grew, leading to the creation of the Labour Party. From the 1870s a number of working-class 'Lib–Lab' candidates were supported by trade unions and the Liberal Party, but demands for separate representation increased. At the 1892 general election, three working men were elected without Liberal support: Keir Hardie in South West Ham, John Burns in Battersea and Havelock Wilson (a seamen's union leader from

Sunderland) in Middlesbrough. A meeting in Bradford in 1893 – after an industrial defeat for woollen workers in the town's Manningham Mills – founded the Independent Labour Party, with Hardie as its first chairman.

The ILP was initially slow to make headway in the north, where workers in many parts remained surprisingly supportive of the Liberals, despite it being their bosses' party. Unions had little appetite for socialist ideology. In part this was the influence of nonconformism, which favoured personal enterprise and advancement rather than equality and common endeavour. Coal and cotton unions were generally hostile to the ILP. Coalfield unions were usually led by Methodists.[21]

Lancashire, always the odd one out, had a tradition of working-class Conservatism. The causes are much debated. Hostility to Irish Catholic immigration played a part. The roots may lie in the county's older history of isolation and insularity. Writer John Morley said of 1860s Lancashire: 'As a rule in the cotton districts where the trade relations between master and man have been ... established on a satisfactory basis, the man, in the truly feudal spirit, takes part with his master, and wears his political colour.'[22] The Conservatives won at least four-fifths of constituencies in Lancashire, Cheshire and High Peak in 1886, 1895 and 1900, before collapsing to 22 per cent in 1906, when their proposals for imperial preference – tariffs that favoured imports from the British Empire against those from the US and Germany – damaged them. Lancashire's Conservatism persisted. As late as 1955–70, only 35 per cent of Lancashire's MPs were Labour compared with 56 per cent in Yorkshire and 76 per cent in the north-east, even though the class composition was similar.[23]

In 1900 left-wing organisations formed the Labour Representation Committee to sponsor parliamentary candidates. Support for the LRC was boosted by the 1901 Taff Vale case, a dispute between strikers and a railway company that ended with the union being ordered to pay £23,000 damages. The judgment in effect made strikes illegal by opening union funds to sequestration. More unions joined the LRC, realising that they needed representation in parliament to change the law. The 1906 election was a landslide for the Liberals – the last time they won a majority in their own right – in which the LRC also won twenty-nine seats, helped by a secret pact not to split the opposition vote. The Conservative prime minister, Arthur Balfour, lost his Manchester East seat. In their first post-election meeting, the Labour group's MPs adopted the name 'The Labour Party'. The ILP, which had played a central role, immediately signed up.

Under prime ministers Henry Campbell-Bannerman (1905–8) and Asquith (1908–16) the Liberals passed reforms that created Britain's basic welfare state. After some prevarication, the government met the unions' demand to legislate to overturn fully the Taff Vale ruling. Asquith, who took over when Campbell-Bannerman resigned because of ill-health, was born in Morley to a Yorkshire nonconformist family, though he moved to London at age eleven. The government's dominant figure was David Lloyd George, chancellor of the exchequer, born in Chorlton-on-Medlock, Manchester, to Welsh parents.

The People's Budget of 1909 proposed taxes on lands and incomes of the wealthy to fund old-age pensions, national insurance and unemployment assistance. It was blocked for a year by the Conservative-dominated House of Lords, leading to two general elections in 1910 and the Parliament Act 1911, limiting the Lords' power of veto. The Liberals depended on Irish Nationalists for a majority, forcing Asquith to introduce a third home rule bill in 1912. Ulster unionists led by Sir Edward Carson threatened armed resistance. This issue, along with the question of women's suffrage, was unresolved when the First World War broke out. 'The lamps are going out all over Europe, we shall not see them lit again in our lifetime,' foreign secretary Sir Edward Grey told a friend. He was MP for Berwick-upon-Tweed and came from the same Northumberland aristocratic family as Lord Grey, the prime minister who enacted the Reform Act 1832.

Volunteer soldiers were recruited heavily from northern industrial cities, Scotland and Ireland. It was argued that more men would enlist if they knew they were going to serve beside friends and relatives. Edward Stanley, seventeenth Earl of Derby, recruited a 'pals' battalion in Liverpool and many other cities and towns followed. Among the best-known were the Accrington Pals, a battalion from Accrington, Blackburn, Burnley and Chorley. On the first day of the Battle of the Somme, 1 July 1916, 235 of them were killed and 350 wounded out of 700.[24]

Tynesiders were particularly keen to volunteer, reflecting the outer north's martial tradition, an economy geared to armaments and a working-class male obsession with strength and courage. The Royal Northumberland Fusiliers and Durham Light Infantry raised many battalions. In Newcastle, the lord mayor rebuked women handing out white feathers because there was 'no need to distribute white feathers amongst the young men of Tyneside'.[25] Tyneside Scots and Irish raised four battalions each and were mauled at the Somme.[26] Of eighty Scottish officers only ten survived, with similar losses among the Irish. Bradford was also among places that suffered huge casualties there. A month later it suffered a second tragedy when the Low Moor Munitions Company's factory in the city exploded, killing 339 and injuring 60.[27]

Cities and towns including Hull, Liverpool, Sheffield and Jarrow were subject to Zeppelin raids, though fewer than in the south. Scarborough was bombarded by the German navy. Zeppelins were not always accurate. One attacked Nottingham, which its captain thought was Manchester. Bolton suffered thirteen deaths in a raid by a Zeppelin whose captain thought he was attacking Derby.[28] West Hartlepool was bombed in 1916 by a Zeppelin captained by Marlene Dietrich's uncle Max. It was shot down by Second Lieutenant Ian Pyott, solo pilot of a biplane, who became a national hero.[29]

Women worked in munitions, aircraft factories and formerly male occupations such as engineering and transport. Liverpool docks proved a step too far, however: moves in 1916 for women to become porters were defeated by the dock labourers' union.[30] On Tyneside, Swan Hunter and Wigham Richardson's Low Walker yard had a shell shop where hundreds of women worked on high-explosive devices. At the war's end, the women were thanked for their efforts with a lavish party and gold bracelets and brooches – and then sacked to make way for men returning from the forces.[31]

North-east industry was at full stretch trying to meet wartime demand for coal, coke, steel, iron, ships and engineering products. In 1914–18 Armstrong Whitworth produced 13,000 guns, 47 warships and 230 armed merchant ships. Its workforce grew from 25,000 to 60,000. Its chairman was John Meade Falkner, a 6-foot 9-inch giant of a businessman who also wrote the children's adventure story *Moonfleet*. Armstrong Whitworth built two ice-breakers for the Russians. Their construction was supervised by a young Russian engineer called Yevgeny Zamyatin, who was also a talented novelist and playwright.[32]

Demand for uniforms meant that Bradford's woollen mills were in full production. The war, however, loosed Lancashire's grip on British India, the biggest outlet for its cotton goods. A Burnley manufacturer had warned a royal commission: 'On India we rely, and if we lose India, Lancashire is practically ruined.'[33] In Liverpool, the quantity of merchandise shipped through the port was high, but in 1918 the number of ships using it was scarcely half the pre-war total. Many merchant ships were sunk and in 1915 a German submarine torpedoed the *Lusitania* on her voyage from New York to Liverpool, killing 1,201.[34]

Production of cotton, wool and coal peaked on the eve of the war. Several northern industries enjoyed a brief post-war boom as pent-up demand and investment were released, but Britain was soon to buckle under a 1920–22 recession that proved deeper for the UK than the great depression of 1930–3.

CHAPTER 27

SING AS WE GO

Gracie Fields, in her best-known film *Sing As We Go!* (1934, script by J.B. Priestley), plays a high-spirited, resourceful heroine made redundant from her job in a Lancashire cotton mill, who is forced to seek work in Blackpool. After misadventures punctuated by songs and romantic complications, she helps to reopen the factory, which is saved by adopting a new synthetic fibre. She leads workers back through the gates in the same manner as they left, singing the title song with gusto.[1] 'Our Gracie' was herself a Rochdale mill girl who became an international singing and acting star of the industrial age, bringing hope and humour to millions.

There were few such fairy tales for the interwar north. This was a dreadful time for many, notably on Tyneside and in Lancashire mill towns. Industries that had been core in the nineteenth century suffered a steep decline: coal, shipbuilding, cotton and, to some extent, iron, steel and wool. Areas where these were concentrated suffered long-term depression. It was a time of unemployment, means-testing of benefits, and hunger marches. The jobless rate was two or three times that seen in regions where new industries were developing, mainly the south-east and midlands.

The modern north–south divide took vivid shape, with the north cast as England's economic laggard. Yet even in the north, there was a divide between those in and out of work. For those in employment there was growth in real wages, shorter hours and even paid holidays despite two recessions. White-collar and middle-class occupations continued to expand. The consumer economy grew. New suburbs were created by private and public housebuilding. Tourists flocked to seaside resorts: Blackpool was attracting more than seven million overnight visitors a year by the later 1930s. By 1939 surveys in Liverpool and York found that 40 per cent of the population visited the cinema at least once a week. With tickets costing only sixpence, it was affordable for most.[2]

The 1918 election resulted in a landslide victory for David Lloyd George's coalition government, comprising mainly Conservatives and coalition Liberals. Lloyd George promised to make Britain 'a fit country for heroes to live in'.[3] Many wartime controls were lifted. Railways, shipping, even coalmines were returned to private hands. There was a vigorous, if short-lived, programme to extend health and educational services, raise pensions and spread universal unemployment insurance. A subsidised housing programme was launched by Liberal minister Christopher Addison, which, with reluctant Treasury support, achieved more than two hundred thousand publicly built houses between 1919 and 1922, a modest start in dealing with the Victorian era's legacy of slum housing.[4]

The year 1918 also saw a serious outbreak of influenza, nicknamed 'Spanish flu', which killed 238,000 in the UK and 50 million to 100 million worldwide. In the absence of a National Health Service, the response was decentralised and uncoordinated. Lloyd George almost became a victim. He was taken ill on a visit to Manchester, where he was returning to his birthplace to receive the keys to the city. He spent a week confined to bed in isolation and needed a respirator. His valet later described his condition as 'touch and go'.[5]

A brief, speculative boom took place in 1919–20, particularly in cotton, shipbuilding, shipping and engineering. Investors borrowed unwisely to finance amalgamations that created bloated companies.

A total of 238 cotton mills, comprising 42 per cent of spinning capacity, changed hands.[6] 'All over Lancashire there could be heard whispers of fortunes that left the riches of pre-war days far behind,' wrote Benjamin Bowker in *Lancashire under the Hammer* (1928). Half the cotton-spinning industry, he said, was 'cast on to the gaming tables' as local syndicates traded in mill company shares at inflated prices.[7] Merchant bankers used Northumberland Shipbuilding Company, at Howdon, on the Tyne, to build the UK's largest shipyard combine. It went into receivership in 1926.

The boom ended abruptly when the government raised the key interest rate from 6 to 7 per cent. Investment halted, prices began to fall and unemployment to rise. Ministers came under pressure to curb national debt and public spending. The 1919 budget had ballooned to more than £2.5 billion, compared with planned spending of £200 million in 1914.[8] The first victim of cuts was Addison's housing programme; he resigned. A review by a committee of businessmen under Sir Eric Geddes cut what was left of the social reforms.

Some core industries had lost markets as a result of the war. In cotton, India had doubled production, so that by 1929 UK cotton exports to India dropped to 42 per cent of the pre-war level; market share was also lost to Japan. The impact was felt particularly in Oldham, Blackburn and Accrington.[9] In shipbuilding, record tonnage was launched in 1920, but in 1921 300 ships were cancelled. Unemployment reached 25 per cent of insured workers in Northern Ireland, 21 per cent in Scotland and 18 per cent each in north-east England and the midlands.[10] Short-time working in cotton protected north-west jobs in the short term, though it delayed reductions in capacity.

There was a wave of strikes in 1919–21 in the cotton, iron and coal industries, and by police and railway workers, as people sought to protect living standards. In 1921, 85,872 working days were lost through strikes, the second highest in UK history after the 162,263 lost in the general strike year of 1926 – and nearly three times the

29,474 lost in 1979's 'winter of discontent'.[11] The Emergency Powers Act 1920 enabled ministers to make emergency regulations and set up courts of summary jurisdiction if strikes threatened the supply of essentials. The economy began to stabilise after 1922, but the north's share of British economic output dropped from 30 to 25 per cent between 1921 and 1931, while that of London and the south-east increased from 35 to 39 per cent.[12]

The coalition collapsed in 1922 and an election was won by the Conservatives under Andrew Bonar Law. Labour more than doubled its seats and overtook the divided Liberals. The Tories went on to spend all but eight of the next forty-two years as the largest party, with Labour as the main opposition and the Liberals falling to third. Labour's breakthrough was achieved under the leadership of John Robert Clynes, a former Oldham cotton piecer who had begun working in a mill aged ten – a self-taught man who loved to quote Shakespeare and Milton in parliamentary debates. Less than a month later, Clynes was defeated in a leadership challenge by the more charismatic Ramsay MacDonald. Bonar Law stepped down after seven months because of a terminal illness and was replaced by Stanley Baldwin. Baldwin called an election in 1923 to seek a mandate for protectionist policies, but the result was a hung parliament. MacDonald formed the first Labour government with tacit Liberal support.

His cabinet included northerners such as Arthur Henderson, home secretary, an iron moulder who was born in Glasgow and raised in Newcastle. An imperturbable figure nicknamed 'Uncle Arthur', Henderson won the Nobel Peace Prize in 1934 and uniquely served three separate terms as Labour leader in different decades (1908–10, 1914–17, 1931–2). He was elected five times at by-elections in different constituencies, giving him the record for the number of comebacks from losing a previous seat. Philip Snowden, chancellor of the exchequer, was a West Riding Methodist and teetotaller. Clynes was leader of the Commons. They were mostly moderates, though the party had been divided over its direction since the Russian Revolution. Radicalism was stronger on Clydeside than in the north. The government lasted only nine months. Its biggest achievement was a housing act pushed through by Scottish socialist John Wheatley, minister for health, which increased the subsidy for houses built at controlled rents. It enabled a huge expansion of municipal housebuilding: 521,700 houses were built under it before the subsidy was abolished in 1933.[13]

Baldwin's Conservatives won the 1924 election by a landslide. The Liberals were further eclipsed, cementing the north–south political divide: former southern Liberal voters went Tory while northern Liberal voters went Labour. It became a long-term pattern. In 1925 Winston Churchill, the chancellor, returned Britain to the gold standard at the pre-war parity of $4.86 to the pound, aiming to restore international price stability. But the rate was too high, causing more problems for exporters. The coal industry suffered from deep-seated problems, as a royal commission under Sir Herbert Samuel in 1925–6 discovered. Samuel, a Liberal politician from Liverpool, was the first nominally practising Jew to serve as a cabinet minister (1909) and to become leader of a major British party (Liberal leader 1931–5). He had also been the first high commissioner for Palestine in 1920. Samuel found that some 2,500 mines were divided among 1,400 owners. Many mines were too small to be efficient and owners lacked capital to modernise.[14] The industry experienced repeated strikes. The president of the Miners' Federation of Great Britain was Herbert Smith, a taciturn Yorkshireman who was once said to have cleaned his dentures during negotiations with the government before telling the prime minister: 'Nowt doing.'[15]

The Samuel report advised reorganisation into larger, more viable units, but mine owners were opposed and argued for wage cuts, which were unacceptable to miners – thus postponing a necessary reconstruction. At the end of April 1926 the owners began to lock miners out. The Trades Union Congress ordered a general strike by rail and transport workers, printers, dockers, ironworkers and steelworkers in support of the miners. The government proclaimed a state of emergency and enlisted middle-class volunteers to maintain essential services. There was little violence, though the Flying Scotsman was derailed by striking miners near Newcastle. After nine days, the TUC called off the strike, fearing a drift back to work. The miners stayed out for several months but were eventually forced to accept longer hours and lower wages. Strikes declined afterwards and Britain has never had another general strike. Memories of what many miners saw as the TUC's betrayal were still raw as late as the 1984–5 coal strike.

The economic climate turned harsh again as the 1929 Wall Street crash led to the great depression. Countries raised tariffs and world trade shrank by a third. The impact in Britain, which had not experienced a 1920s boom, was less severe than in countries such as the US, but again it was concentrated in older industrial areas. By 1930, almost 30 per cent of insured workers were unemployed in the north-west and 25 per cent in the north-east, compared with just under 10 per cent in London.[16]

New industries such as electricals, motor cars, bicycles, aircraft, rayon (initially known as artificial silk), hosiery, plastics, chemicals, stainless steel and scientific instruments accounted for 16 per cent of output in 1930.[17] Some happened in the north. The chemicals industry expanded in Lancashire, Cheshire and Teesside, including building the Brunner, Mond (later Imperial Chemical Industries) plant at Billingham, near Stockton. Sheffield made the most of its invention of stainless steel (though the Gillette safety razor killed its cut-throat razor trade). Most, however, were in the south midlands or the home counties. These light industries needed little but supplies of power and semi-skilled labour. Development of the national electricity grid meant that industry no longer needed to be near coalfields. Herbert Austin's car factory was at Longbridge, Birmingham, while William Morris's was at Cowley, Oxford. Ford moved from Trafford Park to Dagenham in 1931.

J.B. Priestley in *English Journey* (1934) described the north as 'the industrial England of coal, iron, steel, cotton, wool, railways ...

sooty dismal little towns, and still sootier grim fortress-like cities'. By contrast, he described the new region north-west of London: 'America, I supposed, was its real birthplace. This is the England of arterial and by-pass roads, filling stations and factories that look like exhibition buildings, of giant cinemas and dance-halls and cafés, bungalows with tiny garages … as near to a classless society as we have yet got. Unfortunately, it is a bit too cheap.'[18]

MacDonald's second minority government in 1929 was engulfed by economic crisis. Snowden, chancellor again, was a rigid exponent of orthodox finance and would not permit deficit spending. The cabinet split over unemployment benefit cuts and MacDonald formed a national government with Conservatives and Liberals, leading to his expulsion from Labour, which was routed at the 1931 election. The Treasury was forced to abandon the gold standard, after which the pound fell by 25 per cent, making exports more competitive. In 1932, 10 per cent tariffs were introduced on all imports except those from the Empire. Baldwin took over from MacDonald in 1935.

The economy began to recover from 1932. Average unemployment during the 1930s was half that of the US and Britain avoided the rise of fascism seen in other European countries, but life remained tough in parts of the north. The government passed the Special Areas Act 1934 (a euphemism: they were originally intended to be known as 'distressed areas'), designating west Cumberland, Tyneside and most of County Durham, Scotland's central belt, west Monmouthshire and most of Glamorgan, but not Lancashire. Commissioners were appointed to promote development in these areas, but the budget was only £2 million. Whitehall officials were keener on encouraging workers to migrate south. Harold Macmillan, progressive Conservative MP for Stockton, criticised the legislation as defeatist.[19]

Sir Malcolm Stewart, commissioner for England and Wales, resigned in frustration two years later, when unemployment was still 25 per cent in Durham and Tyneside and 35 per cent in west

Cumberland. Efforts to persuade industrialists to invest in special areas had failed, he said. In the previous year more than two hundred new factories had been established in Greater London, but just two in Durham and Tyneside. He called for direct subsidies to attract manufacturers, coupled with an embargo on factory construction in Greater London.[20] Neville Chamberlain, the chancellor, legislated for rent and tax rebates and Treasury loans in 1937. The result was the construction of trading estates where firms could lease premises at Team Valley near Gateshead, Treforest in South Wales and North Hillingdon outside Glasgow. By the war, about four thousand people were working at Team Valley – an improvement, but less than the 30,000 each in estates at Slough and Park Royal in west London.[21] Chamberlain sidestepped the idea of an embargo on London by appointing a Royal Commission on the Distribution of the Industrial Population under his old cabinet colleague and fishing friend, former Salford MP Sir Anderson Montague-Barlow. It did not report until 1940.[22]

An enduring image was the 1936 Jarrow March, in which 200 unemployed walked to London to petition for the right to work. Jarrow had been devastated by the closure of Palmers' shipyard. Unemployment reached almost 73 per cent. A proposal to build a steelworks in Jarrow was blocked by Teesside firms in the Iron and Steel Federation. The town's Labour MP was Ellen Wilkinson, who had taken Jarrow from the Conservatives at the 1935 election. Nicknamed 'Red Ellen' or the 'Fiery Particle', she was a working-class, university-educated Mancunian who had started out on the hard left and was a founder member of the Communist Party of Great Britain. She left the CPGB when Labour proscribed it and became Labour MP for Middlesbrough East, switching to Jarrow after she lost her seat in 1931. Later she was minister for education in the post-war government. The marchers won sympathy on their 280-mile journey and were welcomed, fed and accommodated along the route, often by Conservative-run councils. Baldwin refused to meet them, however. The march was unsuccessful, but helped to shape post-war attitudes to employment and social justice.

Another indelible image was created by Walter Greenwood's novel *Love on the Dole: A Tale of the Two Cities* (1933), which became an immediate bestseller. For many it symbolised the cruelty of a system that condemned millions to poverty. Greenwood had been a clerk in a Salford textile firm. Forced into unemployment at twenty-nine, he spent nine months supported by his mother and sister while he wrote the book. It was originally to be called 'The Lovers'. Changing the title proved fortuitous. Novelist Phyllis Bentley observed that 'the very title ... seems to compress the whole of the post-war era into a single significant phrase'.[23] The book centres on the Hardcastle family. Harry, the son, is sacked soon after he has made his girlfriend pregnant. Sally, the daughter, falls for a Labour activist, Larry, who dies after a police attack on protesting workers. Sally ends up selling her chastity to a businessman to get jobs for her father and brother. The book became a successful play, but efforts to turn it into a film were blocked in 1936 by the British Board of Film Censors, which disliked its radicalism and supposed sexual immorality. In 1940 a sanitised version was made as home-front propaganda. Greenwood briefly became a celebrity. Asked if fame had changed him, he replied that he wanted only to get back to Salford rather than 'live soft' in London, though soon he ditched his Salford fiancée (who sued him successfully for breach of promise), relocated to the capital and married an American actress.[24]

George Orwell, in *The Road to Wigan Pier* (1937), described conditions in the coalfields: 'Every afternoon several hundred men risk their necks and several hundred women scrabble in the mud for hours ... searching eagerly for tiny chips of coal. In winter they are desperate for fuel; it is more important almost than food.'[25] Seebohm Rowntree in 1936 repeated his 1899 survey of poverty in York. He found that the proportion of the working class living in extreme poverty had fallen from more than 15 per cent to 7 per cent, despite a big rise in unemployment. Nonetheless, 18 per cent could not afford adequate nutrition and basic housing, clothing, heat and light. Overall, the working-class standard of living had risen by a third.[26]

Even in the worst-hit areas, as Orwell noted, people settled down to life on the dole. Britain's welfare system, though hardly generous, was one of the world's most developed. Life could be particularly hard for women who had to feed and clothe families on less money than before. Young people grew up and married while on the dole. There were cheap luxuries even for the poor. Crowds flocked to football and cricket. Cinemas and dance halls were inexpensive. Greyhound racing began at Manchester's Belle Vue Stadium in 1926. Football pools companies Littlewoods and Vernons, which ran betting pools based on predicting outcomes of top-level matches, were founded in Liverpool in the 1920s. Professional boxing boomed. There were great expectations of Manchester's Black middleweight Len Johnson becoming a champion, but a British Boxing Board colour bar prevented him from having the opportunity.[27] For the middle classes there was tennis and golf. Some sports clubs discriminated on grounds of class or ethnicity. In 1932 the country's second Jewish golf club opened at Whitefield, near Manchester, in response to discrimination at other clubs.[28] Rambling became popular and there was pressure to open moors and mountains to public access. In April 1932, a mass trespass on Kinder Scout in the Peak District was organised by the Lancashire branch of the British Workers' Sport Federation, a Communist Party offshoot, which led to a battle with gamekeepers. Five trespassers received prison sentences. Curiously, Kinder had been offered as a park to Manchester City Council in 1901, but declined because of the cost of railing it off.[29]

Radio broadcasts began in the 1920s; by 1939 more than eight million British households had licences.[30] Manchester was chosen as the headquarters of the BBC's north region. Regional stations were intended to capture characteristics distinctive to their territories, which provoked rivalries in a region stretching from the Scottish border to the Potteries. Manchester also became the northern centre of national newspaper production, a 'second Fleet Street', starting with the northern edition of the *Daily Mail* in 1900. By 1940, when the *Daily Telegraph* and *Sunday Times* began publishing in the city, seven dailies and four Sundays were printing locally.[31]

The 1920s also saw Britain experience one of its biggest housing booms. Almost 4.2 million homes were built in England and Wales between the wars, expanding the stock by a third. More than a quarter were built by local authorities.[32] Manchester bought an estate at Wythenshawe in 1926 and planned a garden city to house 100,000 with jobs, schools, shops and leisure facilities. Wythenshawe's population passed 35,000 in 1935 and reached its target in 1964.[33] Community facilities did not keep pace, however, and only a fifth of new residents were former slum dwellers, who struggled to afford the higher rents. Other ambitious schemes included Quarry Hill flats in Leeds. In Liverpool, which had pioneered council house building in 1869, there were complaints that estates such as Huyton and Norris Green lacked bus and tram services, shops and pubs, and were too far from the docks, where most manual workers were employed.[34] Private housebuilding helped to create new suburban areas in several cities, such as Willerby and Anlaby Park on the west side of Hull. Manchester grew suburbs such as Brooklands, Timperley, Gatley and Cheadle. Populations of industrial centres began to fall; Manchester's peak was in 1931.[35] Slum clearance progressed slowly, nonetheless.

Britain had five thousand cinemas by 1939.[36] Unlike pubs, cinemas offered entertainment suitable for unaccompanied women and for children. *The Singing Fool* (1928), with Al Jolson in blackface, was the first talkie shown in many English cities. Crowds were moved by a scene in which a dying son asks Jolson, his father, to sing 'Sonny Boy'. Dorothy Armstrong recalled seeing it in Bradford in 1929, aged five, with her sister, mother and aunt: 'My mother was so emotionally overcome she had to lean against the wall outside the theatre and sob for several minutes. She told me later that on the tram coming home, the conductor took one look at the four of us, with red swollen eyes and said: "I know where you lot have been, it's like this every night."[37]

Most films were American, but Lancastrians Gracie Fields and George Formby junior were home-grown stars. Fields landed a lucrative Hollywood deal, yet insisted that the four pictures be filmed in Britain. When she became seriously ill with cervical cancer in 1939, she received 600,000 cards and letters from well-wishers, including one from Queen Elizabeth.[38] During the Second World War, her Italian husband, Monty Banks, faced internment, so she went with him to America. That provoked harsh press criticism, though she toured incessantly to entertain British troops.

Formby's films followed a formula in which he portrayed a gormless Lancashire innocent who wins through in an unfamiliar environment (in horse racing, the TT races, as a spy or a policeman) and in doing so wins the heart of an attractive middle-class girl, usually from the clutches of a caddish type with a moustache. His wife and manager Beryl regularly gave a 'hands-off-my-husband' warning to female co-stars. The BBC banned his suggestive songs 'When I'm Cleaning Windows' and 'With My Little Stick of Blackpool Rock'. According to his producer Basil Dean, Formby 'didn't act gormless as many successful Lancashire comedians have done, he was gormless'.[39] Nonetheless, he managed to symbolise the working classes, the people and the nation. Whatever was thrown at him, he came through smiling, which people loved.

For much of Britain, economic recovery was in the air by 1933 and obvious by 1935. In large parts of the north, it would take rearmament and another world war to revive its industries. The number of registered unemployed in the north fell from 830,000 to 60,000 between January 1939 and January 1942.[40] The big question was how long this accidental solution would last.

CHAPTER 28

HOPES DISAPPOINTED

In Dick Clement and Ian La Frenais's television comedy *Whatever Happened to the Likely Lads?*, first broadcast in 1973–4, beer-drinking, traditional male Terry Collier (James Bolam) returns from five years in the army to a Tyneside rapidly becoming unrecognisable. Terraced houses and busy factories have given way to high-rise blocks, flyovers and suburban estates. This was a time when familiar features of northern working-class life – pubs, factories, collieries, chapels, the Co-op – were disintegrating. 'None of our memories is intact,' mourns Terry. His mate Bob Ferris (Rodney Bewes), a former electrician, is changing with the times. He works in management, got engaged to librarian Thelma, bought a semi-detached house on a new estate, plays badminton, takes skiing holidays and fancies himself as a wine buff. He insists he is no less working class than Terry: 'You still want to live like that, you like the old working-class struggle against the odds. What you won't realise is that some of us won the struggle and it's nothing to be ashamed of.'[1]

The decades after the Second World War were a time of unprece-dented affluence, social change, trade union battles, immigration, deindustrialisation, urban transformation, economic dislocation and renewal, as well as anxiety about nuclear annihilation and Britain's place in the world. There was growing concern about the north–

south economic divide. As the *Likely Lads* illustrates, changes were down not just to impersonal economic forces, utopian planners and the actions of politicians such as Margaret Thatcher. They also involved working-class northerners such as Bob choosing to embrace a middle-class lifestyle. The changes affected everyone and Britain is still grappling with their implications.

The war meant that northern factories, steelworks, shipyards and coalmines were for a time important again. Engineers geared up for military production. Roy Chadwick designed the Lancaster bomber for Manchester's Avro; it was co-manufactured with Metropolitan Vickers and others. Trafford Park increased its workforce from 50,000 to 75,000 and Ford's former car factory there reopened to make Merlin engines.[2] A Royal Ordnance Factory in Chorley employed 35,000.[3] Work for those involved in the war effort could be gruelling. When a metallurgist dropped dead over lunch at a Sheffield steelworks, a friend said: 'He was a member of ninety-two committees.'[4]

Urban children were evacuated, though many returned home before bombing began. There were mismatches, such as when Catholic families from Liverpool were despatched to Calvinist rural Wales.[5] Liverpool, centre of the Battle of the Atlantic, was the most heavily bombed northern city, but its docks remained open. Offices of Littlewoods and Vernons, the football pools companies, were commandeered by intelligence services to open mail and examine it for cryptic messages.[6] Hull was bombed repeatedly. Manchester and Sheffield suffered raids that caused extensive damage to their city centres. Helping to keep up morale was BBC radio comedy *It's That Man Again* (*ITMA*) starring Liverpudlian Tommy Handley, a fast-talking figure around whom other characters orbited. These included Mrs Mopp, the office cleaner ('Can I do you now, sir?'), bibulous Colonel Chinstrap, and Funf, the incompetent German spy. Among fighting forces, the 50th Northumbrian Division was so dependable that it was barely rested as it fought in North Africa, Italy and the D-Day invasion, which caused resentment.[7]

The collective effort needed to win the war fuelled demand for better housing, employment and living standards. A 1942 report by William Beveridge formed the basis of the post-war welfare state put in place by Clement Attlee's Labour government, elected by a landslide in 1945. Beveridge was elected as Liberal MP for Berwick-upon-Tweed in a 1944 by-election, but defeated the following year, after which he was made a peer. Labour created the National Health Service and legislated to nationalise and universalise sickness, unemployment and retirement benefits that had previously existed unevenly. It nationalised coal, rail, steel, some road transport, electricity and gas, which impressed the public less. A 1951 Gallup poll found approval only for nationalisation of health and coal, with other industries seen as having suffered under public ownership.[8] There were some social tensions amid austerity and rationing, notably antisemitic riots that took place in 1947 in cities such as Liverpool and Manchester, triggered by headlines about the hanging in Palestine of two captured British sergeants, but also fuelled by a widespread belief that Jews were making a killing from the black market.[9]

Regional policy gave a modest stimulus to private-sector investment. The Distribution of Industry Act 1945 mandated the Board of Trade to build factories in enlarged versions of the old special areas, renamed 'development areas'. These focused on the north-east, west Cumberland and south and north-east Lancashire, as well as parts of Wales and Scotland. By 1950 more than £30 million had been spent in northern England and almost a thousand factories built, both publicly and privately financed, creating 200,000 jobs.[10] The world's first stored-program computer, known as 'Baby', was created at Manchester University in 1948. Based on it, the government placed a contract worth £35,000 a year with Manchester firm Ferranti to make the first commercially available computer, the Ferranti Mark 1.[11]

Manchester-born Ellen Wilkinson, minister for education, raised the school-leaving age from fourteen to fifteen and oversaw the creation of grammar schools and secondary moderns under the wartime coalition's Education Act 1944. She resisted the introduction of comprehensive schools (first known as 'multilateral' schools) favoured by some in Labour, though the first comprehensive was created at Windermere in 1945.[12] During the bitter winter of early 1947, Wilkinson succumbed to a bronchial disease and died after an overdose of medication, which the coroner at her inquest declared was accidental. There has been speculation ever since that it may have been suicide.

People were desperate for enjoyment. First-class cricket reached its record audience in 1947, when almost three million paid to watch.[13] An all-time peak of 41.3 million people attended Football League matches in the 1948–9 season.[14] Post-war football stars included Preston's Tom Finney, Blackpool's Stanley Matthews and Newcastle's Jackie Milburn. The Burnden Park disaster in 1946, in which thirty-three were crushed to death at an FA Cup tie in Bolton, was quickly forgotten in a society numbed by wartime deaths. The north-west was to suffer a further tragedy in 1958 when an aircraft carrying the Manchester United football team, nicknamed the 'Busby Babes', crashed in trying to take off from a slush-covered runway in Munich. Twenty-three of the forty-four people on board died.

Dance halls thrived. Victorian resorts such as Blackpool also reached their peak. In the summer of 1947, half a million people flocked to Butlin's five holiday camps. Future Labour leader Hugh Gaitskell (Winchester and Oxford) paid his first visit to a Butlin's camp (Filey) at the party's Scarborough conference in 1948 as a guest of the National Union of Mineworkers. He noted: 'Very efficient, organised, pleasure holiday making. Everybody agreed they would not go there!'[15] The Peak District, site of the Kinder Scout trespass in 1932, was designated the UK's first national park in April 1951, followed that year by the Lake District, Snowdonia and Dartmoor.

Winston Churchill regained power narrowly in 1951 by promising to end austerity. Optimism was fuelled by the coronation of

Queen Elizabeth II and talk of a new Elizabethan age. The thirty-year post-war boom was under way with full employment and rising prosperity. It was a deferential, conservative era. The *Eagle* comic, starring Dan Dare, was launched in 1950 by Marcus Morris, an Anglican vicar in Southport, to counter what he saw as the moral corruption of 'over-violent and obscene' American horror comics. Sales reached two million by the mid-1950s.[16] Andy Capp, an unreconstructed working-class cartoon character created by Hartlepool's Reg Smythe, first appeared in the *Daily Mirror* in 1957. 'Look at it this way, honey,' Andy says in an early cartoon, leaning nonchalantly against the wall as his wife Florrie sits battered on the floor. 'I'm a man of few pleasures and one of them 'appens to be knockin' yer about.'[17] (In recent times, Florrie is more likely to be seen dragging Andy by his scarf.) Alan Turing, mastermind behind the cracking of the German Enigma code, who was working on the Ferranti computer project in Manchester, was arrested in 1952 and prosecuted for homosexual acts. He accepted organo-therapy treatment as an alternative to prison, rendering him impotent and making him grow breasts. He died by suicide in 1954.

As the global boom relieved former depressed areas, Churchill's government wound down regional policy. Poverty and inequality persisted in many places, nonetheless. Richard Hoggart, brought up in the Hunslet district of Leeds, warned in *The Uses of Literacy* (1957) that the innate decency of working-class life was being undermined by consumerism's excesses and mass culture, which gave people cheap, sensationalist entertainment. The late 1950s and early 1960s brought to prominence northern writers from modest backgrounds, including Shelagh Delaney, Stan Barstow, Keith Waterhouse, John Braine and David Storey. Some were helped by wider access to secondary education, but Delaney, raised in Salford, failed her eleven-plus and left school at sixteen to work in an engineering factory. Aged just nineteen when *A Taste of Honey* was first performed at London's Theatre Royal Stratford East in 1958, she was nicknamed 'the Françoise Sagan of Salford' and 'an angry young woman', referring to the 'angry young man' genre exemplified by John Osborne's *Look Back in Anger*.[18] For many of these writers, change could not come quickly enough and they were not, on the whole, motivated by political radicalism. John Braine, in *Room at the Top*, portrayed the rise of an ambitious young man, Joe Lampton. Its success made Braine rich and enabled him to give up his job as a West Riding librarian and move to a large house in Surrey. 'What I want to do is to drive through Bradford in a Rolls-Royce with two naked women on either side of me covered in jewels,' he told an interviewer.[19] 'He would like it to be known,' he told the *Express*, 'that he couldn't be less angry.'[20]

Churchill was followed by Anthony Eden and then Harold Macmillan. A journalist from Bolton, Geoffrey Moorhouse, wrote: 'No one who lived in Lancashire, Yorkshire, and in the north-east during the late 1950s and early 1960s could fail to be aware that these areas were gradually falling behind the national average in many ways – in tolerable housing conditions, in mortality, in invest-ment, and, above all, in employment.'[21] By the late 1950s, Britain was a net importer of cotton cloth for the first time since the Industrial Revolution. Mill owners – the heirs of Cobden and Bright – pleaded for protection from low-wage Asian producers. Peter Thorneycroft, president of the Board of Trade, told them: 'The government has no featherbed to offer you and very little shelter in the harsh winds of competition which are blowing through the world today.'[22] However, Macmillan, nervous about losing north-west seats after a by-election defeat in Rochdale, hurriedly negotiated voluntary import quotas with India, Pakistan and Hong Kong. Development areas were replaced by smaller 'development districts' aimed at unemployment blackspots. Regional aid recovered from £3.6 million in 1958–9 to £11.8 million in 1961.[23] Tightening loca-tion controls led to car-makers Ford, Standard-Triumph and Vauxhall setting up assembly plants on Merseyside, where the jobless rate was high. These measures helped to shore up the Tory vote as

Macmillan won by a landslide in 1959, gaining seats in the booming midlands and London.

Independent Television was launched in 1955. Granada, founded by Sidney Bernstein, was among the initial franchisees, covering the north-west and Yorkshire on weekdays, while ABC provided the weekend service. Tyne Tees followed two years later and Yorkshire Television was split from Granada in 1967. Granada began a soap opera in 1960 created by a working-class writer, Tony Warren. He initially wanted to call it *Florizel Street*, which according to some accounts was dropped because a tea lady said it sounded like a toilet cleaner. Producers, torn between *Jubilee Street* and *Coronation Street*, opted for the latter. Initial reviews were not encouraging, but by October 1961 it was the country's most popular programme.[24] Its success owed much to the quality of early scripts and performances, and its portrayal of a fast-disappearing way of life.

Things got harder for Macmillan. In response to pressure on sterling in 1961, Selwyn Lloyd, the chancellor, a Methodist liberal from the Wirral, imposed a credit squeeze and moratorium on state investment. One result was redundancies in the north-east's shipyards, including at Hartlepool, where the collapse of William Gray & Co. threw 1,400 men out of work and ended shipbuilding in the town. Britain became obsessed in the 1950s and 1960s by data showing that economic growth was lagging behind continental competitors, notably France and Germany. The scale of post-war reconstruction was greater there and a large agricultural workforce in France, Germany and Italy was displaced by mechanisation and moved into industrial employment, which had already happened in Britain. The catching-up finished by the early 1970s, since when UK and continental growth rates have been similar.[25] The UK applied to join the European Economic Community in 1961. Its application was vetoed by French president Charles de Gaulle in 1963. That was repeated in 1967 when de Gaulle vetoed a second application under Labour prime minister Harold Wilson.

Macmillan retired on ill-health grounds and was replaced by Alec Douglas-Home. He lost narrowly in 1964 to Wilson, who increased his majority in 1966. Wilson played on his Yorkshire pedigree, although his springboard was Merseyside, where he was first elected as MP for Ormskirk in 1945, switching to Huyton in 1950. Labour created regional planning councils, which lacked powers and democratic legitimacy. They consisted of selected business leaders and local government representatives such as T. Dan Smith, Labour leader of Newcastle City Council from 1960 to 1965. Regional industrial subsidies increased tenfold and a Regional Employment Premium shaved about 8 per cent off manufacturers' payroll costs in assisted areas.[26] Office developments were restricted in London and Birmingham, though many jobs simply shifted from central London to the capital's fringes. The *Manchester Guardian*'s dropping of Manchester from its title in 1959 and move to the capital in 1964 was symptomatic of a wider southwards shift. During the 1950s and 1960s, the north's share of national output fell from 28 to 25 per cent, while that of London and the south-east increased from 34 to 36 per cent.[27]

In the 1960s, feelings about the modernism that dominated postwar urban planning soured. Politicians wanted, for the best of reasons, to demolish Victorian slums. Architects followed Swiss pioneer Le Corbusier in seeking to replace these with an ordered landscape of towers, avenues and walkways. People were either moved out to new estates or rehoused in concrete multi-storey blocks. Cities such as Bradford, Newcastle and Leeds tore up large parts of their historic centre to accommodate the car. The Preston Bypass, opened in 1958, marked the start of Britain's motorway network.

Sheffield's Park Hill flats, built between 1957 and 1961 by architects Jack Lynn and Ivor Smith, were modelled on Le Corbusier's Unité d'Habitation in Marseille, a vast housing megastructure. The architects hoped that walkways stretching the entire length of the thirteen-storey complex would be seen as 'streets in the sky', recapturing the intimate feel of the old terraces. People across Britain became disenchanted with high-rise blocks, many of which were shoddily built and became synonymous with vandalism and juvenile delinquency. 'It's a dump. An absolute dump. I've come out of a dump into a super-dump,' said one Park Hill resident.[28] A gas explosion that devasted east London's Ronan Point in May 1968 shook public confidence. In August that year, the Ministry of Housing said it would discourage the building of more tower blocks. The era was summed up for many in 1974 when T. Dan Smith, who wanted to turn Newcastle into 'the Brasilia of the north', was convicted of taking bribes from Yorkshire architect John Poulson and sentenced to six years in jail. Poulson was jailed for seven years.

Peterlee (named after a former miners' leader) and Newton Aycliffe in County Durham were among England's first fourteen officially designated new towns in the late 1940s, followed later by Skelmersdale, Runcorn, Washington and Warrington. Central Lancashire New Town was the largest and most oddly named new town, designated in 1970, linking Chorley, Leyland and Preston. The name never caught on (the housing minister, Anthony Greenwood, thought it should be called 'Redrose') and its development corporation lasted only fifteen years, half the planned lifespan.[29] Cities created overspill estates such as Kirkby near Liverpool, whose population mushroomed from 3,000 in 1951 to 52,000 a decade later.[30] Half the population was under fifteen and there were complaints about vandalism. The BBC's television police series *Z Cars*, a work of social realism created in 1962, was set in 'Newtown', based on Kirkby. Lancashire Police advised on it, but were horrified by the harsh picture it created, which led the chief constable to call for the series to be cancelled. The BBC dropped the screened acknowledgement to the police, but the series reached an audience of almost seventeen million.[31]

The 1960s brought a more assertive youth culture. An early sign came in 1955 when Bill Haley appeared at the Liverpool Odeon: 140 seats were wrecked and police were called as ecstatic teenagers danced barefoot in the aisles.[32] The Beatles had their first hit with 'Love Me Do' in 1962 and before long there was a fan frenzy dubbed 'Beatlemania'. The extent of the 1960s youthquake is often exaggerated, though. Many young people had conventional aspirations. The Beatles and other Merseybeat musicians boosted Liverpool's self-confidence, but as they became global stars they were seen less in the city.

Edward Heath won a surprise victory for the Conservatives in the 1970 election, ushering in a tumultuous decade of strikes, IRA bombs and stagflation. Chancellor Anthony Barber, MP for Altrincham and Sale and son of a Doncaster businessman, cut taxes and eased credit controls, creating the short-lived 'Barber boom'. Heath declared five states of emergency in three years (out of eleven during the twentieth century) as he sought to get on top of industrial troubles.[33] Wilson had tried and failed to control unofficial strikes through proposals in the white paper *In Place of Strife*, drawn up by Barbara Castle, Blackburn MP and employment secretary, which was killed by cabinet opposition. It did much to kill her career as well.

The main union leaders were northerners, including Vic Feather, general secretary of the Trades Union Congress – the Bradford-born son of a French-polisher – and the 'terrible twins': Hugh Scanlon from Manchester, head of the engineering workers, and transport union leader Jack Jones, son of a Liverpool docker. Personally, Heath got on with them better than Wilson had. On one strange evening in 1969, Heath had invited leading trade unionists to dinner. It went swimmingly and Heath was persuaded to show off his skills on his new piano. 'Play "The Red Flag" for Jack [Jones],' said Feather – which Heath cheerfully did.[34] Heath and Jones had first met on the banks of the Ebro three decades earlier, during one of the bloodiest battles of the Spanish civil war, where Jones was a soldier and Heath part of a student delegation visiting to support the Republican cause. But both Labour and the Conservatives made a mistake in thinking they could curb strikes by getting union leaders onside. The pressure was from workers who wanted their share of rising prosperity. Despite talk of a 'British disease', Britain lost fewer working days per 1,000 workers during the 1970s than Canada, Italy, Australia, the US and Ireland.[35]

It was a tough time for northern manufacturers, many of whose products were uncompetitive. New container vessels were too wide for the Manchester Ship Canal, which hit Trafford Park and made the city's docks virtually redundant by the 1980s. Heath's government cut regional subsidies and relaxed location controls over factories and offices, but later extended development-area status to Tyneside and Wearside and introduced assisted-area status for previously overlooked towns and cities such as Sheffield.[36] Heath took Britain into the Common Market on 1 January 1973, but industrial travails were mounting. The Industrial Relations Act 1971, which created a court to restrict strikes, was undermined by unions' refusal to register. The National Union of Mineworkers, led by Lancashire moderate Joe Gormley, won an unexpected victory in a national strike in 1972 – the first official miners' strike since 1926 – winning a 27 per cent pay rise. It also brought to prominence Yorkshire militant Arthur Scargill, who was involved in the mass picket of Saltley fuel depot in Birmingham. A miners' overtime ban in 1973 forced Heath to impose a three-day week to conserve electricity. When another national strike began in February 1974, Heath called an election using the slogan 'Who governs Britain?', which resulted in a hung parliament.

A weary Wilson returned to office and then won a three-seat majority in a snap election in October, but there was little relief from Britain's problems. Chancellor Denis Healey, MP for Leeds East and raised in Keighley, tried to spend his way out of stagflation until forced to cut spending and raise taxes. Wilson, with his party deeply divided over Europe, called a referendum in 1975 on whether to remain in the EEC. He took a back seat in the campaign. His adviser Bernard Donoughue wrote that Wilson was 'basically a north of England, nonconformist puritan. The continentals, especially from France and southern Europe, were to him alien.'[37] The country voted to stay in by 67.23 per cent to 32.77 per cent. The weakest Yes vote was in Scotland and Northern Ireland. In England, the Yes vote was slightly higher in the south (71.6 per cent) than in the north (67.4 per cent). The lowest Yes votes in England were in Tyne and Wear (62.9 per cent), South Yorkshire (63.4 per cent), Durham (64.2 per cent), Greater Manchester (64.5 per cent) and Merseyside (64.8 per cent).[38]

Wilson, drinking heavily and convinced that MI5, the CIA and the South African Bureau of State Security were plotting to undermine him, resigned in 1976 and was replaced by James Callaghan. Healey was forced to seek a $3.9 billion loan from the International Monetary Fund, which meant more cuts. Shipbuilding was nationalised in 1977, but British Shipbuilders was no better at winning orders than its private-sector predecessors. Hull's fishing industry was wrecked by cod wars with Iceland. In 1979 Dunlop selected its Speke tyre plant on Merseyside for closure, making 2,300 workers redundant. Kirkby Manufacturing and Engineering, a flagship cooperative that had been backed by left-wing former industry secretary Tony Benn, collapsed. In the 1978–9 'winter of discontent', private and public-sector unions mounted strikes for pay rises above the government's 5 per cent limit, including Liverpool gravediggers. In Hull, striking lorry drivers achieved a blockade so complete that it was dubbed 'Stalingrad'. Salt, sugar and dairy products had to be rationed in shops. Animals starved on farms and cargoes froze in the docks.[39] A Gallup poll found that 84 per cent of the public thought the unions had become too powerful, paving the way for Tory reforms.[40]

Margaret Thatcher, forever divisive, came to power in May 1979. While clearly a shift to the right, this was less abrupt than is sometimes portrayed. Labour under Callaghan had already adopted monetarist policies. Thatcherism was more a set of attitudes, instincts and themes – including the Methodism of her Grantham upbringing – than an ideology. It evolved over time. Argument still rages over how far Thatcher can be blamed for destroying much of the north's heavy industry. Critics blame over-tight monetary policy, coupled with tax rises and spending cuts, while supporters point to North Sea oil, which made the pound a strong petrocurrency. UK unemployment doubled to almost 12 per cent after the 1980–1 recession. The corollary was that, from the mid-1980s, it fell faster than in France, Germany or Italy.[41] New investment included Nissan's Sunderland car factory, opened in 1985, which became one of the world's most efficient. Deindustrialisation happened in many countries, though it was felt keenly in Britain, it having started the Industrial Revolution. The decline in industrial employment was not significantly greater under Thatcher (1.9 per cent a year, 1979–90) than subsequently under Labour (1.8 per cent a year, 1997–2005).[42]

Among notable figures was Thatcher's favourite builder, Newcastle-born Lawrie Barratt. Architecture critics hated Barratt houses, but his business methods – cheap mass production, attention to social surveys and aggressive marketing – worked. By the end of the 1970s he was the country's biggest housebuilder. Barratt did not live in one himself: he had long since moved to an eighteenth-century mansion in rural Northumberland. Neither did Thatcher. She bought a five-bedroom Barratt home in Dulwich, but never spent more than a night or two there.[43]

Thatcher's ministers moved cautiously to change labour laws, conscious of Heath's failure. Employment acts banned secondary picketing and required an 80 per cent ballot majority for a closed shop (1980); they tightened closed shop restrictions, made it easier to sack disruptive workers and made unions liable to be sued if they pursued an unlawful dispute (1982); and they required unions to hold a secret ballot before calling a strike (1984). A fourteen-week national steel strike over pay in 1980, including mass picketing of the private firm Hadfields in Sheffield, ended with the Iron and Steel Trades Confederation – led by Bill Sirs, a moderate from Hartlepool – accepting a deal well short of its demands. Later that year, Consett works in County Durham was shut with the loss of 3,400 jobs. Ian

MacGregor, a tough Scots-American aged sixty-seven, became chairman of British Steel and made 90,000 redundant before moving to chair the National Coal Board. Steel productivity boomed, enabling British Steel to be privatised in 1988.

The decisive battle was the 1984–5 miners' strike over pit closures, which began with a walkout at Cortonwood Colliery in Yorkshire on 6 March. Scargill, now NUM president, made the strike official across Britain on 12 March. Crucially, the leadership did not call a national ballot, without which miners in Nottinghamshire, Leicestershire, South Wales and parts of Lancashire kept working. The government had built up ample coal stocks and used police to protect working miners. The strike ended in defeat for the NUM on 3 March 1985, significantly weakening the trade union movement. The much-reduced coal industry was privatised in 1994.

Northern cities appeared to be in terminal crisis by the 1980s. There were riots in 1981 in inner-city areas including Liverpool's Toxteth and Manchester's Moss Side, sparked by resentment among young Black people against what they saw as police harassment. Left-wing councils were at odds with the government, including Sheffield, led by David Blunkett, a former Methodist lay preacher who was blind from birth. Sheffield refused to become an enterprise zone. Blunkett signed a 'peace treaty' with Sheffield's Soviet twin city, Donetsk, and had Rowntree vending machines ripped out from the town hall as punishment for the firm's South African connections. He kept bus fares low by increasing council rates. Blunkett had little interest in chattering-class issues, fearing that placing a special emphasis on the rights of women and minorities would 'sap the energy of the class struggle'.[44]

Most councils, including Sheffield, ultimately backed off from defying the government's cap on rate rises. Seeds of recovery were sown in several cities in the mid-1980s. In Sheffield, a public–private committee was formed to regenerate the Lower Don Valley. It also launched a campaign to attract new industry, investment and jobs to the city. Manchester City Council under Graham Stringer embraced public–private partnership, eagerly bidding for investment against 'competitor cities'. Among areas revived was what became known as the Gay Village, largely the creation of local developer Carol Ainscow.[45] The city's turnround was under way well before the IRA bombing in 1996, which gave further impetus to regeneration.

Liverpool was in a sorry state, with unemployment reaching 20 per cent, double the national average. Apart from the Toxteth riots, Tate & Lyle's sugar works closed with the loss of 1,500 jobs. The docks had declined dramatically. Chancellor Geoffrey Howe suggested to colleagues that Liverpool be allowed to go into 'managed decline', but Michael Heseltine, environment secretary, persuaded Thatcher to allow him to create a taskforce of civil servants and business people. Heseltine arranged for Liverpool to stage a National Garden Festival in 1984 and oversaw the government-appointed Merseyside Development Corporation's redevelopment of Albert Dock. The city council, however, became dominated by the hard-left Militant group under the *de facto* leadership of deputy leader Derek Hatton. It set an illegal 'deficit budget' in 1985, which led to forty-seven councillors being disqualified from office.

The performance of Liverpool and Everton football clubs helped to keep up morale, but Liverpool's success was marred by two disasters. At the 1985 European Cup final at Brussels' Heysel stadium, thirty-nine Juventus fans died when pressed against a collapsing wall, trying to escape rampaging Liverpool fans. The tragedy resulted in English clubs being banned from all European competitions. In 1989, ninety-six Liverpool fans died at an overcrowded FA Cup semi-final in Sheffield's Hillsborough stadium. Police fed the press false stories suggesting that Liverpool hooliganism had caused the disaster. An inquest in 2016 ruled that the fans were unlawfully killed due to grossly negligent failures by police and ambulance services.

Thatcher was succeeded by John Major in 1990. The 1990–1 recession, affecting most of the Western world, was felt in the UK mainly in southern England. This led to a temporary shrinking of the economic divide, though it merely reduced the south's lead over the north in output per head to the already high level of the mid-1980s.[46] Recovery in the north was patchy. Financial services growth in Manchester and Leeds left Liverpool, Bradford and Sheffield behind. Unemployment remained high in parts of the north-east. In 1997, Major's government was swept aside by 'New' Labour under Tony Blair, MP for Sedgefield.

CHAPTER 29

THE TWENTY-FIRST CENTURY

'It's only the rich, the elite, who want to stay,' Paul Noble, a fifty-seven-year-old steel erector in Hartlepool who voted to leave the European Union in the 2016 referendum, told the *Financial Times*. He gave his reasons: 'Immigration; erosion of powers; European despots and dictators telling us what to do all the time.' There was more. 'Redcar steel; they didn't lift a hand. The fishing industry; they gave our sea away.' He added that tanks and trains for UK use were made overseas. 'It's as if they want big industry in Britain to be finished.'[1]

Northern towns were central to the UK's 51.89 to 48.11 per cent vote for Brexit. Hartlepool's Leave vote share was almost 70 per cent. Other places with a high tally included Doncaster, Barnsley, Rotherham, Hull, Blackpool and Burnley. Without northern England and the west midlands, Remain would have won. Accumulated grievances fuelled the revolt. Immigration was cited even in places with few migrants – Hartlepool's foreign-born share of population was below 3 per cent compared with the 13 per cent England and Wales average. Decline underlaid the anger. Hartlepool remained haunted by the demise of traditional industries, some lost decades ago, and its male jobless rate was more than double the national average.

The north caused further shock at the 2019 general election, accounting for almost half of Conservative gains as parts of the 'red wall' of Labour seats in the north, midlands and north-east Wales crumbled, disrupting a voting pattern going back decades in some cases. 'We made Redcar Bluecar,' proclaimed prime minister Boris Johnson, who achieved a net gain of forty-eight seats to reach a Tory majority of eighty, the biggest since Thatcher.[2] Redcar constituency, created in 1974, had never before voted for a Tory. Others to fall included Sedgefield, Blyth Valley, Don Valley, Bishop Auckland, Workington, Leigh, Scunthorpe and Great Grimsby. Anger over Labour's support for a second referendum, the unpopularity of left-wing leader Jeremy Corbyn, and an implausibly high-spending manifesto were advanced as reasons for failure. The Tories subsequently won Hartlepool in a by-election.

It was not meant to be this way when Tony Blair, MP for Sedgefield, County Durham, and the most pro-EU prime minister since Heath, was elected with a landslide majority of 179 in 1997, the highest Labour has ever achieved. Blair was the first Labour premier with a north-east seat since Ramsay MacDonald. To some he seemed the ideal politician to lead outer Britain against the party of the south. He was born in Edinburgh, raised partly in Durham, represented a northern seat and yet had what his ally Peter Mandelson called 'southern appeal'.[3] His centrist 'New' Labour philosophy was an attempt to marry market economics with social justice. The phrase 'New Labour, New Britain' was devised as a conference slogan in 1994 by Alastair Campbell, Blair's Keighley-born media chief.[4]

In the event, New Labour's regional policy yielded mixed results. Devolved parliaments or assemblies were created in Scotland, Wales, Northern Ireland and London, but plans for an assembly in north-east England were rejected by 78 per cent to 22 per cent in a 2004 referendum. Opponents said it would be an expensive talking shop with little power. A key figure in the No campaign was Durham-born Dominic Cummings, later to head Vote Leave in the EU referendum and serve as chief adviser to Johnson. He employed populist tactics such as touring with an inflatable white elephant and suggesting that rejecting the assembly would mean more money for the National Health Service.[5] The defeat ended Labour's English devolution plans. Further proposed referendums in the north-west and in Yorkshire and Humber were dropped.

Blair played down the north–south divide. 'There obviously are differences and variations [between] north and south and there is no point in pretending those don't exist,' he said in 1999. 'But what we actually found when we looked into it was that some of the differences between regions and within regions were every bit as great as the difference that people traditionally talk about as the north–south divide.'[6] Victoria Wood joked that Blair had solved the north–south divide by 'making everything the south'.[7] The issue remained sensitive, however. Under New Labour, financial services output increased at twice the overall growth rate, while manufacturing's share of economic output dropped from just under a fifth (19 per cent) to a tenth. In the north, manufacturing shrank from 24 to 15 per cent of output.[8]

Regional policy focused on supply-side measures to narrow gaps in productivity and involved creating regional development agencies (RDAs) in all nine English regions. Blair's Labour has been seen as making a Faustian bargain: encouraging the City to boom under light-touch regulation in order to fund a sharp rise in public spending, notably on health and education. In the north, public spending was calculated to account for some 60 per cent of economic output and 75 per cent of new jobs.[9]

Northern cities continued their regeneration. Manchester and Leeds developed significant financial and professional services sectors, while city-centre living became popular for young graduates. Manchester hosted the Commonwealth Games in 2002. The BBC chose MediaCity at Salford Quays in 2006 as the place to which it would relocate staff from London. On Tyneside, Gateshead Millennium Bridge opened in 2001, the Baltic Centre for

Contemporary Art in 2002 and the Sage Gateshead concert venue in 2004. Liverpool was European Capital of Culture in 2008. However, mill towns, seaside towns and former mining areas struggled. In 2001 there were riots between white and south Asian youths in Oldham, Bradford, Leeds and Burnley.

Gordon Brown succeeded Blair in 2007, but the good times came to a juddering halt with the financial crisis and the 2008–9 recession. Northern regions had, by some indicators, made a distinctly modest relative economic advance during the New Labour years. The employment rate among those sixteen and over rose in the north-east from 53 per cent of the population in 1997 to 55 per cent in 2010 and in the north-west from 56 to 57 per cent, but in Yorkshire and the Humber it was static at 57 per cent. Call centre or distribution jobs were widely seen as inferior to industrial jobs they replaced. Output per head grew in the north-east from 74 to 76 per cent of the UK average and in the north-west from 86 to 89 per cent, but in Yorkshire and the Humber it dipped from 85 to 83 per cent. London, meanwhile, advanced from 156 to 169 per cent.[10]

The first casualties of the crisis were two overstretched mortgage lenders, Newcastle-based Northern Rock (chaired by Northumberland aristocrat Matt Ridley) and Bradford & Bingley. Both subsequently had to be nationalised. Their failure undermined confidence in a post-industrial future. The north's dependence on public spending left it vulnerable when cuts began under David Cameron's Conservative–Liberal Democrat coalition, elected in 2010, the first peacetime coalition since 1931. Cameron talked of 'rebalancing' the economy away from public spending, housing and finance, a vague idea that also involved attempting to reduce reliance on London and the south-east.[11] Labour's RDAs were abolished and replaced by local enterprise partnerships (LEPs) covering smaller areas. Other initiatives included a £3.2 billion Regional Growth Fund, under which public and private bodies could bid for investment, and 'city deals', bespoke packages of funding and powers agreed between central and local government.

In his austerity plans, chancellor George Osborne opted for spending cuts over tax rises by a ratio of four to one. Urban municipalities bore the brunt. By March 2015 net public service spending per person by local authorities had shrunk by 27 per cent in the north-east and London, compared with 16 per cent in the south-east.[12] Former industrial communities were hit by curbs to disability and other benefits. London and the south-east quickly recovered, with house prices rising sharply as the Bank of England's quantitative easing programme pumped money into the economy. Cameron's enterprise tsar, Lord Young, was forced to resign in November 2010 after saying in an interview that, from where he sat, people 'have never had it so good' than during the 'so-called recession'.[13] London achieved twice the growth rate (17 per cent) of any other UK region or nation between 2010 and 2014, while Northern Ireland (1 per cent) and the three northern English regions (3–4 per cent) brought up the rear.[14]

Osborne proposed the creation of a 'Northern Powerhouse' in a speech at Manchester's Museum of Science and Industry in June 2014, with investments in science and transport aimed at realising the potential for connecting cities from Liverpool to Hull.[15] He offered devolution deals to city-regions that opted for elected mayors. 'Metro mayors' have since been elected for places including Greater Manchester, Liverpool city region, Tees Valley, North of Tyne, Sheffield city region and West Yorkshire.

Cameron won an overall majority in 2015, but met his downfall in the 2016 EU referendum. Every English region voted to leave except London. Out of seventy-two counting areas in the north, fewer than a dozen voted Remain, including Liverpool, Manchester, Harrogate, York and a prosperous part of rural Cumbria (though even Greater Manchester produced an overall majority for Leave). Leave voters tended to have lower qualifications and be older; the Brexit vote was higher in areas with low incomes, high unemployment and a tradition of manufacturing employment. Opinion polling by Lord Ashcroft found that Brexit voters believed leaving the EU was 'more likely to bring about a better immigration system, improved border controls, a fairer welfare system, better quality of life, and the ability to control our own laws'.[16] The north's relatively higher Leave vote was little surprise: even in the 1975 referendum, the No vote share had been higher than in the south. This was far from the first time in history that traditionalist sentiment has been stronger in the north. It carried echoes of northern royalism in the seventeenth-century civil wars and conservative grievances that lay behind the 1536 Pilgrimage of Grace.

Cameron was succeeded by home secretary Theresa May, who decided to hold a snap election in 2017 and lost her party's majority. She actually increased the Conservative share of the vote by six percentage points to 42.4 per cent, equalling Thatcher's performance in 1983, but her hopes of gains across the north were disappointed. She won just two seats there from Labour, Middlesbrough South and Cleveland East. Labour under Corbyn saw its vote share rise by a third to 40 per cent. It captured twenty-seven English seats, including seven in the north, achieving a net gain of twenty-one. In Stockton South, Labour ousted James Wharton, who had been Cameron's minister for the Northern Powerhouse. It also toppled Nick Clegg, former Liberal Democrat leader and deputy prime minister, in Sheffield. Hamstrung by a hung parliament, May saw her draft EU withdrawal agreement rejected three times by the Commons. She resigned in 2019 and was replaced by Boris Johnson, former foreign secretary.

The north's economy underperformed that of the south during Cameron's and May's governments. While employment rates continued to improve between 2010 and 2019 in the north-east (from 55 to 56 per cent), north-west (57 to 60 per cent) and Yorkshire and Humber (57 to 59 per cent), gains were only half those of London (60 to 65 per cent) and less than the English average (58 to 62 per cent). Output per head shrank in the north-east from 76 per cent of the UK average in 2010 to 67 per cent in 2017. In the north-west it shrank from 89 to 87 per cent and in Yorkshire and Humber from 83 to 80 per cent.[17]

That did not stop Johnson from breaching Labour's 'red wall' at the 2019 election. The term, coined by data strategist James Kanagasooriam, refers to a group of post-industrial, Brexit-leaning seats that had not had a Conservative MP in decades. The Conservatives' share of the vote had been creeping up since 2005. The make-up of some had changed: seats such as Bishop Auckland, once dominated by heavy industry, were becoming more prosperous commuter towns.

The loss of northern seats caused a serious headache for Labour, particularly after the collapse of its Scottish vote following the 2014 independence referendum. It broke a broad pattern seen since the nineteenth century, whereby the Anglican-dominated, conservative south voted Tory and the nonconformist north largely voted at first Liberal and then Labour. Corbyn was replaced as Labour leader by Keir Starmer from the party's centre-right. The new leadership blamed losses on a mix of the party's anti-Brexit position, animosity towards Corbyn and a lack of economic credibility.

Johnson's slogans such as 'get Brexit done' and 'levelling up' had a simple appeal while leaving policy details of the latter vague. Visiting Sedgefield after his victory, Johnson pledged: 'I want the people of the north-east to know that we in the Conservative party, and I, will repay your trust. Everything I do as your prime minister will be devoted to repaying that trust.'[18] A cautious manifesto had pledged just £3 billion a year in extra public spending, compared with an equivalent of £83 billion by 2023–4 from Labour.

Johnson affirmed support for the High Speed 2 north–south rail line and a Northern Powerhouse Rail fast link between Manchester and Leeds, and earmarked £100 billion for regional skills and infrastructure over five years. Later he was accused of betrayal when the Leeds leg of the HS2 rail link was cancelled and NPR scaled back. Eight locations in England, including the Humber, Liverpool city region and Teesside, have been designated as freeports, or special economic zones with incentives to stimulate investment. The government launched a £4.8 billion Levelling Up Fund that councils could bid for, on top of a £3.6 billion Towns Fund. Both were accused of favouring Tory-held areas: chancellor Rishi Sunak's Richmond constituency was rated a higher priority under the Levelling Up Fund's criteria than struggling former mining towns.[19] The government did not, however, pledge to restore local authority budgets, hit hard since 2010.

The coronavirus pandemic complicated the question of whether there was substance to Johnson's 'levelling up' policies. He promised to lead a 'One Nation Conservative administration', though it appeared more nationalistic and populist than the liberal form of open Conservatism advocated by the likes of Ken Clarke and John Major. (The phrase originated with Benjamin Disraeli, who sought to improve the lives of the poor.) His main challenge was to satisfy new-found northern voters, who are more likely to demand higher public spending and intervention in industry, without alienating traditional low-tax, small-state Conservatives. 'People here didn't vote to see factories closed down,' said one Tory MP elected for the first time. Dean Simms, a forty-seven-year-old steelworker at Redcar until the plant closed in 2015 with the loss of 3,000 jobs, said he had voted Tory for the first time, as had his dad. 'I just hope they do what they're supposed to do,' he added. Johnson acknowledged the challenge: 'We must understand now what an earthquake we have created. We have to grapple with the consequences.' Revealingly, he added: 'We have to change our own party.'[20] How much of this agenda will survive his political demise is uncertain.

Northerners could be forgiven a weary sigh as once again a government pledged measures to close an economic divide that has become an increasingly pressing political issue. Each administration has introduced new policies while doing little to evaluate and learn from what has worked or not worked in the past. It is a cycle the north appears doomed to repeat.

POSTSCRIPT

Can we ever be rid of the north–south divide, which casts the north as the back end of the English economy's pantomime horse?

Margaret Thatcher claimed to have abolished it. 'The north–south divide has gone,' she told parliament in 1989 after visiting the region, where she found that 'business is flourishing, business men are optimistic, unemployment is falling'.[1] That took bravado – something she rarely lacked – after a decade in which the north's factories, coalmines and shipyards took a beating. She was not the only one trying to wish it away. Ken Clarke, then paymaster-general, declared that talk of a north–south divide was 'a ridiculous simplification' and added: 'It reinforces the cloth cap and brass band image the south has of the north, which does the area no service at all.'[2]

The phrase entered the modern political lexicon in 1980 when John Lee, a Lancashire Conservative MP, told the Commons: 'Those of us who represent the regions are increasingly aware of the north–south divide [cheers from the Labour benches], as twenty-first-century industry is increasingly sucked towards the south-east – the Channel tilt. Unless that trend is positively corrected, we shall in future years need a United Kingdom version of the Brandt report.'[3] He was referring to a work by ex-German chancellor Willy Brandt on the gap between the global north and south. While Thatcher denied the

English divide's existence, her ally Lord Young said: 'The two present growth industries – the City and tourism – are concentrated in the south. It's our turn, that's all.'[4] The divide was certainly not gone. Boris Johnson has been just one of many leaders to grapple with it.

A divide, both economic and cultural, has existed throughout history. The south, with richer farmland, has generally had stronger growth except perhaps for about a hundred years from the late eighteenth to late nineteenth century. In another exception, east Yorkshire enjoyed economic development and population growth in the twelfth and thirteenth centuries, with several monasteries founded. But for the most part, since at least the tenth century, wealth and power have been concentrated in the south.

Southern views of the north have often been disparaging. William of Malmesbury in the twelfth century blamed Northumbria's fall on 'the prevalence of degenerate manners'.[5] Polydore Vergil, an Italian historian at Henry VII's court, described northerners as 'savage and more eager than others for upheavals'.[6] In the seventeenth century, 'to put Yorkshire of a man' served as a phrase for cheating, while dramatist Henry Carey titled his 1736 ballad opera *A Wonder, or, An Honest Yorkshireman*.[7]

The Industrial Revolution added the perceived horrors of industrial townscapes to older notions of the north as harsh and bleak. Working-class radical movements in the 1830s and 1840s revived the idea that northerners were rebellious and truculent. In *North and South*, Elizabeth Gaskell gave a more balanced view. She portrayed northerners as independent, practical, calculating, enterprising and adventurous, but sometimes materialistic, philistine and selfish. Southerners were genteel, stable, graceful, devoted to the land, respectful of social hierarchy, yet could be conservative and snobbish.

As George Orwell noted: 'It was the industrialisation of the north that gave the north–south antithesis its peculiar slant.' That had created the self-made northern businessman – the Rouncewell or Bounderby of Dickens. 'The northern business man, with his hateful "get on or get out" philosophy, was the dominant figure of the nineteenth century, and as a sort of tyrannical corpse he rules us still,' wrote Orwell in *The Road to Wigan Pier*. 'This kind of cant is nowadays a pure anachronism, for the northern business man is no longer prosperous.'[8]

Northern industries had a torrid time in the interwar years and again in the 1980s. The Second World War and broad prosperity in the post-war decades stabilised matters for a while, but deindustrialisation gathered pace after the 1970s oil crisis. The north was slower to create new high-technology and services jobs.

For a while in the 1950s and 1960s, northern life became culturally fashionable, a fresh wind blowing through English creative complacency – the years of Richard Hoggart's *The Uses of Literacy*, kitchen-sink dramas such as *A Taste of Honey* and *A Kind of Loving*, the success of The Beatles and television series such as *The Likely Lads* and *Z Cars*. But as the economic picture darkened, so did portrayals. Alan Bleasdale's television series *Boys from the Blackstuff* was a tragi-comic drama of high-unemployment Liverpool. The film *Brassed Off* portrayed the struggles of a colliery brass band amid pit closures, while *The Full Monty* and *Little Voice* were feelgood musicals, masking pain. *Shameless* was an unsentimental council-estate comedy and *The League of Gentlemen* satirised Pennine small-town eccentricity.

Since the 1930s, governments of all the main parties have sought to tackle the north's problems with an ever-changing roster of regional polices and regeneration initiatives, often half-hearted and inconsistent. Incentives to lure international manufacturers faltered when branch factories were often the first to close as the parent company hit trouble. Such projects became rarer. Efforts to revive cities made better progress, creating financial, professional and business services jobs. Post-industrial towns, mining villages and seaside resorts have proved harder to regenerate.

Much as many would love to wish the north–south divide away, this is no time to give up. It may be fanciful to expect politicians to stop tearing up their predecessors' initiatives, but we must at least hope that new ones will be based on evaluating what has worked best in the past and in other places. Local politicians – though not everywhere – have become better at working with other local authorities. It is as well not to rely overly on national politicians. If there is to be a revival, it will depend on the talents, energy and enterprise of northerners.

As for closing the cultural gap, does anyone really want to? Britain already has enough clone towns, surely.

REFERENCES

Introduction

1. Ian Jack, *The Country Formerly Known as Great Britain: Writings 1989–2009* (Cape, 2009), 303.
2. 'North of England Economic Indicators', Office for National Statistics, 5 November 2014.
3. 'Estimates of the Population for the UK, England and Wales, Scotland and Northern Ireland', ONS, 24 June 2020; Frank Geary and Tom Stark, 'What Happened to Regional Inequality in Britain in the Twentieth Century?', *Economic History Review* 69, I (2016), table 1; Tom Hazeldine, *The Northern Question: A History of a Divided Country* (Verso, 2020), 1; 'Regional gross value added (income approach)', table 1, ONS, 12 December 2018.
4. 'GDP (current US$)', World Bank, data.worldbank.org, accessed 21 April 2021. UK GDP divided by a fifth to equate to northern England's share.
5. Graham Turner, *The North Country* (Eyre & Spottiswoode, 1967), 14; quoted in Dave Russell, *Looking North: Northern England and the National Imagination* (Manchester University Press, 2004), 15.
6. Helen Jewell, *The North–South Divide: The Origins of Northern Consciousness in England* (Manchester University Press, 1994), 11.
7. Jewell, *The North–South Divide*, 15.
8. Jewell, *The North–South Divide*, 23–4.
9. British Bandsman, 7 December 1963; quoted in Paul Barker, 'Cloth caps and chips it isn't', *New Statesman*, 9 January 1998; and in Russell, *Looking North*, 2.
10. Stuart Maconie, *Pies and Prejudice: In Search of the North* (Ebury, 2007), 2.

11. Donald Horne, *God is an Englishman* (Angus & Robertson, 1969), 22–3; quoted in Russell, *Looking North*, 26.
12. Bede, *Ecclesiastical History of the English People*, trans. A.M. Sellar (George Bell, 1907), 157.
13. Jewell, *The North–South Divide*, 208.
14. Norman Davis, ed., *Paston Letters and Papers of the Fifteenth Century* (Oxford, 1971), I, 198; quoted in Jewell, *The North–South Divide*, 46.
15. G.W.S. Barrow, 'Northern English Society in the Twelfth and Thirteenth Centuries', *Northern History* 4 (1969), 1–28; quoted in Eric Musgrove, *The North of England: A History from Roman Times to the Present* (Basil Blackwell, 1990), 2.
16. Thomas Babington Macaulay, *The History of England from the Accession of James II* (Macmillan, 1913), 374–6; quoted in Musgrove, *The North of England*, 3.
17. Musgrove, *The North of England*, 1, 4–5.

BEGINNINGS

Chapter 1: First Northerners to the Romans

1. Yorkshire Archaeological and Historical Society, 'Palaeolithic Yorkshire – Mammoth and Other Ancient Elephant Finds', www.yas.org.uk; Yorkshire Dales National Park, 'Victoria Cave', yorkshiredales.org.uk.
2. Press release, 'Yorkshire's Oldest New Addition to the "Jurassic World"', University of Manchester, 1 June 2015, manchester.ac.uk.
3. 'Waverley Wood Handaxe', British Museum/BBC, *A History of the World*, bbc.co.uk.
4. 'Palaeolithic Art and Archaeology of Creswell Crags', University of Durham, dur.ac.uk.
5. 'Howick', Archaeological Research Services, archaeologicalresearchservices.com.
6. Starr Carr archaeology project, starcarr.com.
7. Jan Harding, 'Thornborough, North Yorkshire: Neolithic and Bronze-Age monument complex' (Archaeology Data Service, 2008), archaeologydataservice.ac.uk.
8. Francis Pryor, *Britain BC* (HarperCollins, 2003), 150–3.
9. Jewell, *The North–South Divide*, 8–10; Barry Cunliffe, *Iron Age Communities in Britain* (4th edn, Routledge, 2005), 70–124; Cyril Fox, *The Personality of Britain* (2nd edn, 1933), 25.
10. Gary Lock and Ian Ralston, 'An Atlas of Hillforts in Britain and Ireland', hillforts.arch.ox.ac.uk.
11. 'Lindow Man', British Museum, britishmuseum.org.
12. Nicki Howarth, *Cartimandua: Queen of the Brigantes* (History Press, 2008), 33.

13. Howarth, *Cartimandua*, 56.
14. Tacitus, *Annals*, 12.37.
15. Tacitus, *Histories*, 3.45; *Annals*, 12.40; Howarth, *Cartimandua*, 121–32.
16. *Histories*, 3.45.
17. Howarth, *Cartimandua*, 47–8.
18. Howarth, *Cartimandua*, 67. There is some debate about whether Venutius' first rebellion in 57 actually happened or whether all the events took place in 69, since descriptions by Tacitus of the two rebellions in the *Histories* and *Annals* are similar.
19. *Histories*, 3.45.
20. *Histories*, 3.45.
21. Tacitus, *Agricola*, 17.
22. Patricia Southern, *Roman Britain: A New History 55 BC–AD 450* (Amberley, 2013), 129; Guy de la Bédoyère, *Roman Britain: A New History* (Thames & Hudson, 2013), 43.
23. *Agricola*, 30.
24. *Agricola*, 37.
25. David Mattingly, *An Imperial Possession: Britain in the Roman Empire* (Penguin, 2007), 154–8.
26. *Historia Augusta*, 'Antoninus Pius', 5.4.
27. Mattingly, *An Imperial Possession*, 159.
28. Southern, *Roman Britain*, 263–7.
29. Anthony Birley, *The African Emperor: Septimius Severus* (Batsford, 1988), 1–7.
30. Cassius Dio, *Roman History*, 77.11.
31. Southern, *Roman Britain*, 242.
32. Dio, *Roman History*, 77.14.
33. Southern, *Roman Britain*, 249.
34. Bédoyère, *Roman Britain*, 64.
35. Mattingly, *An Imperial Possession*, 523.
36. Southern, *Roman Britain*, 304–5.
37. Bédoyère, *Roman Britain*, 73.
38. Ammianus Marcellinus, *Roman History*, 27.8.1–10.
39. Zosimus, *New History*, 6.5.3.
40. Vindolanda Tablet, 164.
41. Tablet 291.
42. Tablet 346.
43. Mike Ibeji, 'Vindolanda', BBC History, bbc.co.uk.
44. Mattingly, *An Imperial Possession*, 93.
45. Bédoyère, *Roman Britain*, 207.
46. Mattingly, *An Imperial Possession*, 195–6.
47. Mattingly, *An Imperial Possession*, 214.
48. Bédoyère, *Roman Britain*, 261.

Chapter 2: The Kingdom of Northumbria

1. Barbara Yorke, *Kings and Kingdoms of Early Anglo-Saxon England* (Routledge, 1997), 87.
2. Ernst Dümmler, ed., *Alcuini Epistolae, Monumenta Germaniae Historica, Epistolae Aevi II* (Weidmann, 1895), no. 16; Dorothy Whitelock, trans., English Historical Documents, Vol. 1, c. 500–1042, 2nd edn (Eyre Methuen, 1979), no. 197; cited in Yorke, *Kings and Kingdoms of Early Anglo-Saxon England*, 93.
3. Bede, *Ecclesiastical History*, book II, chapter 5; Robert Colls, ed., *Northumbria History and Identity 547–2000* (History Press, 2007), ix.
4. Robin Fleming, *Britain after Rome: The Fall and Rise 400 to 1070* (Penguin, 2010), 39–40.
5. Nicholas Higham and Martin Ryan, *The Anglo-Saxon World* (Yale, 2013), 98.
6. Fleming, *Britain after Rome*, 50–60; Higham and Ryan, *The Anglo-Saxon World*, 78–87.
7. Higham and Ryan, *The Anglo-Saxon World*, 87–91.
8. 'The Fine-scale Genetic Structure of the British Population', *Nature*, 18 March 2015.
9. Bede, *Ecclesiastical History*, V.24.
10. Bede, *Ecclesiastical History*, I.34.
11. Max Adams, *The King in the North: The Life and Times of Oswald of Northumbria* (Head of Zeus, 2013), 5.
12. Adams, *The King in the North*, 27–9.
13. Nicholas Higham, *The Kingdom of Northumbria, AD 350–1100* (Sutton Press, 1993), 111–12.
14. Bede, *Ecclesiastical History*, II.2.
15. Paul Gething and Edoardo Albert, *Northumbria: The Lost Kingdom* (History Press, 2012), 14; Adams, 76–9; Higham, 112.
16. Higham, *The Kingdom of Northumbria*, 113; Adams, *The King in the North*, 81–96.
17. Higham, *The Kingdom of Northumbria*, 113–15; Adams, *The King in the North*, 97–102.
18. Higham, *The Kingdom of Northumbria*, 115; Adams, *The King in the North*, 104.
19. Higham, *The Kingdom of Northumbria*, 115; Adams, *The King in the North*, 105–7.
20. Higham, *The Kingdom of Northumbria*, 115; Adams, *The King in the North*, 107–8.
21. Higham, *The Kingdom of Northumbria*, 115–18; Adams, *The King in the North*, 108–13.
22. Bede, *Ecclesiastical History*, II.13.
23. Adams, *The King in the North*, 4.

24. Bede, *Ecclesiastical History*, III, 9–13; Yorke, *Kings and Kingdoms of Early Anglo-Saxon England*, 78.
25. Adams, *The King in the North*, 365–6.
26. Adams, *The King in the North*, 141–59; Higham, *The Kingdom of Northumbria*, 125.
27. Bede, *Ecclesiastical History*, III.17.
28. Bede, *Ecclesiastical History*, III.6.
29. Bede, *Ecclesiastical History*, III.6.
30. Adams, *The King in the North*, 235–7.
31. Bede, *Ecclesiastical History*, III.14.
32. Adams, *The King in the North*, 285–7; Higham, 130.
33. Adams, *The King in the North*, 302–3; Higham, 134.
34. Adams, *The King in the North*, 311–21; Higham, 135.
35. Dan Jackson, *The Northumbrians: North East England and Its People* (Hurst, 2019), 11–12.
36. Adams, *The King in the North*, 373.
37. Bede, *Ecclesiastical History*, IV.26.
38. Higham, *The Kingdom of Northumbria*, 145–7.

Chapter 3: Bede, Hilda and the Golden Age

1. Bede, The *Ecclesiastical History* of the English People, ed. Judith McClure and Roger Collins (Oxford, 1994), introduction, xvi–xvii.
2. Nicholas Higham and Martin Ryan, *The Anglo-Saxon World* (Yale, 2013), 170.
3. Jo Story, 'Bede, St Cuthbert and the Northumbrian *Folc*', in Colls, ed., *Northumbria History and Identity*, 54.
4. Higham and Ryan, *The Anglo-Saxon World*, 167.
5. 'Bede's Death Song' in Bede's *A History of the English Church and People*, trans. Leo Shirley-Price (Penguin, 1955).
6. Higham and Ryan, *The Anglo-Saxon World*, 168.
7. Higham and Ryan, *The Anglo-Saxon World*, 160.
8. Richard Gameson, *From Holy Island to Durham: The Contexts and Meanings of the Lindisfarne Gospels* (Third Millennium, 2013), 93; British Library, *Lindisfarne Gospels*, bl.uk.
9. Bill Griffiths, 'The Start of Everything Wonderful: The Old English Poetry of Northumbria', in Colls, *Northumbria History and Identity*, 39.
10. Griffiths in Colls, *Northumbria History and Identity*, 37.
11. Bede, *Ecclesiastical History*, IV.24.
12. Griffiths in Colls, *Northumbria History and Identity*, 35–6.
13. Higham and Ryan, *The Anglo-Saxon World*, 221.
14. Gething and Albert, *Northumbria: The Lost Kingdom*, 87–100.
15. Gething and Albert, *Northumbria: The Lost Kingdom*, 118–25.
16. Fleming, *Britain after Rome*, 61–2.
17. Fleming, *Britain after Rome*, 65–75.

18. Fleming, *Britain after Rome*, 75–80.
19. Fleming, *Britain after Rome*, 64.
20. Adams, *The King in the North*, 6–7.
21. Adams, *The King in the North*, 9.
22. Bede, *Ecclesiastical History*, II.20.
23. Bede, *Ecclesiastical History*, III.24.
24. Adams, *The King in the North*, 316.
25. Bede, *Ecclesiastical History*, IV.23.
26. Bede, *Ecclesiastical History*, IV.23.
27. Bede, *Ecclesiastical History*, III.25.

Chapter 4: Life with the Danes

1. The Saxon Chronicle, trans. James Ingram (Longman, Hurst, Rees, Orme and Brown, 1823), entry for 793 CE.
2. Katherine Holman, *The Northern Conquest: Vikings in Britain and Ireland* (Signal, 2007), 23.
3. R.M. Ballantyne, *Erling the Bold: A Tale of the Norse Sea-Kings* (James Nisbet, 1869), 437; quoted in Thomas Williams, *Viking Britain: A History* (Collins, 2017), 43.
4. Jayne Carroll, Stephen Harrison and Gareth Williams, *The Vikings in Britain and Ireland* (British Museum, 2014), 8.
5. Whitelock, *English Historical Documents*; quoted in Williams, *Viking Britain*, 31.
6. Holman, *The Northern Conquest*, 3.
7. Max Adams, *Aelfred's Britain: War and Peace in the Viking Age* (Head of Zeus, 2017), 146.
8. Williams, *Viking Britain*, 188.
9. E.A. Freeman, *The History of the Norman Conquest of England* (Clarendon Press, 1867–79), 51; cited in Williams, *Viking Britain*, 175.
10. *The Saxon Chronicle*, trans. Ingram, entry for 876 CE.
11. David Rollason, *Northumbria 500–1100: Creation and Destruction of a Kingdom* (Cambridge, 2003), 211–55.
12. Rollason, *Northumbria*, 228; Matthew Townend, *Viking Age Yorkshire* (Blackthorn, 2014), 58–60.
13. Holman, *The Northern Conquest*, 71–2.
14. Townend, *Viking Age Yorkshire*, 143.
15. Simon Keynes and Michael Lapidge, trans., *Alfred the Great: Asser's Life of King Alfred and Other Contemporary Sources* (Penguin, 1983), 125; quoted in D.M. Hadley, *The Vikings in England: Settlement, Society and Culture* (Manchester University Press, 2006), 16.
16. Nicholas Brooks, 'England in the Ninth Century: The Crucible of Defeat', *Transactions of the Royal Historical Society* (1979), 29, 1–20; cited in Adams, *Aelfred's Britain*, 117.

17. Holman, *The Northern Conquest*, 143–4.
18. Richard Hall, 'York', in Stefan Brink and Neil Price, eds, *The Viking World* (Routledge, 2008), 376; cited in Williams, *Viking Britain*, 296.
19. Holman, *The Northern Conquest*, 157–64.
20. Hadley, *The Vikings in England*, 214–23.
21. Matthew Townend, *Language and History in Viking Age England* (Turnhout: Brepols, 2002), 181–5.
22. Townend, *Viking Age Yorkshire*, 136–45.
23. Townend, *Viking Age Yorkshire*, 175.
24. Higham, *The Kingdom of Northumbria*, 184.
25. Williams, *Viking Britain*, 278–81.
26. Adams, *Aelfred's Britain*, 241.
27. Williams, *Viking Britain*, 286–7; Higham, *The Kingdom of Northumbria*, 192–3.
28. Clare Downham, *Viking Kings of Britain and Ireland: The Dynasty of Ívarr to AD 1014* (Dunedin, 2007), 115; Alex Woolf, *From Pictland to Alba: Scotland, 789–1070* (Edinburgh University Press, 2007), 187–8; Adams, *Aelfred's Britain*, 440.
29. Williams, *Viking Britain*, 297; Higham, *The Kingdom of Northumbria*, 211–15.
30. 'The Chronicles of John of Wallingford' in Joseph Stevenson, ed., *Church Historians of England* (Seeleys, 1853–8), II, 2, 549; quoted in Jewell, *The North–South Divide*, 33.

Chapter 5: William, the North's Nemesis

1. Elisabeth van Houts, trans., *The Gesta Normannorum Ducum of William of Jumieges, Orderic Vitalis, and Robert of Torigni* (Clarendon, 1992–5), 122–5; R.H.C. Davis and Marjorie Chibnall, *The Gesta Guillelmi of William of Poitiers* (Clarendon, 1998), 22–9; quoted by Marc Morris, *The Norman Conquest* (Hutchinson, 2012, Windmill, 2013), 82; Teresa Cole, *The Norman Conquest: William the Conqueror's Subjugation of England* (Amberley, 2016), 151.
2. Morris, *The Norman Conquest*, 15–16; Cole, *The Norman Conquest*, 217.
3. Morris, *The Norman Conquest*, 51–2; Cole, *The Norman Conquest*, 153.
4. Morris, *The Norman Conquest*, 82; Cole, *The Norman Conquest*, 160.
5. Richard Huscroft, *The Norman Conquest: A New Introduction* (Pearson Longman, 2009), 138; Cole, *The Norman Conquest*, 202.
6. Anne Williams, *The English and the Norman Conquest* (Boydell, 1995), 19–20; Morris, *The Norman Conquest*, 211–15; Huscroft, *The Norman Conquest*, 140; Cole, *The Norman Conquest*, 204–5.
7. Huscroft, *The Norman Conquest*, 142; Williams, *The English and the Norman Conquest*, 16–17; Morris, *The Norman Conquest*, 211.

8. Morris, *The Norman Conquest*, 217–20; Cole, *The Norman Conquest*, 206–7; Huscroft, *The Norman Conquest*, 142–3; Higham, *The Kingdom of Northumbria*, 242–3.

9. Cole, *The Norman Conquest*, 207; Huscroft, *The Norman Conquest*, 143; Rollason, *Northumbria 500–1100*, (Cambridge University Press, 2003), 283; Higham, *The Kingdom of Northumbria*, 243–4; Morris, *The Norman Conquest*, 222–4.

10. Marjorie Chibnall, trans., *The Ecclesiastical History of Orderic Vitalis* (Clarendon, 1969–83), ii, 222–3.

11. Cole, *The Norman Conquest*, 208–10; Rollason, *Northumbria 500–1100*, 283; Huscroft, *The Norman Conquest*, 143–4; Higham, *The Kingdom of Northumbria*, 244–6; Morris, *The Norman Conquest*, 225–9.

12. Cole, *The Norman Conquest*, 210–2; Huscroft, *The Norman Conquest*, 144–5; Rollason, *Northumbria 500–1100*, 283–4; Morris, *The Norman Conquest*, 229–31, 313–14.

13. *The Saxon Chronicle*, Ingram, trans., entry for 1069.

14. Chibnall, *Orderic Vitalis*, ii, 230–3; quoted in Morris, *The Norman Conquest*, 229.

15. Higham, *The Kingdom of Northumbria*, 246.

16. Paul Dalton et al., *Conquest, Anarchy and Lordship: Yorkshire 1066–1154* (Cambridge University Press, 2002), 22–5.

17. Richard Muir, *The Yorkshire Countryside: A Landscape History* (Keele University Press, 1997), 120–1; Hugh M. Thomas, *The Norman Conquest: England After William the Conqueror* (Rowman & Littlefield, 2008), 94–6.

18. Morris, *The Norman Conquest*, 314.

19. Muir, *The Yorkshire Countryside*, 120.

20. Brian K. Roberts, *The Making of the English Village* (Longman, 1987), 84, 212–14.

21. R.R. Darlington and P. McGurk, ed., and J. Bray and P. McGurk, trans., *The Chronicle of John of Worcester: The Annals from 450 to 1066* (Clarendon, 1995), 10–11; Jane Sayers and Leslie Watkiss, trans., *Thomas of Marlborough, History of the Abbey of Evesham* (Clarendon, 2003), 166–7; Morris, *The Norman Conquest*, 230.

22. Chibnall, *Orderic Vitalis*, ii, 232–3; Morris, *The Norman Conquest*, 230–1.

23. Cole, *The Norman Conquest*, 212–14.

24. Huscroft, *The Norman Conquest*, 147.

25. Williams, *The English and the Norman Conquest*, 150–4; Rollason, *Northumbria 500–1100*, 285–6.

26. Huscroft, *The Norman Conquest*, 148–9.

27. Sayers and Watkiss, trans., *Thomas of Marlborough*, 176–7; quoted in Morris, *The Norman Conquest*, 285–6.

28. David Rollason, ed., *Simeon of Durham, Libellus de Exordio atque Procursu iustius, hoc est Dunhelmensis ecclesie* (Oxford University Press, 2000),

218–21; Joseph Stevenson, *The Historical Works of Simeon of Durham* (Seeleys, 1855), 152; Morris, *The Norman Conquest*, 290; Rollason, *Northumbria 500–1100*, 284.

29. Huscroft, *The Norman Conquest*, 152.
30. Morris, *The Norman Conquest*, 306–26.
31. Williams, *The English and the Norman Conquest*, 212–13; Huscroft, *The Norman Conquest*, 324–5.
32. Higham and Ryan, *The Anglo-Saxon World*, 418.
33. Morris, *The Norman Conquest*, 338.
34. Huscroft, *The Norman Conquest*, 326.
35. Chibnall, *Orderic Vitalis*, iv, 94–5.

FRONTIER REGION

Chapter 6: A Violent Border

1. George MacDonald Fraser, *The Steel Bonnets: The Story of the Anglo-Scottish Border Reivers* (HarperCollins, 1995, first published 1971), 76–7.
2. Daniel Defoe, *A Tour Through England and Wales*, Vol. II (Dent, 1928), 252.
3. Rollason, *Northumbria 500–1100*, 277.
4. MacDonald Fraser, *The Steel Bonnets*, 43.
5. J.C. Russell, *British Medieval Population* (University of New Mexico Press, 1948), 53–4, 132; cited in Musgrove, *The North of England*, 97.
6. Keith Stringer, 'Emergence of a Nation-State', in Jenny Wormald, ed., *Scotland: A History* (Oxford, 2005), 41–7; Michael Lynch, *Scotland: A New History* (Pimlico, 1992), 80–3; Neil Oliver, *A History of Scotland* (Weidenfeld & Nicolson, 2009), 76–7; Alistair Moffat, *The Borders: A History of the Borders from Earliest Times* (Deerpark, 2002), 141–88.
7. Wormald, *Scotland*, 48; Oliver, *A History of Scotland*, 77–9; Lynch, *Scotland*, 84–7; Musgrove, *The North of England*, 123.
8. Marc Morris, *A Great and Terrible King: Edward I and the Forging of Britain* (Hutchinson, 2008, Windmill, 2009), 229–61; Michael Prestwich, *Edward I* (Yale, 1997), 356–76.
9. Morris, *A Great and Terrible King*, 284–300; Prestwich, *Edward I*, 469–76.
10. Morris, *A Great and Terrible King*, 301–44; Prestwich, *Edward I*, 476–503.
11. D.M. Broome, 'Exchequer migrations to York in the thirteenth and fourteenth centuries', in A.G. Little and F.M. Powicke, eds, *Essays in Medieval History Presented to Thomas Frederick Tout* (Manchester University Press, 1925), 291–300; cited in Musgrove, *The North of England*, 132–3.
12. Geoffrey Richardson, *The Lordly Ones: A History of the Neville Family and Their Part in the Wars of the Roses* (Baildon, 1998), 13, 16.
13. Alexander Rose, *Kings in the North: The House of Percy in British History* (Weidenfeld & Nicolson, 2002, Orion, 2003), 26–7, 35–43.

14. Ian Mortimer, *The Imperfect King: The Life of Edward III* (Jonathan Cape, 2006, Vintage, 2008), 262–3.
15. Mortimer, *The Imperfect King*, 290.
16. Jackson, *The Northumbrians*, 38.
17. Moffat, *The Borders*, Graham Robb, *The Debatable Land: The Lost World Between Scotland and England* (Picador, 2018), 67–8.
18. Moffat, *The Borders*, 246–7.
19. Robb, *The Debatable Land*, 77.
20. Robb, *The Debatable Land*, 79–81.
21. Moffat, *The Borders*, 244.
22. Robb, *The Debatable Land*, 80.
23. Moffat, *The Borders*, 251.
24. Robb, *The Debatable Land*, 127–8.
25. Moffat, *The Borders*, 264–6.
26. Moffat, *The Borders*, 266.
27. MacDonald Fraser, *The Steel Bonnets*, 1.

Chapter 7: John and the Northern Barons

1. David Carpenter, *Struggle for Mastery: The Penguin History of Britain 1066–1284* (Penguin, 2004), 274–5.
2. Musgrove, *The North of England*, 112–13.
3. Musgrove, *The North of England*, 6.
4. Marc Morris, *King John: Treachery, Tyranny and the Road to Magna Carta* (Hutchinson, 2015, Windmill, 2016), 3.
5. John Gillingham, 'The Anonymous of Béthune, King John and Magna Carta', in J.S. Loengard, ed., *Magna Carta and the England of King John* (Woodbridge, 2010); cited in Morris, *King John*, 294.
6. Stephen Church, *King John: England, Magna Carta and the Making of a Tyrant* (Macmillan, 2015, Pan, 2016), xx.
7. Ralph V. Turner, *King John: England's Evil King* (History Press, 2009), 23; Morris, *King John*, 184–6.
8. Church, *King John*, xx.
9. Church, *King John*, 209.
10. Carpenter, *Struggle for Mastery*, 264.
11. Richard Huscroft, *Ruling England 1042–1217* (Pearson Longman, 2005), 148.
12. J.C. Holt, *The Northerners: A Study in the Reign of King John* (Oxford, 1961), 144; Carpenter, *Struggle for Mastery*, 271.
13. Morris, *King John*, 129; Church, *King John*, 147.
14. Church, *King John*, 185.
15. Carpenter, *Struggle for Mastery*, 272.
16. Morris, *King John*, 93–4.
17. Musgrove, *The North of England*, 107–17.

18. Holt, *The Northerners*, 31–2.
19. Holt, *The Northerners*, 34.
20. Holt, *The Northerners*, 89; Morris, *King John*, 220; Turner, *King John*, 174–5.
21. Carpenter, *Struggle for Mastery*, 286.
22. Church, *King John*, 209–11.
23. Holt, *The Northerners*, 100.
24. Carpenter, *Struggle for Mastery*, 287; Huscroft, *Ruling England*, 150.
25. Musgrove, *The North of England*, 108.
26. Turner, *King John*, 180–5; Carpenter, *Struggle for Mastery*, 289–96.
27. Musgrove, *The North of England*, 108.
28. Huscroft, *Ruling England*, 195–7.
29. Carpenter, *Struggle for Mastery*, 289–90.

Chapter 8: The Wars of the Roses

1. Alan Crosby, *A History of Lancashire* (Phillimore, 1998), 35.
2. Trevor Royle, *The Wars of the Roses: England's First Civil War* (Little, Brown, 2009, Abacus, 2010), 14–15; Alison Weir, *Lancaster and York: The Wars of the Roses* (Jonathan Cape, 1995, Vintage, 2009), 196–7.
3. Weir, *Lancaster and York*, 415–17.
4. Musgrove, *The North of England*, 163.
5. Musgrove, *The North of England*, 155, 165–7.
6. Weir, *Lancaster and York*, 9–10; R.L. Storey, 'The North of England', in S.B. Chrimes et al., ed., *Fifteenth Century England 1399–1509* (Sutton, 1995), 132–3.
7. Weir, *Lancaster and York*, 25, 84.
8. Michael Hicks, *Essential Histories: The Wars of the Roses* (Osprey, 2003), 12; Weir, 40–1.
9. Royle, *The Wars of the Roses*, 183–5; Weir, *Lancaster and York*, 90–100.
10. Weir, *Lancaster and York*, 136.
11. Weir, *Lancaster and York*, 178.
12. Weir, *Lancaster and York*, 252–3.
13. Royle, *The Wars of the Roses*, 264; Weir, *Lancaster and York*, 257.
14. Weir, *Lancaster and York*, 264.
15. Royle, *The Wars of the Roses*, 284; Weir, *Lancaster and York*, 287.
16. Royle, *The Wars of the Roses*, 288.
17. Michael Hicks, *Richard III: The Self-Made King* (Yale, 2019), 40–3; Chris Skidmore, *Richard III: Brother, Protector, King* (Weidenfeld & Nicolson, 2017), 38.
18. Hicks, *Richard III*, 107–8.
19. Hicks, *Richard III*, 139–43; Musgrove, *The North of England*, 171.
20. Musgrove, *The North of England*, 172; Hicks, *Richard III*, 156–8.
21. A.J. Pollard, *The Wars of the Roses* (Macmillan, 1988), 70–1.
22. Hicks, *Richard III*, 248, 252–3.

23. Skidmore, *Richard III*, 180–92; Hicks, *Richard III*, 258–60.
24. Hicks, *Richard III*, 263.
25. Dan Jones, *The Hollow Crown: The Wars of the Roses and the Rise of the Tudors* (Faber & Faber, 2014), 287; Hicks, *Richard III*, 276–7.
26. Skidmore, *Richard III*, 285–6; Hicks, *Richard III*, 342–4.
27. N. Pronay and J. Cox (eds), *The Crowland Chronicle Continuations 1459–86* (Sutton, 1986), 170–1, quoted in Hicks, *Richard III*, 326, and Skidmore, *Richard III*, 258.
28. Hicks, *Richard III*, 387–90.
29. Pollard, *The Wars of the Roses*, 39.

Chapter 9: Tudor Rebels

1. S.T. Bindoff, *Tudor England* (Penguin, 1991), 207.
2. John Guy, *Tudor England* (Oxford, 1988), 352.
3. David Loades, *The Tudor Court* (Batsford, 1986), 193–202; cited in Musgrove, *The North of England*, 184, 186, 190.
4. R. Schofield, 'The Geographical Distribution of Wealth in England 1334–1649', *Economic History Review* 18 (1965), 483–510; cited in Musgrove, *The North of England*, 185.
5. Christopher Daniell, *Atlas of Early Modern Britain* (Routledge, 2013), Map 90; Bruce M.S. Campbell, 'North–South Dichotomies, 1066–1550', in Alan R.H. Baker and Mark Billinge, eds, *Geographies of England: The North–South Divide, Material or Imagined* (Cambridge, 2010), 161; cited in Hazeldine, *The Northern Question*, 34.
6. Musgrove, *The North of England*, 17, 185.
7. Francis Bacon, *History of the Reign of King Henry VII*, reproduced in Henry Craik, ed., *English Prose*, Vol. II: *Sixteenth Century to the Restoration* (Macmillan, 1916), bartleby.com.
8. Thomas Penn, *The Winter King: The Dawn of Tudor England* (Allen Lane, 2011), xix–xxi.
9. Stephen Duxbury, *The Brief History of Lancashire* (History Press, 2011), 50–1.
10. Duxbury, *The Brief History of Lancashire*, 51–2; G.R. Elton, *England Under the Tudors* (Methuen, 1955), 27–8.
11. Anthony Fletcher and Diarmaid MacCulloch, *Tudor Rebellions* (Routledge, 2016), 18–19.
12. Musgrove, *The North of England*, 192.
13. Penn, *The Winter King*, 156.
14. C.J. Harrison, 'The Petition of Edmund Dudley', *English Historical Review* 87 (1972), 82–99; quoted in Guy, *Tudor England*, 64.
15. Polydore Vergil, *Anglica Historia*, ed. Denys Hay (Royal Historical Society Camden Society, 3rd series, 74; 1950), 127; quoted in Guy, *Tudor England*, 66.

16. Penn, *The Winter King*, xxi, 349–50.
17. Machiavelli, *Lettere familiari*, ed. E. Alvisi, (Florence, 1883), 293; quoted in Penn, *The Winter King*, 352.
18. C.H. Miller, *The Complete Works of St Thomas More*, 3, 2, no. 19 (New Haven, 1963–97); cited in Penn, *The Winter King*, 359.
19. Penn, *The Winter King*, 375–6; G.R. Elton, *England Under the Tudors*, 57.
20. Guy, *Tudor England*, 62–3, 89–91, 98–9; Elton, *England Under the Tudors*, 82–3.
21. Guy, *Tudor England*, 151, 156–7, 181–2; G.R. Elton, *Reform and Reformation: England 1509–1558* (Arnold, 1977), 211–20.
22. Elton, *Reform and Reformation*, 201–2, 237–8, 257; Guy, *Tudor England*, 176, 179; Musgrove, *The North of England*, 201–2; Fletcher and MacCulloch, *Tudor Rebellions*, 26, 39.
23. Fletcher and MacCulloch, *Tudor Rebellions*, 27–9.
24. Fletcher and MacCulloch, *Tudor Rebellions*, 29–38; R.W. Hoyle, *The Pilgrimage of Grace and the Politics of the 1530s* (Oxford, 2001), 4–11.
25. Guy, *Tudor England*, 149–50.
26. Elton, *Reform and Reformation*, 260–71.
27. Hoyle, 17, 28–9, 43; Fletcher and MacCulloch, *Tudor Rebellions*, 38–48; Guy, *Tudor England*, 151–2.
28. Fletcher and MacCulloch, *Tudor Rebellions*, 50–2; Elton, *Reform and Reformation*, 271–2.
29. Duxbury, *The Brief History of Lancashire*, 56–7.
30. T.N. Toller, ed., *Correspondence of Edward, Third Earl of Derby* (1890), cited in Christopher Haigh, *Reformation and Resistance in Tudor Lancashire* (Cambridge, 1975), 108–9.
31. Alan Crosby, *A History of Lancashire* (Phillimore, 1998), 52; Haigh, *Reformation and Resistance in Tudor Lancashire*, 225–94.
32. Helen Castor, *Elizabeth I: A Study in Insecurity* (Allen Lane, 2018, Penguin, 2019) 66–7; Haigh, *Reformation and Resistance in Tudor Lancashire*, 222.
33. Guy, *Tudor England*, 272.
34. Fletcher and MacCulloch, *Tudor Rebellions*, 101.
35. Guy, *Tudor England*, 273–4; Fletcher and MacCulloch, *Tudor Rebellions*, 101–2.
36. Fletcher and MacCulloch, *Tudor Rebellions*, 102–3.
37. K.J. Kesselring, *The Northern Rebellion of 1569: Faith, Politics and Protest in Elizabethan England* (Palgrave Macmillan, 2007), 1.
38. Fletcher and MacCulloch, *Tudor Rebellions*, 105.
39. Guy, *Tudor England*, 275.
40. Fletcher and MacCulloch, *Tudor Rebellions*, 108.
41. E.A.J. Honigman, *Shakespeare: The 'Lost Years'* (Manchester University Press, 1999).
42. Michael Wood, *Shakespeare* (Basic Books, 2003), 80.

43. Terence G. Schoone-Jongen, *Shakespeare's Companies: William Shakespeare's Early Career and the Acting Companies 1577–1594* (Routledge, 2016), 162; Honigman, *Shakespeare: The 'Lost Years'*, 21–2, 31–4.

44. Wood, *Shakespeare*, 80.

45. The Shakespeare North Playhouse, shakespearenorthplayhouse.co.uk.

46. Stephen Bowd, 'In the Labyrinth: John Dee and Reformation Manchester', *Manchester Region History Review* 19 (2008), 17–43, research. ed.ac.uk.

47. Bowd, 'In the Labyrinth', 17–43.

Chapter 10: Witchcraft and Civil Wars

1. Philip C. Almond, *The Lancashire Witches: A Chronicle of Sorcery and Death on Pendle Hill* (I.B. Tauris, 2012), 2–3.

2. Julian Goodare, 'A Royal Obsession with Black Magic Started Europe's Most Brutal Witch Hunts', *National Geographic*, 17 October 2019.

3. Stephen Pumfrey, 'Potts, Plots and Politics: James I's Daemonologie and The Wonderfull Discoverie of Witches in the Countie of Lancaster', in Robert Poole, ed., *The Lancashire Witches: Histories and Stories* (Manchester University Press, 2002), 23.

4. James Sharpe, 'Introduction: The Lancashire Witches in Historical Context', in Poole, ed., 3.

5. Pumfrey, in Poole, ed., 26–7.

6. Duxbury, *The Brief History of Lancashire*, 62.

7. John Swain, 'Witchcraft, Economy and Society in the Forest of Pendle', in Poole, ed., 73–87.

8. Michael Mullett, 'The Reformation in the Parish of Whalley', in Poole, ed., 88–104.

9. Pumfrey, in Poole, ed., 36–9; Almond, *The Lancashire Witches*, 70–1.

10. Lumby, in Poole, ed., 58–69; Almond, *The Lancashire Witches*, 80–106; see also Jonathan Lumby, *The Lancashire Witch-Craze: Jennet Preston and the Lancashire Witches 1612* (Carnegie, 1995).

11. Almond, *The Lancashire Witches*, 49–52.

12. Almond, *The Lancashire Witches*, 132–6, 139–47.

13. Almond, *The Lancashire Witches*, 151–5.

14. Pumfrey, in Poole, ed., 38.

15. Stephen Bull, *'A General Plague of Madness': The Civil Wars in Lancashire, 1640–1660* (Carnegie, 2009), 90.

16. Charles Carton, *The Experience of the British Civil Wars* (Routledge, 1992), 211–14; 'The Impact of the Fighting', in J.S. Morrill, ed., *The Impact of the English Civil War* (Collins & Brown, 1991), 20; Jack Binns, *Yorkshire in the Civil Wars: Origins, Impact and Outcome* (Blackthorn, 2004), ix; Blair Worden, *The English Civil Wars: 1640–1660* (Weidenfeld & Nicolson, 2009), 73.

REFERENCES

17. Musgrove, *The North of England*, 228–36; J.S. Morrill, 'The Northern Gentry and the Great Rebellion', *Northern History* 15 (1979), 66–87; Worden, *The English Civil Wars*, 46.

18. Trevor Royle, *Civil War: The Wars of the Three Kingdoms 1638–1660* (Little, Brown, 2004), 84–115.

19. David Hey, *Yorkshire from AD 1000* (Longman, 1986), 177; Binns, *Yorkshire in the Civil Wars*, 21–2.

20. Binns, *Yorkshire in the Civil Wars*, 13.

21. Binns, *Yorkshire in the Civil Wars*, 35.

22. Bull, 'A General Plague of Madness', 390.

23. Binns, *Yorkshire in the Civil Wars*, 55–6.

24. Jackson, *The Northumbrians*, 41–2.

25. Bull, 'A General Plague of Madness', 157–61.

26. Bull, 'A General Plague of Madness', 213–34; Royle, *Civil War*, 288–90.

27. Binns, *Yorkshire in the Civil Wars*, 86–95; Hey, *Yorkshire from AD 1000*, 179.

28. Bull, 'A General Plague of Madness', 301.

29. Andrew Marvell, 'Upon Appleton House, to my Lord Fairfax'.

30. Jackson, *The Northumbrians*, 42.

31. Bull, 'A General Plague of Madness', 383–8.

32. Bull, 'A General Plague of Madness', 410.

33. Binns, *Yorkshire in the Civil Wars*, 192–3.

34. Stuart Hylton, *A History of Manchester* (Phillimore, 2003), 37; N.J. Frangopulo, ed., *Rich Inheritance: A Guide to the History of Manchester* (Manchester Education Committee, 1962), 31, 211–13.

35. Duxbury, *The Brief History of Lancashire*, 86–8.

36. Jackson, *The Northumbrians*, 42; 'Ten things you (probably) didn't know about Bonnie Prince Charlie and the Jacobites', BBC History Extra, December 30 2020, historyextra.com.

37. Duxbury, *The Brief History of Lancashire*, 89–90.

38. Duxbury, *The Brief History of Lancashire*, 90–4; Jackson, *The Northumbrians*, 42.

39. T.M. Devine, *The Scottish Nation 1700–2007* (Allen Lane, 1999, Penguin, 2000), 43.

40. Katie Wales, *Northern English: A Social and Cultural History* (Cambridge University Press, 2006), 133–5; Jackson, *The Northumbrians*, 42–3.

41. Alistair Moffat and George Rosie, *Tyneside: A History of Newcastle and Gateshead from Earliest Times* (Mainstream, 2006), 68–9; Jackson, *The Northumbrians*, 42–3.

42. Hylton, *A History of Manchester*, 38; Frangopulo, ed., *Rich Inheritance*, 32–4, 194.

43. Hylton, *A History of Manchester*, 43–4; Duxbury, *The Brief History of Lancashire*, 96.

44. Duxbury, *The Brief History of Lancashire*, 96–7.

45. Hylton, *A History of Manchester* 44.
46. Duxbury, *The Brief History of Lancashire*, 97; Hylton, *A History of Manchester*, 44–5.

INDUSTRIAL REVOLUTION

Chapter 11: Why the North?

1. William Dodd, *A Narrative of the Experiences and Sufferings of William Dodd, a Factory Cripple, Written by Himself* (1851), in James R. Simmons and Janice Carlisle, eds, *Factory Lives: Four Nineteenth-Century Working-Class Autobiographies* (Ontario, 2007); quoted in Emma Griffin, *Liberty's Dawn: A People's History of the Industrial Revolution* (Yale, 2013), 24.
2. Benjamin Shaw, *The Family Records of Benjamin Shaw, Mechanic of Dent, Dolphinholme and Preston, 1772–1841*, ed. Alan G. Crosby (Record Society of Lancashire and Cheshire, 1991), 38, 42, 45; quoted in Griffin, *Liberty's Dawn*, 41–2.
3. Alexis de Tocqueville, *Journeys to England and Ireland*, trans. George Lawrence and K.P. Mayer, ed. K.P. Mayer (Transaction, 2003), 107–8.
4. Emma Griffin, *A Short History of the British Industrial Revolution* (Palgrave Macmillan, 2010), 53–62; Joel Mokyr, *The Enlightened Economy: Britain and the Industrial Revolution 1700–1850* (Penguin, 2009), 302–5.
5. Fred Singleton, *Industrial Revolution in Yorkshire* (Dalesman, 1970), 45–6.
6. Andrew Ure, *The Philosophy of Manufactures, Or, An Exposition of the Scientific, Moral, and Commercial Economy of the Factory System of Great Britain* (1835), 309–13, 378, 380–4, 399, 379–402; quoted in Griffin, *A Short History of the British Industrial Revolution*, 145.
7. Charles Dickens, *Hard Times*, chapter five (Penguin Classics edition, 1995), 28.
8. Paul Bairoch, 'International Industrialisation Levels from 1750 to 1980', *Journal of European Economic History* 11 (1982), 296, reproduced in Paul Kennedy, *The Rise and Fall of the Great Powers* (Vintage, 1989), 149.
9. Sue Wilkes, *Narrow Windows, Narrow Lives: The Industrial Revolution in Lancashire* (Tempus, 2008), 56, 61.
10. Michael Winstanley, 'The Factory Workforce', in Mary B. Rose, ed., *The Lancashire Cotton Industry: A History Since 1700* (Lancashire County Books, 1996), 122.
11. Friedrich Engels, *The Condition of the Working Class in England*, ed. David McLellan (Oxford, 1993, first published 1845), 16.
12. Sven Beckert, *Empire of Cotton: A New History of Global Capitalism* (Allen Lane, 2014, Penguin, 2015), ix.
13. Beckert, *Empire of Cotton*, xv–xvii.

REFERENCES

14. Robert C. Allen, *The British Industrial Revolution in Global Perspective* (Cambridge, 2009); Judy Z. Stephenson, '"Real" Wages? Contractors, Workers, and Pay in London Building Trades, 1650–1800', *The Economic History Review* 71, no. 1 (February 2018), 106–32; Jane Humphries and Benjamin Schneider, 'Spinning the Industrial Revolution', *The Economic History Review* 72, no. 1 (February 2019); Robert C. Allen, 'Real Wages Once More: A Response to Judy Stephenson', *The Economic History Review* 72, no. 2 (May 2019).
15. Joel Mokyr, *A Culture of Growth: The Origins of the Modern Economy* (Princeton, 2016).
16. Joel Mokyr, *The Enlightened Economy*, 1–123.
17. E.A. Wrigley, *Continuity, Chance and Change: The Character of the Industrial Revolution in England* (Cambridge, 1988), 84; cited in Roger Osborne, *Iron, Steam & Money: The Making of the Industrial Revolution* (Bodley Head, 2013, Pimlico, 2014), 216.
18. Edward Baines, *History of the Cotton Manufacture in Great Britain* (H. Fisher, R. Fisher and P. Jackson, 1835), 84–112.
19. Rose, ed., *The Lancashire Cotton Industry*, 1–28.
20. Allen, *The British Industrial Revolution in Global Perspective*, 204–5; Osborne, *Iron, Steam & Money*, 217.
21. E.J. Buckatzsch, 'The Geographical Distribution of Wealth in England 1086–1843', *The Economic History Review* 3 (1950–1), 180–202; cited in Musgrove, *The North of England*, 256–7.
22. Mokyr, *The Enlightened Economy*, 359.
23. Mokyr, *The Enlightened Economy*, 361; Osborne, *Iron, Steam & Money*, 14–15, 222.
24. Osborne, *Iron, Steam & Money*, 295–303.
25. Mokyr, *The Enlightened Economy*, 365–91.
26. Thomas Carlyle, *Past and Present* (Chapman & Hall, 1843), Book 1, Chapter 1.
27. Griffin, *A Short History of the British Industrial Revolution*, 144–5.
28. Anon, *An Exposition of the Nefarious System of Making and Passing Spurious Coin … Being the Confessions of a Coiner* (Preston), quoted in Griffin, *Liberty's Dawn*, 24–5.
29. Shaw, *The Family Records of Benjamin Shaw*, 40; quoted in Griffin, *Liberty's Dawn*, 44.
30. Sue Wilkes, *Narrow Windows, Narrow Lives*, 15–20.
31. Mokyr, *The Enlightened Economy*, 274–5, 309–37; Griffin, *Liberty's Dawn*, 84–106; Wilkes, *Narrow Windows, Narrow Lives*, 58–60.
32. Mokyr, *The Enlightened Economy*, 274–5, 309–37; Osborne, *Iron, Steam & Money*, 71, 323–8; Griffin, *A Short History of the British Industrial Revolution*, 82–3; Wilkes, *Narrow Windows, Narrow Lives*, 55–7.
33. Mokyr, *The Enlightened Economy*, 333.
34. George Orwell, *The Road to Wigan Pier* (Penguin edition, 1986), 104.

35. Asa Briggs, *The Age of Improvement* (Longman, 2000), 42.
36. Walter White, *A Month in Yorkshire* (Chapman & Hall, 1858), 15–16; quoted in Russell, *Looking North*, 34.
37. Elizabeth Gaskell, *North and South* (Penguin edition, 1970), 72, 96.

Chapter 12: Cotton Empire

1. 'This land of long chimneys', attributed to cotton manufacturer Thomas Ashton, 1837, in Beckert, *Empire of Cotton*, 80; Chris Aspin, *The Cotton Industry* (Shire Album, 2003), 3.
2. Allen, *The British Industrial Revolution in Global Perspective*, 182; Phyllis Deane and W.A. Cole, *British Economic Growth, 1688–1959* (Cambridge University Press, 1969), 143, 166, 187; G.H. Wood, 'Real Wages and the Standard of Comfort since 1850', *Journal of the Royal Statistical Society* 72 (1910), 596–9.
3. Engels, *The Condition of the Working Class in England*, 21.
4. Léon Faucher, *Manchester in 1844: Its Present Condition and Future Prospects* (Simpkin, Marshall and Abel Heywood, 1844), 15–16; quoted in Hazeldine, *The Northern Question*, 45–6.
5. John Brown, *A Memoir of Robert Blincoe* (J. Doherty, 1832), quoted in Osborne, *Iron, Steam & Money*, 324–5.
6. Geoffrey Timmins, *Four Centuries of Lancashire Cotton* (Lancashire County Books, 1996), 3–4.
7. Alfred P. Wadsworth and Julia de Lacy Mann, *The Cotton Trade and Industrial Lancashire, 1600–1780* (Manchester University Press, 1931), 15.
8. Osborne, *Iron, Steam & Money*, 161–2; Wadsworth and Mann, *The Cotton Trade and Industrial Lancashire*, 449–71; Duxbury, *The Brief History of Lancashire*, 127–9.
9. Allen, *The British Industrial Revolution in Global Perspective*, 188–93; Baines, *History of the Cotton Manufacture in Great Britain*, 155–63; Wadsworth and Mann, *The Cotton Trade and Industrial Lancashire*, 476–82; Duxbury, *The Brief History of Lancashire*, 129–32.
10. C. Aspin and S.D. Chapman, *James Hargreaves and the Spinning Jenny* (Helmshore Local History Society, 1964), 48–9; cited in Allen, *The British Industrial Revolution in Global Perspective*, 193.
11. Osborne, *Iron, Steam & Money*, 175–8; Allen, *The British Industrial Revolution in Global Perspective*, 206–7; Duxbury, *The Brief History of Lancashire*, 140–6.
12. Thomas Carlyle, *Chartism* (James Frases, 1840), 85; quoted in R.S. Fitton, *The Arkwrights: Spinners of Fortune* (2012 edition, Derwent Valley Mills Educational Trust, first published 1989, Manchester University Press), 1.
13. Samuel Smiles, *Self-Help* (John Murray, 1860), 36; quoted in Fitton, *The Arkwrights*, 1.

14. Fitton, *The Arkwrights*, 51.

15. Osborne, *Iron, Steam & Money*, 195.

16. Osborne, *Iron, Steam & Money*, 196–7.

17. Quoted in Fitton, *The Arkwrights*, 219.

18. D. Bythell, *The Handloom Weavers* (Cambridge University Press, 1968), 254, cited in Rose, ed., *The Lancashire Cotton Industry*, 13.

19. Osborne, *Iron, Steam & Money*, 80.

20. Rose, ed., *The Lancashire Cotton Industry*, 14.

21. Winstanley in Rose, ed., *The Lancashire Cotton Industry*, 123–30.

22. Wilkes, *Narrow Windows, Narrow Lives*, 58–60.

23. Wilkes, *Narrow Windows, Narrow Lives*, 61, 65.

24. Michael Anderson, *Family Structure in Nineteenth-Century Lancashire* (Cambridge University Press, 1971), 37–8, cited by Winstanley in Rose, ed., *The Lancashire Cotton Industry*, 147–8.

25. Winstanley in Rose, ed., *The Lancashire Cotton Industry*, 147–53.

26. Andrew Marrison, 'Indian Summer, 1870–1914', in Rose, ed., *The Lancashire Cotton Industry*, 244.

27. Marrison in Rose, ed., *The Lancashire Cotton Industry*, 245–6; Aspin, *The Cotton Industry*, 31; S. Toms, 'Oldham Capitalism and the Rise of the Lancashire Textile Industry' (White Rose Research Online, 2007).

28. University of Exeter, 'Poetry of the Lancashire Cotton Famine 1861–5', cottonfaminepoetry.exeter.ac.uk.

29. Marrison in Rose, ed., *The Lancashire Cotton Industry*, 238–64.

30. Marguerite Dupree, 'Foreign Competition and the Interwar Period', in Rose, ed., *The Lancashire Cotton Industry*, 265.

31. Timmins, *Four Centuries of Lancashire Cotton*, 74–86.

Chapter 13: Engine Power

1. Jane Carlyle, *Letters*, ed. Alexander Carlyle (John Lane, 1903), Vol. I, no. 78; quoted in Norman Atkinson, *Sir Joseph Whitworth: 'The World's Best Mechanician'* (Sutton, 1996), 119.

2. David Waller, 'Why We Should Never Listen to the Luddites', 23 August 2017, davidwallerwriter.com; Simon Winchester, *Exactly: How Precision Engineers Created the Modern World* (William Collins, 2018), 119–25.

3. E.A. Wrigley, 'English County Populations in the Later Eighteenth Century', *Economic History Review*, 60, no. 1 (2007), table 5, 54–5; reproduced in Griffin, *A Short History of the British Industrial Revolution*, 55.

4. Griffin, *A Short History of the British Industrial Revolution*, 123–5.

5. Benjamin Disraeli, *Sybil, Or the Two Nations* (David Bryce, 1853), 120; quoted in Griffin, *A Short History of the British Industrial Revolution*, 105.

6. Michael W. Flinn, *The History of the British Coal Industry: 1700–1830*, Vol 2, *The Industrial Revolution* (Oxford, 1984), table 1.2, 26; S. Pollard, 'A New Estimate of British Coal Production, 1750–1850', *Economic History Review*, 33, no. 2 (1980), 212–35, table 14, 229; cited in Griffin, *A Short History of the British Industrial Revolution*, 109.

7. Osborne, *Iron, Steam & Money*, 64.

8. Osborne, *Iron, Steam & Money*, 71.

9. Osborne, *Iron, Steam & Money*, 249–52.

10. David Hey, *A History of Sheffield* (Carnegie, 1998), 190–1.

11. Hey, *Yorkshire from AD 1000*, 271.

12. Hey, *A History of Sheffield*, 196.

13. Singleton, *Industrial Revolution in Yorkshire*, 45–8.

14. Mokyr, *The Enlightened Economy*, 103, 137.

15. Jackson, *The Northumbrians*, 48–50.

16. *Newcastle Journal*, 14 May 1859; quoted in Henrietta Heald, *William Armstrong: Magician of the North* (McNidder & Grace, 2012), 104.

17. David Dougan, *The Great Gun-Maker: The Life of Lord Armstrong* (Sandhill, 1971), 67–8; quoted in Jackson, *The Northumbrians*, 50.

18. Dan Bogart, 'Turnpike Trusts and the Transportation Revolution in 18th Century Britain', *Explorations in Economic History*, 2, no. 4 (October 2005), 479–508; Bogart, 'Did Turnpike Trusts Increase Transportation Investment in Eighteenth-century England?', *Journal of Economic History*, 65, no. 2 (June 2005), 439–68; cited in Mokyr, *The Enlightened Economy*, 205.

19. Osborne, *Iron, Steam & Money*, 259.

20. Griffin, *A Short History of the British Industrial Revolution*, 120; Osborne, *Iron, Steam & Money*, 266–7; Mokyr, *The Enlightened Economy*, 209.

21. Griffin, *A Short History of the British Industrial Revolution*, 121.

22. Osborne, *Iron, Steam & Money*, 271–3.

23. David Ross, *George & Robert Stephenson: A Passion for Success* (History Press, 2018), 11–33; Osborne, *Iron, Steam & Money*, 275.

24. Ross, *George & Robert Stephenson*, 55–8, 61–3, 79–80; Osborne, *Iron, Steam & Money*, 276–7.

25. Osborne, *Iron, Steam & Money*, 277–9; Ross, *George & Robert Stephenson*, 110–20.

26. Frances Anne Kemble, *Records of a Girlhood* (R. Bentley & Son, 1878), Vol. 2, 158; quoted in Ross, *George & Robert Stephenson*, 116.

27. H.M. Walmsley, *The Life of Sir Joshua Walmsley* (Chapman & Hall, 1879), 72; quoted in Ross, *George & Robert Stephenson*, 120.

28. T.R. Gourvish, 'Railways 1830–70: The Formative Years', in Michael J. Freeman and Derek H. Aldcroft, eds, *Transport in Victorian Britain* (Manchester University Press, 1988), 57; cited in Griffin, *A Short History of the British Industrial Revolution*, 121.

29. Osborne, *Iron, Steam & Money*, 280.

30. Max Adams, *The Prometheans: John Martin and the Generation that Stole the Future* (Quercus, 2010), 185; quoted in Jackson, *The Northumbrians*, 90.

31. Mokyr, *The Enlightened Economy*, 214–15.

32. Mokyr, *The Enlightened Economy*, 216.

33. Ross, *George & Robert Stephenson*, 8, 84.

34. Combined totals for north, north-west and Yorkshire–Humberside standard statistical regions. Frank Geary and Tom Stark, 'Regional GDP in the UK, 1861–1911: New Estimates', *Economic History Review*, 68, no. 1 (2015), table 3; cited in Hazeldine, *The Northern Question*, 71.

Chapter 14: Trouble at th'Mill

1. Phyllis Bentley, *Inheritance* (Victor Gollancz, 1932), 286.

2. Keith Waterhouse, *Billy Liar* (Penguin, 2010, first published 1959), 31.

3. T.B. Macaulay, 'Southey's Colloquies', *Edinburgh Review* 50 (1830), 528–65; cited in Musgrove, *The North of England*, 266–7.

4. William Cobbett, *Rural Rides* (Everyman, 1973, first published 1822–6), Vol. 2, 290; cited in Musgrove, *The North of England*, 267.

5. Robert Tombs, *The English and Their History* (Allen Lane, 2014, Penguin, 2015), 426.

6. Engels, *The Condition of the Working Class in England*, 31.

7. Duncan Bythell, *The Handloom Weavers* (Cambridge, 1969), 96–106; cited in Robert Poole, *Peterloo: The English Uprising* (Oxford, 2019), 42, 205.

8. Hazeldine, *The Northern Question*, 52–3.

9. B.R. Mitchell and Phyllis Deane, *Abstract of British Historical Statistics* (Cambridge, 1962), 8–10, 366, 388, 402–3; cited in Tombs, *The English and Their History*, 426.

10. Robert Poole, *Peterloo*, 80–1.

11. A. Read, *The Peterloo Massacre* (James Wroe, 1819), 5.

12. Poole, *Peterloo*, 310.

13. Poole, *Peterloo*, 1–2.

14. Robert Reid, *The Peterloo Massacre* (Windmill, 2018, originally published 1989), 275–6.

15. Poole, *Peterloo*, 391; Tombs, *The English and Their History*, 437.

16. K. Theodore Hoppen, *The Mid-Victorian Generation, 1846–1886* (Oxford, 1998), 96; quoted in Tombs, *The English and Their History*, 433.

17. R.P. Hastings, 'Poverty and the Poor Law in the North Riding of Yorkshire, c. 1780–1837', University of York, *Borthwick Papers* 61 (1982), 33; cited in Tombs, *The English and Their History*, 439.

18. Donald Winch and Patrick O'Brien, eds, *The Political Economy of British Historical Experience, 1688–1914* (British Academy, 2002), 359–60; cited in Tombs, *The English and Their History*, 441.

19. Martin Daunton, *Wealth and Welfare: An Economic and Social History of Britain, 1851–1951* (Oxford, 2008), 525–6; cited in Tombs, *The English and Their History*, 442.

20. Tombs, *The English and Their History*, 442.

21. Michael S. Edwards, *Purge This Realm: A Life of Joseph Rayner Stephens* (Epworth Press, 1994), 44–5; quoted in Hazeldine, *The Northern Question*, 63.

22. Sir William Francis Patrick Napier, *The Life and Opinions of General Sir Charles James Napier* (J. Murray, 1857), 32; quoted in Hazeldine, *The Northern Question*, 63.

23. Tombs, *The English and Their History*, 452, 511.

24. F.M.L. Thompson, ed., *The Cambridge Social History of Britain, 1750–1950* (Cambridge, 1990), Vol. 2, 5, 132–3; cited in Tombs, *The English and Their History*, 450.

25. Constable Educational Series, 1860, in Suzanne Baudemont, *L'Histoire et la légende dans l'école élémentaire victorienne* (Klincksieck, 1980), 157; quoted in Tombs, *The English and Their History*, 467.

26. Tombs, *The English and Their History*, 467.

27. Iain Gateley, *A Cultural History of Alcohol* (Gotham, 2009), 248.

28. Peter Burne, *The Teetotaler's Companion; or, A Plea for Temperance* (Arthur Hall, 1847); quoted in Pascal Tréguer, 'The Authentic Origin of the Word "teetotal"', wordhistories.net.

29. F.M.L. Thompson, *The Rise of Respectable Society: A Social History of Victorian Britain, 1830–1900* (Harvard, 1988), 197; quoted in Tombs, *The English and Their History*, 471–2.

30. Keith Laybourn, *A History of British Trade Unionism* (Sutton, 1992).

31. Engels, 'England in 1845 and in 1885', *Commonweal* (March 1885), 12–14.

Chapter 15: Hail to the Sheep

1. Susan Rose, *The Wealth of England: The Medieval Wool Trade and Its Political Importance 1100–1600* (Oxbow, 2018), 3.

2. Alan Butler, *Sheep* (O Books, 2006), 39.

3. Rose, *The Wealth of England*, 87.

4. Marjorie Chibnall, *Anglo-Norman England 1066–1166* (Blackwell, 1986), 134–6, cited in Musgrove, *The North of England*, 96.

5. Musgrove, *The North of England*, 102.

6. Butler, *Sheep*, 42–4.

7. Rose, *The Wealth of England*, 18.

8. Rose, *The Wealth of England*, 33.

9. Butler, *Sheep*, 55–7; Rose, *The Wealth of England*, 52–9.

10. Butler, *Sheep*, 80–1.

11. Musgrove, *The North of England*, 96–7.

REFERENCES

12. Herbert Heaton, *The Yorkshire Woollen and Worsted Industries* (Clarendon, 1920), 44; cited in Musgrove, *The North of England*, 185.
13. Gary Firth, *A History of Bradford* (Phillimore, 1997), 18–20.
14. Keith Sugden, Sebastian A.J. Keibek and Leigh Shaw-Taylor, 'Adam Smith Revisited: Coal and the Location of the Woollen Manufacture in England before Mechanization, c. 1500–1820', econsoc.hist.cam.ac.uk.
15. Butler, *Sheep*, 100.
16. Defoe, *A Tour Through England and Wales*, Vol. II, 194.
17. Defoe, *A Tour Through England and Wales*, Vol. II, 203–6.
18. Fred Singleton, *Industrial Revolution in Yorkshire* (Dalesman, 1970), 22.
19. Singleton, *Industrial Revolution in Yorkshire*, 29–30, 35.
20. Butler, *Sheep*, 106–7.
21. Singleton, *Industrial Revolution in Yorkshire*, 30.
22. Singleton, *Industrial Revolution in Yorkshire*, 30–5; E.J. Connell and M. Ward, 'Industrial Development 1780–1914', in Derek Foster, ed., *A History of Modern Leeds* (Manchester University Press, 1980), 146–7.
23. Singleton, *Industrial Revolution in Yorkshire*, 37.
24. Ephraim Lipson, *The History of the Woollen and Worsted Industries* (A. and C. Black, 1921), 158; cited in Singleton, *Industrial Revolution in Yorkshire*, 152.
25. Singleton, *Industrial Revolution in Yorkshire*, 145–79; Firth, *A History of Bradford*, 64.
26. Singleton, *Industrial Revolution in Yorkshire*, 80, 85; Butler, *Sheep*, 175.
27. Firth, *A History of Bradford*, 67.
28. Butler, *Sheep*, 177–8.
29. Connell and Ward, in Foster, ed., *A History of Modern Leeds*, 159–60.
30. Singleton, *Industrial Revolution in Yorkshire*, 195.
31. National Wool Textile Export Corporation, Facts and Figures (1944); cited in Firth, *A History of Bradford*, 115.
32. Firth, *A History of Bradford*, 114.

IMMIGRATION AND SLAVERY

Chapter 16: Migrant Land

1. David Olusoga, *Black and British: A Forgotten History* (Macmillan, 2016), 450–1; *Liverpool Echo*, 6 June 1919, quoted in Jacqueline Jenkinson, '"All in the same uniform?" The Participation of Black Colonial Residents in the British Armed Forces in the First World War', *Journal of Imperial and Commonwealth History*, 40, no. 2, 207–30; *Liverpool Evening Express*, 'Negro in Dock: No Evidence How He Got into Water' (10 June 1919).
2. 'Viv Richards, Learie Constantine & Wes Hall: West Indies cricketers who charmed Lancashire', 2 October 2017, bbc.co.uk.
3. Olusoga, *Black and British*, 29; Peter Fryer, *Staying Power: The History of Black People in Britain* (originally published 1984, Pluto, 2018), 1.

4. 'Africans in Roman York?' University of Reading (26 February 2010), reading.ac.uk; Olusoga, *Black and British*, 30–1.

5. 'Ivory Bangle Lady', Yorkshire Museum, yorkshiremuseum.org.uk; Olusoga, *Black and British*, 31–2.

6. Olusoga, *Black and British*, 16.

7. Rozina Visram, *Asians in Britain: 400 Years of History* (Pluto, 2002), 2, 18–33.

8. Olusoga, *Black and British*, 85–6.

9. Hakim Adi, *The History of the African and Caribbean Communities in Britain* (Hodder Wayland, 1995), 24; Fryer, *Staying Power*, 60–1.

10. Adi, *The History of the African and Caribbean Communities in Britain*, 24–5.

11. Barclay Price, *The Chinese in Britain: A History of Visitors and Settlers* (Amberley, 2019), 35.

12. Price, *The Chinese in Britain*, 147–9.

13. Frangopulo, ed., *Rich Inheritance*, 113.

14. Chris Daniell 'Early Medieval York', in Patrick Nuttgens, ed., *The History of York: From Earliest Times to the Year 2000* (Blackthorn, 2001), 78–9.

15. Frangopulo, ed., *Rich Inheritance*, 114.

16. Todd M. Endelman, *The Jews of Britain 1656 to 2000* (University of California, 2002), 80.

17. Harold Pollins, *Economic History of the Jews in England* (Associated University Presses, 1982), 91; Frangopulo, ed., *Rich Inheritance*, 114.

18. Endelman, *The Jews of Britain*, 128–30.

19. Endelman, *The Jews of Britain*, 132.

20. Olusoga, *Black and British*, 409; Jeffrey Green, *Black Edwardians: Black People in Britain 1901–14* (Taylor & Francis, 1998), 4.

21. Visram, *Asians in Britain*, 169, 196–8.

22. Olusoga, *Black and British*, 427–48.

23. Ernest Marke, *In Troubled Waters: Memoirs of My Seventy Years in England* (Karia, 1975), 32.

24. Marke, *In Troubled Waters*, 30–1.

25. Olusoga, *Black and British*, 450–1, 454–8; Fryer, *Staying Power*, 302–8.

26. Visram, *Asians in Britain*, 201–22; Michael H. Fisher, Shompa Lahiri, Shinder Thandi, *A South-Asian History of Britain* (Greenwood, 2007), 134; Olusoga, *Black and British*, 465–6.

27. Visram, *Asians in Britain*, 222–3; Fisher et al., *A South-Asian History of Britain*, 135–7.

28. 'When Gandhi met Darwen's mill workers', 23 September 2011, bbc.co.uk.

29. Endelman, *The Jews of Britain*, 184–5.

30. Frangopulo, ed., *Rich Inheritance*, 115.

31. Endelman, *The Jews of Britain*, 196–203.

32. Endelman, *The Jews of Britain*, 223–5.

33. Visram, *Asians in Britain*, 234–52; Fisher et al., *A South-Asian History of Britain*, 150–2.

34. Jo-Anne Lee and John Lutz, *Situating: Critical Essays for Activists and Scholars* (McGill-Queen's Press, 2005); cited in Olusoga, *Black and British*, 490–4.

35. Olusoga, *Black and British*, 495–6.

36. Olusoga, *Black and British*, 496–7; Fryer, *Staying Power*, 373–7.

37. Price, *The Chinese in Britain*, 144–5.

38. Price, *The Chinese in Britain*, 171–2.

39. Diane Frost and Richard Phillips, *Liverpool '81: Remembering the Riots* (Liverpool University Press, 2011), 32; quoted in Olusoga, *Black and British*, 516–17.

40. Olusoga, *Black and British*, 517.

Chapter 17: Tainted Wealth

1. 'Liverpool and the Transatlantic Slave Trade', Merseyside Maritime Museum, liverpoolmuseums.org.uk.

2. Anthony Tibbles, *Liverpool and the Slave Trade* (Liverpool University Press, 2018), 1; statistics from David Eltis and David Richardson, *The Atlas of the Transatlantic Slave Trade* (New Haven, CT, 2010) and the Trans-Atlantic Slave Trade Database.

3. Tibbles, *Liverpool and the Slave Trade*, 4–5; Kenneth Morgan, 'Liverpool's Dominance in the British Slave Trade, 1740–1807', in David Richardson, Suzanne Schwarz and Anthony Tibbles, eds, *Liverpool and Transatlantic Slavery* (Liverpool University Press, 2007), 15.

4. Fryer, *Staying Power*, 51–3.

5. 'World of Domesday: The Social Order', National Archives, nationalarchives.gov.uk.

6. Tibbles, *Liverpool and the Slave Trade*, 3.

7. Tibbles, *Liverpool and the Slave Trade*, 3.

8. Tibbles, *Liverpool and the Slave Trade*, 3–4.

9. Tibbles, *Liverpool and the Slave Trade*, 61–5; Morgan, in Richardson et al., eds, *Liverpool and Transatlantic Slavery*, 15.

10. Tibbles, *Liverpool and the Slave Trade*, 13–15.

11. Jane Longmore, '"Cemented by the Blood of a Negro"? The Impact of the Slave Trade on Eighteenth-century Liverpool', in Richardson et al., eds, *Liverpool and Transatlantic Slavery*, 227–51.

12. Nicholas J. Radburn, 'William Davenport, the Slave Trade, and Merchant Enterprise in Eighteenth-Century Liverpool' (PhD thesis, Victoria University of Wellington, New Zealand, 2009); Tibbles, *Liverpool and the Slave Trade*, 65; general discussion of profitability in Kenneth Morgan, *Slavery, Atlantic Trade and the British Economy, 1660–1800* (Cambridge, 2000).

13. Fryer, *Staying Power*, 42–3; Tibbles, *Liverpool and the Slave Trade*, 67–8, 72.

14. Olusoga, *Black and British*, 204–5; Adam Hochschild, *Bury the Chains: The British Struggle to Abolish Slavery* (Macmillan, 2005, Pan, 2006), 79–82.
15. Hochschild, *Bury the Chains*, 95–7.
16. Adam Smith, *The Wealth of Nations, Books I–III* (Penguin, 1986, first published 1776), 488–9.
17. Kenneth Morgan, *Slavery in the British Empire: From Africa to America* (Oxford University Press, 2007), 157; Olusoga, *Black and British*, 208.
18. Thomas Clarkson, *The History of the Rise, Progress and Accomplishment of the Abolition of the African Slave-Trade by the British Parliament* (Longman, Hurst, Rees and Orme, 1808), Vol. I, 388, 409–10, 417–18; Seymour Drescher, *Capitalism and Antislavery: British Mobilization in Comparative Perspective* (Oxford University Press, 1987), 72; quoted in Hochschild, *Bury the Chains*, 117–21.
19. Robert D. Bass, *The Green Dragoon: The Lives of Banastre Tarleton and Mary Robinson* (Henry Holt, 1957), 290–1, 294, 299; quoted in Hochschild, *Bury the Chains*, 183–4.
20. Tibbles, *Liverpool and the Slave Trade*, 88–9.
21. Tibbles, *Liverpool and the Slave Trade*, 91–3.
22. Tibbles, *Liverpool and the Slave Trade*, 95, 102.
23. Olusoga, *Black and British*, 344, 351; *The Economist*, 19 January 1861, quoted in Lance E. Davis and Stanley L. Engerman, *Naval Blockades in Peace and War: An Economic History Since 1750* (Cambridge University Press, 2006), 127.
24. Olusoga, *Black and British*, 352–3.
25. Tibbles, *Liverpool and the Slave Trade*, 102; Olusoga, *Black and British*, 356–7.
26. Olusoga, 360–2; see also Mary Ellison, *Support for Secession: Lancashire and the American Civil War* (University of Chicago Press, 1973).
27. Bill Cash, *John Bright: Statesman, Orator, Agitator* (Bloomsbury, 2011), 146; Olusoga, *Black and British*, 362–3.
28. Olusoga, *Black and British*, 363–4.
29. *The Anti-Slavery Reporter*, 5 February 1863, 43–4; Norman Longmate, *The Hungry Mills: The Story of the Lancashire Cotton Famine 1861–5* (Maurice Temple Smith, 1978), 254; Olusoga, *Black and British*, 364–5.
30. Tibbles, *Liverpool and the Slave Trade*, 104.
31. 'Is this James Johnson?', Gallery Oldham, galleryoldham.org.uk.
32. Marika Sherwood, *After Abolition: Britain and the Slave Trade since 1807* (I.B. Tauris, 2007), 45–57.
33. David Richardson, 'The British Empire and the Atlantic Slave Trade, 1660–1807', in P.J. Marshall, ed., *The Oxford History of the British Empire: Volume II: The Eighteenth Century* (Oxford, 1998), 440–64.
34. Klas Rönnbäck, 'On the Economic Importance of the Slave Plantation Complex to the British Economy during the Eighteenth Century: A Value-added Approach', *Journal of Global History* 13, no. 3, (November 2018).

REFERENCES

35. Tibbles, *Liverpool and the Slave Trade*, 77; Morgan, *Slavery, Atlantic Trade and the British Economy*, 97.

Chapter 18: Irish Influence

1. John Belchem, *Irish, Catholic and Scouse* (Liverpool University Press, 2007), 3–4.
2. 'One in Four Britons Claim Irish Roots', Guinness/ICM Research poll, 16 March 2001, news.bbc.uk.
3. Donald MacRaild, *The Irish Diaspora in Britain, 1750–1939* (Palgrave Macmillan, 2011), 24–5.
4. MacRaild, *The Irish Diaspora in Britain*, 7, 24; Kerby A. Miller, *Emigrants and Exiles: Ireland and the Irish Exodus to North America* (Oxford University Press, 1988), 291.
5. Graham Davis, *The Irish in Britain, 1815–1914* (Gill & Macmillan, 1991), 42–4; MacRaild, *The Irish Diaspora in Britain*, 50.
6. Frank Neal, 'Lancashire, the Famine and the Poor Laws', *Irish Social and Economic History* 22 (1995), 33; quoted in MacRaild, *The Irish Diaspora in Britain*, 50.
7. Tristram Hunt, *Building Jerusalem: The Rise and Fall of the Victorian City* (Weidenfeld & Nicolson, 2004, Phoenix, 2005), 20.
8. Christine Kinealy, *This Great Calamity: The Irish Famine, 1845–52* (Gill & Macmillan, 1994), 33–5; MacRaild, *The Irish Diaspora in Britain*, 51–2.
9. Mervyn Busteed, *The Irish in Manchester c. 1750–1921: Resistance, Adaptation and Identity* (Manchester University Press, 2016), 150.
10. James Phillips Kay, *The Moral and Physical Condition of the Working Classes Employed in the Cotton Manufacture in Manchester* (Cass & Co., 1970, first published 1832), 21–2, 27; quoted in Busteed, *The Irish in Manchester*, 26–7.
11. Dean Kirby, *Angel Meadow: Victorian Britain's Most Savage Slum* (Pen & Sword History, 2016), 51.
12. Hunt, *Building Jerusalem*, 32.
13. Busteed, *The Irish in Manchester*, 30–1; Tristram Hunt, *The Frock-Coated Communist: The Revolutionary Life of Friedrich Engels* (Allen Lane, 2009, Penguin, 2010), 232–3.
14. Pauline Millward, 'The Stockport Riots of 1852: A Study of Anti-Catholic and Anti-Irish Sentiment', in R. Swift and S. Gilley, eds, *The Irish in the Victorian City* (Croom Helm, 1985), 207–25; Busteed, *The Irish in Manchester*, 63.
15. MacRaild, *The Irish Diaspora in Britain*, 177–81.
16. *Cowdroy's Weekly Gazette and Manchester Advertiser*, 18 July 1807; quoted in Busteed, *The Irish in Manchester*, 88–9.
17. MacRaild, *The Irish Diaspora in Britain*, 90–109.
18. MacRaild, *The Irish Diaspora in Britain*, 58–9.

363

19. Arthur Redford, *Labour Migration in England* (Manchester University Press, 1926), 161–2; Davis, *The Irish in Britain*, 105.

20. Davis, *The Irish in Britain*, 112–13; MacRaild, *The Irish Diaspora in Britain*, 170–3.

21. MacRaild, *The Irish Diaspora in Britain*, 142–51.

22. Sharon Lambert, *Irish Women in Lancashire 1922–1960: Their Story* (University of Lancaster, 2001), 15–29.

23. Davis, *The Irish in Britain*, 193; MacRaild, *The Irish Diaspora in Britain*, 125–6.

24. Busteed, *The Irish in Manchester*, 211–18; Davis, *The Irish in Britain*, 193–5; MacRaild, *The Irish Diaspora in Britain*, 126–7.

25. Belchem, *Irish, Catholic and Scouse*, 178; MacRaild, *The Irish Diaspora in Britain*, 129.

26. MacRaild, *The Irish Diaspora in Britain*, 138; Busteed, *The Irish in Manchester*, 262.

27. Belchem, *Irish, Catholic and Scouse*, 312–14; MacRaild, *The Irish Diaspora in Britain*, 138.

28. Lambert, *Irish Women in Lancashire*, 1.

29. J.B. Priestley, *English Journey* (Heinemann/Gollancz, 1934), 249.

30. Lambert, *Irish Women in Lancashire*, 83–98.

THE VICTORIAN AGE

Chapter 19: The Great Cities

1. Nikolaus Pevsner, *The Buildings of England: Northumberland* (Penguin, 1957), 56; quoted in Jackson, *The Northumbrians*, 103.

2. Robert Vaughan, *The Age of Great Cities* (Jackson & Walford, 1843), 1.

3. Asa Briggs, *Victorian Cities* (Penguin, 1968, first published 1963), 59.

4. Briggs, *Victorian Cities*, 16.

5. Parliamentary Papers VII (1843), 'Select Committee on Smoke Prevention. II. Minutes of Evidence', 62; quoted in Hunt, *Building Jerusalem*, 21.

6. Alexis de Tocqueville, *Journeys to England and Ireland* (Faber, 1958, first published 1835), 94; quoted in Hunt, *Building Jerusalem*, 26.

7. C. Turner Thackrah, *The Effects of the Principal Arts, Trades, and Professions, and of Civic States and Habits of Living, on Health and Longevity* (1959 edition, first published 1831), 5–6; quoted in Hunt, *Building Jerusalem*, 26.

8. John Ruskin, *The Stones of Venice*, in Cook and Wedderburn, eds, *Collected Works*, X (George Allen & Unwin, 1903), 459; quoted in Hunt, *Building Jerusalem*, 122.

9. *Edinburgh Review*, L (1829), 539–40; cited in Hunt, *Building Jerusalem*, 130.

10. *Manchester Guardian*, 20 August 1845; quoted in Hunt, *Building Jerusalem*, 132.

11. Hunt, *Building Jerusalem*, 167.
12. Hylton, *A History of Manchester*, 110–18.
13. Briggs, *Victorian Cities*, 56.
14. Robert Southey, *Letters from England* (Longman, Hurst, Rees and Orme, 1808), II, 97; quoted in Briggs, *Victorian Cities*, 89.
15. Benjamin Disraeli, Coningsby (William Blackwood, 1844); quoted in Briggs, *Victorian Cities*, 93.
16. Hylton, *A History of Manchester*, 143–7, 152–6.
17. Briggs, *Victorian Cities*, 136–7; Hunt, *Building Jerusalem*, 189–91, 224–6; Hylton, *A History of Manchester*, 166–8.
18. Briggs, *Victorian Cities*, 138.
19. Briggs, *Victorian Cities*, 140.
20. Firth, *A History of Bradford*, 77.
21. Firth, *A History of Bradford*, 89–98.
22. Firth, *A History of Bradford*, 90–1.
23. Firth, *A History of Bradford*, 98.
24. Briggs, *Victorian Cities*, 87, 147.
25. C.J. Morgan, 'Demographic Change, 1771–1911', in Fraser, ed., *A History of Modern Leeds*, 65–6.
26. Briggs, *Victorian Cities*, 162.
27. Hey, *A History of Sheffield*, 235.
28. Hey, *A History of Sheffield*, 235–41.
29. Hey, *A History of Sheffield*, 222–3, 254–5.
30. Moffat and Rosie, *Tyneside*, 232, 254.
31. Jackson, *The Northumbrians*, 190–1; Moffat and Rosie, *Tyneside*, 251–4.
32. *The Civil Engineer and Architect's Journal* XI, (November 1848), 353.
33. W. Clark Russell, *The North East Ports and Bristol Channel: Sketches of the Towns, Docks, Ports, and Industries of Newcastle-upon-Tyne, Sunderland, the Hartlepools, Middlesbro', Bristol, Cardiff, Newport and Swansea* (Andrew Reid, 1883); quoted in Jackson, *The Northumbrians*, 100.
34. Peter Aughton, *Liverpool: A People's History* (Carnegie, 1993), 110.
35. John Belchem, *Merseypride: Essays in Liverpool Exceptionalism* (Liverpool University Press, 2000), 11.
36. Belchem, *Merseypride*, 155–76.
37. Aughton, *Liverpool*, 163.
38. Hunt, *Building Jerusalem*, 386–7.
39. Briggs, *Victorian Cities*, 23.

Chapter 20: Friends or Rivals

1. Turner, *The North Country*, 231.
2. Crosby, *A History of Lancashire*, 20–5; Duxbury, *The Brief History of Lancashire*, 18–19.
3. Crosby, *A History of Lancashire*, 33.

4. Crosby, *A History of Lancashire*, 35.
5. R. Schofield, 'The Geographical Distribution of Wealth in England 1334–1649', *Economic History Review* 18 (1965), 483–510, cited in Musgrove, *The North of England*, 15; Crosby, *A History of Lancashire*, 50.
6. Lancs CCC, 'The Early Years' (1864–1883), lancashirecricket.co.uk.
7. 'Beside the Roses the Ashes Paled into Insignificance', ESPN Cricinfo, 2 February 2006, espncricinfo.com.
8. Maconie, *Pies and Prejudice*, 181–2.
9. *Leeds Mercury*, 22 September 1894; quoted in William Marshall, 'The Creation of Yorkshireness: Cultural Identities in Yorkshire c. 1850–1918' (PhD thesis, University of Huddersfield, 2011), 57, 66.
10. John K. Walton, *Fish and Chips and the British Working Class, 1870–1940* (Leicester University Press, 1992), 121.
11. William Moss, *The Liverpool Guide* (Crane and Jones, 1796), 1; quoted in Belchem, *Merseypride*, 37.
12. W.H. Chaloner, 'The Cotton Industry to 1820', in J.H. Smith, ed., *The Great Human Exploit* (Phillimore, 1973), 17–24; cited in Alan Kidd and Terry Wyke, eds, *Manchester: Making the Modern City* (Liverpool University Press, 2016), 72.
13. Thomas Baines, *History of the Commerce and Town of Liverpool, and of the Rise of Manufacturing Industry in the Adjoining Counties* (Longman, Brown, Green and Longmans 1852), 840; quoted in Belchem, *Merseypride*, 38.
14. 'Calm down yourself', *Guardian*, 10 July 1999.
15. John Kerrigan, 'Introduction', in P. Robinson, ed., *Liverpool Accents: Seven Poets and a City* (Liverpool University Press, 1996), 2; quoted in Belchem, *Merseypride*, 41.
16. 'Popular Scouse words and where they originate from', *Liverpool Echo*, 17 July 2019.
17. Aughton, *Liverpool: A People's History*, 214; Belchem, *Merseypride*, 34–5.
18. John Parkinson-Bailey, *Manchester: An Architectural History* (Manchester University Press, 2000), 127; Nikolaus Pevsner, *Lancashire, The Industrial and Commercial South* (Penguin, 1969), 267.
19. Hylton, *A History of Manchester*, 178.
20. Maconie, *Pies and Prejudice*, 99.
21. Alan Bennett, *Writing Home* (Faber & Faber, 1994), 144.
22. Maconie, *Pies and Prejudice*, 95.
23. 'A rivalry with roots in kings and coal', *Guardian*, 23 October 2005.
24. Bill Lancaster, 'The North East, England's Most Distinctive Region?', in Bill Lancaster, Diana Newton and Natasha Vall, eds, *An Agenda for Regional History* (Northumbria University Press, 2007), 33.
25. 'Fight like "scene from Braveheart"', 12 March 2002, news.bbc.co.uk.
26. Priestley, *English Journey*, 287–350; 'Is J.B. Priestley to blame for the grim up north stereotype?', 26 November 2014, bbc.co.uk.

Chapter 21: York, Lost Capital

1. Paul Chrystal, *York Then & Now* (History Press, 2010), 7.
2. W.J. Shiels, 'York in the Seventeenth Century', in Patrick Nuttgens, ed., *The History of York: From Earliest Times to the Year 2000* (Blackthorn, 2001), 177.
3. Richard Hall, *York* (Batsford/English Heritage, 1996), 26–7; Patrick Ottaway, 'Roman York', in Nuttgens, ed., *The History of York*, 1–7, 12–13.
4. Hall, *York*, 31.
5. Ottaway, in Nuttgens, ed., *The History of York*, 28–32.
6. Hall, *York*, 31.
7. Hall, *York*, 34; Richard Hall, 'Anglo-Saxon and Viking-Age York', in Nuttgens, ed., *The History of York*, 43–4.
8. Hall, in Nuttgens, ed., *The History of York*, 50.
9. Musgrove, *The North of England*, 49.
10. Rollason, *Northumbria*, 228; Townend, *Viking Age Yorkshire*, 58–60.
11. Hall, in Nuttgens, ed., *The History of York*, 51.
12. Williams, *Viking Britain*, 294–6; Hall, *York*, 37.
13. Hall, in Nuttgens, ed., *The History of York*, 55–7.
14. Williams, *Viking Britain*, 282.
15. Adams, *Aelfred's Britain*, 440, Williams, *Viking Britain*, 297; Higham, *The Kingdom of Northumbria*, 211–15.
16. Chris Daniell, 'Early Medieval York', in Nuttgens, ed., *The History of York*, 68–70.
17. Daniell, in Nuttgens, ed., *The History of York*, 80–3.
18. Daniell, in Nuttgens, ed., *The History of York*, 78–9.
19. Daniell, in Nuttgens, ed., *The History of York*, 90, 99; Hall, *York*, 41.
20. Barrie Dobson, 'Later Medieval York', in Nuttgens, ed., *The History of York*, 103.
21. Hall, *York*, 45; Dobson, in Nuttgens, ed., *The History of York*, 104–14.
22. Hall, *York*, 45; Claire Cross, 'Tudor York', in Nuttgens, ed., *The History of York*, 146–56.
23. Cross, in Nuttgens, ed., *The History of York*, 170.
24. Musgrove, *The North of England*, 8.
25. Shiels, in Nuttgens, ed., *The History of York*, 192–9; Hall, *York*, 45.
26. Daniel Defoe, *A Tour Through England and Wales*, Vol. II (Dent, 1928), 234.
27. Hall, *York*, 48; Alison Sinclair, 'Eighteenth Century York', in Nuttgens, ed., *The History of York*, 215–43.
28. Edward Royle, 'Nineteenth Century York', in Nuttgens, ed., *The History of York*, 244.
29. Royle, in Nuttgens, ed., *The History of York*, 258–9; Chrystal, *York Then & Now*, 9.
30. Chrystal, *York Then & Now*, 35.

31. Patrick and Bridget Nuttgens, 'Twentieth Century York', in Nuttgens, ed., *The History of York*, 316.

Chapter 22: Northern Women

1. The Grace Darling website, gracedarling.co.uk; H.C.G. Matthew, 'Darling, Grace Horsley (1815–1842)', *Oxford Dictionary of National Biography* (Oxford University Press, 2004).
2. Eva Hope, *Grace Darling: Heroine of the Farne Islands* (Adam & Co., 1875), chapter I.
3. Russell, *Looking North*, 39, 92.
4. Juliet Barker, *The Brontës* (Abacus, 2010, first published Weidenfeld & Nicolson, 1994), xvii.
5. Elizabeth Gaskell, *The Life of Charlotte Brontë* (Smith, Elder & Co., 1857), Vol. I, 11; Russell, *Looking North*, 87–8; Barker, *The Brontës*, xix.
6. Daniel S. Burt, *The Literature*, 100: *A Ranking of the Most Influential Novelists, Playwrights, and Poets of All Time* (Infobase, 2008), 224.
7. Barker, *The Brontës*, 772.
8. 'Anne Brontë's grave error corrected', 30 April 2013, bbc.co.uk.
9. Jenny Uglow, *Elizabeth Gaskell* (Faber & Faber, 1993), 191–2.
10. Uglow, *Elizabeth Gaskell*, 214.
11. Uglow, *Elizabeth Gaskell*, 322–42.
12. Uglow, *Elizabeth Gaskell*, 361.
13. Russell, *Looking North*, 79–106.
14. Miranda Seymour, *In Byron's Wake: The Turbulent Lives of Lord Byron's Wife and Daughter Annabella Millbanke and Ada Lovelace* (Simon & Schuster, 2018), 150, 153, 160, 186.
15. Linda Lear, *Beatrix Potter: The Extraordinary Life of a Victorian Genius* (Allen Lane, 2007, Penguin, 2008), 81–129.
16. Helen Mathers, *Patron Saint of Prostitutes: Josephine Butler and a Victorian Scandal* (History Press, 2014), 109–10.
17. Millicent Fawcett and E.M. Turner, *Josephine Butler: Her Work and Principles, and Their Meaning for the Twentieth Century* (Association for Moral & Social Hygiene, 1927), 1.
18. Josephine Butler, *Recollections of George Butler* (J.W. Arrowsmith, 1892), 183.
19. Mathers, *Patron Saint of Prostitutes*, 81.
20. Mathers, *Patron Saint of Prostitutes*, 129–31.
21. Jacqueline Broad, 'Mary Astell', 28 March 2018, oxfordbibliographies.com.
22. Harold L. Smith, *The British Women's Suffrage Campaign* (Longman, 2010, first published 1998), 10.
23. Emmeline Pankhurst, *My Own Story* (Hearst's, 1914), 38.
24. 'Annie Kenney: Statue to mark "overlooked" suffragette', 21 October 2018, bbc.co.uk.

25. June Purvis, *Emmeline Pankhurst: A Biography* (Routledge, 2002), 194.
26. Martin Pugh, *The Pankhursts* (Vintage, 2008, first published Allen Lane, 2001), 287–8; Purvis, *Emmeline Pankhurst*, 248–9.
27. Paul Bartley, *Emmeline Pankhurst* (Routledge, 2002), 231–7; Purvis, *Emmeline Pankhurst*, 361–3; Smith, *The British Women's Suffrage Campaign*, 34, 60–1.
28. Purvis, *Emmeline Pankhurst*, 318–35.
29. Purvis, *Emmeline Pankhurst*, 316.
30. Purvis, *Emmeline Pankhurst*, 341.
31. Judith Godden, *Lucy Osburn, A Lady Displaced: Florence Nightingale's Envoy to Australia* (Sydney University Press, 2006).
32. Helen Berry, 'Gertrude Bell: Adventurer, Diplomat, Mountaineer and Anti-suffragette', *BBC History Magazine*, September 2013, historyextra.com; Jackson, *The Northumbrians*, 72–3.

Chapter 23: At Leisure

1. Priestley, *English Journey*, 263.
2. 'Cities Outlook 1901', Centre for Cities, July 2012.
3. Edward Royle, *Modern Britain: A Social History 1750–2011* (Bloomsbury, 3rd edn, 2012), 295.
4. Dan Jackson, *The Northumbrians*, 131–66.
5. Wilkes, *Narrow Windows, Narrow Lives*, 143.
6. Seebohm Rowntree, *Poverty: A Study of Town Life* (Macmillan, 1901), 133–4.
7. Juliet Barker, *Wordsworth: A Life* (Penguin, 2001), 490–1.
8. 'Circus keeper killed by Barney the leopard', *Bolton News*, 10 October 2002, theboltonnews.co.uk.
9. Lee Jackson, *Palaces of Pleasure: From Music Halls to the Seaside to Football, How the Victorians Invented Mass Entertainment* (Yale, 2019), 56.
10. G.J. Mellor, *The Northern Music Hall* (Frank Graham, 1970), 23.
11. Mellor, *The Northern Music Hall*, 17; 'City Varieties', Historic England, historicengland.org.uk.
12. Mellor, *The Northern Music Hall*, 27.
13. Richard Anthony Baker, *British Music Hall: An Illustrated History* (Pen & Sword, 2014), 26–8.
14. Baker, *British Music Hall*, 123–5; Mellor, *The Northern Music Hall*, 89.
15. Barry Anthony, *The King's Jester* (I.B. Taurus, 2010), 17.
16. Hickory J. Wood, *Dan Leno* (Methuen, 1905), 83–4; Gyles Brandreth, *The Funniest Man on Earth: The Story of Dan Leno* (Hamish Hamilton, 1977), 4.
17. Baker, *British Music Hall*, 33.
18. Baker, *British Music Hall*, 90–2.
19. Mellor, *The Northern Music Hall*, 88–9.

20. Baker, *British Music Hall*, 171–4.
21. Baker, *British Music Hall*, 114–15, 154.
22. Mellor, *The Northern Music Hall*, 66–7.
23. Baker, *British Music Hall*, 49–50.
24. Lee Jackson, *Palaces of Pleasure*, 87–8.
25. Jackson, *Palaces of Pleasure*, 90.
26. Jackson, *Palaces of Pleasure*, 83–4, 90–1.
27. Jackson, *Palaces of Pleasure*, 122, 124, 146; Robert Nicholls, *The Belle Vue Story* (Neil Richardson, 1992), 5; 'The World on Fire … Pyrodramas at Belle Vue, Manchester, c. 1850–1950', in David Mayer and John M. MacKenzie, eds, *Popular Imperialism and the Military: 1850–1950* (Manchester University Press, 1992), 180.
28. Jackson, *Palaces of Pleasure*, 200–18.
29. Anne Pimlott Baker, 'Bainbridge, Emerson Muschamp (1817–1892)', *Oxford Dictionary of National Biography* (Oxford University Press, 2004); Bill Lancaster, *The Department Store: A Social History* (Leicester University Press, 1995), chapter I; Bill Lancaster, 'Sociability and the City', in Robert Colls and Bill Lancaster, eds, *Newcastle upon Tyne: A Modern History* (Phillimore, 2001), 330.
30. John Styles, 'Clothing the North: The Supply of Non-elite Clothing in the Eighteenth Century North of England', *Textile History* 25, no. 2 (1994).
31. Robert Roberts, *The Classic Slum: Salford Life in the First Quarter of the Century* (Penguin, 1990, first published by Manchester University Press, 1971), 39.
32. Standish Meacham, *A Life Apart: The English Working Class, 1890–1914* (Harvard University Press, 1977), 84.
33. Tony Naylor, 'Of course food isn't grim up north', *Guardian*, 6 January 2015.
34. Mellor, *The Northern Music Hall*, 107.
35. www.settlevictoriahall.org.uk.
36. Baker, *British Music Hall*, 244–5.
37. Sue Smart and Richard Bothway Howard, *It's Turned Out Nice Again! The Authorized Biography of the Two George Formbys, Father and Son* (Melrose, 2011), 32.
38. Jeffrey Richards, *Stars in their Eyes: Lancashire Stars of Stage, Screen and Radio* (Lancashire County Books, 1994), 8–9.
39. Obituary, 'Eric Sykes', 8 July 2012, independent.ie.
40. A.J.P. Taylor, *Essays in English History* (Hamilton, 1976), 312.
41. Walter Greenwood, *Lancashire* (Robert Hale, 1951), quoted in Charles Nevin, *Lancashire, Where Women Die of Love* (Mainstream, 2004), 10.
42. Quoted in Paul Morley, *The North: (And Almost Everything In It)* (Mainstream, 2013), 293.
43. Russell, *Looking North*, 237.
44. 'Sheffield FC: Over 150 years of history', 24 October 2007, fifa.com.

45. 'One letter, two meetings and 12 teams – the birth of league football', 26 February 2013, bbc.co.uk.
46. Russell, *Looking North*, 237–8.
47. Russell, *Looking North*, 238.
48. Russell, *Looking North*, 239.
49. 'Heroes of the Tyne', 24 September 2014, bbc.co.uk; Dan Jackson, *The Northumbrians*, 155–6.
50. Russell, *Looking North*, 240.
51. Russell, *Looking North*, 240.
52. J.M. Kilburn, *History of Yorkshire County Cricket Club* (Yorkshire CCC, 1950), 123; Richard Holt, 'Heroes of the North: Sport and the Shaping of Regional Identity', in J. Hill and J. Williams, eds, *Sport and Identity in the North of England* (Keele University Press, 1996), 147.

Chapter 24: Engineers or Poets?

1. Arthur Conan Doyle, 'On the Geographical Distribution of British Intellect', *Nineteenth Century* 24 (1988), 184–95, arthur-conan-doyle.com.
2. William Wordsworth, *The Prelude* (1805), VIII.
3. Defoe, *A Tour Through England and Wales*, Vol. II, 269–70.
4. Wordsworth, *A Guide through the District of the Lakes* (published as anonymous introduction to a book of engravings 1810; published as separate volume 1822; definitive edition 1835).
5. Simon Bainbridge, *Mountaineering and British Romanticism: The Literary Cultures of Climbing, 1770–1836* (Oxford University Press, 2020), 3.
6. Wordsworth, *The Prelude* (1805), XII.
7. Adam Roberts, 'Did Wordsworth really betray Coleridge? The strange events of 27th December 1806' (Wordsworth Grasmere, 27 December 2015), wordsworth.org.uk.
8. Dan Jackson, *The Northumbrians*, 85.
9. Juliet Barker, *Wordsworth*, 484–5.
10. Barker, *The Brontës*, 303–5; Elizabeth Gaskell, *The Life of Charlotte Brontë* (Smith, Elder, 1857), Vol. 1, 172.
11. 'Lakes and Moors: The Power of Northern Landscapes', *The Matter of the North* (2 September 2016), bbc.co.uk.
12. 'New Year Letter', Faber 1941; Humphrey Carpenter, *W.H. Auden: A Biography* (George Allen & Unwin 1981), 13, 23.
13. Keith Sagar, *The Laughter of Foxes: A Study of Ted Hughes* (Liverpool University Press 2006, first published 2000), 3.
14. Russell, *Looking North*, 99.
15. Russell, *Looking North*, 101.
16. 'Anthony Burgess's fictional Manchesters', The International Anthony Burgess Foundation (29 September 2020), anthonyburgess.org.
17. Russell, *Looking North*, 152.

18. Russell, *Looking North*, 148.
19. Letter to the organiser, Canon Gorton, quoted in *Musical Times*, July 1903.
20. Russell, *Looking North*, 209–12.
21. Dave Russell, *Popular Music in England, 1840–1914: A Social History* (Manchester University Press, 2nd edn, 1997), 194.
22. Russell, *Popular Music in England*, 263–4.
23. *Slaithwaite Guardian and Colne Valley News*, 21 January 1898; quoted in Stephen Etheridge, 'The North of England: An Outline of a Musical Region', bandsupper.wordpress.com.
24. Russell, *Looking North*, 222.
25. Ronald Parkinson, *John Constable: The Man and His Art* (V&A, 1998), 22.
26. Simon Schama, *A History of Britain, 1776–2000: The Fate of Empire* (BBC, 2003), 96; quoted in Dan Jackson, *The Northumbrians*, 75.
27. 'Annie Swynnerton: Painting Light and Hope', Manchester Art Gallery, manchesterartgallery.org.
28. David Duggleby, 'The Staithes Group', davidduggleby.com.
29. 'Barbara Hepworth', The Hepworth Wakefield, hepworthwakefield.org.
30. Whitney Chadwick, *Women Artists and the Surrealist Movement* (Thames and Hudson 1985), 67.
31. 'A guide to L.S. Lowry', christies.com.
32. 'His life', thelowry.com.
33. Matthew Sperling, 'The pull of Hockney's pool paintings', *Apollo* 4, February 2017.
34. Tim Adams, 'David Hockney review – sunshine superman', *Observer*, 12 February 2017.
35. Kate Brown, 'Damien Hirst Is Still the UK's Richest Artist – With a Net Worth of $384 Million, According to the *Sunday Times*'s "Rich List"', 18 May 2020, news.artnet.com.
36. 'The Angel of the North', Gateshead Council, gateshead.gov.uk.

Chapter 25: Divided Tongues

1. A.C. Crawley, *The Wakefield Pageants in the Townley Cycle* (Manchester University Press, 1968).
2. Russell, *Looking North*, 112.
3. David Crystal, *The Stories of English* (Allen Lane, 2004, Penguin, 2005), 5.
4. Crystal, *The Stories of English*, 34.
5. Katie Wales, *Northern English: A Social and Cultural History* (Cambridge University Press, 2006), 41.
6. Crystal, *The Stories of English*, 73.
7. Wales, *Northern English*, 55.
8. Melvyn Bragg, *The Adventure of English: The Biography of a Language* (Hodder & Stoughton, 2003), 28.
9. Crystal, *The Stories of English*, 194–5.

10. Russell, *Looking North*, 112; Wales, *Northern English*, 18, 48.
11. Wales, *Northern English*, 33, 49, 61; Crystal, *The Stories of English*, 216–17; Jewell, *The North–South Divide*, 198.
12. Jewell, *The North–South Divide*, 147; Wales, *Northern English*, 76.
13. Crystal, *The Stories of English*, 222–42; Bragg, *The Adventure of English*, 99; Wales, *Northern English*, 68.
14. Crystal, *The Stories of English*, 243–8.
15. Jewell, *The North–South Divide*, 200.
16. Crystal, *The Stories of English*, 262.
17. Bragg, *The Adventure of English*, 203–10; Crystal, *The Stories of English*, 365–87.
18. Bragg, *The Adventure of English*, 210–11; Crystal, *The Stories of English*, 381–7.
19. Crystal, *The Stories of English*, 468–74; Wales, *Northern English*, 203.
20. Wales, *Northern English*, 104–14; Crystal, *The Stories of English*, 484–5.
21. Russell, *Looking North*, 117–31; Wales, *Northern English*, 94–9.
22. Russell, *Looking North*, 119.
23. Wales, *Northern English*, 127–41.
24. Wales, *Northern English*, 144–5.
25. Russell, *Looking North*, 134–5; Crystal, *The Stories of English*, 473.

TWENTIETH CENTURY AND BEYOND

Chapter 26: Abrupt Reversal

1. 'Rutherford's Legacy – the Birth of Nuclear Physics in Manchester', University of Manchester, 2 November 2017, manchester.ac.uk; 'Rutherford: splitting the atom', 30 September 2009, bbc.co.uk.
2. Lawrence James, *The Decline and Fall of the British Empire* (Little, Brown, 1994), 202.
3. Combined totals for north, north-west, Yorks–Humberside standard statistical regions. Frank Geary and Tom Stark, 'Regional GDP in the UK, 1861–1911: New Estimates', *Economic History Review*, 68, no. 1 (2015), table 3; cited in Hazeldine, *The Northern Question*, 71–2.
4. Timmins, *Four Centuries of Lancashire Cotton*, 58.
5. Pre-war interview reported in Benjamin Bowker, *Lancashire Under the Hammer* (Hogarth Press, 1928); quoted in Kidd and Wyke, *Manchester: Making the Modern City*, 99.
6. *St James's Gazette*, 18 December 1893, quoted in Hazeldine, *The Northern Question*, 73.
7. Kidd and Wyke, *Manchester*, 97; C.B. Phillips and J.H. Smith, *Lancashire and Cheshire from AD 1540* (Longman, 1994), 245; Michael Nevell, *The Archaeology of Trafford* (Trafford Metropolitan Borough with University of Manchester Archaeological Unit, 1997), 130–3.

8. Quoted in Hylton, *A History of Manchester*, 190.
9. B.R. Mitchell, *European Historical Statistics, 1750–1970* (Palgrave Macmillan, 1975), 399–401.
10. Hey, *A History of Sheffield*, 196–7.
11. Richard Hough, *The Big Battleship* (Periscope, 2003), 14; quoted in Roy Hattersley, *The Edwardians* (Abacus, 2006, first published Little, Brown, 2004), 448.
12. Moffat and Rosie, *Tyneside*, 288–90.
13. Julian Corbett, *Maritime Operations in the Russo-Japanese War 1904–1905* (Naval Institute Press, 2015), Vol. 2, 31–5.
14. Moffat and Rosie, *Tyneside*, 285–7.
15. Hattersley, *The Edwardians*, 449–53; Moffat and Rosie, *Tyneside*, 288–90.
16. Duxbury, *A Brief History of Lancashire*, 170–3.
17. Hattersley, *The Edwardians*, 72.
18. Quoted in Firth, *A History of Bradford*, 113.
19. 'The Lost World of Mitchell and Kenyon', British Film Institute, bfi.org.uk.
20. Hazeldine, *The Northern Question*, 87.
21. Musgrove, *The North of England*, 306–9.
22. John Morley, 'The Chamber of Mediocrity', *Fortnightly Review* (December 1868), 690.
23. Musgrove, *The North of England*, 310.
24. Duxbury, *A Brief History of Lancashire*, 172–3.
25. Neil Storey, *Newcastle Battalions in Action on the Somme* (Tyne Bridge, 2016), 37; quoted in Jackson, *The Northumbrians*, 52.
26. Moffat and Rosie, *Tyneside*, 302–4.
27. Firth, *A History of Bradford*, 114.
28. Hylton, *A History of Manchester*, 192–3.
29. 'Story of 20-year-old pilot who shot down a Zeppelin as it bombed Hartlepool, 100 years ago', *Northern Echo*, 31 October 2016, thenorthernecho.co.uk.
30. Aughton, *Liverpool: A People's History*, 181.
31. Moffat and Rosie, *Tyneside*, 308.
32. Moffat and Rosie, *Tyneside*, 305–10.
33. D.A. Farnie, *The English Cotton Industry and the World Market, 1815–1896* (Clarendon, 1979), 81; quoted in Hazeldine, *The Northern Question*, 89.
34. Aughton, *Liverpool: A People's History*, 181–2.

Chapter 27: Sing As We Go

1. *Sing As We Go!* (1934), British Film Institute, screenonline.org.uk.
2. E.H. Carter and R.A.F. Mears, *A History of Britain*, book VII: *Liberal England, World War and Slump, 1901–38* (Stacy International, 2011, ed. David Evans; originally published 1937), 164–5.
3. Speech in Wolverhampton, 24 November 1918.

REFERENCES

4. Kenneth O. Morgan, *The Oxford History of Britain* (Oxford University Press, updated edition 2010), 595–6.
5. 'Coronavirus: Boris Johnson hospital stay and parallels to Lloyd George', 8 April 2020, bbc.co.uk.
6. Charles Loch Mowat, *Britain Between the Wars 1918–1940* (Methuen, 1955), 24–5.
7. Bowker, *Lancashire under the Hammer*, 32–42; quoted in Hazeldine, *The Northern Question*, 91.
8. Carter and Mears, *A History of Britain*, book VII, 183.
9. Mowat, *Britain Between the Wars*, 282–3.
10. Mowat, *Britain Between the Wars*, 275, 280.
11. 'Labour Disputes, Annual Estimates, UK', Office for National Statistics, ons.gov.uk.
12. Combined total for north, north-west and Yorks–Humberside standard statistical regions. Frank Geary and Tom Stark, 'What Happened to Regional Inequality in Britain in the Twentieth Century?', *Economic History Review*, 69, no. I (2016), table 1; cited in Hazeldine, *The Northern Question*, 92.
13. Mowat, *Britain Between the Wars*, 176.
14. Carter and Mears, *A History of Britain*, book VII, 187.
15. Jack Lawson, *The Man in the Cap: The Life of Herbert Smith* (Methuen, 1941), 203, 253; quoted in Hazeldine, *The Northern Question*, 94–5.
16. Mowat, *Britain Between the Wars*, 275.
17. Mowat, *Britain Between the Wars*, 272.
18. Priestley, *English Journey*, 399, 401–3.
19. House of Commons Debate, 14 November 1934, Vol. 293; C2002; Fredric Miller, 'The Unemployment Policy of the National Government', *Historical Journal*, 19, no. 2 (1976), 469; cited in Hazeldine, *The Northern Question*, 107.
20. Third Report of the Commissioner for the Special Areas (England and Wales), 1936, Cmd 5303, Part I and Appendix IV; cited in Hazeldine, *The Northern Question*, 111–12.
21. Hazeldine, *The Northern Question*, 112; Moffat and Rosie, *Tyneside*, 334–5.
22. Robert Self, *Neville Chamberlain: A Biography* (Ashgate, 2006), 231; cited in Hazeldine, *The Northern Question*, 112.
23. Salford University, Greenwood papers, WPG 3/1, review in the *Evening Chronicle*, 21 June 1933; quoted in Richard Overy, *The Morbid Age* (Penguin, 2010), 74.
24. Ibid, WPG 3/5/1, review in *The People*, quoted in Overy, *The Morbid Age*, 73; Chris Hopkins, *Walter Greenwood's Love on the Dole: Novel, Play, Film* (Liverpool University Press, 2018), 214–15.
25. George Orwell, *The Road to Wigan Pier* (Penguin, 1989, first published 1937), 96.

26. Seebohm Rowntree, *Poverty and Progress: A Second Social Survey of York* (Longmans, Green, 1941), 453, 457; cited in Edward Royle, *Modern Britain: A Social History 1750–2011* (Bloomsbury, 3rd edn, 2012), 201–2.

27. Dave Russell, 'Culture, Media and Sport', in Kidd and Wyke, eds, *Manchester*, 292.

28. Russell, in Kidd and Wyke, eds, *Manchester*, 288–9.

29. Phillips and Smith, *Lancashire and Cheshire from AD 1540*, 352–4.

30. Carter and Mears, *A History of Britain*, book VII, 167.

31. Russell, in Kidd and Wyke, eds, *Manchester*, 282–5.

32. Mowat, *Britain Between the Wars*, 458–9.

33. Hylton, *A History of Manchester*, 195–6; Kidd and Wyke, eds, *Manchester*, 336.

34. Aughton, *Liverpool: A People's History*, 183; Alexander Tulloch, *The Story of Liverpool* (History Press, 2008), 113–14.

35. Kidd and Wyke, eds, *Manchester*, 331.

36. Carter and Mears, *A History of Britain*, book VII, 164.

37. Firth, *A History of Bradford*, 126–7.

38. David Bret, *Gracie Fields: The Authorized Biography* (Robson, 1995), 76.

39. Robert Murphy, *Realism and Tinsel: Cinema and Society in Britain, 1939–1948* (Routledge, 1989), 193.

40. Combined total for north-eastern, north-western and northern Ministry of Labour divisions. British Labour Statistics Historical Abstract 1886–1968 (1971) table 162; cited in Hazeldine, *The Northern Question*, 113.

Chapter 28: Hopes Disappointed

1. Phil Wickham, *The Likely Lads* (Basingstoke, 2008), 1–3, 39–43, 49; quoted in Dominic Sandbrook, *State of Emergency. The Way We Were: Britain 1970–1974* (Allen Lane, 2010, Penguin, 2011), 50–1, and *Seasons in the Sun: The Battle for Britain, 1974–1979* (Allen Lane, 2012, Penguin, 2013), 25–6.

2. Hylton, *A History of Manchester*, 204.

3. Angus Calder, *The People's War: Britain 1939–45* (Jonathan Cape, 1969), 325.

4. James Landale Hodson, *The Sea and the Land* (Victor Gollancz, 1945), 254; quoted in Calder, *The People's War*, 336.

5. Richard Padley and Margaret Cole, eds, *Evacuation Survey* (Routledge, 1940), 236–7; cited in Calder, *The People's War*, 41.

6. Tulloch, *The Story of Liverpool*, 121.

7. Jackson, *The Northumbrians*, 55–8.

8. David Kynaston, *Austerity Britain 1945–51* (Bloomsbury, 2007), 536–7.

9. Kynaston, *Austerity Britain*, 270.

10. 'Programming Redevelopment after World War II', parliament.uk.

11. Hylton, *A History of Manchester*, 220.

12. Paul Addison, *Now The War is Over: A Social History of Britain 1945–51* (Pimlico, 1995), 150.

13. Paul Addison, *Now The War is Over*, 120.

14. David Kynaston, *Family Britain 1951–57* (Bloomsbury, 2009), 186.

15. Kynaston, *Austerity Britain*, 267.

16. Dominic Sandbrook, *Never Had It So Good: A History of Britain from Suez to the Beatles* (Little, Brown, 2005, Abacus, 2006), 409–10.

17. David Kynaston, *Modernity Britain 1957–62* (Bloomsbury, 2015), 74.

18. Sandbrook, *Never Had It So Good*, 195.

19. Humphrey Carpenter, *The Angry Young Men: A Literary Comedy of the 1950s* (Allen Lane, 2002), 160; quoted in Sandbrook, *Never Had It So Good*, 205.

20. *Daily Express*, 23 May 1957; quoted in Sandbrook, *Never Had It So Good*, 205.

21. Geoffrey Moorhouse, *Britain in the Sixties: The Other England* (Penguin, 1964), 14–15; quoted in Hazeldine, *The Northern Question*, 125.

22. John Singleton, *Lancashire on the Scrapheap* (Oxford, 1991), 130; Kynaston, *Family Britain*, 120; Hazeldine, *The Northern Question*, 126.

23. Peter Scott, 'The Worst of Both Worlds: British Regional Policy, 1951–64', *Business History* 38, no. 4 (1966), 44; cited in Hazeldine, *The Northern Question*, 127–8.

24. Sandbrook, *Never Had It So Good*, 399–401.

25. Tombs, *The English and Their History*, 791–5.

26. Hazeldine, *The Northern Question*, 134.

27. Combined total for north, north-west and Yorks–Humberside standard statistical regions. Frank Geary and Tom Stark, 'What Happened to Regional Inequality in Britain in the 20th Century?', *Economic History Review*, 68, no. 1 (2016), table 1; cited in Hazeldine, *The Northern Question*, 136.

28. Dominic Sandbrook, *White Heat: A History of Britain in the Swinging Sixties* (Little Brown, 2006, Abacus, 2007), 620.

29. 'How Preston was nearly renamed Redrose', *Lancashire Post*, 26 March 2020, lep.co.uk.

30. Kynaston, *Modernity Britain*, 447–8.

31. Sandbrook, *Never Had It So Good*, 405.

32. Aughton, *Liverpool: A People's History*, 200.

33. Tombs, *The English and Their History*, 801.

34. Edward Heath, *Travels: People and Places in My Life* (Sidgwick & Jackson, 1977), 39; Jack Jones, *Union Man* (HarperCollins, 1986), 70, 215; quoted in Sandbrook, *State of Emergency*, 105.

35. Chris Wrigley, 'Trade Unions, Strikes and the Government', in Richard Coopey and Nicholas Woodward, eds, *Britain in the 1970s: The Troubled Economy* (UCL Press, 1996); cited in Sandbrook, *State of Emergency*, 98.

36. Hazeldine, *The Northern Question*, 140.
37. Bernard Donoughue, 'Harold Wilson and the Renegotiation of the EEC Terms of Membership, 1974–5: A Witness Account', in Brian Brivati and Harriet Jones, eds, *From Reconstruction to Integration: Britain and Europe since 1945* (Leicester University Press, 1993), 204; quoted in Sandbrook, *Seasons in the Sun*, 320.
38. David Butler and Uwe Kitzinger, *The 1975 Referendum* (Macmillan, 1976), 266–9.
39. Andy Beckett, *When the Lights Went Out: Britain in the Seventies* (Faber & Faber, 2009), 485.
40. Sandbrook, *Seasons in the Sun*, 759.
41. Tombs, *The English and Their History*, 812.
42. Ken Coutts, Andrew Glynn, Bob Rowthorn, 'Structural Change under New Labour', *Cambridge Journal of Economics*, 31 (2007), 845–61; cited in Tombs, *The English and Their History*, 819.
43. Dominic Sandbrook, *Who Dares Wins: Britain, 1979–1982* (Allen Lane, 2019, Penguin, 2020), 28–30.
44. Sandbrook, *Who Dares Wins*, 584–5.
45. Kidd and Wyke, eds, *Manchester*, 381.
46. David Smith, *North and South: Britain's Economic, Social and Political Divide* (Penguin, 2nd edn, 1994), 167, 336; cited in Hazeldine, *The Northern Question*, 176.

Chapter 29: The Twenty-first Century

1. 'Demise of Hartlepool's economy has seen anti-EU feeling grow', *Financial Times*, 23 June 2016.
2. 'Boris Johnson jokes "we made Redcar Bluecar" as Tories win huge majority', Teesside Live, 13 December 2019, gazetteliveco.uk.
3. 'Labour's great divide', *Guardian*, 6 January 1999.
4. Tony Blair, *A Journey* (Random House, 2010), 85.
5. 'Dominic Cummings honed strategy in 2004 vote, video reveals', *Guardian*, 12 November 2019; 'How to win a referendum', 10 May 2016, bbc.co.uk.
6. 'Notion of north–south divide simplistic, says Blair', *Guardian*, 6 December 1999.
7. *Victoria Wood with All the Trimmings*, BBC One, 25 December 2000.
8. Stephen Burgess, 'Measuring Financial Sector Output and Its Contribution to UK GDP', *Bank of England Quarterly Bulletin*, 2011, Q3, 234; 'Regional GVA NUTS1', ONS December 2014, table I.3; cited in Hazeldine, *The Northern Question*, 179.
9. Coutts et al., 'Structural Change under New Labour', University of Oxford, Department of Economics, Economics Series Working Papers 312 (February 2007), 845–61; cited in Tombs, *The English and Their History*, 851.

10. 'Employment rate (16 and over)', ONS, accessed 21 April 2021; 'Regional gross value added (income approach)', table 3, ONS, 12 December 2018.

11. David Cameron speech, 'Transforming the British economy: Coalition strategy for economic growth', 28 May 2010, gov.uk.

12. Carl Emmerson and Gemma Tetlow, 'UK Public Finances: From Crisis to Recovery', *Fiscal Studies*, 36, no. 4 (2015), 574; David Innes and Gemma Tetlow, 'Central Cuts, Local Decision-making: Changes in Local Government Spending and Revenues in England, 2009–10 to 2014–15', IFS, March 2015, 9; excludes transport spending; cited in Hazeldine, *The Northern Question*, 185.

13. 'Cameron adviser quits over "never had it so good" claim', 19 November 2010, bbc.co.uk.

14. Regional GVA (income approach), ONS, table 1, deflated using the implied deflators in ONS data set, 'Regional gross value added (production approach) constrained data tables', table 3; cited in Hazeldine, *The Northern Question*, 187.

15. 'Chancellor: "We need a Northern Powerhouse"', 23 June 2014, gov.uk.

16. 'How the United Kingdom voted on Thursday … and why', 24 June 2016, lordashcroftpolls.com.

17. 'Employment rate (16 and over)', ONS, accessed 21 April 2021; 'Regional gross value added (income approach)', table 3, ONS, 12 December 2018.

18. 'Boris Johnson promises to repay trust of voters who switched to Tories', *Financial Times*, 14 December 2019.

19. 'UK chancellor accused of playing politics over "levelling-up"', *Financial Times*, 3 March 2021.

20. '"New dawn" as Conservatives turn Redcar into Bluecar', *Financial Times*, 13 December 2019.

Postscript

1. *Hansard*, 14 March 1989, publications.parliament.uk.

2. *Sunday Times*, 11 January 1987, *Yorkshire Evening Post*, 26 January 1987, *Yorkshire Post*, 28 January 1987; quoted in Jewell, *The North–South Divide*, 2.

3. *Hansard*, 20 November 1980; quoted in Hazeldine, *The Northern Question*, 166.

4. 'Across the North–South Divide', *Business*, September 1987; quoted in Hazeldine, *The Northern Question*, 166.

5. William of Malmesbury, *Chronicle of the Kings of England*, trans. J.A. Giles (Henry G. Bohn, 1847), book I, chapter III; quoted in Jewell, *The North–South Divide*, 37.

6. Vergil, *Anglica Historia*, 11; quoted in Jewell, *The North–South Divide*, 58.

7. Hey, *Yorkshire from AD 1000*, 5; Michael Bradford, *The Fight for Yorkshire* (Hutton, 1988), 24; Arnold Kellett, *Basic Broad Yorkshire* (Smith Settle, 1991), 109; cited in Russell, *Looking North*, 34.
8. Orwell, *The Road to Wigan Pier*, 104.

SELECT BIBLIOGRAPHY

Adams, Max, *The Prometheans: John Martin and the Generation that Stole the Future* (Quercus, 2010).

Adams, Max, *The King in the North: The Life and Times of Oswald of Northumbria* (Head of Zeus, 2013).

Adams, Max, *Aelfred's Britain: War and Peace in the Viking Age* (Head of Zeus, 2017).

Addison, Paul, *Now The War is Over: A Social History of Britain 1945–51* (Pimlico, 1995).

Adi, Hakim, *The History of the African and Caribbean Communities in Britain* (Hodder Wayland, 1995).

Allen, Robert C., *The British Industrial Revolution in Global Perspective* (Cambridge, 2009).

Almond, Philip C., *The Lancashire Witches: A Chronicle of Sorcery and Death on Pendle Hill* (I.B. Tauris, 2012).

Aspin, Chris, *The Cotton Industry* (Shire Album, 2003).

Atkinson, Norman, *Sir Joseph Whitworth: 'The World's Best Mechanician'* (Sutton, 1996).

Aughton, Peter, *Liverpool: A People's History* (Carnegie, 1993).

Baines, Edward, *History of the Cotton Manufacture in Great Britain* (H. Fisher, R. Fisher and P. Jackson, 1835).

Baker, Alan R.H. and Billinge, Mark, ed., *Geographies of England: The North–South Divide, Material or Imagined* (Cambridge, 2010).

Baker, Richard Anthony, *British Music Hall: An Illustrated History* (Pen & Sword, 2014).

Barker, Juliet, *The Brontës* (Abacus, 2010, first published Weidenfeld & Nicolson, 1994).

Barker, Juliet, *Wordsworth: A Life* (Penguin, 2001).

Beckert, Sven, *Empire of Cotton: A New History of Global Capitalism* (Allen Lane, 2014, Penguin, 2015).

Beckett, Andy, *When the Lights Went Out: Britain in the Seventies* (Faber & Faber, 2009).

Bede, *Ecclesiastical History of the English People*, trans. A.M. Sellar (George Bell, 1907); also ed. Judith McClure and Roger Collins (Oxford, 1994); and trans. Leo Shirley-Price (Penguin, 1955).

Belchem, John, *Merseypride: Essays in Liverpool Exceptionalism* (Liverpool University Press, 2000).

Belchem, John, *Irish, Catholic and Scouse* (Liverpool University Press, 2007).

Bindoff, S.T., *Tudor England* (Penguin, 1991).

Binns, Jack, *Yorkshire in the Civil Wars: Origins, Impact and Outcome* (Blackthorn, 2004).

Birley, Anthony, *The African Emperor: Septimius Severus* (Batsford, 1988).

Blair, Tony, *A Journey* (Random House, 2010).

Bragg, Melvyn, *The Adventure of English: The Biography of a Language* (Hodder & Stoughton, 2003).

Briggs, Asa, *Victorian Cities* (Penguin, 1968, first published 1963).

Bret, David, *Gracie Fields: The Authorized Biography* (Robson, 1995).

Briggs, Asa, *The Age of Improvement* (Longman, 2000).

Brink, Stefan and Price, Neil, eds, *The Viking World* (Routledge, 2008).

Bull, Stephen, 'A General Plague of Madness': The Civil Wars in Lancashire, 1640–1660 (Carnegie, 2009).

Busteed, Mervyn, The Irish in Manchester c. 1750–1921: Resistance, Adaptation and Identity (Manchester University Press, 2016).

Butler, Alan, Sheep (O Books, 2006).

Butler, David and Kitzinger, Uwe, The 1975 Referendum (Macmillan, 1976).

Calder, Angus, The People's War: Britain 1939–45 (Jonathan Cape, 1969).

Carroll, Jayne, Harrison, Stephen and Williams, Gareth, The Vikings in Britain and Ireland (British Museum, 2014).

Carpenter, David, Struggle for Mastery: The Penguin History of Britain 1066–1284 (Penguin, 2004).

Carpenter, Humphrey, W.H. Auden: A Biography (George Allen & Unwin, 1981).

Carter, E.H. and Mears, R.A.F., A History of Britain, Book VII: Liberal England, World War and Slump 1901–38 (Stacy International, 2011, ed. David Evans; originally published 1937).

Cash, Bill, John Bright: Statesman, Orator, Agitator (Bloomsbury, 2011).

Castor, Helen, Elizabeth I: A Study in Insecurity (Allen Lane, 2018, Penguin, 2019).

Chibnall, Marjorie, trans., The Ecclesiastical History of Orderic Vitalis (Clarendon, 1969–83).

Chrimes, S.B. et al., ed., Fifteenth Century England 1399–1509 (Sutton, 1995).

Chrystal, Paul, York Then & Now (History Press, 2010).

Church, Stephen, King John: England, Magna Carta and the Making of a Tyrant (Macmillan, 2015, Pan, 2016).

Cole, Teresa, The Norman Conquest: William the Conqueror's Subjugation of England (Amberley, 2016).

Colls, Robert, ed., Northumbria History and Identity 547–2000 (History Press, 2007).

Colls, Robert and Lancaster, Bill, eds, *Newcastle upon Tyne: A Modern History* (Phillimore, 2001).

Crosby, Alan, *A History of Lancashire* (Phillimore, 1998).

Crystal, David, *The Stories of English* (Allen Lane, 2004, Penguin, 2005).

Cunliffe, Barry, *Iron Age Communities in Britain* (4th edn, Routledge, 2005).

Dalton, Paul et al., *Conquest, Anarchy and Lordship: Yorkshire, 1066–1154* (Cambridge University Press, 2002).

Daniell, Christopher, *Atlas of Early Modern Britain* (Routledge, 2013).

David, Graham, *The Irish in Britain, 1815–1914* (Gill & Macmillan, 1991).

Defoe, Daniel, *A Tour Through England and Wales*, Vols I and II (Dent, 1928).

De la Bédoyère, Guy, *Roman Britain: A New History* (Thames & Hudson, 2013).

De Tocqueville, Alexis, *Journeys to England and Ireland*, trans. George Lawrence and K.P. Mayer, ed. K.P. Mayer (Transaction, 2003).

Devine, T.M., *The Scottish Nation 1700–2007* (Allen Lane, 1999, Penguin, 2000).

Dougan, David, *The Great Gun-Maker: The Life of Lord Armstrong* (Sandhill, 1971).

Downham, Clare, *Viking Kings of Britain and Ireland: The Dynasty of Ívarr to AD 1014* (Dunedin, 2007).

Duxbury, Stephen, *The Brief History of Lancashire* (History Press, 2011).

Elton, G.R., *England Under the Tudors* (Methuen, 1955).

Elton, G.R., *Reform and Reformation: England 1509–1558* (Arnold, 1977).

Endelman, Todd M., *The Jews of Britain 1656 to 2000* (University of California, 2002).

Engels, Friedrich, *The Condition of the Working Class in England*, ed. David McLellan (Oxford, 1993, first published 1845).

Faucher, Léon, *Manchester in 1844: Its Present Condition and Future Prospects* (Simpkin, Marshall and Abel Heywood, 1844).

Firth, Gary, *A History of Bradford* (Phillimore, 1997).

Fisher, Michael H., Lahiri, Shompa and Thandi, Shinder, *A South-Asian History of Britain* (Greenwood, 2007).

Fitton, R.S., *The Arkwrights: Spinners of Fortune* (2012 edition, Derwent Valley Mills Educational Trust, first published 1989, Manchester University Press).

Fleming, Robin, *Britain after Rome: The Fall and Rise 400 to 1070* (Penguin, 2010).

Fletcher, Anthony and MacCulloch, Diarmaid, *Tudor Rebellions* (Routledge, 2016).

Foster, Derek, ed., *A History of Modern Leeds* (Manchester University Press, 1980).

Frangopulo, N.J., ed., *Rich Inheritance: A Guide to the History of Manchester* (Manchester Education Committee, 1962).

Freeman, E.A. *The History of the Norman Conquest of England* (Clarendon Press, 1867–79).

Fryer, Peter, *Staying Power: the History of Black People in Britain* (originally published 1984, Pluto, 2018).

Gameson, Richard, *From Holy Island to Durham: The Contexts and Meanings of the Lindisfarne Gospels* (Third Millennium, 2013).

Gaskell, Elizabeth, *The Life of Charlotte Brontë* (Smith, Elder, 1857).

Gething, Paul and Albert, Edoardo, *Northumbria: The Lost Kingdom* (History Press, 2012).

Green, Jeffrey, *Black Edwardians: Black People in Britain 1901–14* (Taylor & Francis, 1998).

Griffin, Emma, *A Short History of the British Industrial Revolution* (Palgrave Macmillan, 2010).

Griffin, Emma, *Liberty's Dawn: A People's History of the Industrial Revolution* (Yale, 2013).

Guy, John, *Tudor England* (Oxford, 1988).

Hadley, D.M. *The Vikings in England: Settlement, Society and Culture* (Manchester University Press, 2006).

Haigh, Christopher, *Reformation and Resistance in Tudor Lancashire* (Cambridge, 1975).

Hall, Richard, *York* (Batsford/English Heritage, 1996).

Hattersley, Roy, *The Edwardians* (Abacus, 2006, first published Little, Brown, 2004).

Hazeldine, Tom, *The Northern Question: A History of a Divided Country* (Verso, 2020).

Heald, Henrietta, *William Armstrong: Magician of the North* (McNidder & Grace, 2012).

Hey, David, *Yorkshire from AD 1000* (Longman, 1986).

Hey, David, *A History of Sheffield* (Carnegie, 1998).

Hicks, Michael, *Richard III: The Self-Made King* (Yale, 2019).

Hicks, Michael, *Essential Histories: The Wars of the Roses* (Osprey, 2003).

Higham, Nicholas, *The Kingdom of Northumbria*, AD 350–1100 (Sutton Press, 1993).

Higham, Nicholas and Ryan, Martin, *The Anglo-Saxon World* (Yale, 2013).

Hill, J. and Williams, J., eds, *Sport and Identity in the North of England* (Keele University Press, 1996).

Hochschild, Adam, *Bury the Chains: The British Struggle to Abolish Slavery* (Macmillan, 2005, Pan, 2006).

Holman, Katherine, *The Northern Conquest: Vikings in Britain and Ireland* (Signal, 2007).

Holt, J.C., *The Northerners: A Study in the Reign of King John* (Oxford, 1961).

Honigman, E.A.J., *Shakespeare: The 'Lost Years'* (Manchester University Press, 1999).

Hope, Eva, *Grace Darling: Heroine of the Farne Islands* (Adam & Co, 1875).

Horne, Donald, *God is an Englishman* (Angus & Robertson, 1969).

Howarth, Nicki, *Cartimandua: Queen of the Brigantes* (History Press, 2008).

Hoyle, R.W., *The Pilgrimage of Grace and the Politics of the 1530s* (Oxford, 2001).

Hunt, Tristram, *Building Jerusalem: The Rise and Fall of the Victorian City* (Weidenfeld & Nicolson, 2004, Phoenix, 2005).

Hunt, Tristram, *The Frock-Coated Communist: The Revolutionary Life of Friedrich Engels* (Allen Lane, 2009, Penguin, 2010).

Huscroft, Richard, *Ruling England 1042–1217* (Pearson Longman, 2005).

Huscroft, Richard, *The Norman Conquest: A New Introduction* (Pearson Longman, 2009).

Hylton, Stuart, *A History of Manchester* (Phillimore, 2003).

Jack, Ian, *The Country Formerly Known as Great Britain: Writings 1989–2009* (Cape, 2009).

Jackson, Dan, *The Northumbrians: North East England and Its People* (Hurst, 2019).

Jackson, Lee, *Palaces of Pleasure: From Music Halls to the Seaside to Football, How the Victorians Invented Mass Entertainment* (Yale, 2019).

Jewell, Helen, *The North–South Divide: The Origins of Northern Consciousness in England* (Manchester University Press, 1994).

Jones, Dan, *The Hollow Crown: The Wars of the Roses and the Rise of the Tudors* (Faber & Faber, 2014).

Kesselring, K.J., *The Northern Rebellion of 1569: Faith, Politics and Protest in Elizabethan England* (Palgrave Macmillan, 2007).

Kidd, Alan and Wyke, Terry, eds, *Manchester: Making the Modern City* (Liverpool University Press, 2016).

Kirby, Dean, *Angel Meadow: Victorian Britain's Most Savage Slum* (Pen & Sword History, 2016).

Kynaston, David, *Austerity Britain 1945–51* (Bloomsbury, 2007).

Kynaston, David, *Family Britain 1951–57* (Bloomsbury, 2009).

Kynaston, David, *Modernity Britain 1957–62* (Bloomsbury, 2015).

Lambert, Sharon, *Irish Women in Lancashire 1922–1960: Their Story* (University of Lancaster, 2001).

Laybourn, Keith, *A History of British Trade Unionism* (Sutton, 1992).

Lear, Linda, *Beatrix Potter: The Extraordinary Life of a Victorian Genius* (Allen Lane, 2007, Penguin, 2008).

Loch Mowat, Charles, *Britain Between the Wars 1918–1940* (Methuen, 1955).

Lumby, Jonathan, *The Lancashire Witch-Craze: Jennet Preston and the Lancashire Witches 1612* (Carnegie, 1995).

Lynch, Michael, *Scotland: A New History* (Pimlico, 1992).

Macaulay, Thomas Babington, *The History of England from the Accession of James II* (Macmillan, 1913).

MacDonald Fraser, George, *The Steel Bonnets: The Story of the Anglo-Scottish Border Reivers* (HarperCollins, 1995, first published 1971).

Maconie, Stuart, *Pies and Prejudice: In Search of the North* (Ebury, 2007).

MacRaild, Donald, *The Irish Diaspora in Britain, 1750–1939* (Palgrave Macmillan, 2011).

Marke, Ernest, *In Troubled Waters: Memoirs of My Seventy Years in England* (Karia, 1975).

Mathers, Helen, *Patron Saint of Prostitutes: Josephine Butler and a Victorian Scandal* (History Press, 2014).

Mattingly, David, *An Imperial Possession: Britain in the Roman Empire* (Penguin, 2007).

Mellor, G.J., *The Northern Music Hall* (Frank Graham, 1970).

Moffat, Alistair, *The Borderers: A History of the Borders from Earliest Times* (Deerpark, 2002).

Moffat, Alistair and Rosie, George, *Tyneside: A History of Newcastle and Gateshead from Earliest Times* (Mainstream, 2006).

Mokyr, Joel, *The Enlightened Economy: Britain and the Industrial Revolution 1700–1850* (Penguin, 2009).

Mokyr, Joel, *A Culture of Growth: The Origins of the Modern Economy* (Princeton, 2016).

Morgan, Kenneth, *Slavery in the British Empire: From Africa to America* (Oxford University Press, 2007).

Morgan, Kenneth O., *The Oxford History of Britain* (Oxford University Press, updated edition 2010).

Morley, Paul, *The North: (And Almost Everything In It)* (Mainstream, 2013).

Morrill, J.S., ed., *The Impact of the English Civil War* (Collins & Brown, 1991).

Morris, Marc, *A Great and Terrible King: Edward I and the Forging of Britain* (Hutchinson, 2008, Windmill, 2009).

Morris, Marc, *The Norman Conquest* (Hutchinson, 2012, Windmill, 2013).

Morris, Marc, *King John: Treachery, Tyranny and the Road to Magna Carta* (Hutchinson, 2015, Windmill, 2016).

Mortimer, Ian, *The Imperfect King: The Life of Edward III* (Jonathan Cape, 2006, Vintage, 2008).

Muir, Richard, *The Yorkshire Countryside: A Landscape History* (Keele University Press, 1997).

Musgrove, Eric, *The North of England: A History from Roman Times to the Present* (Basil Blackwell, 1990).

Nevin, Charles, *Lancashire, Where Women Die of Love* (Mainstream, 2004).

Nuttgens, Patrick, ed., *The History of York: From Earliest Times to the Year 2000* (Blackthorn, 2001).

Oliver, Neil, *A History of Scotland* (Weidenfeld & Nicolson, 2009).

Olusoga, David, *Black and British: A Forgotten History* (Macmillan, 2016).

Osborne, Roger, *Iron, Steam & Money: The Making of the Industrial Revolution* (Bodley Head, 2013, Pimlico, 2014).

Pankhurst, Emmeline, *My Own Story* (Hearst's, 1914).

Penn, Thomas, *The Winter King: The Dawn of Tudor England* (Allen Lane, 2011).

Phillips, C.B. and Smith, J.H., *Lancashire and Cheshire from AD 1540* (Longman, 1994).

Pollard, A.J., *The Wars of the Roses* (Macmillan, 1988).

Pollins, Harold, *Economic History of the Jews in England* (Associated University Presses, 1982).

Poole, Robert, ed., *The Lancashire Witches: Histories and Stories* (Manchester University Press, 2002).

Poole, Robert, *Peterloo: The English Uprising* (Oxford, 2019).

Prestwich, Michael, *Edward I* (Yale, 1997).

Price, Barclay, *The Chinese in Britain: A History of Visitors and Settlers* (Amberley, 2019).

Priestley, J.B., *English Journey* (Heinemann/Gollancz, 1934).

Pryor, Francis, *Britain BC* (HarperCollins, 2003).

Pugh, Martin, *The Pankhursts* (Vintage, 2008, first published Allen Lane, 2001).

Purvis, June, *Emmeline Pankhurst: A Biography* (Routledge, 2002).

Read, A., *The Peterloo Massacre* (James Wroe, 1819).

Reid, Robert, *The Peterloo Massacre* (Windmill, 2018, originally published 1989).

Richardson, David, Schwarz, Suzanne and Tibbles, Anthony, eds, *Liverpool and Transatlantic Slavery* (Liverpool University Press, 2007).

Richardson, Geoffrey, *The Lordly Ones: A History of the Neville Family and Their Part in the Wars of the Roses* (Baildon, 1998).

Robb, Graham, *The Debatable Land: The Lost World Between Scotland and England* (Picador, 2018).

Roberts, Brian K., *The Making of the English Village* (Longman, 1987).

Roberts, Robert, *The Classic Slum: Salford Life in the First Quarter of the Century* (Penguin, 1990, first published by Manchester University Press, 1971).

Rollason, David, *Northumbria 500–1100: Creation and Destruction of a Kingdom* (Cambridge, 2003).

Rose, Alexander, *Kings in the North: The House of Percy in British History* (Weidenfeld & Nicolson, 2002, Orion, 2003).

Rose, Mary B., ed., *The Lancashire Cotton Industry: A History Since 1700* (Lancashire County Books, 1996).

Rose, Susan, *The Wealth of England: The Medieval Wool Trade and Its Political Importance 1100–1600* (Oxbow, 2018).

Ross, David, *George & Robert Stephenson: A Passion for Success* (History Press, 2018).

Royle, Trevor, *Civil War: The Wars of the Three Kingdoms 1638–1660* (Little, Brown, 2004).

Royle, Trevor, *The Wars of the Roses: England's First Civil War* (Little, Brown, 2009, Abacus, 2010).

Russell, Dave, *Popular Music in England, 1840–1914: A Social History* (Manchester University Press, 2nd edn 1997).

Russell, Dave, *Looking North: Northern England and the National Imagination* (Manchester University Press, 2004).

Sagar, Keith, *The Laughter of Foxes: A Study of Ted Hughes* (Liverpool University Press, 2006, first published 2000).

Sandbrook, Dominic, *Never Had It So Good: A History of Britain from Suez to the Beatles* (Little, Brown, 2005, Abacus, 2006).

Sandbrook, Dominic, *White Heat: A History of Britain in the Swinging Sixties* (Little Brown, 2006, Abacus, 2007).

Sandbrook, Dominic, *State of Emergency. The Way We Were: Britain 1970–1974* (Allen Lane, 2010, Penguin, 2011).

Sandbrook, Dominic, *Seasons in the Sun. The Battle for Britain, 1974–1979* (Allen Lane, 2012, Penguin, 2013).

Sandbrook, Dominic, *Who Dares Wins: Britain, 1979–1982* (Allen Lane, 2019, Penguin, 2020).

Seymour, Miranda, *In Byron's Wake: The Turbulent Lives of Lord Byron's Wife and Daughter Annabella Millbanke and Ada Lovelace* (Simon & Schuster, 2018).

Sherwood, Marika, *After Abolition: Britain and the Slave Trade since 1807* (I.B. Tauris, 2007).

Singleton, Fred, *Industrial Revolution in Yorkshire* (Dalesman, 1970).

Skidmore, Chris, *Richard III: Brother, Protector, King* (Weidenfeld & Nicolson, 2017).

Smiles, Samuel, *Self-Help* (John Murray, 1860).

Smith, Harold L., *The British Women's Suffrage Campaign* (Longman, 2010, first published 1998).

Southern, Patricia, *Roman Britain: A New History 55 BC–AD 450* (Amberley, 2013).

The Saxon Chronicle, trans. James Ingram (Longman, Hurst, Rees, Orme and Brown, 1823).

Thomas, Hugh M., *The Norman Conquest: England After William the Conqueror* (Rowman & Littlefield, 2008).

Tibbles, Anthony, *Liverpool and the Slave Trade* (Liverpool University Press, 2018).

Timmins, Geoffrey, *Four Centuries of Lancashire Cotton* (Lancashire County Books, 1996).

Tombs, Robert, *The English & Their History* (Allen Lane, 2014, Penguin, 2015).

Townend, Matthew, *Language and History in Viking Age England* (Turnhout: Brepols, 2002).

Townend, Matthew, *Viking Age Yorkshire* (Blackthorn, 2014).

Tulloch, Alexander, *The Story of Liverpool* (History Press, 2008).

Turner, Graham, *The North Country* (Eyre & Spottiswoode, 1967).

Turner, Ralph V., *King John: England's Evil King* (History Press, 2009).

Uglow, Jenny, *Elizabeth Gaskell* (Faber & Faber, 1993).

Van der Kiste, John, *William and Mary* (Sutton, 2003).

Visram, Rozina, *Asians in Britain: 400 Years of History* (Pluto, 2002).

Wadsworth, Alfred P. and de Lacy Mann, Julia, *The Cotton Trade and Industrial Lancashire, 1600–1780* (Manchester University Press, 1931).

Wales, Katie, *Northern English: A Social and Cultural History* (Cambridge University Press, 2006).

Weir, Alison, *Lancaster and York: The Wars of the Roses* (Jonathan Cape, 1995, Vintage, 2009).

Wilkes, Sue, *Narrow Windows, Narrow Lives: The Industrial Revolution in Lancashire* (Tempus, 2008).

Williams, Anne, *The English and the Norman Conquest* (Boydell, 1995).

Williams, Thomas, *Viking Britain: A History* (HarperCollins, 2017).

Winchester, Simon, *Exactly: How Precision Engineers Created The Modern World* (William Collins, 2018).

Wood, Michael, *Shakespeare* (Basic Books, 2003).

Woolf, Alex, *From Pictland to Alba: Scotland, 789–1070* (Edinburgh University Press, 2007).

Worden, Blair, *The English Civil Wars: 1640–1660* (Weidenfeld & Nicolson, 2009).

Wormald, Jenny, ed., *Scotland: A History* (Oxford, 2005).

Wrigley, E.A., *Continuity, Chance and Change: The Character of the Industrial Revolution in England* (Cambridge, 1988).

Yorke, Barbara, *Kings and Kingdoms of Early Anglo-Saxon England* (Routledge, 1997).

ACKNOWLEDGEMENTS

I wish I could go back in time and thank all the northerners, sung and unsung, locally born or adopted, whose lives inspired me and shaped my world. Their stories deserved to be told and it has been a big responsibility to try to do them proud. More wryly, I should also express my gratitude to coronavirus lockdowns for providing the time to hasten the final stages of this project.

Massive thanks go to the brilliant team at HarperNorth, whose arrival on the publishing scene is such an important boost for the region. Jon, Gen, Alice, Megan and their colleagues have been tremendously supportive – thoughtful, constructive, kind and encouraging. Jonathan de Peyer, senior commissioning editor for non-fiction, has assembled a splendid list of independently-minded books. It is a privilege to be part of it. He also guided this first-timer expertly through the publishing processes. My agent Andrew Lownie, a formidable historian, helped me to shape the proposal in a way that put the likely readers front and centre.

My parents made many sacrifices to help me to become the first person in our family to go to university. They are not around to see this book, but I hope they would be pleased by what their efforts to give me a good education have produced. Above all, I thank my wife Carola for casting her critical novelist's eye expertly over everything

I have written. She is from Liverpool and I am from Manchester, but despite this, we have worked harmoniously. I could not have done it without her.

My former colleagues at the *Financial Times*, *Scotland on Sunday* and the *Goole Times* have been an inspiration and a model of rigorous, independent journalism. All my family and friends have been patient and supportive in listening to me talk about my hopes for this project. Thank you.

INDEX

Huyton, Merseyside 306, 315

Ida, King of Bernicia (founder of Northumbrian royal family) 20
Idle, Eric 259
Independent Labour Party 292
India
  cotton trade and 137, 138, 142, 295, 298
  First World War and 182, 185
  independence movement 183–4
  north of England, contribution of Indian migrants to 257
  passport controls and immigration from 183
  post-war immigration into Britain from 172, 199, 257
  Romani immigration into Britain from 179
  Second World War and 185
  servants and ayahs (nannies) arrive with English families returning from 179
Industrial Relations Act (1971) 318
Industrial Revolution ix, x, xi, xvi, 81, 121–73, 197, 224, 313, 320, 334. See also cotton, coal, iron, steel, chemicals, shipbuilding, road–building, canals, railways
  arms manufacture and 149–50
  Britain, reasons for development in 125–8
  child labour and 131–2
  inventors and 126, 127, 131, 136, 154
  migration and 124, 141, 148, 171, 172

north, reasons for development in 128–9
north-south divide and 132
'organic' phase 145–6
precision engineering and 144–5, 146–9
scientists in 128, 149–50
steamships 150
transport and 150–4
women and 131
working conditions and 123–5
Ireland x, 5, 9, 13, 74
  English Civil Wars and 109, 110, 113, 115
  Elizabeth I and 103
  Great Famine 180, 199–200
  Irish Christianity 23, 25, 39, 40
  migration into Northern England from see Irish, migration into northern England of
  Northumbrians and 20–1
  Vikings in 44, 46
Irish, migration into northern England of 124, 180, 199–207, 203–4
  backlash against 200–1
  destinations of 200
  de Valera in Manchester 205
  Engels and Mary Burns 201
  female migration 203–4
  Fenians 204–5
  Great Famine and 180, 199–200
  home rule and 205
  industrial expansion, Irish male workers and 202–3
  IRA 205–6, 207
  'Manchester Martyrs' 205
  nationalist movements 204–5
  Protestant migration 202
iron
  deposits in north 145

midlands technologies and 126
Ironopolis, Middlesbrough becomes known as 148
Iron Age 5–6
Isle of Man 21, 185, 254, 255, 256
Ismay, Joseph Bruce 290
Issa, Mohsin and Zuber 187
It's That Man Again 309
Ivar 'the Boneless' 44, 50, 51, 52
Ivory Bangle Lady 179

Jacobite revolts 116–19
James II, King of Scotland 84
James VI of Scotland and I of England, King 103–4, 233
  border wars, ends 72–3
  Gunpowder Plot and 106
  witchcraft obsession 106
James VII of Scotland and II of England, King 114–17
Jameson, Storm 267
Jarrow 60, 232, 277, 294
  March (1936) 248–9, 303–4
Jervaulx Abbey 167
Jewel, Jimmy 259
Jews
  antisemitic riots (1947) 310
  Cromwell invites to resettle (1650s) 181
  eastern European immigration 181–2
  expulsion from England (1290) 181
  First World War and 184
  King John taxes money-lenders 77
  nineteenth-century communities 181
  Second World War internment 184–5
  synagogue, first northern 181

Harper North

BOOK CREDITS

HarperNorth would like to thank the following staff
and contributors for their involvement in making
this book a reality:

Laura Amos	Graham Holmes
Hannah Avery	Ben Hurd
Fionnuala Barrett	Megan Jones
Claire Boal	Jean-Marie Kelly
Caroline Bovey	Samantha Luton
Charlotte Brown	Taslima Khatun
Sarah Burke	Ben McConnell
Alan Cracknell	Alice Murphy-Pyle
Jonathan de Peyer	Adam Murray
Anna Derkacz	Genevieve Pegg
Tom Dunstan	Agnes Rigou
Kate Elton	Florence Shepherd
Sarah Emsley	Zoe Shine
Mick Fawcett	Emma Sullivan
Nick Fawcett	Katrina Troy
Simon Gerratt	Phillipa Walker
Monica Green	David Wardle
Tara Hiatt	Kelly Webster

For more unmissable reads,
sign up to the HarperNorth newsletter at
www.harpernorth.co.uk

or find us on Twitter at
@HarperNorthUK

Harper
North